Thinking Through the Language Arts

Thinking Through the Language Arts

DENISE D. NESSEL

Reading/Language Arts Consultant
San Francisco, California

MARGARET B. JONES

Reading/Language Arts Coordinator
Avon Grove School District
West Grove, Pennsylvania

CAROL N. DIXON

Director, Education Reading Clinic
Co-director, South Coast Writing Project
University of California at Santa Barbara

Macmillan Publishing Company
New York
Collier Macmillan Publishers
London

Copyright © 1989 by Macmillan Publishing Company, a division of Macmillan, Inc.

Printed in the United States of America

Macmillan Publishing Company
866 Third Avenue, New York, New York 10022

Collier Macmillan Canada, Inc.

Library of Congress Cataloging-in-Publication Data

Nessel, Denise D., 1943-
    Thinking through the language arts / Denise D. Nessel, Margaret B. Jones, Carol N. Dixon.
        p.   cm.
    Includes bibliographies and index.
    ISBN 0-02-386601-2
    1. Language arts (Elementary)   2. Language arts—Correlation with content subjects.   I.   Jones, Margaret B., 1928-   .   II. Dixon, Carol.   III. Title.
LB1576.N37 1989
372.6—dc19   88-1477
                                                                              CIP

Printing: 1 2 3 4 5 6 7   Year: 9 0 1 2 3 4 5

ACKNOWLEDGMENTS

The editor gratefully acknowledges permission to reprint material appearing in this volume:

Page 126. Ginn and Company. Theodore Clymer et al., *Ginn Reading Program,* Level 9, Teacher's edition, 1982, excerpt from selection "The Mystery Sneaker." Reprinted by permission of Ginn and Company.

Pages 121–24. Harcourt Brace Jovanovich, Inc. "The Giant Beet," from *People and Places,* HBJ Bookmark Reading Program, Eagle Edition by Margaret Early, Elizabeth K. Cooper, and Nancy Santeusanio. Copyright © 1983 by Harcourt Brace Jovanovich, Inc. Reprinted by permission of Harcourt Brace Jovanovich, Inc.

Page 215. D. C. Heath & Company. M. Johnson et al., *Far and Away,* The READ Series, 1971, excerpt from selection "U.S.S. Fish," published by Litton Educational Publishing, Inc. Reprinted by permission of D. C. Heath & Company.

Page 254. Houghton Mifflin Company. Edmund Henderson, *Teaching Spelling,* p. 41. Copyright © 1985 by Houghton Mifflin Company. Used by permission.

Pages 211–20. Lantern Press, Inc. *Danger in the Deep* by Charles Coombs from Young Readers Water Sports Stories, copyright 1952 by Lantern Press, Inc. Reprinted by permission of Lantern Press, Inc.

Pages 152–53, 154. *The New York Times.* "Fast Food: A Nutritional Trap" by Jane E. Brody, September 19, 1979. Copyright © 1979 by The New York Times Company. Reprinted by permission.

Pages 152–53, 154. The Readers Digest. "How Good Are Fast Foods?" by Jane E. Brody (*Readers Digest,* February, 1980). Reprinted with permission from the February 1980 *Readers Digest.* Originally appeared in *The New York Times.*

Pages 156–57. Seymour Reit. "The Hard Way" by Seymour Reit, as published in *Free Rein* (Allyn and Bacon, 1978). Copyright © 1978 by Seymour Reit. Reprinted by permission of Seymour Reit.

Pages 280–81. Scott, Foresman & Company. "D'Nealian manuscript alphabet" and "D'Nealian cursive alphabet" from *D'Nealian Handwriting,* Book 2, by Donald N. Thurber. Both figures reprinted by permission of Scott, Foresman & Company.

Pages 279–80. Zaner-Bloser, Inc. Zaner-Bloser student desk alphabet card used by permission of Zaner-Bloser, Inc., Columbus, Ohio. Copyright 1987.

Page 344. Western Publishing Company, Inc. "Stars," from Golden Book Encyclopedia. Copyright © 1969 by Western Publishing Company, Inc. Used by permission.

Joanne Chancer. Class dictated stories based on *A House is a House for Me, Q is a Duck,* and *Nate the Great,* reprinted by permission of Joanne Chancer.

Classroom work by numerous students reprinted by permission of the individual students and their parents or guardians.

Photographs by Margaret B. Jones. 1988.

To our students,
who have been our best teachers

Preface

Listening, speaking, reading, and writing are the cornerstones of language arts. Each process may be analyzed separately, to understand how each is developed and refined, but connections must also be made among the four. Comprehending and using language are intimately related processes. In this book we address each of the four language arts, suggesting how each may be taught to develop communication abilities and how all may be developed concurrently. We also identify common denominators, showing how the language arts are related to one another and how developing skill in one reinforces skillful use of the others. Furthermore, we emphasize that comprehension and use of language are basic to learning in all subjects.

We consider all four language processes equally important to include in the language arts program. However, we know that reading is often separated from the other language arts in terms of established curricula, teaching materials, and scheduled instructional time. Although this division is understandable to some extent, we think it has the effect of lessening the teacher's chances of developing a fully integrated language arts program. Good reading instruction extends beyond the basic teaching of reading to guide students in the reading of content-area texts, reference materials, and good literature of all types. Considered in this light, reading instruction exerts an important influence on students' comprehension and use of language across the curriculum. The teacher who knows how to guide reading effectively will be in an advantageous position to make important connections between reading and the other language arts. He or she will thus be able to develop students' language abilities fully.

Throughout this book, our intent is to provide suggestions that are unified by a philosophy of what is basic to good instruction. We believe that good teaching, above all, leads students to think, both critically and creatively, about what they hear, read, say, and write. When students use their intellects with sense and purpose, day after day, they learn far more than the content at hand.

They acquire the habit of inquiry, developing competence and confidence in tackling new information and new problems; they learn to learn. That is why we have chosen to examine language arts methodology in detail, for what the teacher does with this important subject can help students to develop active, inquiring minds.

Also basic to our philosophy is the conviction that the student's own purposes are the strongest forces for motivating and sustaining learning. We believe teaching is most effective when it is not obviously didactic. We think students need to be given the chance to seek answers to their own questions and to work together to solve their own problems. Good teachers work as guides, setting directions and often leading the way, but they are always sensitive to what the students bring with them and what the students, as individuals, hope to achieve. Earl Kelley, whose works we cite in this book, stated it well:

> Now it comes about that whatever we tell the learner, he will make something that is all his own out of it, and it will be different from what we held so dear and attempted to "transmit." He will build it into his own scheme of things, and relate it uniquely to what he already uniquely holds as experience. Thus he builds a world all his own, and what is really important is what he makes of what we tell him, not what we intended.

All students are naturally curious about all sorts of things, in school and out. Teachers will be most successful if they can build on students' natural drive to learn and can show learners how to use the language arts to discover and describe their worlds.

This is a practical book. It is based on the many hours we have spent in classrooms, teaching students and working with teachers to improve instruction. Yet we cite scholarly works often, as we believe that practice is best when it is based on sound theory and research. We call attention to recent works and also to the writings of master teachers from years past, whose insights about teaching and learning are ever relevant. We give many examples of actual lessons, often including teacher-student dialogue, to describe what goes on during effective instruction. Student work is included liberally, to show the results of the procedures we advocate. A number of activities, references, and additional suggested readings—both theoretical and practical—are given at the ends of chapters to encourage further thought.

Our discussions and examples are presented primarily with elementary and middle/junior high school students in mind. However, the same principles are applicable to language arts instruction at any grade level. We hope our ideas provide useful perspectives to teachers. We wish to encourage all to think through what they are doing when they teach thinking through the language arts.

Special thanks go to the colleagues who welcomed us into their classrooms to teach and observe and who shared ideas with us that are reflected in this book: Ellen Milgrim and the teachers from the West Chester Area School District, West Chester, PA; Marie Conner, Gregory Metzger, Roger Morrill, Gloria Nieweg, and Elizabeth Sharon from the Avon Grove School District, West Grove, PA; the teachers from the Newark School District and the Indian River School District in Delaware; Sheridan Blau, John Boettner, Joanne Chancer, Laurie Guitteau, Jack Phreaner, and Nancy Shepherd from the California South Coast Writing Project Santa Barbara, CA; Sandra Bonace, Geoffrey Carvey, Pamela Grinnell, Susan Hillway, Kathleen Kurtz, Ricci Lambert, and Julie Slocum-Nuckolls, graduate students at the University of California at Santa Barbara.

Thanks also to those who reviewed the manuscript and offered suggestions that helped us to shape the final draft: W. Dorsey Hammond (Oakland University, Rochester, Michigan); Leslie Rex-Kerish and Mary Kimber (Univeristy of California at Santa Barbara); MaryAnne Hall (Georgia State University); Edward E. Hakanson (Drake University); Karla Hawkins Wendelin (The University of Nebraska-Lincoln); Helen E. Jones (Fairmont State College); Mary Jo Lass (California State University-Long Beach); Carolyn L. Piazza (Florida State University); Harry W. Sartain (The University of Pittsburgh); and Timothy Shanahan (The University of Illinois at Chicago).

We add a special note of recognition to Russell G. Stauffer, whose philosophy of education has influenced our work and whose dedication to children's learning we respect and admire.

D. D. N.
M. B. J.
C. N. D.

Contents

5 **Reading Expository Text**

SECTION III **Active Involvement in Writing**

6 **Private Writing**

7 **Public Writing**

SECTION IV

Refining Expressive Abilities   247

8   Spelling and Handwriting   249

9   Grammar and Language Usage   287

Thinking Through the Language Arts

Language acquisition takes place without conscious planning or formal instruction, through natural interactions with people and things in the environment.

1

Language Arts for Active Thinking: An Overview

Most teachers agree that the purpose of language arts instruction is to help students comprehend and use language skillfully and effectively. There is also basic agreement that because students must comprehend and use both oral and written language, teachers ought to give instruction in listening, speaking, reading, and writing. But there the agreement seems to end.

So much can be included in the category of language arts that teachers from school to school have different notions about what constitutes an appropriate program. To some, language arts means primarily grammar and the mechanics of writing, such as spelling and punctuation. Others believe that composition and the study of literature are priorities. From one classroom to the next, activities may range from dictionary exercises to creative drama, from reading poetry to practicing handwriting. Word games, puppet shows, spelling lessons, and literature projects all have been a part of language arts.

With many possible instructional goals and activities and many materials to choose from, teachers are often overwhelmed with planning a coherent program. There simply seems to be too little time to accomplish all that seems necessary and desirable. There are no easy solutions to this problem, but for language arts, as for all subjects, good teaching stems from clear thinking. The most effective teachers give deliberate thought to their work. These teachers pay particular attention to the objectives they set, the materials they use, the activities they design, and the expectations they have of their students.

The purpose of this book is to provide direction to teachers who must decide on an approach to teaching language arts. To start, let us consider how children develop the ability to comprehend and use language before they come to school.

Foundations of Language Development

Language is a code. Within its system, one thing (a set of sounds or printed symbols) stands for something else (e.g., an object, a concept, an emotion). When it follows a consistent pattern, the code can be understood by others. Acquiring the code is a process that may begin even before birth as the fetus begins to respond to the sounds in its environment. From the earliest days of infancy, the child gradually expands and refines his or her ability to understand and produce the code. This process takes place not through conscious planning or formal instruction but through natural interactions with people and things in the environment.

Psycholinguistics is the branch of research that is concerned with the ways in which language is acquired and used. By observing young children, psycholinguists have greatly expanded our understanding of how language is acquired, of how the environment influences the process of acquisition, of the stages children go through as they develop the ability to use language, and of the problems that may arise in various language-learning contexts. Three major theories have contributed to our understanding of language development: behaviorist, nativistic, and cognitive.

Theories of Language Development

Some researchers, known as behaviorists, believe that language acquisition can be explained in terms of a stimulus-response-reinforcement or conditioning model. This school of thought, based on the work of scientists such as Pavlov and B. F. Skinner, holds that the child hears a sound or a set of sounds (stimulus) and responds with imitation. As that response is reinforced by either a positive or a negative reaction, the child's language behavior is modified or shaped. Through a process called successive approximation, the child's language comes gradually to match that of the social group who is providing the stimuli and reinforcers. Although behavioral theory explains some of what occurs as children acquire language, it does not adequately explain children's ability to invent language forms that they have not heard. The child who says "Allgone cookie" is inventing, not imitating.

A second approach to explaining language development is based on the work of scientists such as Lennenberg. This nativistic, or genetic, theory is grounded on the assumption that people are biologically predisposed to acquire language. Proponents of this theory argue that all languages consist of certain universals. These common features are phonology (a consistent sound system); morphology (a consistent system for combining sounds into larger, meaningful units such as words); syntax (a finite system of rules for ordering words in utterances); and semantics (consistent, culture-based rules for creating an infinite number of utterances that have an infinite variety of meanings). The nativistic theorists assume that acquisition of these universals takes place in an orderly, systematic fashion that is only partially explained by what language learners actually hear in their environments. Although this theory accounts for much of what occurs during language development, it does not adequately account for individual differences in the acquisition of language.

Other theorists are particularly interested in the interaction between thought and language. These cognitive theorists aim to discover how one influences the other. Those who take this perspective have debated the question as to which comes first: does language make thought (conceptual development) possible, or does thought produce language as a vehicle for communication? One group, represented by researchers such as Piaget, believes that thought and language develop independently. They claim that thought develops in the form of mental schemata, which are like unstated hypotheses about objects and phenomena. These schemata are based on sensorimotor interactions with the environment, and they develop without the aid of language. Gradually, language is acquired to label experiences and to communicate with others. The opposite view is based on work by theorists such as Vygotsky, Bruner, and Luria, who argue that thought and language develop simultaneously and that it is the development of language that actually enables higher-order thought to take place. In this view, language is regarded as a verbal mediator or middleman that organizes and clarifies thought.

None of these theories seems to account completely for language acquisition and development, but each adds to our understanding of the process. Knowing the basic principles of each can help teachers to recognize the theoretical bases of different instructional approaches. Teachers can then make informed decisions about which approaches to use in the classroom.

Stages of Language Development

Although almost all children acquire the ability to comprehend and use language, not all develop in exactly the same way or at the same rate. Research has nonetheless identified a progression of stages of language development that most children appear to pass through. Following is a list of the stages, with the skills typically acquired at each level. Research, however, shows that age ranges vary widely when individual children are considered (DiVesta, 1974; Phelps-Terasaki, Phelps-Gunn, and Stetson, 1983).

Prelanguage or Prelinguistic (Birth to Ten Months) Infants as young as one month can have a highly sophisticated ability to differentiate among sounds of the language, but their ability to control sound production is much less well developed. The first phase of development, frequently called the babbling stage, is usually characterized by sound production that signals distress (through crying) or pleasure (through cooing, gurgling). Gradually, sound production is refined, coming closer and closer to the phonological system of the language that the child hears regularly. The child then begins producing utterances that sound very much like words. Parents and others respond with positive attention to these pseudowords; the attention results in the child's increased attempts to communicate.

Stage 1 (Ten Months to Eighteen Months) The child is gaining control over the production of recognizable words and acquires a communication vocabulary of up to fifty words. These words are usually related to objects, animals, people, or events in the immediate environment, although children use a variety of types of words (Nelson, 1973). Some show a preference for referential words that name or categorize (doggie, bottle); others use utterances related to social events (bye-bye, night-night). This kind of talk is known as *holophrastic speech;* it is called this because the one- or two-word utterance may contain the meaning of a whole phrase or sentence.

Stage 2 (Eighteen Months to Twenty-four Months) This stage of speech is characterized by two-word utterances and short phrases (go car, mommy kiss). Such utterances are called *telegraphic speech.* As with a telegram, the language patterns typically consist only of key words, but the omission of nonessential words does not result from conscious choice, in contrast to the way an adult purposely structures a telegram. The child's vocabulary increases dramatically at this stage to about three hundred words and includes verbs and negative forms. More complete communication is now possible. During this stage, children often engage in playful monologues (go car; car go, go, go; car go) as they try out various words and patterns.

Stage 3 (Twenty-four Months to Thirty Months) At this stage, the child's vocabulary typically increases to over 450 words. Utterances are composed of longer phrases and short simple sentences (Milk all gone. Where Daddy go?) and include adjectives (pretty dolly, bad puppy). Conceptual overextensions (such as applying the term *doggie* to all four-legged animals) are common and may result from lack of exposure to appropriate labels. Conceptual underextensions (such as the failure to use *doggie* for both a Cocker Spaniel and a Great Dane) are also typical and may reveal inadequately developed concepts. The child at this stage is attentive to labeling and often asks for confirmation through his or her intonation (doggie?).

Stage 4 (Thirty Months to Thirty-six Months) The child's speaking vocabulary continues to increase. Vocabularies at this stage average about one thousand words. Sentence complexity also increases with the child's use of such sophisticated linguistic devices as embedded clauses (Guess what Jimmy did today.). Children who live in a language-rich environment show rapid growth in vocabulary and syntactical diversity at this stage.

Stage 5 (Thirty-six Months to Fifty-four Months) The child is able to communicate effectively within the family and other familiar social groups. His or her typical speaking vocabulary at this stage includes at least two thousand words. The child uses a variety of sentence patterns and shows a grasp of coordinating and subordinating relationships (Jimmy pushed me down and I hurt my arm. I got two kinds when the ice cream truck came.). Although further language abilities will continue to develop, the child at this stage has firmly established the foundations for learning to communicate orally and for beginning to deal with language in print.

Knowledge of this developmental progression helps the teacher to understand the considerable learnings that children have accrued before they have entered school. The outline of stages also illustrates the way those learnings have occurred in a process of exploration and discovery within natural communication settings. Although most children progress as just described, some develop quite rapidly; others proceed at a slower pace; and still others show signs of disorder (delayed growth accompanied by gaps in the process). The teacher needs to recognize that individual differences exist within any group of children. Special attention must be given to those who have special needs.

Uses of Language

Whereas some researchers have concentrated on the stages of language acquisition, others have focused on the uses or functions of language. Halliday (1975) has identified seven functions that appear to be universal. Each language has features that are

1. *Instrumental:* the language contains statements for expressing basic needs and desires. A person will state, "I want ..." "I need ..."
2. *Regulatory:* communication is used to control the behavior of others. A person will demand, "Do this." "Get out."
3. *Interactional:* some statements are intended to get someone else to agree to one's goals. A person will suggest, "Let's play school."
4. *Personal:* some utterances are indications of personal intent. A person will declare, "I'm going to be a teacher." "I will get a new jacket."
5. *Imaginative:* some cues indicate that the communication is pretend or fictional. A person may state, "Once upon a time ..."
6. *Heuristic:* some statements pose questions or suggest hypotheses. A person may say, "I wonder if ..." "Why won't ..."
7. *Informative:* some statements are intended to convey information. A person will claim, "This is a ..."

As children gain proficiency in language, they learn to use it in these different ways. At the same time, they also must learn to change register—that is, to vary tone, form, and content to suit different situations. A child sharing crayons with a good friend might make the forceful instrumental statement, "I want the purple one next!" without offending the friend. However, the same desire should be stated differently to a less familiar companion if the social encounter is to proceed smoothly ("Please pass me the purple one."). Developing this awareness of audience and context is a key to successful use of language and is one of the goals of language arts instruction. As children increase their awareness of the functions of language, they must be empowered to achieve their own purposes through changing register appropriately.

In another analysis of the functions of language, Britton (1970) presents findings that have implications for classroom instruction (see also Pradl, 1982). First, Britton makes a distinction between the *participant* and *spectator* roles that the language user assumes. Essentially, the participant role is associated with language that is used to meet one's immediate goals. It is the role that one assumes, for example, when one talks with a sales clerk while making a purchase. By contrast, the spectator role is associated with language that is used to reflect on experience. One assumes this role when one describes the encounter with the sales clerk at a later time.

This distinction between roles is central to Britton's perspective on the functions of language. He claims that there are three functions: transactional, poetic, and expressive. Transactional discourse mainly involves language associated with the participant role; it consists of "getting-things-done" language that would be found in, for example, a business context. Poetic discourse mainly involves language associated with the spectator role; it is the language of literature or of any communication that has the goal of shaping an experience to highlight and elaborate selective aspects of that experience. Expressive discourse may involve use of both the participant and spectator roles. The primary purpose of this third type of language is neither to accomplish a goal nor to shape an experience. Rather, it is highly personal language that is used to communicate attitudes, feelings, and reactions.

According to Britton, the expressive mode is the foundation on which children refine and extend their ability to use language. Expressive language itself becomes richer and more varied as children gain experiences in talking and writing. As children hear and read different forms of discourse, they gradually learn to use language to achieve transactional and poetic purposes. The informal talk and writing of expressive language, as well as of the other forms of discourse, thus all have an important place in the classroom.

Insights from Second-Language Study

Researchers who have studied how children acquire a first (native) language have in recent years also been interested in how children master a second language. Second-language researchers have responded to a great need to discover ways of teaching students from other cultures who have little or no knowledge of English. The discoveries have implications for teaching children whose first language is English.

Acquisition versus Learning   Several of the second-language theorists distinguish between language acquisition and language learning (Krashen and Terrell, 1983). *Acquisition* is defined as the natural, informal process of responding to the language one hears and thereby coming to understand and to produce that language. *Learning* is defined as what one accomplishes through a conscious, rather formal attempt to master the rules of the language. The learning process involves, for example, studying vocabulary or discovering the ways in which sentences are formed.

Ease and fluency of communication appear to be enhanced by the natural process of language acquisition. The more formal learning of language, by contrast, seems to help the person to develop a "monitor" or internal editor that alerts him or her to the need for revising speech or written work to produce a better final product (Krashen and Terrell, 1983). The monitor is most helpful in situations for which the language user has time to revise and polish. Such situations include the rehearsing of a speech or the editing of a first written draft. However, if the monitor is constantly responding during extemporaneous speech or rough-draft writing, the result may actually be decreased fluency and blocked communication. Discoveries suggest that if the goal is to build confidence and fluency, language activities should simulate the process of acquisition, but if the goals are precision and accuracy, activities should involve greater attention to conscious learning. Both kinds of activities have their place in the language arts program.

Affective Variables   Theorists of second-language acquisition have also suggested the existence of a psychological constraint that they call the *affective filter*. The affective filter is defined as a set of attitudinal factors that may interfere with language production. A person's age and the type of instruction received both seem to influence the strength of the affective filter. For instance, children often gain fluency in a second language more readily than adults. This may be partially the result of children's lower levels of self-consciousness when they try to speak a new language. Teenagers and adults are more likely to be embarrassed by their awkwardness with a new language and hence have a higher affective filter that tends to inhibit speech. This same affective filter may operate in many unfamiliar language situations, even when the learners are using their native language. Instruction that causes any child to feel inadequate or embarrassed may easily limit the production of language.

The best kind of instruction lowers the affective filter while still encouraging children to refine their own language productions. Research on language acquisition suggests several useful guidelines for teachers. First, children need time to absorb a language before they can be expected to produce that language. They must also be allowed to respond and express at their own individual pace. Next, children need to get positive response for making attempts at production, even if the attempts include errors. Indeed, errors should be considered a normal, natural, and necessary part of the process of learning to use language. Furthermore, children need to have considerable control over what will or will not be attempted at any given time. Finally, children need a certain amount of meaningful repetition and practice; they should have the chance to hear and use language in a variety of useful contexts so that they may gradually refine and shape their own efforts. Effective instruction creates these conditions in the classroom.

Task Demands   As teachers consider affective variables, they should also think about the demands that various classroom activities make on students. An activity that is too difficult can be frustrating; one that is too easy may lead to restlessness and boredom. Second-language educator Cummins (1982) has identified two interacting dimensions of task demands. These are shown in Figure 1.

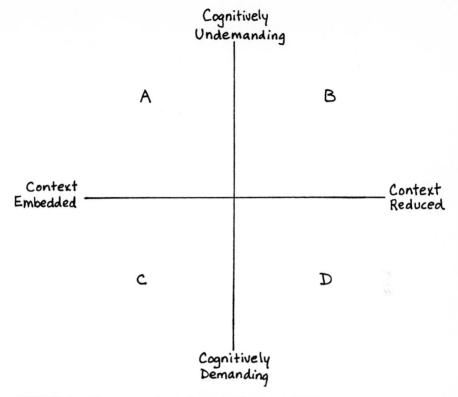

FIGURE 1   Dimensions of task demands (Cummins, 1982)

The horizontal axis of the diagram essentially represents the familiarity of the task. A context-embedded task might involve talking with one's mother at the breakfast table; a context-reduced task might involve addressing the class on one's first day at a new school. The vertical axis of the model represents the level of thinking required by the task. A cognitively undemanding task might involve copying a list of telephone numbers; a cognitively demanding task might involve planning a science experiment to test a hypothesis. Classroom activities may be categorized on these two dimensions simultaneously and thus may be categorized in one of the four quadrants of the diagram—A, B, C, or D.

By analyzing classroom activities in this way, teachers may estimate the relative difficulty of activities for different students. For example, activities that are context-embedded for native English speakers may be context-reduced (and thus may be more difficult) for students from another language and/or culture group. Activities that are cognitively undemanding for native English speakers could be more demanding for the student who is learning English as a second language, simply because of the language requirements of the task. Most children, regardless of their native language, are better able to function at a demanding cognitive level when the task is embedded in a familiar context. Children may become restless with activities that are both undemanding and context-reduced. Such tasks may seem like meaningless busywork. An analysis of task demands can help the teacher plan meaningful activities that are challenging and yet not frustrating.

Language Development
and Classroom Instruction

In planning a language arts program, teachers must realize that almost all children come to school with well-developed receptive and expressive language abilities. The typical kindergartner has acquired language by listening and is able to speak with considerable skill. Many children in the preschool years have also been attentive to language in print; some have explored reading and writing and are able to perform both activities. Most children have an intuitive grasp of the different functions of language. There will be individual differences among students, in terms of rate of development and in terms of familiarity with the English that is used in the classroom, but all children will have gained language ability through having taken an active, problem-solving approach. Their inquisitive minds have led them to explore, discover, and learn. It is the school's job to build on this early, active involvement with language. Teachers must help children refine and extend what they already know.

A Philosophy of Teaching

To make informed decisions about what to do in the classroom, the teacher needs to establish a philosophy of teaching that will lead to a consistent approach to refining and extending children's language development. The ideas presented in this book are based on a philosophy that includes these beliefs:

- *In teaching language arts, process is as important as content.* The content of lessons in language arts may vary considerably. Students may work with fiction, nonfiction, poetry, drama, or other forms of discourse. The quality of the content should be high; for instance, teachers should expose students to good literature and should encourage them to speak and write fully about what is most important to them. But simply attending to the quality of the content is not enough. Once decisions are made, teachers must also decide what students will do with the content so as to improve their ability to use the four language processes: listening, speaking, reading, and writing.

  Some classroom activities are more effective than others because they involve students actively in the meaningful use of language processes. For example, students who are writing sentences to incorporate each of their spelling words are not as fully involved with the process of writing as are students who are keeping journals or writing plays to be performed for the class. The sentence-writing activity is not necessarily a poor one; it is just not the best one for engaging students in the writing process. The writing process involves not only sentence formation but also other considerations, including how to organize a set of ideas.

Teachers who are attentive to the process dimension are thoughtful and selective about the activities they include in their programs. Their decisions are based on their understanding of language processes and on their desire to give students the best opportunities for further acquisition and learning. Teachers recognize, too, that students also use language in other subjects and in their daily lives outside of school. Students therefore have many opportunities to extend and refine what is taught during the time designated for language arts.

- *Language arts instruction should be based on principles of integration that reflect the relationships existing among the language processes.* Listening, speaking, reading, and writing are closely related processes, because each is a facet of language ability. Listening and reading are receptive processes; speaking and writing are expressive processes. Speaking and listening are ways of using oral language; reading and writing are ways of using language in print. Because of the close relationships, growth in one area usually affects growth in all the others; for example, the student who reads widely will tend to speak, listen, and write with greater skill and confidence.

Some approaches to instruction will fragment these four processes into separate sets of skills to be mastered. However, a skills approach tends to limit students to consider only isolated elements of language. For example, students may only practice using a certain mark of punctuation or may state the main ideas of a series of unrelated paragraphs. Mastery of isolated elements, though sometimes useful, will not necessarily result in overall competence with language. Consider an analogous situation: learning to play basketball. The novice player must practice shooting, dribbling, and passing, but a good performer of such drills will not necessarily be a good player; actual play requires fluid, coordinated use of all the specific skills and reflects an ability that is learned only from playing. Similarly, the student of language arts must learn to make fluid, coordinated use of the language processes in situations for which communication (rather than mastery of skills) is the goal.

In an integrated program, students are given many opportunities for such coordinated activity. For example, they will work on a project that requires a mix of reading, discussion, and writing. Although specific instruction in each area may be given, attention to isolated language elements does not dominate the program. Instead, the emphasis is on active involvement in communication.

In developing an integrated program, it is especially important for the teacher to recognize that reading is one of the language arts. Although teachers generally agree with this assertion, they may find it difficult in the real world of school to coordinate reading with the other language arts. In many schools, reading is taught as a separate subject; students may have one teacher for reading and a different teacher for language arts. Even when the same teacher is responsible for both subjects, there may be separate curricula and different textbooks for each area. The tendency to separate reading from the other language arts makes it hard for teachers to set coordinated instructional goals. However, even when such a division is maintained, it is possible to engage students in well-rounded activities. Natural connections among the language processes can be used to develop comprehension and expressive abilities, to foster appreciation for literature, and to enhance learning in other subjects.

• *Language arts instruction is best when it involves conscious efforts at developing students' ability to think.* Each of the language processes may be used in simple, mechanical ways that do not reflect real thinking; language may also be used in complex, purposeful ways that reflect the highest levels of thought. At one extreme, it is possible to memorize, copy, read, or repeat words without even understanding the meaning of the words. At the other extreme, it is possible to grasp the most subtle meanings and express the most sophisticated ideas in an elegant fashion. The best language arts instruction requires students to use an array of higher-level mental processes.

All students will profit from instruction that emphasizes process, integration, and thinking. However, not all students will be ready to learn or to accomplish the same things at the same time. At all grade levels, some children will come to school with a rich background of language experiences, having been nurtured in homes filled with reading material and extensive talk. Other children will not have had opportunities to hear stories, enjoy books, or converse with a variety of articulate adults. Still others will come from environments in which English is a second language; they and their families may have only a rudimentary grasp of oral English and little or no experience with English in its written form.

Children will have different levels of readiness to handle the demands of the language arts curriculum. The teacher must be attentive to individual strengths and weaknesses and must be prepared to set different goals for different children and adjust activities and expectations accordingly. At the same time, the ultimate goal is the same for all students: they must learn to use the alert and inquiring minds with which they come to school.

Promoting Active Involvement

Before reading the rest of this chapter, put your own alert and inquiring mind to work so that you can experience for yourself one kind of active, thoughtful involvement that will require the use of the four language processes. The following is a story for you to read. The text is interrupted with directions for writing and discussing. You will need to work with one or more partners.

You will begin by reading the first part of the story. Then you will be asked some questions that will require you to speculate about coming events. Write your answers, and then compare notes with your partner(s) before reading on.

THE BEGGAR AND THE GAZELLE[1]

Once upon a time there was a man so poor that he had to beg for his daily food. He had no home and had to sleep in the open every night, finding what shelter he could in a doorway or under a wagon on the street.

One morning, as the beggar awoke, cold and hungry, he saw a peddler coming along the street, pulling a cart behind him. Nearing the beggar, the peddler paused and cried out, "Gazelles! Gazelles! Miniature gazelles for sale!"

"Don't bother stopping here," said the beggar. "I am a poor man, with no money to buy a gazelle."

"Ah, my good sir," said the peddler, "my prices are very reasonable. And, as you will see, these animals are very fine indeed. Please, just take a look."

And so the beggar walked around to the back of the cart, where several tiny gazelles were crowded together in a cage. He peered through the bars, and as he did so, one of the creatures looked straight at him with large, soft eyes and said in a quiet voice, "Buy me. You will not regret it."

The beggar was startled at the animal's plea and suddenly became curious. He dug through his pockets and, finding a few pennies, he went back and showed these to the peddler, saying, "I have only this small amount to offer, but if you will accept it, I shall be pleased to buy one of your gazelles."

"Fine! Fine!" cried the peddler, who believed that an early sale, for whatever price, meant good luck for the rest of the day. He accepted the coins, released the creature, and went on his way.

In a few moments, the beggar was alone on the street with his purchase. He scratched his head and looked down at the gazelle, who was standing by his side.

"Well! I have given my last few coins for you, though why I have done so, I'm sure I don't know," said the beggar.

"You have given me my freedom," said the gazelle quietly, its eyes shining. "And now I will help you. In fact, I intend to make you a rich man!"

"Hah!" said the beggar, amused and skeptical at this news. "And what must I do for this wealth?"

"Nothing, for the moment," replied the gazelle. "Just wait here. I shall return to you shortly." And the gazelle scampered away, heading towards the desert that lay outside the town.

The beggar looked after the animal with dismay.

"What a fool I've been!" he muttered to himself. "My last money is gone, and now so is the gazelle! It has played a trick on me, with its talk of riches, just to keep me from tying it up again. Yes, I'm sure of it. Now it has escaped, and I have nothing at all in the whole world!"

Still cold and hungry, the beggar sat in the street, shaking his head in disbelief at what he had done.

---

[1] This story is an old folktale that is part of the oral tradition of several cultures, especially those of the Middle East and Africa. This version is a retelling of the tale as it appears in I. Shah, *World Tales* (New York: Harcourt Brace Jovanovich, 1979, pp. 218–21).

What do you think will happen next? Why do you think so? Write your predictions and your reasons here.

Discuss your ideas with your partner.

Read on.

While the beggar sat in the street, the gazelle ran through the desert until it reached a grand encampment of tents near an oasis. The creature made its way to the largest and finest structure of all, which belonged to a great sheik.

The gazelle trotted in gracefully and bowed low to the noble sheik, who was reclining on a richly woven carpet.

"Greetings to you, sir!" said the gazelle. "I come on behalf of a wealthy merchant, Sheik Abdul, who was bringing his caravan to this very oasis in hopes of offering you his finest wares. Unfortunately, a band of thieves attacked us last night, and my master has lost a great deal, including most of his clothing. He asks if you would kindly send him some garments so that he may come before you in proper attire."

"Of course, of course!" said the good sheik. "I have here a set of clothes I just had made for myself. Take them to your master and tell him I am most sorry to hear of his misfortune. You must bring him here soon so that I may entertain him and soothe him in the wake of his terrible loss."

"Thank you, sir," said the gazelle. "Oh, yes. My master asked me to give you this in exchange for whatever you might be able to send him. I hope it pleases you."

On the elegant carpet the gazelle placed a large, sparkling emerald, worth more than the entire contents of the good sheik's tent. Then the creature gathered up the clothes, bowed once again, and ran off.

The nobleman was awed by the fiery green jewel, for he had seen nothing like it in all his world. He thought to himself, "Well, well! Despite his loss, this Abdul must certainly be a very wealthy man! Hmmm. Perhaps he would be a good match for my daughter. It is time for her to marry, and I must make sure to provide her with a husband of means."

The gazelle at once brought the clothes to the beggar, who was overjoyed with the fine garments.

"This has turned out to be a lucky day after all!" cried the beggar, who had never before had a complete set of new clothes to wear.

"This is only the beginning," said the gazelle. "Come with me."

The tiny creature led the way to an abandoned building on the edge of town and pointed out a loose brick in one of the walls. When the beggar removed the brick and peered into the wall, he saw a cache of gold and silver and precious gems, a fortune greater than he had ever dreamed of.

"What luck! What luck!" cried the beggar, filling his pockets and dancing about with sheer delight.

"That is nothing," said the gazelle. "But there is more than enough to buy you a horse and whatever else you desire for now. You must be quick about it, though, for we have an appointment to keep."

The beggar made several purchases, among them a fine, white stallion. Freshly bathed, dressed in his new finery, and mounted astride his swift horse, he was a new man, fit to meet any nobleman in the land. Soon he was galloping into the desert behind the gazelle, his pockets jingling with coins and gems and small treasures.

When they came near the oasis, the gazelle stopped and said, "Please wait here. I shall be back in a few moments."

"Yes, yes," said the beggar, looking at the tents in the distance with some interest. "I will be here when you return."

The gazelle went once again to the nobleman's tent and bowed low before the good sheik. When it raised its head, there lay on the carpet a gleaming ruby of great value.

"My master hopes you will be able to receive him so that he may thank you in person for your kindness," said the gazelle quietly. "He respectfully offers this small gift to your daughter and hopes you will allow her to accept it as a token of his esteem for her."

The noble sheik was once again amazed at such a show of wealth. Ruby in hand, he smiled broadly and said, "I shall be delighted to receive this Sheik Abdul. Tell him to come immediately. And tell him, too, that my daughter accepts this gift with thanks and is, herself, eager to see the man who may soon become her husband."

What did you read that supported or contradicted your predictions? Discuss your findings with your partner.

What do you think will happen next? Why do you think so? Write your predictions and your reasons here.

Discuss your predictions with your partner.

Read on.

The gazelle returned to the beggar and explained that he must now take the identity of Sheik Abdul, a wealthy merchant whose caravan had been set upon by robbers. The beggar readily agreed, thinking the new role far preferable to the one he was used to. Before long, Sheik Abdul was lounging at the nobleman's side, luxuriating in the feel of the thick carpets and soft pillows that servants had brought for his comfort.

The two men became friends immediately and talked long into the night over coffee and sweets. When they had told one another many jokes and stories and had discussed more serious matters, the noble sheik at last mentioned his daughter.

"Abdul, my friend," he said, "you would do me great honor if you would accept the hand of my lovely daughter. I can think of no man more suitable as a husband than you, and I would be most pleased to have you as a son-in-law. What do you say?"

Sheik Abdul, delighted at his continuing good fortune, eagerly agreed to the marriage, for he had seen the charming young woman earlier in the evening, and she had smiled most warmly at him.

And so the wedding took place soon after, with a feast and many festivities. The couple was given a large, newly furnished tent. There they lived in comfort and happiness, attended by their own servants. Each evening, as they slept, the gazelle lay quietly at the entrance, guarding them and watching over them.

As the months passed, Sheik Abdul became quite used to his new, luxurious life. He ate well, had the company of a lovely wife, and was surrounded by wealth. But the more satisfied he became, the less he remembered the reason for his good fortune. He devoted his days to idle pleasures and quite forgot about the gazelle.

What do you think will happen next? Why do you think so? Write your predictions and your reasons here.

Discuss your ideas with your partner.

Read on.

One day the gazelle went to Sheik Abdul's wife and said to her, "Dear mistress, I am feeling quite ill. Would you go to your husband and ask him to prepare me a bowl of dates and honey? I believe I could recover my strength if he would do this for me."

And so the lady went at once to her husband, saying "Abdul! Abdul! Come quickly! The gazelle is ill and needs your help. It has asked that you prepare it a bowl of dates and honey."

"What?" cried Sheik Abdul, with some annoyance. "Why are you so worried about something that only cost me a few pennies? The creature can take care of itself. I do not have time to be making dates and honey for it!"

The lady returned to the gazelle and explained gently that her husband was very busy and could not come. "May I get you the dates and honey?" she asked.

"No, mistress, no," said the gazelle in a small voice. "Oh! I am feeling so weak, I am afraid I will die. Please, mistress, please beg your husband to do as I ask."

And so the lady went once again to Sheik Abdul and, with great agitation, said, "Husband! You must prepare a bowl of dates and honey for the gazelle, and you must do so immediately or it will surely die!"

"I will hear no more of this!" said Sheik Abdul angrily. "If you are so worried about that gazelle, then take it a bowl of milk. But do not bother me again with the matter. I am busy!"

The lady returned to find the gazelle lying on the ground, panting softly. It raised its head weakly as the woman knelt at its side.

"I am sorry, dear gazelle," said Abdul's wife. "My husband will not come."

Hearing these words, the gazelle closed its eyes, dropped its head to the ground, and died.

What do you think will happen next? Why do you think so? Write your predictions and your reasons here.

Discuss your ideas with your partner.

Read on.

That evening, Sheik Abdul noticed that his wife was unusually quiet. Impatiently he asked her, "What is the matter with you?"

"The gazelle died today," she replied sadly. "And I know its death was the result of your neglect. I have lost all respect for you, Abdul, and no longer wish to live as your wife. Tomorrow I will return to my father's tent."

"What foolishness is this?" cried Sheik Abdul. "Put the matter out of your mind, wife. I told you it is of little importance! Now I am going to bed, and I advise you to do the same. You will have forgotten all about it in the morning."

Sheik Abdul fell asleep at once and slept soundly for some hours. But then he had a dream. He saw the gazelle before him, and its large, soft eyes were open wide. The creature spoke quietly, but its voice filled Abdul's head.

"You gave me my freedom," said the gazelle, "and for that I was deeply grateful. I gladly provided you with wealth and comfort and a loving wife. I asked only one favor of you in all that time—a bowl of dates and honey. Oh, why did you refuse me?"

Shame and remorse came upon Sheik Abdul, and he cried out, "But I told my wife to bring you a bowl of milk!"

"Ah," said the gazelle very softly, "but that was not the same thing." And it vanished.

Filled with terror, Sheik Abdul awakened and found himself huddled in the street, dressed in rags, cold and hungry in the pale morning light.

As you responded to this story, you became actively involved. You anticipated outcomes, searched for clues, revised your predictions, and constructed meanings. You read with purpose—a self-determined purpose—to confirm or reject your hypotheses about the outcome of the tale. The story may have developed as you expected or may have taken a surprising turn. Either way, you wanted to read on to find out what happened next. You were motivated because you were making your own interpretations, evaluating events from your own point of view, and making decisions based on your unique experiences and knowledge. Your involvement heightened your attention and interest, and it sharpened your reading. In your written responses, you had something to say about what you thought and believed. As you discussed your ideas with a partner, what you read and wrote took on new meaning as you listened, reflected, and talked things through. You used all four language processes in a purposeful, coordinated way, and your participation required thinking.

Setting Priorities for Instruction

The process of stimulating active involvement is at the heart of good teaching. The best lessons are the ones that generate lively responses and that provoke students' curiosity to learn more. Usually, students become interested and willing to take an active part only when they see a reason to become involved. They become engaged when it is important for them to do so. In a similar fashion, you read to the end of the story not just because it was there to read but because once you were involved, it became important for you to know the outcome.

Effective learners are not passive receivers of information. They are actively engaged in learning and are motivated by their individual purposes. They read to find out and write to communicate; they listen attentively and speak confidently; they raise questions and eagerly seek answers. Such zestful learning occurs when the teacher sets the right priorities. These priorities include *attitude, meaning,* and *mechanics.*

Attitude   To learn well, students must want to learn and must believe that they can learn. Enthusiasm and confidence are the basic features of a positive attitude toward learning. Parental encouragement contributes a great deal toward students' attitudes, but what the teacher does is also very important. A teacher's enthusiasm is contagious; a teacher's sincere praise raises confidence; a teacher's skillful use of the right kinds of activities can lower students' "affective filters" and make them eager to learn.

If students are to have positive attitudes toward the language arts, they must be inspired to value reading, writing, listening, and speaking. Lively discussions will lead them to understand and appreciate what they read. Engaging presentations and thrilling stories will make them eager to listen. Receptive audiences will make them want to speak and write. Each child must be challenged to find out about a fascinating world, filled with great ideas to discover and express. Each child must experience the genuine excitement that learning can create.

Master teachers have always recognized the vital connection between attitude and learning. Almost a century ago, William James (1899) stated that

> in teaching, you must simply work your pupil into such a state of interest in what you are going to teach him that every other object of attention is banished from his mind; then reveal it to him so impressively that he will remember the occasion to his dying day; and finally fill him with devouring curiosity to know what the next steps in connection with the subject are. (p. 4)

Kelley (1951), Ashton-Warner (1963), Cullum (1967), Torbe and Medway (1981) and many others through the years have expressed the same theme. The

Effective learners are not passive receivers of information. They are thoroughly and actively engaged in learning and are motivated by their individual purposes. The best lessons generate lively response and provoke students' curiosity to learn more.

common thread in these works, echoing John Dewey, is that the process of teaching and learning is best when it involves an exhilarating exchange among individuals who respect one another and who want to learn together. When the classroom atmosphere is charged with enthusiasm and filled with the excitement of what the world of knowledge has to offer, students cannot help wanting to be part of it. They will learn the content, and they will also learn much more besides—they will acquire a love of learning and achieving that can influence them for the rest of their lives.

Meaning   Students will not be able to sustain positive attitudes if they perceive their work to be pointless. Enthusiasm for learning can be maintained only if students are engaged in meaningful pursuits. Walter Loban, eminent educator and an authority on language arts, speaks often of the need for classroom endeavors that have "evident, meaningful purpose" to the students. That is, the activity must be purposeful, the purpose must make sense, and both sense and purpose must be readily apparent to the students.

Of course, what is meaningful to teachers may not be meaningful to students. For instance, the teacher may fully understand a concept that is fuzzy to the students, or the teacher may give what is intended to be a meaningful assignment that the students perceive simply as busywork. In fact, teachers always run the danger of falsely assuming that students fully understand a lesson.

If teachers are not attentive to the students' perceptions, the students may feel stranded and muddled. Holt (1964) describes his own realization of this pitfall of teaching:

> I used to feel that I was guiding and helping my students on a journey that they wanted to take but could not take without my help. I knew the way looked hard, but I assumed they could see the goal almost as clearly as I and that they were almost as eager to reach it.... [But] the valiant and resolute band of travelers I thought I was leading toward a much-hoped-for destination turned out instead to be more like convicts in a chain gang, forced under threat of punishment to move along a rough path leading nobody knew where and down which they could see hardly more than a few steps ahead. (pp. 23–24)

Two conditions are necessary for conducting a lesson that has an evident and meaningful purpose. First, the teacher must give careful thought to goals, sequences of activities, task demands, and expected outcomes. Good planning, based on clear thinking, is an essential prerequisite to a good lesson. Second, once the lesson is in progress, the teacher must be attentive to how students are making sense of what is being taught. Such awareness comes about most readily when teachers allow students the freedom to ask questions, to admit confusion, and to take the risk of making some errors. Having created such an open environment, teachers must be receptive listeners and alert observers. Teachers can thereby discover what is clear to students and what is still a jumble. Monitoring the students' responses, the teacher must decide whether to continue as planned or whether to adjust the activities so that students will achieve a greater sense of clarity and meaning.

Mechanics   Specific skill instruction is an important part of a good language arts program, but mastery of the skills (e.g., spelling, punctuation, specific comprehension skills) should not be the ultimate goal. More important is that such mechanics be learned and practiced within a broader context of interesting, meaningful endeavors that involve reading, writing, speaking, and listening.

If students approach learning with enthusiasm and perceive the sense of what they are doing, they can develop the important mechanics of language with relative ease. For instance, if young children are eager to learn to read and are given interesting, meaningful texts (such as stories they dictate themselves or good children's literature), they can become skillful readers naturally and easily. If students have real audiences for their writing (for example, readers of a school newspaper) and can write about what they know, they will see a reason for learning to spell and punctuate and compose orderly sentences. Skillful use of the conventions of writing develops naturally if students are truly writers. Under the guidance of a good teacher, students will acquire a solid command of specific skills, and their work on skills will be a natural extension of their involvement in purposeful and enjoyable projects, games, and activities.

Language Arts and Thinking

By promoting active student involvement and by giving attention to priorities, the language arts teacher will help students develop as thinkers. There is no need for a special thinking "program" based on a hierarchy of thinking skills. In fact, trying to teach thinking in isolation from the regular day-to-day activities is about as useful as trying to teach music or art appreciation without supplying students with melodies or paintings to consider. Thinking should not be isolated and taught separately from the language arts; it is an integral part of language comprehension and use. One group of educators concluded as follows:

> We remained suspicious of attempts to identify and teach any set of intellectual strategies or repertoire of behaviors that might be identified as "thinking skills." We felt that the idea of a "thinking skill" is a pseudo-concept which misrepresents and trivializes the authentic intellectual activity that we call "thinking." As a group, we embraced Dewey's dictum that "There is no method for thinking; thinking is the method."
>
> Our skepticism about a skills approach to teaching thinking does not mean, of course, that we don't want to direct our teaching to enhancing the quality of thinking that our students engage in. We do believe that we can describe qualitative differences in thought and that such descriptions as we are accustomed to using are adequate to characterize advances in thinking. This is to say that we have a responsibility as teachers to foster more mature, more complex, more discriminating, more critical, and more penetrating thought on the part of our students.[2]

This is a perceptive statement that, no doubt, echoes what many other teachers have also concluded. Teachers are responsible for developing students' cognitive abilities, but the responsibility cannot be met by assigning work from skill kits or programs.

Use of such special materials may indeed lead both teachers and students to a false sense of accomplishment. The teacher sets aside time for the program and assigns the exercises; students complete the work; and everyone seems satisfied that thinking abilities are thereby developed. But the question of transfer remains: Will students reason better about the subjects they study just because they have worked through special skill exercises? Such transfer cannot be assumed. Students must also be expected to think when they are reading, writing, listening, and speaking about their regular school work.

Special programs are useful not because they teach thinking but because the authors have made attempts to translate theories of cognition into practice. In so doing, the authors of these programs suggest the kinds of thinking that students need to do on a regular basis. For instance, a program may provide

---

[2] Sheridan Blau, "Teaching Thinking Skills." *South Coast Writing Project Newsletter* (Santa Barbara, CA: Spring, 1985).

activities involving cognitive processes such as seeing relationships, logical reasoning, and synthesizing. However, no matter how interesting the material, such exercises are usually more valuable as models for the teacher than as classroom activities. That is, students will improve their thinking to the extent that they are given the chance to see relationships, reason logically, and synthesize information in their regular language arts and content area work. They will be more likely to perform well if the teacher plans activities specifically to elicit such thinking within the regular day-to-day activities. For detailed discussions of how regular classroom work provides a base for developing thinking abilities, see Marzano and Hutchins (1985) and Raths et al. (1986).

There are a number of special programs on the market that may be useful as models. Each program identifies a set of specific cognitive processes. Some of the more commonly listed processes are these:

- Anticipating (predicting, hypothesizing)
- Classifying/categorizing
- Comparing/contrasting ideas, facts, concepts
- Discovering relationships
- Analyzing processes
- Making judgments
- Using evidence to support an argument
- Forming concepts
- Drawing conclusions
- Making inferences
- Applying knowledge to novel situations
- Reasoning inductively and deductively
- Ordering information (e.g., by attributes, priorities)
- Solving problems
- Interpreting meanings
- Visualizing a process, event, setting, character
- Making decisions

If teachers gain an understanding of such processes, these teachers will be better able to plan their own lessons to include attention to thinking. Such teaching can go far beyond a skills approach, because the emphasis is on thinking about subjects (issues, problems) rather than on exercises that supposedly develop specific thinking skills in isolation. This emphasis on process applied to curriculum content also places the teaching responsibility where it belongs— on the teacher rather than on the materials. The teacher cannot simply assign tasks and assume that the use of materials will inevitably result in thinking and learning. Instead, the teacher must take the initiative to ensure that students become actively involved in using a wide range of mental processes as they listen, speak, read, and write. That is, to induce students to think, teachers themselves must be actively engaged in thinking as well. For an elaboration of this point, see Schön (1983) and Sternberg (1987).

To provide opportunities for active involvement, teachers must be attentive to what students bring with them to class (life experiences, knowledge, language abilities, attitudes). It is only by using what students already know that teachers can help pupils learn to listen, speak, read, write, and think more effectively. Just as you used your experience and knowledge to think your way through "The Beggar and the Gazelle," students, under the guidance of a thoughtful teacher, will use what they have, to think their way through stories they read, explanations they hear, films they view, papers they write, and discussions they have.

Section Previews

In the pages that follow, we examine specific methods of promoting active involvement in the language arts. Our intent is to describe a way of teaching that will enable students to have positive attitudes toward learning, that will keep their attention on purpose and meaning, and that will help them develop skill in the use of language.

Section I examines the processes of oral language (listening and speaking) as well as the process of viewing as it is used with stimuli such as illustrated books, films, and television. The chapters in this section describe methods that promote active involvement with these processes. We give attention to the process of listening for appreciation (notably when the content is literature) and to the process of listening for informational purposes (as when students learn about science or social studies). The material on speaking gives suggestions for engaging students in a variety of enjoyable activities that develop language and thinking abilities. Connections between oral language, viewing, reading, and writing are emphasized.

Section II is devoted to a description of the reading process and the instructional implications that follow from an understanding of it. We emphasize that the way teachers perceive and guide reading has a powerful influence not only on students' growth as readers but, equally important, also on their attitudes toward reading and thus toward much of what they do in school. The chapters in this section describe methods that are used to develop motivated, thinking readers. We emphasize the ways in which reading instruction can develop and extend the same kinds of thinking processes that children employ when they listen, view, and speak. Suggestions for integrating writing activities with reading lessons are also given.

Section III discusses the process of writing as it is used for students' own private purposes (such as in keeping a journal) and for purposes that require attention to an audience (such as in writing a report). The chapters in this section describe methods for teaching that help students to develop confidence and competence as writers. We suggest ways in which students can be encouraged to respond to one another's writing. We emphasize connections between oral language, reading, and writing, and show the ways in which writing develops and extends thinking abilities.

Section IV explores ways for teachers to help students refine their abilities to express themselves in speech and writing. We give suggestions for teaching spelling, handwriting, grammar, and usage. Our emphasis is on helping students learn the conventions of expression so that they can speak and write with greater clarity and precision.

Section V presents suggestions for designing a language arts program with attention to process, integration, and thinking. There are guidelines for setting instructional goals and evaluating student progress, first for each of the language processes and then for the overall program. Illustrative plans show how reading, listening, speaking, and writing may be used in an integrated fashion to further learning.

Suggested Activities

1. Select a children's picture storybook (for example, *Sky Dog* by Brinton Turkle, *Harry the Dirty Dog* by Gene Zion, or *Blueberries for Sal* by Robert McCloskey) in which the conclusion seems inevitable. Analyze the structure of the story. Why could you anticipate the ending so easily? Which thinking processes did you use?

2. Examine two language arts texts intended for the same grade level. Which one would you rather use to teach a class of academically talented students? Why? Analyze the instructional priorities that led you to make your decision.

3. If you were going to tell the story "The Beggar and the Gazelle" to a multi-ethnic group of children, what changes might you make? List these and give your reasons. What thinking processes did you use when making these decisions?

4. Interview a teacher of language arts. Ask what the teacher teaches, which materials are used, how time is allotted, and so on. Analyze the teacher's responses. Which beliefs about teaching seem to guide the teacher's decisions?

References

Ashton-Warner, S. *Teacher*. New York: Simon and Schuster, 1963.
Britton, J. *Language and Learning*. London: Penguin, 1970.
Cullum, A. *Push Back the Desks*. New York: Citation Press, 1967.

Cummins, J. "The Role of Primary Language Development in Promoting Educational Success for Language Minority Students" in *Schooling and Language Minority Students: A Theoretical Framework*. Los Angeles: Evaluation, Dissemination and Assessment Center, California State University at Los Angeles, 1982.

DiVesta, F. *Language, Learning, and Cognitive Processes*. Monterey, CA: Brooks/Cole, 1974.

Halliday, M. *Learning How To Mean—Explorations in the Development of Language*. London: Edward Arnold, 1975.

Holt, J. *How Children Fail*. New York: Dell, 1964.

James, W. *Talks to Teachers on Psychology and to Students on Some of Life's Ideals*. New York: Dover, 1962 (originally published by Henry Holt in 1899).

Kelley, E. *The Workshop Way of Learning*. New York: Harper & Brothers, 1951.

Krashen, S., and Terrell, T. *The Natural Approach: Language Acquisition in the Classroom*. Hayward, CA: Alemany Press, 1983.

Marzano, R. J., and Hutchins, C. L. *Thinking Skills: A Conceptual Framework*. Aurora, CO: Midwest Regional Educational Laboratory, 1985.

Nelson, K. "Structure and Strategy in Learning to Talk" in *Monographs of the Society for Research in Child Development* 38 Serial No. 149, 1973.

Phelps-Terasaki, D.; Phelps-Gunn, T.; and Stetson, E. *Remediation and Instruction in Language: Oral Language, Reading, and Writing*. Rockville, MD: Aspen Systems Corporation, 1983.

Pradl, G. (ed.) *Prospect and Retrospect: Selected Essays of James Britton*. Montclair, NJ: Boynton/Cook, 1982.

Raths, L. E.; Wasserman, S.; and Rothstein, A. *Teaching for Thinking: Theories, Strategies, and Activities*. New York: Teachers College Press, 1986.

Schön, D. A. *The Reflective Practitioner*. New York: Basic Books, 1983.

Sternberg, R. J. "Teaching Critical Thinking: Eight Easy Ways to Fail Before You Begin." *Phi Delta Kappan* 68(February 1987):456–59.

Torbe, M., and Medway, P. *The Climate for Learning*. Montclair, NJ: Boynton/Cook, 1981.

Suggested Readings

Abt, C. *Serious Games*. New York: Viking, 1971.

Bransford, J. D. *Human Cognition: Learning, Understanding and Remembering*. Belmont, CA: Wadsworth, 1979.

California State Department of Education. *English-Language Arts Framework for California Public Schools*. Sacramento: California State Department of Education, 1987.

Chance, P. *Thinking in the Classroom: A Survey of Programs*. New York: Teachers College Press, 1986.

Covington, M., et al. *The Productive Thinking Program: A Course in Learning to Think*. Columbus, OH: Charles Merrill, 1974.

Easterling, J., and Pasanen, J. *Confront, Construct, Complete*. Rochelle Park, NJ: Hayden, 1979.

Feuerstein, R., et al. *Instrumental Enrichment: An Intervention Program for Cognitive Modifiability*. Baltimore: University Park Press, 1980.

Goodlad, J. I. *A Place Called School.* New York: McGraw-Hill, 1984.

Harrison, A. F., and Bramson, R. M. *Styles of Thinking: Strategies for Asking Questions, Making Decisions, and Solving Problems.* New York: Doubleday, 1982.

Maxwell, M. (ed.) *Thinking: The Expanding Frontier.* Philadelphia: Franklin Institute Press, 1983.

Meeker, M. *The Structure of Intellect: Its Interpretation and Uses.* Columbus, OH: Charles Merrill, 1969.

Rubenstein, M. *Patterns of Problem-Solving.* Englewood Cliffs, NJ: Prentice Hall, 1975.

Thelen, J. (ed.) *Ignite! A New Program to Build Higher Level Thinking Skills.* New York: Newsweek/International Reading Association, 1987.

I

Active Involvement in Listening, Viewing, and Speaking

Listening is a major pathway to language and learning. Starting in early childhood, young children acquire the ability to use language from listening to the people around them. As children acquire language, they also learn about the world from their parents, friends, and teachers. Much of this learning is related to visual stimuli; for example, parents point to objects while naming them and comment on events as they occur. In their early years, children watch television and films; through these activities they become exposed to many vicarious visual and auditory experiences. Similar exposure is offered to them when their parents or siblings read aloud from well-illustrated books. These viewing activities help children form concepts and understand the world around them.

Talking is a primary means of self-expression; it is also a pathway to learning. In their early preschool years, children's speech is most often used to express urgent desires (Mama!) and to name things in the immediate environment (Doggie!). As children grow, their use of language is extended in a variety of ways. They continue to name things and express their needs, but they also use language to talk about what they have experienced and what they are looking forward to doing in the future.

They ask questions, relate stories, describe what they have observed, and in many other ways express what is important and interesting to them. These uses of oral language—besides being forms of self-expression—are also ways of learning in that the child can come to a fuller understanding of a concept or phenomenon by talking about it, just as adults often achieve greater insight by talking things through.

When children enter school, the teacher needs to refine and extend children's abilities in listening, viewing, and speaking. Youngsters who are attentive, interested listeners will tend to be successful learners who will also have many opportunities for hearing language that can influence their own speech patterns and styles. Children who are actively attentive to visual stimuli such as picture books, films, and television will profit greatly from viewing. Students who discuss, retell stories, participate in creative drama, and in other ways use oral language freely will develop confidence and competence as speakers.

Although all children come to school with some listening, viewing, and speaking abilities, students may vary considerably in their levels of competence with these processes. Some will be very attentive to visual and auditory stimuli and will also have considerable command of their own oral language. Others will be limited in one or more of these areas, perhaps because they have had limited opportunities to interact with interested adults and peers, or perhaps because they are learning English as a second language and are adjusting to new societal expectations. Whatever a child's level of competence, however, the teacher can help that child make progress.

Other chapters in this book describe oral activities that are parts of lessons in which reading or writing is the major emphasis. For instance, discussions may be held during reading lessons, or students may meet specifically to talk about their writing. However, in this part of the text, the primary emphasis is on activities that are used for developing oral, aural, and viewing abilities. Chapter 2 concentrates on listening and viewing; Chapter 3 concentrates on speaking.

The points of view in this section are consistent with the ideas that are expressed later in the book. The most valuable lessons include meaningful activities that are used not only to improve students' competence with language but also to refine thinking abilities and to help students develop positive attitudes towards learning. The strong relationships between the receptive (listening, reading) and the expressive (speaking, writing) language arts allow many opportunities for lessons that integrate these processes.

Listening and viewing activities help children form concepts and understand the world around them.

2

Developing Listening and Viewing Abilities

Listening may be the most overlooked of the language arts. Reading and writing programs receive much attention, but efforts to develop listening abilities may be limited to exercises in following directions or to isolated games and activities that are not integrated with the overall program. Students are invariably expected to pay attention, but concerted efforts to help them listen effectively are meager. Wilt (1950) found that although teachers expected students to listen over half the time class was in session, the purposes for listening were rarely made clear. Decades later, Elin (1972), Kean and Personke (1976), and Pearson and Fielding (1982) concluded that the art of listening was still neglected in teacher's instructional plans, language arts textbooks, and curriculum guides.

Viewing, as well, has not been accorded much attention. Viewing is a process that needs to be refined and enhanced through a variety of well-planned activities. Too often, classroom viewing experiences are highly similar to home television viewing in that students are allowed to remain passive. Yet illustrations in books, films, filmstrips, and television can be excellent sources of information and can provide much enjoyment if they are used to promote active involvement.

Students should not just be passive receivers of information. This chapter suggests ways of designing listening and viewing activities so that students can develop the ability to be attentive participants who think.

Promoting Effective Listening

Effective listening is developed when the teacher gives constant attention to helping students build good listening habits. There are three main facets to teaching listening: 1) being a good role model for students, 2) arranging an environment that is conducive to listening, and 3) designing a program that includes varied listening experiences with clear purposes.

The Teacher as a Role Model

Children tend to imitate the adults in their worlds. Parents and relatives are their primary models; teachers, too, are significant people who serve as behavior models more than they may realize. What teachers *do* is more important than what they say; how teachers behave as listeners themselves will have a greater impact on children than any verbal directives or admonishments about listening (Penfield, 1970). As Faix (1975) stresses:

> Many of us merely "act out" listening to our students' chattering and formal answering. At this point we need to go deeper ourselves and see how vital our own style is in setting up the support system necessary in helping children develop and grow in self-identity, self-esteem, and other correlates of healthy self and group growth. (p. 410)

A very important listening behavior involves looking directly at the speaker. You can demonstrate the value of this behavior for yourself. Ask a friend to help. Tell your friend to look over your shoulder as you speak for several minutes; then have the friend look you directly in the eye as you talk for another few minutes. Which situation makes you feel that the friend is really listening to you? If you are like most people in this culture, you feel uncomfortable when a speaker is looking past you—it makes you feel as if you are being ignored for someone or something more interesting behind you. You may have a difficult time continuing to talk at all; your voice may peter out, and you may even turn to look at what your friend is concentrating on behind you. It is always distracting and sometimes humiliating to speak to someone who does not offer full visual attention. This is as true for children as for adults. The teacher who always looks past child speakers will be a poor model; that teacher will suggest that respectful attention is unimportant in that classroom. But the teacher who looks directly at students when they talk will demonstrate the value and importance of giving undivided attention to a speaker. (Teachers should, however, be aware of cultural differences in communication styles. Children who come from a culture in which direct eye contact is considered impolite may find it difficult to look directly at a speaker. For information on such cultural differences, see Saville-Troike, 1978).

Another important listening behavior is to grant the speaker a fair chance to be heard. Some people will give speakers only minimal amounts of time and will fulfill only the most basic requirements of social politeness. These people give the impression that they are waiting impatiently to jump back into the conversation. They do not listen—they pause until they can continue speaking. This behavior is distracting. Timid speakers will quickly give up the floor, feeling that their thoughts are being neither heard nor valued. Teachers must not be so eager to move the lesson along that they demonstrate this kind of impatience. Students need to know that their responses are not just filler between successive teacher monologues. Teachers must be sincerely attentive to students' remarks; they must allow their students adequate time to speak. If teachers must interrupt, they should do so politely.

A good listener also conveys a generally accepting attitude toward speakers. We are encouraged when a listener shows obvious interest as well as polite attention. We tend to go on if we perceive that our remarks are being well received. Teachers who clearly want to hear their students will convey a positive attitude in their postures, facial expressions, and body movements. The responsive, accepting teacher will not only encourage students to speak out but will also demonstrate good listening attitudes.

The teacher occasionally has opportunities to become part of a listening audience with the students. During school assemblies or when a guest speaker comes to the classroom, the teacher can demonstrate listening behavior directly. The following two examples illustrate contrasting behavior by teachers.

A storyteller once visited an elementary school class for a special story hour. The teacher asked the students to gather in the back of the room. Some children brought chairs while others sat on the floor. The teacher sat on the floor in the middle of the group, watching attentively, participating as a member of the group to repeat certain refrains, and obviously enjoying the stories. The teacher laughed aloud during a particularly funny story and was as startled as the children at the ending of a scary tale.

The next day the storyteller went to a different classroom. The second teacher also gathered the group in the back of the room, but instead of joining the audience, stood near the guest, in front of the group, and watched the children. This teacher did not react to the stories and often seemed not to be listening at all but rather was preoccupied with the children's behavior. Occasionally, this teacher interrupted the story to reprimand youngsters who were not paying strict attention.

The difference between the two teachers as listening models was pronounced. The first showed students how to listen; the second told students to listen but did not demonstrate good listening behavior. There were also distinct differences in the behavior of the students in the two groups. In the first class, the group was attentive and responsive. When individuals glanced at the teacher, they observed a good listener. In the second class, the children were restless. They too glanced at their teacher, but instead of seeing an attentive listener, they saw a disciplinarian.

With the busy routine of the classroom, it is not always possible for a teacher to be the perfect listener. A disturbance on one side of the room must be handled and may distract the teacher from listening attentively to an individual student. The day's schedule will not always permit leisurely discussions in which everyone has the same chance to be heard. The teacher must intervene, even when that teacher is part of the audience, if individuals are impolite to a guest speaker. Nevertheless, teachers must do their best regularly to be good listening models for their classes.

The Listening Environment

Listeners are strongly affected by the environment. Adults get up to close doors or to turn down televisions when they want to hear one another better. They cannot concentrate well when there are distracting noises around them; nor can they be fully attentive if they are physically uncomfortable. Students are similarly affected by the classroom environment; their attention and concentration can be hampered if their surroundings are not conducive to listening.

To listen well, students need to be comfortable. Even with the best efforts, they will have a hard time listening attentively if they are too hot or too cold, if the sun is in their eyes, or if their seats are uncomfortable. Teachers need to watch for restlessness caused by physical conditions and make adjustments accordingly.

Group lessons and individual activities should be scheduled with foresight so that when students need to listen with maximum attention they are not distracted by what is going on elsewhere in the room or in the school. It is rather unreasonable to expect children to be quietly attentive when the class next door is having a noisy recess in the hall. Similarly, if one group in the class is working on a project that requires group discussion, that group may disturb the other students who may be trying to listen to the teacher's explanations. Distractions are inevitable in a busy school, but teachers can minimize their effects through careful planning.

The teacher's voice is also a significant part of the listening environment. A pleasant, well-modulated voice will induce better attention than a shrill, loud voice or one that is so soft that students must strain to hear it. Teachers do not need to undergo special voice training, but they should be aware of what their voices sound like and should be prepared to make improvements when necessary. It is a good idea to tape your voice from time to time and listen to the recording critically. Do you have the kind of voice you would want to listen to regularly? Is it too loud? Too soft? A dull monotone? Be honest with yourself. Is your voice an asset to the environment?

Finally, the students themselves are a part of the listening environment. Children today are not subjected to the rigid requirements of absolute silence that characterized nineteenth-century schoolrooms, but students still need to learn to maintain a respectful silence as a group when someone is talking. Each teacher has somewhat different expectations, but whether the standards are generally loose or strict, the teacher should require the class to refrain from distracting talk and behavior when attentive listening is the goal.

Environmental factors can be controlled to maximize attentive listening. However, in daily life, people must often be attentive under less than ideal circumstances. In school, there will be some unavoidable distractions—noisy repairs to the building, traffic in the street, or bustling groups in the hall. Under adverse conditions, only well-developed listening strategies will make it possible for the students and the teacher to block out disturbances and stay with the activity successfully. Besides being a model for the class and attending to the environment, teachers must also provide the right kinds of lessons and activities to help students develop useful listening strategies.

Planning the Program

To become effective listeners, students need a variety of listening experiences, each presented for a different purpose. Sometimes the purpose will be to learn information, as when the teacher explains a process or a sequence of events. But teachers will also want to stretch students' imaginations and so will tell fanciful stories and read poetry. Sometimes students need to follow oral directions or to listen to other students' ideas. Whatever the activity, it is essential for the teacher to have clear objectives and to make sure the students also have clear purposes to guide their listening. Students must know what is expected of them if they are to listen effectively (Kennedy and Weener, 1971).

The purpose of an activity will determine the level of attention that is required of students. Sometimes the teacher may want to encourage "escape" listening; hence, soothing music or soft, rhythmical poetry can calm a restless group or be a welcome background during a needed rest period. Often, teachers read to students or tell stories. The children are not expected to attend to every detail but are encouraged just to enjoy the literature. Other times, teachers may explain a concept in science or social studies and expect students to remember the information and use it. Or the teacher may conduct a discussion and expect students to make critical judgments about the ideas. Students should have varied experiences so that they can learn to adjust their level of attention to different purposes for listening.

Listening for Different Purposes

Purposeful listening should be a regular part of the instructional program. Listening ability cannot be developed with only occasional games or skill drills. Daily activities, arising naturally from ongoing instruction, will give students the meaningful, varied experiences they need if they are to become effective listeners. In this section are descriptions of activities that may be used repeatedly, with different content, to meet curriculum goals in all subject areas. Listening may be a language art, but it is not developed only during the language arts class period. There are many opportunities throughout the school day to help children build good listening habits.

Listening to Appreciate Literature

Hearing a story is a very special experience, different from reading for oneself. For a brief time, the listener shares a view of life with the person who takes the time to read or tell the tale. Folklore, fairy tales, stories of adventure, humor, and mystery are a delight to hear, and all promote a variety of learnings. When students listen with pleasure to good literature, they also gain insights about themselves. Students construct their cognitive view of the world, in part, from the stories they assimilate. They gain versatility with language by listening to the flow and rhythm of a captivating and memorable story. While they listen, students are naturally attentive; they learn good listening habits because the material itself is irresistible. Oral literature also has a decidedly positive effect on students' intellectual growth. Listening to stories can increase students' abilities to anticipate outcomes, recognize cause–effect relationships, follow sequences of events, and derive meaning from descriptions and dialogue.

Oral literature particularly enables students to develop a sense of story (Applebee, 1978; Pradl, 1979). A sense of story leads one to anticipate the direction of a story because one is familiar with stories of that type. Brown (1977b) describes this concept:

> Sense of story is seen as a personal construct which develops and progresses toward a mature internalized representation. This mature internalized representation also aids comprehension in listening and reading and allows the child to make predictions (based on previously accrued expectations) about possible meaning. More precisely, the child's internalized representation of story or sense of story assists the child in predicting what is likely to be said and how it might be said in a given listening situation. And in reading, sense of story helps in predicting what is likely to be stated on the printed page and how it might be written dependent on the kind of material being read. (p. 358)

Citing Piaget and more recent cognitive psychologists, Applebee (1979) connects sense of story to the schemata that shape our conceptualizations and explanations of experience:

> In considering children and stories, the fact that there are such schemata is very important. Schemata guide the child's reactions to literature, and to the extent that literature has any effect or influence upon the child, it is in terms of changes in schemata. This is because a schema functions as a kind of archive of past experience, a record of what has gone before. But just as importantly, this archive of the past is the basis for a set of reasonable expectations about what will come next. (p. 641)

A sense of story is not something that is learned directly; it is acquired through repeated experiences with a variety of different stories. Very young children acquire rudimentary story sense simply from hearing stories at home. Before they enter school, most children have a good idea of what is coming when they hear the phrase "Once upon a time. . . ." School-age children extend their sense of story with each new tale they hear or read; adults broaden their concepts and expectations of story if they continue to read widely. Film, television, and theater also affect one's sense of story; viewers of all ages come to know what to expect of westerns, romantic comedies, cops-and-robbers shows, musicals, and other forms of drama.

Oral literature is of particular value to students who have not yet acquired extensive reading skills. Their listening comprehension is much advanced over their ability to comprehend print (Sticht et al., 1974). They can understand and appreciate the narrated stories that they are unable to read for themselves and can develop auditorily the important sense of story that is so closely tied to reading comprehension abilities (Brown, 1977a; Stein and Glenn, 1982).

The content of traditional oral literature—that is, of folklore and fairy tales—is of significant interest to students (Sallee, 1983). A good told story can stimulate their imaginations and can generate excitement about literature and the desire to read. Story language can also extend students' vocabularies and knowledge of language structure. This solid oral base is vital to the children's future success in comprehending language in print (Pearson and Fielding, 1982; Strickland, 1985; Cochran-Smith, 1984; Sawyer, 1987). For beginning readers especially, and for developing readers of all ages, oral literature provides background, affects attitudes, and contributes to intellectual growth.

Just as it affects success in reading, so can oral literature also help students as they master composing skills. The syntactic elements of good stories, the logic of story structure, and the development of character and action all have a cumulative effect on students. These elements can provide a base from which pupils can compose their own stories (Brown, 1977a; Pradl, 1979). When students write, they must bring order to their ideas. They select, sequence, and choose wording to create the effect they desire. The organization and language of stories they hear can help them write coherently and effectively.

Oral literature is more than rewarding entertainment. Stories play a major role in developing students' skills in language, listening, and thinking. The activities of reading aloud and telling stories should both be included regularly in the language arts program.

Reading Aloud   The importance of surrounding students with books cannot be overemphasized. Having books around and being read to are critical to the development of positive attitudes toward reading (Durkin, 1974; Porter, 1969; Squire, 1968; Sirota, 1971; Botel, 1977). Students will learn to enjoy and value reading if teachers demonstrate a love of books; accordingly, teachers should read in the presence of students and also should read aloud often. There is considerable evidence to suggest that there is "a direct relationship between reading aloud to children and reading performance, language development, and the development of reading interests" (McCormick, 1977, p. 43). Hearing literature is as fundamental to developing reading ability as is anything in the curriculum.

Children who are read to regularly make significantly greater gains in comprehension than do those who do not have this experience. The two critical dimensions seem to be frequency and duration (Cohen, 1968; Porter, 1969; Bailey, 1970). Students must hear literature often over a long period of time. Hearing the teacher read aloud several times a week or daily throughout the year (and throughout the grades) would create an ideal situation.

The book language that children hear is the very language they must understand in order to read themselves. Students learn what books say and how they say it by listening. These listening experiences are probably most important for children who come from homes where reading is not valued, where books are not in evidence, and where parents do not read to their children. Schickedanz (1978) argues that "skills" instruction (for instance, phonics) is easiest for children who have a solid background in listening to others read aloud. As she writes,

They probably already know, at least on an intuitive level, the very skills they are being 'taught,' and have learned to use others as well. [But children who do not have this background] may become terribly lost, not knowing the source of these rules. . . . [The exercises are] isolated from the data-rich context of real reading materials. (p. 52)

Reading aloud to children also enhances their language development. Chomsky (1972) found a positive relationship between the syntactic complexity of books to which a child has been exposed and the child's stage of language development. Explaining this relationship, she stressed that children who hear and read books have an opportunity to learn language that is denied to children who do not have access to books. As children listen to stories, they become familiar with the rich language of literature. They assimilate word meanings, idioms, and common story expressions such as "once upon a time." They often imitate wording and phrasing. In these ways, they extend the boundaries of their language ability.

Reading aloud introduces children to authors or content they might not discover on their own. Teachers know that a read-aloud book becomes a popular choice for children's own reading. For instance, one teacher read Mollie Hunter's *The Kelpie's Pearls* (Funk & Wagnall, 1964) to a class of fifth graders. Interest in the magic, legend, and suspense of these Scottish tales grew rampant. Within days, other Mollie Hunter books were gone from the library shelves: *The Stronghold* (Harper & Row, 1974), *The Walking Stones* (Harper & Row, 1970), *A Stranger Came Ashore* (Harper & Row, 1975), *The Thirteenth Member* (Harper & Row, 1971), and *The Haunted Mountain* (Trophy, 1973) all were eagerly passed from one child to another. Students even placed their names on a waiting list for these books. Teachers tell of similar success with stories by E. B. White, Walter Farley, Robert McCloskey, and other authors. Kipling's *Just So Stories* became a best-loved book in one classroom after the teacher read how the elephant got his trunk in "The Elephant's Child." Teachers' experiences are consistent with research findings; for example, Porter (1969) found that reading aloud to fourth, fifth, and sixth graders affected the students' reading interests as well as their comprehension achievement. The New York City Public Library has conducted surveys in conjunction with its read-aloud programs for reluctant readers. Results show a high correlation between books students heard and the books they checked out of the library (Butler, 1980).

There are ample reasons for allotting time in the language arts program for reading aloud to students. Here are some of the benefits that students derive from read-aloud activities:

1. *Aesthetic:* Children learn to appreciate literature when they enjoy the rhythm of language and the sense of moving into another time and space.
2. *Academic:* Children improve their reading achievement, listening skill, and language ability.

3. *Cognitive:* Children's concepts, knowledge, and thinking abilities are expanded. Vicarious experiences provided by literature broaden children's understanding of the world.
4. *Affective:* Reading aloud is a sure way to establish a bond between listeners and reader.
5. *Stimulative:* Reading aloud encourages children to develop an interest in books and a desire to read for themselves. As they enjoy and learn from read-aloud books at levels beyond their own reading competency, they look forward to the books they will be able to read in the future.

Read-aloud books should be selected with two primary criteria in mind: *content* that will appeal to the class and *language* that is worth reading. Children will most enjoy stories that contain vivid characterization, believable dialogue, and a plot that moves briskly. They will be most captivated by language that is rhythmic, rich, and powerful. For the most part, teachers should choose stories that they themselves find enjoyable and entrancing. Reading aloud, the teacher will then naturally convey his or her own enthusiasm for the content and language of the story.

The teacher should remember, too, that varied selections will broaden students' experiences. The reading of a folk tale could be followed by some realistic fiction. Rachel Field's *Hitty, Her First Hundred Years* (Macmillan, 1969) could be followed by selections from Shel Silverstein's *Where the Sidewalk Ends* (Harper & Row, 1974). When the evening news focuses on the South Pacific, the teacher could read Armstrong Sperry's *Call It Courage* (Macmillan, 1968). When the weather forecaster predicts snow, the class could be introduced to Robert Frost's "Stopping by Woods on a Snowy Evening" or Ezra J. Keats's *The Snowy Day* (Viking, 1962). Sterling North's *Rascal* (Avon, 1975) is a good selection when the class is studying animal life; Scott O'Dell's *Sarah Bishop* (Houghton Mifflin, 1980) is appropriate when they are learning about colonial America. The choices from day to day may include the real and the fantastic, the near and the remote. Through a variety of books, stories, and poems, students can go on trips around the world and can enter into the lives of diverse people and creatures.

A teacher must also be attentive to the students' reactions to books and stories. Sometimes a book the teacher loves will not interest the students, so it will be best to move on to something else. Selective reading is sometimes necessary to maintain the children's interest; a single chapter from a long book might be just the right length for one class. If students seem to dislike a book, the teacher should admit it and try to find out what the source of dissatisfaction is. For instance, one teacher was thrilled with Mildred Taylor's *Roll of Thunder, Hear My Cry* (Bantam, 1978) and was eager to read it to a seventh-grade class. However, the group became increasingly restless at the beginning of the story. After reading only a few pages, the teacher stopped to discuss the story and found that the students were quite lost. The first dozen pages were filled with dialogue in the vernacular of the South, coupled with lengthy descriptions of rural Mississippi. Both features were foreign to the students' experiences, and there was also no incident to capture their imaginations, to provoke curiosity, and to make them wonder what would happen next. The teacher realized that a brief telling of the beginning, without the long (though beautiful) descriptive passages, would prove more effective in getting the students to listen; the reading could begin with the first real action. Hearing a story should be a pleasure, not a chore. Students' reactions give the alert teacher a good idea of the kind of material that will maintain interest and that will make the read-aloud time memorable.

There are so many excellent books and stories available that a comprehensive list cannot be presented here. New titles or new editions of old classics are published regularly. Thus, the best strategies involve checking libraries regularly, surveying literature anthologies, keeping up with book reviews, and asking colleagues and students to recommend their favorite selections. Most important, the teacher should be a wide reader, always on the lookout for a book or story that might interest the class. Some good sources for books to read aloud are listed here:

- American Library Association
  50 East Huron Street
  Chicago, Illinois 60611

- Bulletin of the Center For Children's Books
  The University of Chicago Press, Journals Division
  P.O. Box 37005
  Chicago, Illinois 06037

- The Children's Book Council
  67 Irving Place
  New York, NY 10003

- International Reading Association
  P.O. Box 8139
  Newark, Delaware 19714

- National Council of Teachers of English
  1111 Kenyon Road
  Urbana, Illinois 61801

For effective reading aloud, the following guidelines should be helpful. Other suggestions are given by Trelease (1985) and in articles by Cramer (1975) and Johnson (1983).

1. Before reading aloud to the class, practice the story until you feel comfortable speaking the author's language smoothly and with expression. Become familiar with the material so that you can emphasize certain words

or sentences. As you preview the selection, you can also make decisions about deleting sections, shortening long descriptive passages, or occasionally paraphrasing a portion in order to maintain the listeners' interest.

2. Try to establish a regular time for reading. Adhere to your schedule. Read aloud daily once you start a book; children may lose interest if several days elapse between chapters.

3. To help students set a purpose for listening, tell them that you have a story (poem, book) to share and that you want them to enjoy it with you. If you are continuing a long selection, review the main events with students before beginning. This will help them maintain continuity and will enable them to follow and enjoy the next segment.

4. Do not view reading aloud as the most expendable activity in the classroom program. Do not eliminate it automatically if the day's schedule seems very full. Equally important, do not withdraw it as punishment for misbehavior. Reading aloud is a valuable activity, not just a reward.

5. Seat students informally, perhaps in a cluster or circle, so that they can hear easily and see any illustrations clearly. Have reasonable rules, such as not allowing talking or moving about during reading.

6. Maintain as much eye contact with students as possible. Make them feel that you are sharing the story with each individual. As you read, you should observe students' responses; watch their facial expressions and body language. Adjust your reading to those signals.

7. Read slowly and enunciate clearly. You can create a mood by varying the pitch, tone, and pace of your voice. Once in a while, tape your oral reading so that you can monitor your performance and improve it.

8. Read without stopping to define vocabulary. Do not ask recall questions or make comments. Let the author communicate through you to the listeners. Well-written stories need no explanations; they speak for themselves. Differentiate between read-aloud time and an informational listening activity that has other objectives (see the next section).

9. Although didactic remarks by the teacher are unnecessary during the reading, spontaneous student involvement should be encouraged. Students who are attentive and interested will rather naturally participate. They will supply the next words when you pause; they will gleefully announce that they know what will happen next. Encourage them. Give them opportunities to predict what will happen and to chime in on repeated phrases. Let them laugh, be afraid, and want to cry. The best read-aloud activity is characterized by this kind of student involvement (Lamme, 1976). A sure sign of attention and comprehension occurs when the children become so immersed in the story that they rather naturally help with the telling (Kennedy and Weener, 1971).

10. Adjust story time to the attention span of your listeners and to your own endurance. Fifteen or twenty minutes is probably a suitable length of time for reading aloud. The young or inexperienced listener may tire even sooner. Many readers' voices also begin to fade after steady reading aloud. When you stop, give the audience something to look forward to. Try to finish the session at a suspenseful spot; make your audience eager to hear more.

Most read-aloud activities should be strictly for the enjoyment of students and teacher. Good books should simply be shared. But sometimes, a story may be incorporated into an instructional activity. Here is an example of one such lesson. The goals were both to improve listening through the use of folk literature and to provide a stimulus for writing. First, the teacher asked the fifth graders if anyone had seen a rose blooming at Christmas. In that Pennsylvania town, no one had, and the consensus was that such an occurrence was unlikely. Then students predicted what might happen in the Norse folk tale called "The Christmas Rose." Students thought that the story might involve a rose carved in ice, a girl named Rose, a rose that bloomed and froze, or perhaps an indoor rose that always bloomed at Christmas time. The teacher asked the group to listen to find out if any of those predictions matched the actual story and also to attend to as many details and facts as they could.

The teacher read, stopping three times during the story. At each pause, students took a few minutes to reflect on the story's events, to compare these with their predictions, and to write down whatever facts and details they remembered hearing. At the end of the story, the group reviewed the original predictions and discussed how their first ideas differed from the actual outcome. Then the teacher said, "You have in front of you a number of facts and details from the story, and you also know that this is a folk tale, similar to other folk tales we have been studying. What do you suppose actually happened to cause this story to be told?" After a short discussion, students wrote explanations of how the folk tale may have come about. Here are some of their responses:

The Christmas rose is really a myth to explain the Christmas spirit. People give gifts to each other. They are kind and caring at Christmas. Somebody who was a storyteller decided there had to be a reason. He made up the story of the rose. The rose in the story made people happy.

Well, one Christmas when the snow was all over the ground, one little rose had not died yet. It was still in bloom. It was so unusual in the north land that a story was told about it.

Maybe the rose wasn't the most important part of the story. Maybe what happened was that a little boy risked his life to get firewood or a Christmas tree. When people told about it, it made a better story to add the part about a rose with a rosy light.

The story was to explain why people put lights in their windows at Christmas. The rose with its glow that even lighted the street was like a candle. The light was a symbol of William's bravery and good, kind heart.

While enjoying an interesting Christmas tale, these students were also actively involved in listening. They had purposes for listening; they thought and wrote during the telling; and they discussed and wrote after listening. In so doing, they noted facts and made inferences. Their papers revealed thoughtful attention to meanings and interpretations. The activities kept students actively involved but did not detract from their enjoyment of the tale.

Storytelling   In an earlier age, storytellers were revered members of communities; they described and interpreted life with their tales. Rather than dying out with other trappings of early cultures, the metaphors and images of those stories have remained with us. Archetypal tales have survived for centuries and have crossed cultural barriers. Different versions of "Cinderella," "Don't Count Your Chickens," "Patient Griselda," and other stories still exist throughout the world, as they have for generations (Shah, 1979; Clarkson and Cross, 1980).

Most of us remember the stories that we heard in our childhood from family members or librarians. We were delighted with fanciful creatures, we were apprehensive about witches and wolves, and we were thrilled to hear our favorites again and again. Anyone who has been enthralled with well-told stories knows that the tales and their telling have touched our lives deeply. The old favorites are compelling because they express basic human emotions and motivations that can be interpreted on many levels; what we enjoyed as children takes on new meaning at later stages of life (Bettelheim, 1975; Sale, 1978).

The oral tradition in literature has been extended in modern times by television. We now turn to television for information and entertainment, taking advantage of programs that have visual as well as audio impact. It might seem that storytelling, as a personal, face-to-face interaction, has become outdated and irrelevant. But the opposite is true. Despite the overwhelming influence of television, storytelling still creates a special magic, and storytellers are actually increasing in numbers and popularity. The art has gone beyond the children's room of the public library and children's bedtimes; there are storytelling festivals across the nation, and more and more storytellers are entertaining groups of all ages.

Even though storytelling belongs to an older cultural tradition than reading, it is not part of most school curricula. Many teachers have had little experience as storytellers and have had few opportunities to learn the craft. This is true even if they read aloud to their students frequently. Yet Bettelheim (1975) and Applebee (1979), taking different perspectives, both argue that exposure to the centuries-old oral tradition of literature can have a significant influence on children's intellectual and social development. Mandler and Johnson (1977) also stress the usefulness of memorable folk tales and fables for developing listeners' awareness of story structure. The advantages of telling stories, as well as of reading aloud, are great.

When the book is put aside, the story takes on a life of its own through the teller. Practiced storytellers, well into the absorbing events of a tale, almost become a part of the group that is listening. The audience is aware only of the events, the dialogue, and the magic of the words. Successful storytelling teachers

Listening is a major pathway to language and learning. Storytelling creates a special magic and is an excellent way to improve students' listening skills. The craft of storytelling can be learned. The requirements are simply the desire to learn and the willingness to practice.

can capture and hold the group's attention through eye contact; each listener feels the story is just for himself or herself, and each student responds with more than the usual amount of attention and interest.

Students' imaginations and visualization skills are enhanced significantly when their teachers tell stories. Without a book's illustrations to define characters and setting, listeners' minds are free to picture the people and events in different ways. With the abundance of films, television shows, and well-illustrated books in their lives, students seldom have an opportunity to imagine characters and settings. Learning to visualize, students can come to enjoy their own reading even more, being better able to imagine the happenings when illustrations are not provided.

Well-told stories present excellent models of language for listeners of all ages. Especially when selected from a variety of sources, cultural backgrounds, and historical periods, stories can provide listeners with rich vocabulary and diverse language structures. Many unusual words and language patterns, not common in everyday speech, become meaningful in the context of a good story. The telling enhances students' oral comprehension and builds foundations for comprehending written literature. Hearing stories is especially valuable to those children who have limited listening and speaking vocabularies. Story language is limited only by the teller's ability to select and use words. This skill invariably improves with practice.

The craft of storytelling can be learned. No special drama training, speech lessons, or unique flair is needed. The requirements are simply the desire to learn and the willingness to practice. Farrell and Nessel (1984) suggest seven steps for a narrator to follow in learning a story. The essentials of the strategy, common among storytellers, are these:

1. Choose a story that appeals to you, one you would enjoy telling and that you think the class might like to hear. Also consider the quality of the language. A story with rhythmic, powerful language can create rich verbal effects in the telling.
2. Read the story carefully. Note its construction. Then outline the story, dividing it into parts that represent the events in sequence. Note these in writing; make a list or diagram of the main events.
3. Visualize the setting. Close your eyes. Imagine all the small, interesting details of the various scenes.
4. Visualize the plot. Recreate the sequence of action in your imagination. (Visualizing the action in detail greatly helps in learning the story. You will not have trouble retelling the story if you can see it unfold in your mind's eye.)
5. Read the story aloud. Bring the words to life; read with expression.
6. Put the book aside and tell the story, using your understanding of the structure and your visual images as guides. You need not memorize the story word-for-word, but you may want to use some phrases or sentences from the original. Make the words come alive to project your images of the tale.
7. Practice telling the story. Share it with friends or family. Do not worry about forgetting something or making a mistake. Think of the story as "yours" so that you can tell it comfortably and smoothly.

Learning and telling become easier with each new story. A beginning storyteller may feel self-conscious or nervous and may worry that the "performance" may get bad "reviews." Initial awkwardness soon goes away, though, and assurance comes with practice. Students usually enjoy hearing the same story many times; each time a teacher tells a tale, the narration gets smoother. The class's delight will also bolster confidence. Whether hearing an old favorite or a new story, students will be thrilled and will eagerly ask for more.

Here are four additional suggestions for making storytelling sessions effective:

1. Establish a simple ritual to mark the beginning of a story. Light a candle or ring a small bell. Students will learn that the signal means that a special experience is about to begin. Attention can be obtained quickly and easily, and the occasion will be memorable because of the familiar ritual.
2. Tell the story simply, in your own way. You do not need to create a new and different personality, costumes, props, or special effects. Use your natu-

ral voice, natural gestures, and natural facial expressions. Let the words of the story speak through you; do not "act," but just tell.

3. Avoid teaching while storytelling. Do not stop to ask questions about story details, to point out a moral, or to define a word. Let the story have its own strong impact. Didactic intervention is not necessary.

4. Use a variety of stories. Tell old-time favorite fairy tales and folk tales. Introduce students to characters and stories that exist in the traditions of diverse cultures. Use modern stories. Create stories from memorable personal experiences. Turn a unique classroom event into a story.

There are many sources for stories to tell. Trade books, collections of folk literature, and magazines will all suggest ideas. Librarians are glad to help. Storytellers also enjoy swapping stories, so a good source for new tales is at a gathering of storytellers. These are a few sources for stories and information about storytelling:

Caroline F. Bauer, *Handbook for Storytellers.* American Library Association, 1977.
Sara C. Bryant, *How To Tell Stories to Children.* Boston: Houghton Mifflin, 1924.
Ramon Ross, *Storyteller.* Columbus, OH: Charles Merrill, 1972.
Stith Thompson, *One Hundred Favorite Folktales.* Bloomington, IN: Indiana University Press, 1968.

After the Story When the book is put aside or the storytelling is over, follow-up activities can extend the pleasure of the experience and can also help the students to develop language abilities. The best kinds of post-story activities enhance the literature and encourage students to reflect on the events and characters. Hence, students can enrich their understanding and appreciation of the tale. The emphasis is always on the story, not on practicing skills. In the process, language skills are inevitably developed, however.

When we finish a good book or see a terrific movie, we are eager to talk about it. We want to tell what we thought of it, why it affected us, what it made us think. Similarly, students enjoy talking about a story. They will often do so spontaneously because they are filled with the experience of having heard it. Each will have different reactions and interpretations. Informal discussion can encourage divergent responses. The following kinds of open-ended questions stretch the group's thinking and enrich the meaning of a story:

- What was the most important part of the story to you? Why?
- Which character did you like best? least? Why?
- What do you think the witch (the giant, and so on) looked like?
- Which was the funniest (scariest, saddest) part?
- What did you think when ———?
- Which part did you like best? Why?
- What would you have done when ———?

Given the chance, students will discuss a story with great enthusiasm. One group of sixth graders was entranced with a telling of "The Beggar and the Gazelle" (see Chapter 1), and the listeners offered a wide range of reactions as they reflected on this moving story. Their remarks included these comments:

You're so sad about the gazelle! Why was the beggar so mean to him?

I liked hearing about the trips to the desert where they all lived in the tents.

When the gazelle died, I wanted to cry!

There's a moral, but it's not one of those moral stories. It's a good story.

The full discussion of this tale touched on character motivation, vivid details, comparisons with other stories, reflections on ingratitude, and personal interpretations of the story's events. This story, like all good stories, stimulated thinking and feeling.

The sharing of reactions can take other forms, too. Students might draw a character or scene and show their illustrations to one another. Drawing is especially valuable when the story is told or when the book has no illustrations. Each student will visualize the events differently; pictures will reveal the unique interpretations. For instance, one first-grade class enjoyed hearing "The Squeaky Door," a Puerto Rican folk tale about a little boy who, at bedtime, is repeatedly startled by a closing squeaky door. To soothe his fears, his grandmother places a new animal in his bed each night. As the menagerie grows, so does the noise and confusion. The animals are startled by the door, too, and eventually their antics collapse the bed, causing the house to fall down. After hearing the story, each child drew a representation of the tale. Many showed the bed filled with animals, but each student drew a different combination. Some depicted the door emitting a great squeak. Some showed the boy trying to sleep. Some drew the grandmother. As the children talked about their pictures, they related the details that were most memorable to them.

Sometimes very simple, concrete activities precipitate positive responses to oral literature. For instance, after hearing *Ask Mr. Bear* by Marjorie Flack (Macmillan, 1986), each child can give a neighbor a bear hug. Tasting blueberries will be fun after students hear Robert McCloskey's *Blueberries for Sal* (Viking, 1948). After *Sylvester and the Magic Pebble* by William Steig (Windmill, 1969), children will love to search for their own magic pebbles in the school yard. Hearing Byrd Baylor's *Sometimes I Dance Mountains* (Scribner, 1973) can stimulate impromptu dancing. Children might also pantomime characters' actions; they might trudge down the lane or stalk the large elephant. Such dramatizing gives children a chance to respond to a detail in the story and can also help to reinforce word meanings.

Children also might enact scenes from the story, or write about what they liked most, or take turns retelling and interpreting memorable events. Because any story impresses different listeners in different ways, the follow-up should encourage divergent responses. There is no need for comprehension questions or for making sure that students can recognize and restate a moral. To focus on the meaning is to diminish the fullness and richness of a tale. Any story has many meanings, and these meanings are constructed by the individuals who listen with their own experiences and personalities as the foundation.

Stories through the Grades   Oral literature is not just for the very young. It is enticing for learners of all ages, as a valuable listening activity, and as a stimulant to many reading and writing activities. Students may enjoy reading favorite stories aloud to classmates or family. In so doing, they extend their oral expression and interpretation abilities. They may also compose their own stories as their writing abilities develop. Two examples illustrate how extension activities can be used in multigrade situations.

Abrahamson (1977) reports on an oral literature unit completed by adolescents. The students learned of the craft of storytelling by reading books about techniques, by inviting a storyteller to the class, and by studying a tape they made of the teller's performance. With a librarian's help, they then selected books, practiced reading them, and finally went to first- and second-grade classrooms to read their selections to the youngsters. The children were delighted; the adolescents gained new perspectives on literature and developed their speaking and oral-interpretation skills.

Robinson (1978) conducted a story-writing unit in her high-school English class. Students first visited an elementary school, where they were paired with primary-school students. They then interviewed their charges to find out what kinds of stories the younger children most enjoyed. The older students then studied children's literature and discussed the elements found in a good story. Finally, each composed and illustrated an original story for the primary-school child each had interviewed earlier. With their stories bound into book form, the high-school students returned to the elementary school to read the very personal tales to their little friends.

Oral literature can be a stimulating part of other subjects, too, at all grade levels. A young man once remarked that he had always disliked history because it had seemed to be a dull and uninteresting collection of irrelevant facts to be learned. But in a college history course, he had an instructor who told the *stories* of history—the thrilling travels of the explorers, the agonies of war, the intrigues at court. The young man asked the teacher, "Hey, where did all this good stuff come from?" The instructor's answer: "It's all in the history books. That's what history is!" (By the way, that young man decided to major in history.)

History lessons are natural settings for stories. Who could resist tales of the struggles between Henry II and Thomas à Becket, the shock of Lincoln's assassination, or the determination of nineteenth-century immigrants? So, too, are classic myths fascinating to elementary- and middle-school students when told as tales of adventure and romance. Lewis Carroll's *Through the Looking Glass* (Nelson Doubleday, n.d.) is enjoyable for any age group. The book also provides thought-provoking material for discussion; for instance, the famous exchange between Alice and Humpty Dumpty is an excellent starting point for a discussion of word meanings:

> "When I use a word," Humpty Dumpty said, in a rather scornful tone, "it means just what I choose it to mean—neither more nor less."
>
> "The question is," said Alice, "whether you can make words mean so many different things."
>
> "The question is," said Humpty Dumpty, "which is to be master—that's all."

Science classes can be vividly enlivened if "Newton" appears to tell of his discoveries. Or teachers can relate the exciting story of the race to discover the intricacies of DNA. Smardo (1982) and Hennings (1982) suggest other ways of using literature in elementary-level social studies and science lessons.

The content of the school curriculum is based on the adventures, discoveries, creations, triumphs, and disasters of past and present society. This is exciting material that is too captivating to be relegated only to the pages of a text or the contents of a lecture. Stories bring the substance to life and turn lessons into truly memorable listening experiences.

Listening to Obtain Information

Students are expected to learn a great deal from listening to teachers' explanations and instructions. If students are inattentive or confused, they will miss important information and lose sense of what the class is doing. It is the teacher's responsibility to help students acquire good informational listening habits. This is best accomplished if the students are fully aware of the listening purposes and if they are given opportunities to be active participants rather than passive recipients. This section describes selected listening activities that are designed to give students instructions and information. These activities can help them become purposeful listeners.

Because each student has a different background of experience and knowledge, each student will be at a different level of readiness for learning. The teacher needs to prepare students to listen, to focus their attention, and to help them set clear purposes. Students also need to remain actively involved; accordingly, the lecture or explanation should include opportunities for students to respond and take part. The children furthermore need to review what they have heard. They must discuss, ask questions, and state information in their own words if they are to retain what they have heard. Even if students seem quite attentive, they may not fully understand the material. Therefore, the follow-up activities are as important as that which is done before and during the presentation. Let us consider each of these principles in more detail.

An excellent way to *set purposes* for listening is to have students discuss what they already know about the topic. Calling up familiar knowledge and experiences will help students assimilate new information. One way to do this is to have students predict answers to key questions that are based on the content objectives of the lesson. For instance, assume that the teacher is planning to present information about deep sea diving and intends to emphasize facts about the equipment divers use, the depths to which they dive, and the creatures they find in the ocean. To set the purposes before the students listen to the presentation, the teacher could ask students to predict answers to these questions:

- What equipment do you think divers use?
- How deep do you think divers go?
- What do you think divers see in the ocean?

Students would not necessarily know the right answers, but they would be able to make some reasonable predictions based on whatever they do know about oceans. As they discuss their predictions and give reasons for their ideas, they will be setting purposes for learning, identifying what they know about the topic and what they would like to learn. They will be actively involved; their curiosity will be aroused; and they will be ready to listen. Anticipating what is to come, based on what is known, employs the same kind of thinking process that students need to use when they read (see Chapters 4 and 5). Speculating before listening not only sets the purposes for listening but also directly develops cognitive skills that students use in reading (Stauffer, 1975).

During the presentation, students should stay actively involved. They might take notes or ask questions or discuss or add information. They will be particularly attentive to information that is related to the questions they discussed before listening. As these points come up in the presentation, the group can stop to discuss the information, clarifying what they have heard.

When the explanation is finished, *follow-up activities* may be used to reinforce learning. Further discussion or writing, to review important points, will enable students to state the new information in their own words. Reading or viewing supplementary material can also help to extend and cement learning. There is no "best" follow-up activity; choices depend on the students, on the lesson's objectives, and on the information that has been presented.

The following examples illustrate the principles of setting purposes, presenting the oral material, and ending with follow-up activities. The first example is from a lesson that was conducted in a fourth-grade class. The group was learning about the Revolutionary War era; the teacher's goal was to introduce the class to details about the life of Benjamin Franklin. An interesting account of Franklin's early life provided good information (Lucille Wallower's *Pennsyl-*

vania Primer). To set purposes for listening, the group predicted answers to these questions:

- What do you think Ben Franklin did for a living?
- What do you think were some of the things that Franklin invented?

The group already knew a little about Franklin, so they were able to make reasonable predictions. Some thought Franklin was a farmer; these students claimed that a lot of people were farmers in those days. Others thought he started out being a writer; these students recalled that Franklin had written *Poor Richard's Almanac*. As they made their predictions and gave their reasons, the children became quite interested in learning the actual answers. Thus, their purposes were set; they were ready to learn because they had become actively involved in thinking of possibilities.

The children kept paper handy to write down answers to the pertinent questions as they heard them. They were not expected to write everything but were only to jot down a few words from time to time as they heard relevant information. The purpose for taking notes was to keep students involved while they listened, not to have them transcribe all they would hear.

After listening to the teacher's selection, the children discussed answers to the original questions and decided which of their first predictions were most correct. This review, tied closely to the original purpose-setting discussion, helped the group recall information and state it in their own words. Some used their notes as they talked, but because the children had specific purposes when they started listening, most were able to remember the important points. To reinforce learning, students wrote accounts of Franklin's life, based on what they had heard and discussed. Here are two of their papers (in their original form, before spelling and other such mechanical details were corrected):

When Ben was a boy he worked in a candle shop with his father. Buy the time Ben was five he knew how to read and buy the time he was seven he knew how to wright. Then he went to school for two years. When he was ten his father asked him sence he liked to read so much if he would like to be a printer. Of corce he didn't turn that offer down be cose he liked to print more than make candles. But when he was seventean he ran away to Newark. He couldn't find a job there so he went to Philadeafa. There he got a job as a ausistent printer. Befor that when he first got there he got three big fluffy rolls for three sents and put one under each arm and ate one. He was wearing a raggy old coat with his pockets full of shirts and stockings. He was walking down the street and a lady laughed at him. That same lady was working for his manager and a few years later he maried her and soon he owned the Franklin mint.

When Ben Franklin was four years old he could read. When he was seven years old he could write. When he was ten he joined his father in the candlemaking business. He told his father that he wanted to be a sailor not a candlemaker. So his father said "Since you like to read so much then join your brother as a printer at his printer shop." So Ben printed in his brother's printing shop until he was seventeen then he and his brother started fighting at each other. So Ben ran away and went to Philadelphia. He was hungry so he went to a bakery and asked for three cents worth of bread. He got three rolls of bread. He got a job at a printing shop. Then he got married to Mary Reed. He invented the rocking chair, Franklin stove, grocers arm, speedometer, odometer, bifocals, harmonica, ditto machine, lightning rod, cartoons in newspapers. He also made the first fire insurance, libary, daylight savings time, fire department, hospital, and said lightning is electricity.

Through writing, the students had another chance to review the information they had heard and to state it in their own words. Their papers reveal that they had grasped the essentials of the account and that they had responded to it in their own unique ways. The students had picked up key facts about Franklin's work as a printer and inventor. It is also interesting to see that certain other details were memorable; for instance, students enjoyed the description of Franklin buying three rolls for three cents and marching down the street with them. Later activities reinforced this first lesson.

This next example illustrates a different method of presenting information orally. This lesson was conducted by an elementary-school teacher who aimed to stimulate students' interest in the history of California. First the teacher wrote three names on the chalkboard: Karana/Juana Maria, Mammy Pleasant, and Tamson Donner. Then she told the group that all of these people were women who had been in California in the mid-nineteenth century. She asked the children to speculate about who the women were and what they were remembered for. The children did not know for sure, but they began to think. They reviewed what they knew about California history from previous lessons and from independent reading. They had learned about the missions, the gold rush, the difficult travel conditions, and so on. The consensus was that the three unknowns must have been pioneer women; there were different ideas as to what each woman was known for. As curiosity was aroused, purposes were set: the group wanted to know who those women were!

Then, taking a beaded collar from her bag, the teacher became the ghost of Karana/Juana Maria. She told the group about her life as an Indian girl on a California South Coast island. The audience became captivated. After a few moments of autobiographical information, the ghost said, "Do you have any questions to ask me?" Queries tumbled forth; everyone felt there was only a short time to obtain valuable information before the Indian girl would drift away. When those questions had been answered, the ghost disappeared. The teacher then dipped into her bag and quickly exchanged the beaded collar for a calico bonnet and the personality of the notorious Mammy Pleasant of early San Francisco, an enterprising and powerful businesswoman. What followed was another autobiography, more questions from the listeners, and a second fading away. Then the third ghost, Tamson Donner, appeared in a simple apron, holding a dried flower, to tell of her terrible experiences crossing the mountains in winter and to answer listeners' questions. As a final step, the teacher brought out three books, each presenting the story of one of the three fascinating people the group had "met." The listeners were eager to read the books and learn more.

Another teacher used a similar tactic with his first-grade class. One day, he came to school dressed in sturdy pants and a loose plaid work shirt. A frying pan was affixed to his head as a hat. He had a small canvas bag slung over his shoulder, in which he had put some apple seeds. The children were intrigued with the costume and began asking questions. Speaking "in character," the teacher told the class that he was the ghost of Johnny Appleseed, coming to tell them about his adventures and about his commitment to planting apple trees. As he talked, he gave the children a good deal of information about the life and times of Johnny Appleseed. The students readily accepted the ghost, listened attentively, and continued to ask questions. The simple playacting, which aroused the children's interest and curiosity, led to further discussion, films, and activities related to the legendary figure and American life during his era. It led, as well, to some interesting study of apples and apple trees.

The mode of presentation in these three examples was essentially narrative. The account of Franklin's life reads like a story, and the ghosts of the other illustrations told the stories of their lives. Not all teachers' presentations need to be performed as stories, but narratives are particularly powerful for capturing attention and maintaining interest when the goal is to transmit information. Such presentations are not the same as oral literature; the material is not necessarily literary or poetic. But the effect on listeners is similar—a well-told "story" of a person's life or an event in history can be as memorable as a fairy tale.

The next example is a listening activity that was conducted in a third-grade class to present selected information about ladybugs. The group began with several purpose-setting questions, reproduced here with the students' responses:

What does a ladybug look like?

- like a bug with feelers
- has four legs (six legs, eight legs)
- round, with red (orange, black) dots

Where do you think ladybugs live?

- under bark in trees
- in holes in the ground
- in the grass
- in nests

What do you think ladybugs eat?

- insects
- grass
- leaves
- honey

The students' predictions were all based on first-hand experiences with ladybugs or on inferences based on their knowledge about other animals. The children had good reasons to support their thinking. For instance, some had seen ladybugs near trees and in the grass, so it seemed logical to assume that the creatures lived there. Others knew that birds and other animals built nests or lived in holes in the ground, so it seemed equally logical that ladybugs might do the same.

Giving reasons to support predictions is as important as making the predictions themselves. The reasoning process exercises students' thinking and prepares them to learn something new or to confirm what they already know. There is no surer way of getting students involved than to ask them the following question: What do you think and why do you think so? As the third graders speculated, inferred, and drew tentative conclusions, they did not remain passive; on the contrary, they were active thinkers who were ready to learn.

Students obtained their answers from the teacher's oral explanation. Then they spent a few minutes discussing the information, going back to their original predictions to decide which of the responses were closest to being right. Students were able to revise their first thoughts by using what they had heard. They saw for themselves how much they had learned at this point.

To reinforce and extend learning, students read "Lucky Ladybugs" by Gladys Conklin (from *Sunshine Days,* Allyn & Bacon, Level 13, 1978). This selection contained details about the habits and the life cycle of ladybugs. When the students finished reading, they discussed the article, reviewing and restating the information. They also discussed facts about the life cycle. As a group, the class reviewed the phases and drew these as a life-cycle diagram on the chalkboard. Then each student drew a model of the life cycle, labeling the stages with words the group had learned (egg, larva, pupa, pale ladybug, ladybug).

Each of these lessons followed the same principles. Clear purposes were set; students were actively involved while they were listening; follow-up activities extended and reinforced learning. These are the basics of good informational listening activities. The examples also suggest the variety that is possible when the teacher presents information. Though straightforward explanations (lectures) are often appropriate, there are many other ways to capture students' attention and interest. Stories, demonstrations, dramatizations, and experiments can all be used to highlight important facts that the teacher wants students to learn and remember.

Viewing for Different Purposes

As our society becomes increasingly sophisticated technologically, more and more information is transmitted visually as well as verbally. Films, filmstrips, television, videotapes, computer graphics, diagrams, and billboards all command our attention daily. Sometimes it seems that concepts should be automatically comprehensible because they are pictured. Indeed, some kinds of information may be more understandable because of illustrations; a diagram is usually more effective than a verbal explanation is in presenting a complex process. But we cannot assume that students will understand concepts better just because the ideas are pictured. Children are attracted to bright illustrations, television, and other kinds of visual material, but they may not know how to look carefully and critically.

Viewing, like listening, is a cognitive process. It requires attention to details, skill at making inferences or interpretations, and ability to evaluate pictorial material. Textbook illustrations, maps, charts, and graphs contain information that can be used to develop and reinforce concepts. The pictures accompanying a story represent key events in the narrative. Films and filmstrips enhance learning if students are prepared to view them attentively and thoughtfully.

Effective viewing, like effective listening, is promoted when the teacher pays attention to basic principles. Students need a well-lighted, comfortable environment, clear purposes for viewing, active involvement, opportunities for review, and practice with a variety of viewing experiences. Here are several activities that can develop the cognitive skills associated with comprehending pictorial information.

Responding to a Wordless Picture Book

Wordless picture books tell a story through pictures alone. They give youngsters a chance to exercise the same kind of thinking with narrative material that they use when they listen to stories and when they read stories on their own. Students must make use of visual details, follow the story sequence, anticipate outcomes, note cause–effect relationships, make inferences and judgments, and draw conclusions. An example will illustrate the process.

A group of first graders participated in a lively lesson based on the wordless picture book *April Fools* by Fernando Krahn (E.P. Dutton, 1974). First the

Viewing, like listening, is a cognitive process requiring attention to details, skill at making inferences or interpretations, and ability to evaluate.

teacher read the title aloud and then showed the cover picture, which depicted two boys holding aloft a dragon's head affixed to a plank. Next the group examined the first page, which pictured the same two boys carrying lumber and tools.

To stimulate observing and thinking, the teacher asked, "What do you think will happen in this story?"

AMY: They're going to work.
TEACHER: Why do you think so?
AMY: They have a hammer and a saw and those boards.
CHRIS: They're going to make something.
MARIO: They're going to make a scary head and drive it through town. [This child combined the details from the two illustrations.]
STEVEN: Yes! That's what they're doing.
MARK: They'll make a head.

The teacher revealed the next few pages, on which the boys are shown building something. The children agreed that they had been right in predicting that the boys would be hammering, sawing, and building a scary head. When the teacher showed the next picture, of the completed head, this was the exchange:

MARIO: We were wrong!

TEACHER: Why?

MARIO: It's not a scary head. It's a dragon. [There was general agreement on this point.]

TEACHER: What do you think they'll do now?

AMY: Scare people.

MARIO: No, they're not going to scare people. They're going to fool people. It's that day.

MARK: Yes! It's April Fool's Day.

The next several pages confirmed this prediction. The boys are shown carting the "dragon" around town, poking it in front of people's doors, placing it on a rooftop, and pulling it through the lake, where it resembles the Loch Ness monster. The group examined the pictures, discussed what was going on, and agreed that they had been right. Then they saw that the boys were in the forest, looking bewildered.

TEACHER: What will happen now?

STEVEN: They look lost.

TEACHER: Why do you think so? [The group pointed out details such as the boys pointing in different directions, one boy crying, and the other climbing a tree to look around.] What do you think will happen?

MARK: A real dragon will show them the way home!

AMY: Maybe the people will find them.

MARIO: The people will see the head and come find them.

The last pages of the book confirm the final two predictions. The boys climb a tree with the head; the townspeople see it and rescue them.

These students worked together to grasp the essential points of the picture story: the boys play their tricks, become lost, mark their location, and are found. Using picture clues alone, these children "read" the story. Predicting and discussing, the group used the reading-thinking process (see Chapter 4). They exercised the following specific reading skills: noting details, getting the main ideas, making inferences, and using information to anticipate outcomes. Children of all ages love wordless picture books, and there are many available for these kinds of lessons. Several titles are suggested in Appendix A.

This type of viewing exercise can be done with a variety of materials, with students at all grade levels. For instance, a similar viewing lesson, with a different twist, was done in a middle school language arts class. The teacher had assembled sets of unrelated black and white photographs, including shots of highways, residential areas, city streets, swimming pools, and so on. Students were divided into groups of seven or eight; each group was given a pile of photographs. In each group, one student started with the picture on top and began telling an impromptu story, based on the details of the picture. When the teller ran out of ideas, a second student continued, using the next photograph as a stimulus. Students quickly entered into the spirit of the activity, and the storytelling was lively, often hilarious, especially as the tale passed from one person to another and the new teller was pressed to move the characters into the next scene believably. All listened carefully, enjoying one another's creativity; all participated, eager to add their own ideas. When the small groups were finished (all had been working simultaneously), the teacher asked several to hold up their pictures and retell their stories to the whole class. The stories improved in the retelling; they were more detailed and were related with greater smoothness and expression.

Responding to Filmstrips

The vivid, projected illustrations of filmstrips can be particularly striking, and they can provide excellent visual information as a base for learning. Because the rate of presentation can be controlled easily by the teacher, filmstrips allow students to discuss and ask questions during viewing. This practice encourages active participation in the lesson. Filmstrips can be used to tell a story, to introduce concepts, or to reinforce learning. Thus, they can supplement literature units or lessons in any subject. But filmstrips do not teach automatically; they must be employed purposefully to meet specific objectives.

Students can "read" a story strip just as they "read" a picture book—using the details of pictures to follow the story as it unfolds. Purpose setting and discussion during viewing should focus on the actions of the characters and the sequence of events. Students need to think about what is happening and why, what might happen next, what the characters are like, and what these characters might do. The cognitive activity is the same that the students perform in listening to or in reading a story. The main difference is that in viewing a filmstrip, students will be attending to pictures (rather than to text) most of the time.

With an informational filmstrip, the instructional focus is on the content of the lesson. Students need to know that they are looking for facts (information) rather than following a story. They also need to know, before viewing, what they are looking for. Purpose setting should focus on the concepts or facts that students are to learn. Viewing a filmstrip is like listening for information; even though the pictures can contribute to learning, students still need opportunities to stop, discuss, and clarify as they view.

Filmstrip lessons include components for listening and reading as well as viewing. Most strips contain text that can be read aloud by the teacher or students. For several reasons, it is usually best for the teacher to do most of the reading. When one student is called on to read the captions aloud, everyone else follows the words, too, and only glances at the pictures. The lesson in such cases quickly becomes a dull exercise in oral reading rather than an interesting search for information. Also, few filmstrips control text vocabulary and language;

the material may be expressed in language that is too difficult for the students to read easily, even though they can understand the concepts by listening and viewing. Inexperienced or poor readers may miss information if they must struggle with a difficult text while also trying to process the visual information. Having the teacher read allows students to concentrate on viewing and listening.

To illustrate a good use of a filmstrip, here are the details of a first-grade lesson that was conducted one November day. As part of a unit on the tradition of Thanksgiving, the teacher planned to show a filmstrip that told the story of the first such celebration. Before viewing, the children discussed what they already knew about Thanksgiving. Most mentioned family gatherings, turkey dinners, and a school holiday. Then the children offered predictions about how the first Thanksgiving came to be. A few thought of Indians and Pilgrims, but these children were generally not sure of the origins of the tradition. To find out the reasons for the first celebration, the children then viewed a filmstrip that told the story of the early settlers. The teacher read aloud the captions and enlarged upon them, engaging the class in discussion as they looked at each frame. The children noted details, asked questions, and commented on the different scenes. To summarize what they had seen, the group dictated a short account, which the teacher recorded on chart paper:

THE THANKSGIVING STORY

They went over to America on the Mayflower. The Indians taught the Pilgrims how to plant corn and how to dig clams. The Pilgrims and Indians had a Thanksgiving dinner. The Pilgrims had a Thanksgiving because of all the food at harvest. They played games. The Indians had a race.

The children here had clear purposes for viewing the filmstrip. In addition, they had a chance to discuss and summarize what they saw, during and after viewing. The dictated account allowed them to tell what they had learned in their own words and to have a record of that learning. They were able to reread their account over the next several days.

The filmstrip is a unique way of organizing and presenting information or a story. Once students are familiar with the form, they greatly enjoy making their own filmstrips. This composing activity has distinct advantages. Students must plan what they want to say, choose what they want to illustrate, coordinate script with graphics, and produce a finished product. These activities require careful thought and attention to detail, sequencing, and clarity, while allowing considerable room for original thought and art work. Those who produce a filmstrip also gain an improved sense of what to look for when viewing an unfamiliar strip.

Students can do their planning and drafting on a "story board," an example of which is shown in Figure 2 with the first draft of fourth-grade Linda's story

		Sue the baby koala
1		Once upon a time there was a koala her name was Sue.
2		Sue's mother was a big koala. She had white fur and so did Sue.
3		One day Sue was out on her own and a lion tried to attack her but Sue ran in to the den with her mother.
4		Sue and her mother were eating eucalyptus, then all of a sudden Sue fell out of the tree and hurt her arm badly.
5		the next day some people came and took Sue to there barn and put her in the hay.
6		When Sue woke up She was better but very tired.
7		The next day the people took Sue to a tree and Sue saw her mother and was very happy.
8		Sue and her mother ate leaves for the whole day and were very happy. the end.

FIGURE 2 Fourth grade student's story board for an original filmstrip

and drawings. Linda uses a classic opening and closing, clear sequencing, and appropriate illustrations. She is also attentive to moving her story along with good transitions (One day.... The next day.... When Sue woke up ...). The structure of the story board and the blanks for illustrations help students construct a meaningful, connected story like Linda's. The final step is to draw and color the illustrations on a blank filmstrip.[1] The author then shows the strip to the class, acting as narrator.

An alternative plan is for the author first to show the strip without narration while the other students write their own captions for each frame. Then the author reads the original script, and the group compares notes. Here, for example, is one student's interpretation of Linda's story, written while this student viewed only the illustrations:

SUE, THE BABY KOALA

1. This baby likes to climb.
2. This baby koala likes to sleep on the ground.
3. This lion is the king.
4. This koala fell out of the tree.
5. This koala is a very sleepy koala.
6. This is a house where people live.
7. This is where they eat in the trees.
8. This is the mother and the baby.

An activity such as this one is useful for generating discussion about the interaction of words and pictures. In Linda's filmstrip, the picture in frame 4 was more successful in presenting its message than was the more ambiguous picture in frame 3. The other child wrote a caption for frame 4 that was very similar to the original, but the one she wrote for frame 3 was not at all Linda's intended message. Noting the differences, the class decided that the picture in frame 4 was effective because it showed just what Linda had intended and that the picture for frame 3 should be revised to include the lion actually chasing the koala. Such an activity sharpens students' skills at coordinating text and pictures and helps them view professional filmstrips more carefully and critically.

Responding to Films and Television

Educational films and television programs are natural supplements to the language arts program and to students' studies in science, social studies, and other

---

[1] Blank filmstrips are available in a kit called "Cut and Print, The Filmstrip Maker's Laboratory" (Perfection Form Co., Logan, Iowa 51546).

content areas. Television and movies also offer good opportunities to build skills for viewing and listening. Rather than deploring the influence of these media in students' lives, teachers should take advantage of some of the excellent programs and films that are available. The best of these can show students how to be active, intelligent viewers. May (1979), in a discussion of children who have spent countless passive hours in front of the television set, writes as follows:

> Their minds, dulled by programs that do not build their knowledge by directly involving them through questioning or problem solving techniques, grow up lacking the intellectual framework which allows them to critically judge the values of popular visual entertainment.... [But] if students are introduced to good educational programs which do demand input and thought, they ... will become discriminating viewers who would rather turn off a mediocre television show and read a good book. (p. 245)

Through the intelligent use of films and television, teachers can help students become discriminating viewers.

One eighth-grade teacher made good use of film when the class was studying the Middle Ages. Before viewing a film about that era, the teacher told the class that the story was about a medieval peasant who had been insubordinate to his feudal lord. Explaining the general meaning of the term *insubordination,* the teacher then asked the group what act they thought the peasant might have done and what they thought would happen to him. The group made their predictions based on what they had already studied about the life of peasants and manor owners. They had already discussed the mores and structure of feudal European society.

The pre-viewing discussion helped the group recall concepts and facts about medieval life that they had recently learned. The discussion stimulated curiosity about what would happen to the peasant. Hence, the students knew what they would be watching for. After viewing, the group discussed the events, comparing that which actually happened with what they had thought would happen. Then the teacher wrote on the chalkboard several words that had been used in the film: moat, keep, poaching, bailiff, and herdsman. Each term had been used in a major scene. Reminding the class of the different scenes, the teacher had the group recall the events that would help them understand the meanings of the words. As a follow-up exercise, each student chose one of these words and wrote about how the film had depicted that person or thing. As a final activity, the students took turns reading their papers aloud to one another.

For this lesson, the film was an excellent learning tool. The students watched vivid portrayals of the society they had been studying, and these brought the group's previous lessons to life. Pre-viewing discussion, postviewing review, vocabulary study, and writing all made for a lesson in which students were actively involved.

Films can also be used to extend children's appreciation of and response to literature. If a group has heard or read *Tom Sawyer,* they will have their own ideas of the Mississippi, river boats, and other details of life in the world created by Mark Twain. A film version of that story will provide a wealth of visual images. Students can then compare and contrast these pictures with those that they imagined for themselves. Seeing a film can also stimulate the viewers to read related books. This happens periodically when a film becomes popular. When lines formed outside theaters showing *Mary Poppins,* that book became a favorite; *Star Wars* books have also been enormously popular because of strong interest in the films. Children are just like adults in their responses; everyone is curious to see the film after reading the book, and they will read or reread the book after enjoying the movie.

Film viewing can also stimulate film making. As students become familiar with the medium, they will enjoy producing their own, an activity that requires the use of a number of language arts skills. Students may produce documentaries, original plays, or adaptations of favorite books. Making a film requires thinking, script writing, reading, and rehearsing. It is a particularly purposeful activity because the point of making a film is to show it; students will be remarkably persistent about "getting it right" because they will know that their audience—their peers—will be viewing and judging the production. Cox (1975) stresses the value of having children make films based on books they have read and enjoyed.

Television programs may also be used to enhance and extend learning. Nature or science programs, televised plays, or movies may from time to time tie in directly with what the class is studying. Pre-viewing discussion in school can show students the purposes for viewing at home or in school; follow-up discussion in class can provide a review of concepts and vocabulary.

Because many parents are concerned about their children's viewing habits, teachers must be selective and purposeful in choosing home-viewing assignments. One teacher, who has the support of the students' parents, sometimes uses a television movie as a preview to the reading of a book and sometimes assigns viewing as a follow-up to reading. This teacher guides students to look for similarities and differences between the two media. Students are able to see that some television movies are quite different from the books of the same titles, whereas other television versions closely follow the books. Discussions in this classroom bring out comparisons and contrasts; students' responses are prompted by such questions as the following:

- Did the characters look (speak) as you expected?
- Were the characters the same (in actions, personalities) in both presentations?
- Which presentation (television or book) was more interesting? Why?

- If you could have only viewed or only read, which would you have chosen? Why?

This teacher also occasionally uses the television scripts that are provided in a student newspaper, *Weekly Reader,* as an introduction to a program that the children can watch at home. The students read and discuss the scripts in class before viewing and then discuss or write about the programs after they watch them. The teacher also keeps track of local television programming and encourages students to watch particularly good programs at home.

In one elementary school, the principal and teachers were committed to involving students in the good use of and response to television. Classes were prepared for viewing carefully selected programs in school, and students were encouraged to watch certain specials at home. The children also created their own programs. Every few weeks, one class would be responsible for preparing a short program that was taped and broadcast within the school on a closed-circuit system. The children produced news programs (covering school, community, and national events), weather forecasts, plays, puppet shows, and even commercials. Their efforts required critical viewing of television (to determine the features of a good broadcast), discussion, writing, and rehearsals. As the year progressed, the programs improved in content and quality as the children became more practiced and more thoughtful about their work. They watched television at home more alertly, looking for ideas to use in their own programs; passive, uncritical viewing was reduced. In some communities, public access channels can broaden the possibilities for such well-prepared student programs.

Used properly, television can be an excellent supplement to the language arts program. Lange (1981) reviews a number of studies that have shown how television viewing can stimulate reading, writing, and discussion and can extend school learning. He stresses that teachers cannot afford to ignore the medium of television; nor can they simply assume that all television is "bubblegum for the mind." Rather, teachers need to use television selectively, purposefully, and intelligently to supplement instruction.

Listening and Viewing: Some Conclusions

As described here, listening and viewing activities can help students develop as thinkers. For instance, through hearing and viewing stories, students can develop the ability to follow a narrative sequence, anticipate outcomes, recognize cause–effect relationships, and acquire a general sense of story that influences their comprehension. Similarly, when listening to or viewing informational presentations, students can learn to connect new information to what they already know about a topic; they can also develop concepts that extend their knowledge. The key to success lies not only in the use of specific cognitive processes but also in the purposes students have set for each activity. Tutolo (1977) stresses the importance of setting purposes for listening; this article points out that children need to know in advance what the purpose is and how they are expected to respond. As has been emphasized in this chapter, a particularly good way to have students set purposes for listening and viewing is to have them speculate (hypothesize) about what they might hear or see, so that their own predictions will become their purposes for learning.

While they are actively involved in listening and viewing, students are also developing and refining their oral language abilities—abilities that help them improve their self-expression and that prepare them to deal with the special demands of language in print (Newman, 1986; Teale and Sulzby, 1986). Comprehending material aurally and visually requires the same language and thinking processes that students need to use when they read. The discourse that they hear becomes a basis for the discourse they produce when they speak and write. The processes of listening and viewing are thus intimately related to the processes of speaking, reading, and writing.

As was shown in this chapter (and as will be shown in other chapters), lessons are particularly effective when students are encouraged to use listening and viewing (along with the other language processes) to respond to literature and acquire information. Activities that integrate the receptive (listening, viewing, reading) and the expressive (speaking, writing) processes keep students actively involved in thinking and learning.

Suggested Activities

1. Examine some wordless picture books. Select one that seems suitable for young children and one that seems suitable for children of middle-school age. What different strategies would you use to introduce the books to each group of students? Would it be possible to use both picture books with the older children? How could you do so?

2. Select and read aloud a story to a group of children whose native language is not English. Describe and analyze the experience. How did the children respond?

3. Select an incident from history that has storytelling possibilities. Prepare the story and tell it to a group of middle-school students. Evaluate your performance and describe the students' reactions.

4. Select a film or videotape of a children's story. Plan a purpose-setting activity and a follow-up activity. Teach the lesson and evaluate the students' performance.

References

Abrahamson, R. F. "Storytelling: Oral Interpretation in the Senior High School." Report prepared at the University of Houston, 1977. ERIC Documents, No. ED 144 091.

Applebee, A. *The Child's Concept of Story: Ages Two to Seventeen.* Chicago: University of Chicago Press, 1978.

——————. "Children and Stories: Learning the Rules of the Game." *Language Arts* 56 (September 1979):641–46.

Bailey, G. "The Use of a Library Resource Program for Improvement of Language Abilities of Disadvantaged First Grade Pupils of an Urban Community." Unpublished doctoral dissertation. Boston College, 1970.

Bettelheim, B. *The Uses of Enchantment: The Meaning and Importance of Fairy Tales.* New York: Alfred Knopf, 1975.

Botel, M. *A Comprehensive Reading/Communication Arts Plan.* Harrisburg, PA: Pennsylvania Department of Education, 1977.

Brown, G. "Children's Sense of Story in Relation to Reading and Writing." Unpublished master's thesis. The Ohio State University, 1977.

——————. "Development of Story in Children's Reading and Writing." *Theory into Practice* 16(December 1977):357–62.

Butler, C. "When the Pleasurable is Measurable: Teachers Reading Aloud." *Language Arts* 57(November/December 1980):882–85.

Chomsky, C. "Stages in Language Development and Reading Exposure." *Harvard Education Review* 42(February 1972):1–33.

Clarkson, A., and Cross, G. B. *World Folktales.* New York: Charles Scribner's Sons, 1980.

Cochran-Smith, M. *The Making of a Reader.* Norwood, NJ: Ablex, 1984.

Cohen, D. H. "The Effect of Literature on Vocabulary and Reading Achievement." *Elementary English* 45(February 1968):357–62.

Cox, C. "The Liveliest Art and Reading." *Language Arts* 52(September 1975):771–75.

Cramer, R. "Reading to Children: Why and How." *The Reading Teacher* 28(February 1975):460–63.

Durkin, D. "A Six-Year Study of Children Who Learned to Read in School at the Age of Four." *Reading Research Quarterly* 10(Fall 1974):9–61.

Elin, R. J. "Listening: Neglected and Forgotten in the Classroom." *Language Arts* 49 (February 1972):230–32.

Faix, T. "Listening as a Human Relations Art." *Elementary English* 52(March 1975):409–33.

Farrell, C., and Nessel, D. *Word Weaving: A Teaching Sourcebook.* San Francisco: Zellerbach Family Fund, 1984.

Hennings, D. "Reading Picture Storybooks in the Social Studies." *The Reading Teacher* 36(December 1982):284–89.

Johnson, R. "Reading Aloud: Tips for Teachers." *The Reading Teacher* 36(April 1983):829–83.

Kean, J., and Personke, C. *The Language Arts: Teaching and Learning in the Elementary School.* New York: St. Martin's Press, 1976.

Kennedy, D. K., and Weener, P. "Visual and Auditory Training with the Cloze Procedure to Improve Reading and Listening Comprehension." Unpublished doctoral dissertation. Pennsylvania State University, 1971.

Lamme, L. "Reading Aloud to Young Children." *Language Arts* 53(November/December 1976):886–88.

Lange, B. "ERIC/RCS Report. Television's Role in Education: Is There an Artful Balance?" *Language Arts* 58(January 1981):93–99.

McCormick, S. "Should You Read Aloud to Your Children?" *Language Arts* 54(February 1977):139–43 + .

Mandler, J. M., and Johnson, N. S. "Remembrance of Things Parsed: Story Structure and Recall." *Cognitive Psychology* 9(January 1977):111–51.

May, J. P. "Encouraging Children's Creative Oral Responses Through Non-narrative Films." *Language Arts* 56(March 1979):244–50.

Newman, J. (ed.) *Whole Language: Theory in Use.* Portsmouth, NH: Heinemann, 1986.

Pearson, P. D., and Fielding, L. "Research Update: Listening Comprehension." *Language Arts* 59(September 1982):617–29.

Penfield, D. A. "Learning to Listen: A Broad Demonstration Study." Paper presented at the Conference of the American Educational Research Association. Minneapolis: March, 1970.

Porter, J. "The Effect of a Program of Reading Aloud to Middle Grade Children in the Inner City." Unpublished doctoral dissertation. The Ohio State University, 1969.

Pradl, G. "Learning How to Begin and End a Story." *Language Arts* 56(January 1979):21–25.

Robinson, J. "Writing Children's Books." Unpublished instructional unit. West Chester, PA: West Chester Area School District, 1978.

Sale, R. *Fairy Tales and After.* Cambridge: Harvard University Press, 1978.

Sallee, E. R. "Effects of Adding Folklore to Basal Reading Instruction." *The California Reader* 16(March/April 1983):11–14.

Saville-Troike, M. *A Guide to Culture in the Classroom.* Rosslyn, VA: National Clearinghouse for Bilingual Education, 1978.

Sawyer, W. "Literature and Literacy: A Review of Research." *Language Arts* 64(January 1987):33–39.

Schickedanz, J. A. "Please Read That Story Again." *Young Children* 33(July 1978):49–55.

Shah, I. *World Tales.* New York: Harcourt Brace Jovanovich, 1979.

Sirota, B. "The Effect of a Planned Literature Program of Daily Oral Reading by the Teacher on the Voluntary Reading of Fifth Grade Children." Unpublished doctoral dissertation. New York University, 1971.

Smardo, F. A. "Using Children's Literature to Clarify Science Concepts in Early Childhood Programs." *The Reading Teacher* 36(December 1982):267–73.

Squire, J. (ed.) *Response to Literature.* Urbana, IL: National Council of Teachers of English, 1968.

Stauffer, R. G. *Directing the Reading-Thinking Process.* New York: Harper & Row, 1975.

Stein, N. L., and Glenn, C. G. "Children's Concept of Time: The Development of a Story Schema" in J. Friedman, ed., *The Developmental Psychology of Time.* New York: Academic Press, 1982.

Sticht, T. G.; Beck, L. V.; Hanke, R. N.; Kleiman, G. M.; and James, J. H. *Auding and Reading: A Developmental Model.* Alexandria, VA: Human Resources Research Organization, 1974.

Strickland, D. "Building Knowledge of Stories" in J. Osborn, P. T. Wilson, and R. C. Anderson, eds., *Reading Education: Foundations for a Literate America.* Lexington, MA: Lexington Books/D.C. Heath, 1985.

Teale, W. H., and Sulzby, E. (eds.) *Emergent Literacy: Writing and Reading.* Norwood, NJ: Ablex, 1986.

Trelease, J. *The Read-Aloud Handbook.* New York: Penguin, 1985.

Tutolo, D. "A Cognitive Approach to Teaching Listening." *Language Arts* 54(March 1977):262–65.

Wilt, M. E. "A Study of Teacher Awareness of Listening as a Factor in Elementary Education." *Journal of Educational Research* 43(April 1950):626–36.

Suggested Readings

Bellon, E. C. "Language Development Through Storytelling Activities." *School Media Quarterly* 3(Winter 1975):149–56.

Boothray, B., and Donham, J. "Listening to Literature: An All-School Program." *The Reading Teacher* 34(April 1981):772–74.

Cazden, C. B.; John, V. P.; and Hymes, D. *Functions of Language in the Classroom.* New York: Teachers College Press, 1972.

Chadwick, B. "On Reading Aloud." *English Journal* 71(September 1982):28–29.

Chambers, A. "The Making of a Literary Reader." *Horn Book Magazine* 51(June 1975):301–10.

Chappel, B. *Listening and Learning: Practical Activities for Developing Listening Skills, Grades K–3.* Belmont, CA: Fearon/Lear Siegler, 1973.

Darkatsh, M. "Making Reading to Children an Experience to Remember." *Reading Improvement* 16(Fall 1979):196–97.

Donaldson, M. *Children's Minds.* New York: W. W. Norton, 1979.

Farnsworth, K. "Storytelling in the Classroom: Not an Impossible Dream." *Language Arts* 58(February 1981):162–67.

Hopkins, L. B. *Best of Book Bonanza.* New York: Holt, Rinehart and Winston, 1980.

Kimmelman, L. "Literary Ways Towards Enjoyable Thinking." *Language Arts* 58(April 1981):441–47.

Kotkin, A. J., and Baker, H. C. "Family Folklore." *Childhood Education* 53(January 1977):137–42.

Lee, D. M., and Rubin, J. B. *Children and Language.* Belmont, CA: Wadsworth, 1979.

Mendoza, A. "Reading to Children: Their Preferences." *The Reading Teacher* 38(February 1985):522–27.

Nessel, D. D. "Storytelling in the Reading Program." *The Reading Teacher* 38(January 1985):378–81.

Paullen, B. C. "To Capture Those Captives: Read to Your Students." *English Journal* 63(November 1974):88–89.

Pinnell, G. S. "Ways to Look at the Functions of Children's Language" in A. Jaggar and M. T. Smith-Burke, eds., *Observing the Language Learner.* Urbana, IL: National Council of Teachers of English/International Reading Association, 1985.

Polette, N. *Picture Books for Gifted Programs.* Metuchen, NJ: Scarecrow Press, 1981.

Purves, A., and Monson, D. *Experiencing Children's Literature.* Glenview, IL: Scott, Foresman, 1984.

Rickel, A. V., and Fields, R. B. "Storybook Models and Achievement Behavior of Preschool Children." *Psychology in the Schools* 20(January 1983):105–13.

Rosen, H., and Rosen, C. *The Language of Primary School Children.* London: Penguin, 1973.

Ross, R. R. *Storyteller.* Columbus, OH: Charles Merrill, 1972.

Rouse, J. *The Completed Gesture.* New Jersey: Skyline Books, 1978.

Sanacore, J. "Creative Writing and Storytelling: A Bridge from High School to Preschool." *Phi Delta Kappan* 64(March 1983):509–10.

Shannon, G. "Storytelling and the Schools." *English Journal* 68(May 1979):50–51.

Smith, E.; Goodman, K. S.; and Meredith, R. *Language and Thinking in the Classroom.* New York: Holt, Rinehart and Winston, 1976.

Stahl, M. B. "Using Traditional Oral Stories in the English Classroom." *English Journal* 68(October 1979):33–36.

Vukelich, C. "The Development of Listening Comprehension through Storytime." *Language Arts* 53(November/December 1976):889–91.

Wells, G. (ed.) *Learning Through Interaction.* London: Cambridge University Press, 1981.

Wilcox, L. "The Artistry of Once Upon a Time." *Language Arts* 52(October 1975): 983–86.

Developing an awareness of audience and context is a key to the successful use of language. At all grade levels, children need to be encouraged to use language to describe, explain, and share their views of the world.

3 Developing Speaking Abilities

Just as listening and viewing are somewhat overlooked in language arts programs, so too does speaking tend to be given a minor place in the curriculum. Students are expected to recite or to discuss and occasionally to give oral reports, but they are usually not given the kinds of opportunities that will help them use a range of speaking abilities effectively and comfortably. It is not surprising that so many students are distinctly ill at ease speaking in class and that so many adults are actually fearful of speaking in front of even a small group. Kelley (1951) reminds us of the deplorable "turtle state of mind" that affects so many exchanges between people (Well, I don't want to stick my neck out, but . . .). He attributes such reticence to childhood learning:

> Many hold the attitude that children should be seen and not heard, and that the child is too immature to have a worthwhile opinion. Carried into school, life there too often becomes a matter of listening and reading, but not of giving out. This trains the child to have a low opinion of himself, and to have little respect for his own thinking. He becomes persuaded that what he has to say cannot be of any importance. (p. 76)

Classrooms have not changed greatly since Kelley wrote those words. Students are encouraged to speak freely only in certain limited activities. Much of the time, they are expected to remain quiet and to speak only when they are specifically requested to do so.

Yet the more effectively students can communicate orally, the more easily they will be able to get along in the world. Speech is often the key to making thoughts and feelings clear to others, to getting things accomplished, and even to being accepted socially. Those who speak well tend to feel successful and *are* successful; those who have a difficult time talking with others tend to feel uneasy, unskilled, and frustrated. Confidence and ability with speech may even determine the course of a person's life. Some people will turn down a career advancement because the promotion requires meeting and socializing with new people or speaking in public. Other people are not offered new opportunities because they seem unable to handle greater oral demands. Oral expression is not a minor facet of life—speaking abilities affect the way people are perceived by others and the way they perceive themselves.

It is in school that children first begin to realize that speaking is more than just the familiar, natural behavior they learned at home. They become aware of new demands on them as speakers. These demands may also involve new expectations and perhaps new standards. If children are successful speakers in school, they will tend to see themselves as competent speakers in general. The reverse holds true as well: unsuccessful student speakers will view themselves as incompetent speakers in general. Their abilities and their confidence, developed and fostered to a significant extent in the classroom, affect their oral communication in all facets of their lives.

To a great extent, children's expressive abilities improve naturally as the youngsters mature physically, cognitively, and emotionally. Direct instruction is not necessary for general growth. But children do need many opportunities to speak for a variety of purposes so that they can learn through experience to communicate effectively. They also need direction, encouragement, and specific opportunities to refine their speaking skills.

Just as listening skills cannot be developed adequately through occasional games and isolated activities, so it is that oral expression cannot be refined through occasional exercises or speaking assignments (such as oral reports). Students also need more than question–answer sessions, a limited form of oral discourse that, in its extreme form, is like an oral examination. Children must be given frequent, varied opportunities to converse, discuss, and speak to groups if they are to develop speaking skill and confidence. They need opportunities to speak about things they know well, so that they may experience the confidence that comes from occasionally being an expert. This chapter describes a variety of speaking activities that can broaden students' abilities in oral communication. Connections between speaking and the other language arts are also emphasized; suggestions for integrating speaking with listening, reading, and writing are given.

Speaking for Different Purposes

At all grade levels, children need to be encouraged to use language to describe, explain, and share their views of the world. Through speaking for a variety of purposes, children develop oral-expression abilities and also refine their understanding of the concepts they are using. As Britton (1970) points out, language represents and organizes experience; talking allows us to "construct for ourselves an increasingly faithful, objective and coherent picture of the world" (p. 105). Through talk, children describe current happenings, reflect on the past, and anticipate the future. In so doing, they become actively involved in making meanings. That is, by talking for a variety of purposes, children learn not only to speak more effectively but also to think and learn more effectively.

Purposeful talk can take many forms in the classroom. In this section are several speaking activities that may be adapted for any grade level. In each instance, the activity is structured to some extent; that is, the children's talk is not idle conversation. However, within the overall structure there is much opportunity for children to express their ideas in their own ways and thus to explore different forms and uses of oral expression.

Informal Sharing

Informal sharing allows children to talk about things that are important in their daily lives. In years past, this activity was usually labeled "Show and Tell" because it involved youngsters bringing something into school to display and describe to classmates. Yet children do not need to bring in something special to participate in informal sharing. Each child may simply be given a chance to address the group during a regular sharing time. Some may want to bring a favorite toy and talk about it. Others may choose to talk about a recent experience with the family or may decide to tell the group about something notable that was seen or experienced on the way to school. The topic does not matter; it is the process of speaking to the group that counts. The activity has several features worth considering carefully, for it is one of the best ways of helping children to develop ease and confidence in speaking at all grade levels.

First, the speaker chooses a topic. Subjects are not assigned, though they may be suggested. This self-selection immediately puts the child in control. The topic is invariably something that is of genuine interest to the speaker. Also, there are no particular expectations or rules of performance. Speakers are simply given the chance to talk informally. They can say as much or as little as they like. If they run out of ideas, they can stop gracefully. The audience is receptive; questions and comments from classmates and teacher arise naturally from their curiosity. The speaker is never put on the spot by the audience but rather is encouraged and often urged to tell more. This is exactly the kind of experience students need if they are to develop poise and overcome reticence about speaking in front of a group.

Such meaningful, personal communication is especially important in the early grades, when oral language rather than written language is a primary means of communication. However, as students mature, they still have much of interest to relate about their hobbies, projects, and experiences. Given regular chances to talk informally to the group, students will develop speaking abilities naturally. If these opportunities to talk are part of the classroom routine, students will not fear the experience. Their speaking skills will improve if the environment is informal and relaxed.

Developing the Habit of Notation

Another form of talk that goes beyond informal sharing is described by Landor (1979, 1982)* as "developing the habit of notation." The process Landor devised encourages children to keep an ongoing record of the thoughts, feelings, and experiences that are most important to them. To explore these topics, participating children meet regularly in school (usually once a week for an hour) in groups of six or seven with an adult listener-recorder, who may be the teacher, an aide, or a volunteer. Each group member is given a turn to talk about something significant to him or her. These important things may be events,

---

*This description of Landor's work is based on observation of her program and personal communication as well as on the works cited. Her program, called "Children's Own Stories," is sponsored by the Zellerbach Family Fund (San Francisco, CA).

objects, interactions with people, dreams, things read or heard, feelings, opinions—whatever is foremost in the child's mind.

While one student talks, the listener-recorder takes down the child's words, writing or typing as the child speaks. Other group members draw and listen as they await their turns. Speakers are never criticized for the content or style of their talk or drawing; the group is attentive to and respectful of each member's contributions. The drawn and written works are kept in individual folders for the children. Students may examine their folders at any time and are encouraged to add written material, to reflect on their drawings, and to reread earlier entries to themselves or to others in the group (the listener-recorder may read them if the child is not mature enough to read without assistance). At the end of the year, the pages are bound simply and are given to the owners to keep so that each has a record of what was important to him or her during that school year.

As Landor (1982) says, each individual has a "life history which is made up of the modest daily experiences which are very important [to the individual] but which go unheeded, unheralded, and unrecorded." And yet, as she points out, experiences and inner reflections are the essence of life and therefore compose the "raw materials" that one may use to "become an artist of life"— that is, a person who approaches life with imagination, flexibility, and the confidence to express his or her individuality. By regularly attending to such "raw materials" in a group setting, and by maintaining a record of the sharing, individuals can learn to value their unique perspectives and in so doing may come to value themselves as individuals and as members of a community.

This activity contains several features in common with other language arts activities: it involves sharing with a group, dictating or writing one's ideas, drawing and discussing art work, and keeping an ongoing record of personal thoughts. The unique combination of these activities in a notation program affords children the chance to develop confidence and self-esteem as speakers.

The most significant feature of this program is that children are encouraged to reflect on their lives and to capture in words and drawing the important thoughts, feelings, and experiences that shape their separate individualities. Honored by the presence of an attentive and nonjudgmental audience, children receive a valuable unspoken message: Your ideas are important; you are important. For virtually all children, the chance to be heard and appreciated affects the way they perceive themselves as people and as learners. The ritual of selecting their topics, taking turns at talking, and having their words heard and recorded demonstrates to children in notation groups that they have important things to say to a receptive and sympathetic audience.

No one is ever pressed to reveal private thoughts in a notation group, but when a child chooses to become vulnerable by talking about a sensitive issue, such as the death of a pet or a secret ambition, that person gains strength and self-confidence by becoming safely vulnerable for a short time within a supportive group. That feeling, in turn, tends to make the child more receptive to the other group members when they are talking. As children work together over time, they gain a growing appreciation for each other as individuals, and they extend the boundaries of their communication with one another.

The maintenance of a personal record reinforces the notion that each child has something of value to say in words and pictures. As children see their works collected, they become enthused about adding to the folder and begin to give careful thought to what they will draw and what they will say when it is their turn to have their words recorded. Their reflections on their experience become more deliberate; their words and images become more carefully chosen. Students often wish to add their own writings to the pieces that are prepared by the adult listener-recorder.

Because the work is done in a group setting, children also develop a special sense of community within their respective groups. Because they are allowed to talk about what is most important to them, they come to see the time they spend together as especially valuable, different from the time they may spend together in play, in casual conversation, or in instructional groups. They become supportive and sympathetic of one another. The sense of mutual support creates a firm sense of mutual purpose.

Sometimes the effects of this program on individuals are quite noticeable, as was the case with Marlene (not the child's real name), a fourth-grade girl whose academic work was poor and whose behavior and unkempt appearance prompted considerable teasing by her classmates. As a member of a newly formed notation group, Marlene was withdrawn for weeks, except for a few occasions during which she expressed anger toward other children. She devoted little effort to drawing, and her oral contributions were brief and often delivered with indifference. Gradually, however, she ventured to talk about certain things that were very much on her mind, and the group showed sympathetic interest in what she had to say. The acceptance encouraged Marlene to talk more, and eventually she became an eager and cooperative participant. By the end of the year, she was conversing regularly with others in the group, had established a significant friendship with another girl, and obviously felt a great deal better about herself. Her oral contributions had increased in length, detail, and complexity, and she began to give more attention and effort to writing. Nothing else had changed in her life at school or at home; the improvement seemed to result directly from her participation in the notation group. Marlene's progress in the group also had an effect on her behavior at other times during the school day. For instance, near the end of the year she wrote a story and asked if she could read it aloud to the whole class. She had never before shown such healthy initiative and confidence, and she was rewarded with careful attention and positive response from the teacher and the classmates.

Many other children, both younger and older than Marlene, have shown similar improvement as judged subjectively by the parents and teachers who observed the students' progress after they joined a notation group. The results are not always dramatic, but the children in these groups seem to benefit greatly from the chance to explore what is unique to them as individuals.

Responding to Literature: Pattern Stories

As we saw in Chapter 2, reading aloud and telling stories give children valuable experiences with the forms and language of literature. The pattern stories of children's literature are particularly good for inducing participation and thus for giving young students the chance both to hear and to use language that is different from everyday language. In these stories, the plot follows a predictable pattern; certain words or phrases are repeated throughout. For instance, in Wanda Gag's *Millions of Cats* (Putnam, 1952), the refrain is "Hundreds of cats, thousands of cats, millions and billions and trillions of cats." In Betsy Bang's *The Old Woman and the Red Pumpkin* (Macmillan, 1975), the refrain is "Pumpkin, pumpkin, roll along. I eat tamarinds, I do. I eat plums and rice, I do, while I sing my song."

When they become familiar with these stories through listening, children catch on quickly to the patterns and quite naturally chime in. They derive satisfaction from anticipating succeeding events and saying familiar lines again and again. Confidence grows with each repetition as children realize that they know what is coming next. For young children, grasping the pattern and predicting it accordingly lay the foundations for the more sophisticated prediction that children will use when they learn to read. As they grow older, they will be able to anticipate the words and ideas in more complex pieces of discourse.

Oral participation in pattern stories instills in students a sense of the sounds and rhythms of language. This sense gives children an important foundation for developing skill in reading and writing. Rhyming refrains are pleasing to hear and say, especially if the lines also have a musical rhythm, such as, "I will not eat them here or there. I will not eat them anywhere" (Dr. Seuss, *Green Eggs and Ham,* Beginner Books, 1960). In developing sensitivity to rhythms and patterns, children become more attentive to the way words sound together. The knowledge is useful as they begin reading and writing, for it enables them to perceive and use sound patterns as represented by various letter and word combinations.

Pattern stories can lead to various writing and reading activities. When young children are familiar with a story of this type, they can dictate a favorite part (perhaps a refrain) and watch as the teacher writes the words on the board or a piece of chart paper. Seeing the words written down, children will be eager to read what they know to be familiar. Such dictation is a good precursor or adjunct to the use of dictated experience stories in the early grades (described later in this chapter).

Children can also make up their own variations on pattern stories. For instance, students love the old favorite "I Know an Old Lady Who Swallowed a Fly" (see the book version by Nadine Westcott, published by Little, Brown, 1980). After students have learned the original story-poem, they will enjoy making up new verses involving different animals. Young children may dictate their own versions to the teacher, and older children may write on their own. Several children may contribute verses and illustrations in order to make their own "Old Lady" book. Other suggestions for using pattern stories as a stimulus to writing are given in Chapter 7.

Many additional pattern stories are suitable for the language activities described here. Other good titles include the following:

As I Was Crossing Boston Common, by Norma Farber and Arnold Lobel (Creative Arts Books, 1982).
The House That Jack Built, illustrated by Janet Stevens (Holiday House, 1985).
I Unpacked My Grandmother's Trunk, by Susan Hoguet (E. P. Dutton, 1983).
The Rose in My Garden, by Arnold Lobel (Greenwillow Books, 1984).
"Soap! Soap! Soap!" in *Grandfather Tales,* by Richard Chase (Houghton Mifflin, 1948).
Strega Nona, by Tomie de Paola (Prentice Hall, 1975).
Too Much Noise, by Ann McGovern (Houghton Mifflin, 1967).

Creative Dramatics

Creative dramatics, or improvised drama, is an enjoyable and intellectually stimulating speaking activity. Students enact a story, inventing dialogue and action as they speak. Although the activity is structured in that there is a story to be told, there is room for individual variations. The group may act out the tale repeatedly, exchanging roles, making up new lines, and altering the details with each new improvisation. The purpose is not to produce a formal play but rather to imagine, interpret, and express the story in unique ways.

There are few better activities for putting language to use in a purposeful and meaningful way. Students must choose their words carefully; they must recognize that a princess speaks differently than a giant. The characters must be portrayed effectively through language and action, so there is good reason for being precise and clear. As students play different roles, they have the chance to use different expressions, to create different moods, and to speak as different people. They must also speak clearly and loudly enough to be heard. In the excitement and fun of such creative play, students are not aware that they are practicing speaking skills.

Creative dramatics has other advantages too. There is the opportunity to develop the imagination, to think and plan with a group, and to enhance the pleasure of good literature by enacting it. Taking on different roles allows students to gain insights about different kinds of people. The experience of acting is often more valuable than the experience of reading about or discussing different characters (Wright, 1974). Perhaps most important, creative dramatics is a natural way for children to learn and grow. It is an extension of children's preoccupation with playing out the world as they perceive it and thus coming to understand it.

There are several ways of engaging children in creative dramatics. One of the best is to encourage them to enact a story they have heard. After a group has enjoyed "Little Red Riding Hood" or an episode from *Alice's Adventures in Wonderland,* the students can take turns assuming various roles and playing out the story. Another strategy is to have children make up an original story and act it out. If a group is fascinated with kings and castles, they will need little prompting to invent and portray a magical kingdom. If they love the talking, cunning cat in "Puss in Boots," they will come up with wonderful new adventures for that creature. Even seemingly ordinary events can stimulate original stories. McCaslin (1968) describes a group of fifth graders who invented and enacted a story about an old man they had seen on the way to school. The children imagined that the man was a retired school janitor who, always watchful of the boys and girls in his neighborhood, one day saved a child from being hit by a car in the street. The simple drama was sensitive and moving, a fine portrayal of love and courage. (See also McCaslin, 1984.) Other creative drama activities are described by Cottrell (1987) and Thomas and Dinges (1986).

Creative dramas do not follow exact scripts; the pleasure of imagining and inventing would be lost if children felt that they must memorize lines. But planning and discussion may be needed to get a group started. Discussions can give the players ideas about what to try. For instance, assume that a group of first graders is about to enact their favorite story, "The Three Bears." When the first group of volunteers is ready, the teacher and the rest of the class can prepare the actors by asking them these kinds of questions:

- What are the bears like? How will they act?
- What will be happening at the beginning?
- What do we want to show?
- How will Goldilocks act?
- What will the different characters say? How will they say it?

It is important to let the group decide what they want to do; the questions serve only as a guide to thinking. The players will want to emphasize what is important to them, and they should not be made to feel that there is only one way to enact the story. Sometimes their interpretations will deviate from what they have heard; this is perfectly all right.

After the preliminary decisions, the players will have some ideas about how to proceed. They can speak and act with assurance, having decided what will happen first in the bears' house. They will know what, in general, the different characters will say and do. With just a few ideas as guides, the group will be ready to act; their familiarity with the tale will carry them along. As they get into the spirit of the story, they will invariably add details that they did not discuss. For instance, one first grader added a charming new twist to this story when she played the Great, Huge Bear. When the Small, Wee Bear noted that his porridge was all gone, the Great, Huge Bear said, "That's all right. We'll make you some more." These kinds of personal interpretations are at the heart of creative dramatics.

When the first group finishes its version, the class might take a few minutes to discuss the performance. The goal is not to find fault but to appreciate the interpretation and to consider other directions that different groups might take. These kinds of questions will guide thinking:

- What did you like about this play?
- How did the bears show how they felt? How else could that be done?
- Is there anything else we could show?
- When we perform this story again, what might we change?

Follow-up discussion encourages critical thinking about the dramatizing in re- lation to the story. Again, the emphasis is not on what is right or wrong but rather on different ways that the story might be developed. As students consider what they have seen and think of new possibilities, they will be broadening their response to the tale and deepening their understanding of it. Each new dramatization builds on and enriches earlier performances. Language and action will become finely tuned to express different interpretations of the story.

There are several related activities that help students develop expressive abilities. Visualization exercises, for example, refine students' imaginations and abilities to interpret the stories they hear (Farrell and Nessel, 1984). The group may be told to close their eyes and to imagine that they are walking up the steps of an abandoned house (or entering a dark forest, or flying on a magic carpet). They are asked to look around them to note their surroundings, to think about what they are feeling, and to speculate on what might happen. After everyone has thought for several minutes, the group can discuss the various images and moods that they experienced. Discussion will be lively and inter- esting. Students are sure to have "seen" different things, and they will be eager to describe precisely what their images were. The more practice children have in visualizing, the better able they will be to imagine characters and scenes in stories they hear, to describe them accurately, and to put life into their own dramatizations.

Improvising various real-life situations is another activity that involves the expressive use of language and the same kinds of skills employed in acting out a story. The teacher suggests the scene; volunteers assume roles and invent as they proceed. There is no predetermined story to enact; the performers rely only on the initial directions that get the group started. These kinds of situations lend themselves to improvising:

1. A new child has moved into your neighborhood. Several of you notice the newcomer playing in his (her) front yard. What do you do? What do you say?
2. A group is out in the woods on a hike. You find a birds' nest that has been blown out of a tree. What do you decide to do with it? What do you say?
3. You are exploring an attic filled with trunks and boxes. What do you find? What do you do with it?

Other suggestions can easily be devised to suit the ages and interests of a given class. The most workable situations will be open-ended, allowing children to invent and act out all sorts of happenings and conversations. An imaginary trunk-filled attic would lead some groups to pretend they have found old clothes; others will discover interesting books and papers; some may create a ghost from the past or a magical genie who appears to grant three wishes. Each acted scene will give children the chance to develop a story and tailor their language to fit the situation they have invented.

Puppetry, also, encourages the creative use of language. Puppets can be as simple (made of old socks with faces drawn on or sticks decorated with construction paper figures) or as elaborate as time and resources will allow. They may be used on a "stage" such as a sturdy box, or they may simply be incorporated into creative drama. Puppets can be made to do and say all sorts of interesting things; they extend children's imaginations and expressive abilities. Children who may be quite shy about participating in creative drama will often come out of their protective shells with a puppet to help them, and almost all children will readily accept puppets as regular members of the class.

Other activities can refine and extend children's perceptions of the roles they have assumed. For instance, in one second-grade classroom where children had heard and enacted "The Three Bears," the teacher asked students to assume story roles and then interview one another. Goldilocks interviewed Mama Bear; Mama Bear questioned Papa Bear, and so on. One exchange went like this:

GOLDILOCKS: Baby Bear, why were you upset when I ate your porridge?
BABY BEAR: It was good porridge!
GOLDILOCKS: But it would have been cold when you got home.
BABY BEAR: But I always feed my cold porridge to my pet rabbit, and now he's hungry!

Staying clearly within story boundaries, students elaborated and invented new thoughts, perspectives, and motivations for the characters. While having fun and using their imaginations, these children were also interpreting and exploring the story's meanings in new and cognitively challenging ways.

All of these activities are both stimulating and fun. Children will love the chance to be trolls, princes, and magical creatures; they will want to play at being the neighborhood grocer, the old woman in the house on the corner, or the police coming to the rescue; they will like to make and use puppets; they will wish to enact a story they have heard and then invent new scenes, carrying the story forward in their own imaginations. While they "play," they will be using language expressively and purposefully.

Storytelling and Retelling

When students hear, discuss, and enact stories frequently, they usually want to tell stories themselves. With a little encouragement, they can become storytellers, too, retelling old favorites and making up original tales. At first, their efforts will not meet stringent adult standards, but students will improve gradually with practice and continuing exposure to good oral literature. Telling a story requires attention to sequencing events, describing characters and settings, relating dialogue, and choosing the right words to make the result pleasing and effective. It is an excellent speaking-thinking activity, as Pradl (1979) stresses:

> Encouraging children to tell stories is an important way of not only fostering their personal-social development, but of allowing them to develop a rhythmical sense of order and relatedness to events. In telling stories children are acquiring the formal aspects of what makes a gesture complete, of how experience is organized, and they are acquiring these things in terms of an internalized body-sense ("How does it feel or sound?"), rather than an externally imposed set of rules ("Avoid a succession of loose sentences."). (p. 25)

Other researchers also recognize the value of retelling stories (Zimiles and Kuhns, 1976; Whaley, 1981; Morrow, 1985); they point out that retelling requires active cognitive involvement with story language (vocabulary and syntax) and story structure. The involvement helps students to develop oral-language and comprehension abilities.

Primary-grade students can begin simply, by retelling stories they have heard at school. Bryant (1924), for instance, tells of a class of first graders who, through the year, adopted certain stories as "theirs" to tell. The teacher told stories regularly and frequently, and certain ones became favorites that were requested more than others. Each child who wanted to participate was encouraged to learn a favorite, and soon a number of children were eager to tell "their" stories to anyone who would listen. This same strategy has been used many times since Bryant adopted it over sixty years ago. Children begin with brief, often incomplete retellings, but the more they hear the story and the more they practice retelling it, the better their renditions become. Students should always be praised so that they will want to keep retelling. The experience will help them feel comfortable speaking before a group and will develop their oral-expression and interpretation abilities.

Students' storytelling may be one of the best speaking activities educators can arrange for students. Children will need good models to follow (especially a storytelling teacher), practice, and encouragement, but the effort is worth it. Storytelling is both purposeful and creative. It also has the particular advantages of giving speakers a wide and appreciative audience and the chance to take pride in their speaking accomplishments.

Discussion

Discussion is one of the most loosely used words in education. For instance, the term is commonly used as a synonym for recitation sessions in which the teacher asks questions and students give answers. Teachers also sometimes say, "We discussed X today" when they actually mean, "I told the class about X today, and they asked me some questions to make sure they understood my explanation." That is, teachers use *discussion* to mean *lecture*. Each of these activities can be worthwhile, informative, and interesting, but none can be called discussion. There is a distinction between discussion and other kinds of student talk. To recognize the distinction is important for teachers who are concerned about building effective speaking skills.

A discussion includes some or all of these features:

- Students respond directly to one another most of the time, rather than just to the teacher.
- The purpose of the talk is not necessarily to arrive at the right answer, though consensus about an answer may be a goal.
- The teacher and the group are not always certain of the direction the talk is taking; there is purpose, but the purpose may change.
- The teacher has the feeling that the group can and would continue entirely on their own; intrinsic motivation carries the discussion along.
- The teacher is one of several contributors to the talk; he or she does not speak more often than anyone else.
- There is a certain alertness within the group that is different from simple attentiveness; the atmosphere occasionally becomes electric as ideas tumble forth.
- Participants can become excited, angry, impatient, or clownish; feelings are expressed along with ideas, opinions, and facts.

This is not an all-inclusive list, but it contains many of the features found in classroom discussions. People, indeed, know when they are having a discussion and when they are not—when the talk occurs *outside* the classroom. Everyone has at one time or another cut short a monologue by complaining impatiently, "This is no discussion! You're not listening to me at all!" Everyone has felt the exhilaration of freely sharing ideas and feelings with family and friends. People can remember specific occasions that they can describe only by saying, "Now *that* was a good discussion." Discussion is an exchange on a particular topic about which everyone has an opinion. All participants contribute purposefully; all are responsible for the direction of the talk.

Of all speaking skills, the art of discussion may be the most important to learn. People spend a good deal of time discussing things. They put their heads together to solve problems, to learn what others believe, to evaluate events and ideas, and to persuade others to go along with them. They become persuaded themselves, and they learn new perspectives. If people are too shy to take part, they miss out; if they don't listen, others become impatient; if they are too aggressive, people avoid talking to them at all. But in learning the give-and-take of exchange, people benefit enormously.

Children may be adept at casual conversation with one or two friends, but they are not usually practiced in the art of group discussion. Just as with adults, some are too shy to speak out in front of several classmates; others try to dominate the floor. All need opportunities to participate in discussions so that they will learn to feel comfortable in a group and to be attentive and respectful of one another's opinions.

Teachers can help students by setting the stage properly. Most important, teachers must believe that devoting time to learning discussion skills is in itself important. Holding this attitude, the teacher will plan lessons specifically to teach students to have discussions (in a similar manner, the teacher plans reading lessons or writing lessons so that students will improve their reading and writing skills). Focusing on the process is important; the topic for discussion is secondary when the purpose is to develop skill. This means that the teacher will sometimes be less concerned about students learning a particular body of material than about their conduct while they talk. As students learn the skills, the topic and the process become equally important.

These are some important discussion skills that can be taught:

- listening to others
- contributing purposefully
- respecting other points of view
- responding directly to others
- recognizing agreement and disagreement
- working as a group to achieve consensus
- working as a group to solve a problem

These skills are best learned in actual discussions. One way to direct learning is to devise discussion activities that will give students practice. For instance, take the case of a group of third graders who need to learn to listen to one another. Typically, they all want to talk at once, and no one hears what anyone else says. The teacher decides to plan a discussion specifically for the purpose of teaching them how to listen.

First, the teacher announces the rules: 1) each person will have a chance to give an opinion; and 2) no one can add a new idea until he or she has restated someone else's idea and said whether or not the two are in agreement. Next, the teacher introduces a topic for discussion. The theme is one that will interest the group and about which everyone is sure to have an opinion. An example of a theme: Some people believe television is bad for children; others believe it is good. What do you think? Some responders will immediately be ready with their ideas. The teacher reminds these students of the rules and calls on the first student to state an opinion. The next student must state the first one's idea, say whether or not he or she agrees, and then give the new point of view. The process continues until everyone has had a chance to speak. The teacher eases out of the proceedings, letting the students carry on independently unless they start to deviate from the rules. When the group finishes, they evaluate the results: Was it difficult to listen? Why? What did you learn? How did you feel when someone stated what you said? Did listening to each other help you to form better ideas to offer to the group? (See Stanford and Stanford, 1969, for more such discussion "games.")

This very structured activity probably seems forced and artificial. It *is,* to some extent, but it provides the first step toward helping children learn to conduct themselves appropriately on their own. As students develop and refine their abilities, they must use their skills in more realistic situations, such as in discussing books they read, films they see, ideas they learn in science and social studies, and concerns about current events.

Teacher-directed Recitation

The term *recitation* is used here to describe question-and-answer sessions for which the teacher predetermines the questions and during which students are expected to give certain answers. These exchanges are sometimes useful for reviewing material that students have been studying or for guiding children's thinking in a particular direction. Even during such highly controlled oral sessions, the teacher can do much to improve the way students respond and thus can help them to develop their speaking skills and confidence.

The most significant feature of recitation is that the activity puts students on the spot. The teacher chooses the questions and knows the answers; the students do not know the questions and may or may not know the answers. Even the very best students can experience anxiety during recitation because, even if they know the answers, they are not sure which question is coming next. Less able students may have little or no idea of what the questions might be and are usually quite sure they do not know the answers. They may become frustrated, anxious, or gloomily resigned to failure. The teacher has the "power" in such a circumstance and needs to be particularly careful in wielding it.

An important element in recitation is the amount of time that students are given to respond to a question. Imagine a teacher in front of a classroom, having just asked a question that most of the students should be able to answer. The teacher calls on someone to respond. How much time will the teacher allow for that student to speak before repeating the question or calling on someone else? Three seconds? Five seconds? Twenty seconds? One minute?

Astonishing as it may seem, Rowe (1969, 1986) and others have found that teachers tend to allow only about one second of silence before intervening with a different question, saying "Weren't you listening?" or having someone else try. Students quickly learn what to do—they answer immediately, even if they have to say "I don't know." Rapid exchanges are probably common because teachers often become uncomfortable if there is silence when they are expecting students to talk. Indeed, a long silence in the middle of a lesson has an ominous tone. Everyone becomes jittery when the teacher stops talking, when someone takes "too long" to respond to a question, or when the pace is broken with even a few seconds of utter silence.

Outside of school we note the same phenomenon. Silence bothers people when they are expecting talk. An example of such an expectation was described by Heywood Klein in a news article called "Firms Seek Aid in Deciphering Japan's Culture" (*Wall Street Journal,* September 1, 1983):

> Mr. Diamond [a businessman] recalls holding a press conference [in Japan] to introduce a new soft-focus lens; he gave his presentation, asked for questions and was greeted with a long silence before the first reporter raised his hand. 'I felt like a comedian who's just told his best joke and nobody laughed,' he says. He later learned that Japanese journalists, unlike many of their American counterparts, carefully compose their questions so they don't look silly to their colleagues. (p. 25)

Mr. Diamond was, fleetingly, in a position all classroom teachers have experienced. And yet, consider the reason for the long silence: the responders were *thinking.*

This is precisely what students will learn to do if teachers give them the time. When the question hangs comfortably in the air, students have time to consider, reflect, speculate, and compose. As Rowe (1969, 1986) emphasizes, extending the wait time even to five seconds (preferably more) has the following advantages for students:

- They give longer and better responses.
- They express their ideas with more confidence.
- They look away from the teacher, relax, and concentrate on the topic at hand.
- Their speculative thought increases; they begin to ask questions themselves.
- Reticent students begin responding.
- "Slow" students begin responding.

There are advantages for teachers too:

- They see new value in their students' responses.
- They become more flexible in the responses they allow.
- They see less difference between the "slow" student and the "bright" student.
- They tend to ask better questions. They are giving themselves time to think, too.

Good things happen when teachers moderate the pace of recitation and other such teacher-dominant talk. Silence becomes not an occasion for anxiety but an occasion for thinking.

While waiting for a response (and perhaps counting to five, or seven, or ten), the teacher should also set a relaxed tone and should try not to stare at the student who is the expected responder. Fixed eye contact from the teacher at this point can be intimidating and distracting to the student who is trying to think. The teacher should not seem impatient and should discourage others from waving their hands or calling out for attention. Most important, the teacher should try to remember how everyone feels about being asked a question in front of peers. The teacher should see the situation from the students' perspective. It is disquieting to be put on the spot in front of others. A moment ago the child was content; now people are staring. It seems, suddenly, that everyone else must know, but the child's thoughts have become hopelessly tangled. Students *do* have these reactions. Everyone does. The teacher who remembers this will find good ways to counteract students' anxiety about speaking out and will allow comfortable thinking time.

Talking to Learn

The teacher-directed speaking activities suggested so far all can help students improve expressive abilities and develop firmer understandings of what they are talking about. Less formal talk that is an integral part of subject-matter lessons can also be used specifically to further thinking and concept learning. Such talk is neither teacher-directed recitation nor large-group discussion; rather, it is an exchange among a few students who are given the chance to talk things through on their own.

Torbe and Medway (1981) offer several examples of how this type of talk may be used in the process of thinking and learning. They relate one especially interesting exchange between two eight-year-old boys who talk about gravity. The teacher is not present but has asked the boys to record their conversation on tape. In the recording, neither child has a perfectly clear idea of what gravity is, but they explore the concept by relating it to what they do know. One boy thinks of gravity as a concrete object, comparable to lava, water, or smoke. The other boy claims that gravity is like none of these things; he insists that it is invisible. The second boy is further along in his understanding than the first, and in his own words he carefully helps his classmate try to understand that gravity is a force rather than an observable entity. They do not arrive at a final, correct understanding of the concept, but by talking freely and comfortably, they come closer to grasping the essentials. Listening to their tape later, the teacher was able to discover what they seemed to know and what they didn't know about the concept (valuable information for planning later lessons) and was also able to assess and appreciate the boys' thinking processes as revealed by their conversation.

It is somewhat difficult for teachers to realize the value of allowing children to talk on their own without an adult present to step in and correct misunderstandings. It may seem less troublesome and more efficient to keep students from getting confused by intervening with the correct information. However, as Torbe and Medway point out, there is considerable value in allowing students to talk things through with minimal teacher intervention. These authors recognize that students may get into a "mess" if allowed to discuss things alone. Yet Torbe and Medway conclude that

> if we insist on giving them what they seem to need, devoting our efforts to telling them the knowledge in the best way we can ... we do not keep them out of that mess. The mess is still there: the difference is that it does not show. But we *need* it to show, so that we can learn, by studying the errors, exactly what this particular pupil *does* understand, where she has difficulty, where he needs most help, and so on. Success depends not only on our teaching processes but on their learning processes—which are distinct operations that need to be provided for and are not simply automatically created by teaching. It is in this unpromising material [i.e., free student talk] that the means lie, in the long run, of helping them far more. (p. 41)

This perspective on the value of talking to learn is in line with Britton's (1970) theory of the relationship between language and learning. These researchers all believe that through talking (and writing) students engage in an active process of constructing meanings by connecting new information to what is already known. Discussions involve a kind of exploratory expression in which the direction is set by the students rather than by a supervising teacher.

In the early grades, exploratory talking to learn is best when it is closely connected to activities that the children are doing. Planting seeds, observing a class pet, experimenting with magnets, or engaging in other activities with concrete objects will give children the chance to describe and explain what they see, hear, and feel. Such exploratory talk about immediate experience is a primary means of making sense of that experience, of coming to understand it, and of assimilating it with previous learnings. In later grades, the exploratory talk may go beyond the immediate, concrete present to include reflection on vicarious experiences or discussion of more abstract learnings.

Given the value of this kind of exploratory talk, teachers need to allow students regular opportunities to meet in small groups to discuss what they are doing and learning about. At first, the teacher may meet with groups to encourage such talk, helping students to feel at ease about discussing concepts or issues even when the children feel uncertain about what they know. As students become more comfortable talking freely among themselves, they will be able to proceed with minimal supervision. At times, the groups may tape their discussions, as in the previous example. This allows the teacher to analyze the exchanges at a later time. Whether or not the children's talk is monitored, however, the fact that it is allowed to take place at all will encourage students to become actively involved in thinking and learning.

Speaking for Different Purposes: Some Conclusions

Students need frequent opportunities to speak. Regular informal sharing of personal experiences should be encouraged in all grades. Other speaking activities throughout the grades can include notation groups, participatory telling of pattern stories, creative dramatics, student storytelling (and retelling), discussion, and occasional teacher-directed recitations. Exploratory talk should be encouraged when students are introduced to various concepts that stem from literature units or that are part of other subject curricula (science, mathematics, social studies, etc.). In addition, the teacher needs to encourage oral expression in a variety of other situations, such as those that involve exchanges among students in writing response groups (see Chapter 7), during discussions of stories that children read together (see Chapter 4), and in inquiry reading work groups (see Chapter 11). The goals are to help students develop confidence and skill as speakers, whether they are sharing ideas with just a few others or whether they are making a relatively formal presentation to a larger group.

Ideally, various speaking activities will be integrated with other language processes within a single unit. Here is one example of an extended kindergarten project that features such integration. The activities are listed here with brief explanations of what was accomplished when the group concentrated their attention on pumpkins.

Pumpkins

1. Children examined a pumpkin and described what they saw and felt as they handled the intact fruit and then watched the teacher cut the top and remove the pulp and seeds. As they talked, the children compared features of the pumpkin with other familiar objects and foods, exploring the concept of *pumpkin* by adding new information to knowledge they already possessed. They thought of many words to describe the pumpkin. The teacher listed these words on a large piece of chart paper and then read the list aloud to the group.

2. The group worked together to design a jack-o-lantern, which the teacher cut to their specifications. As they discussed their design and told the teacher how they wanted it to look, their words and directions became more and more precise.

3. The teacher read aloud the version of "Cinderella" in which a pumpkin becomes a coach. Different groups of children improvised dramas of the story, inventing dialogue as they played out the scenes. They used several words and sentences from the story in their dramas and, talking as the characters in the tale, used language patterns that were in some instances different from their usual way of speaking.

4. The group toasted pumpkin seeds and made pumpkin custard. These activities provided students the opportunities for measuring and timing as well as for tasting the finished products. Throughout, language was used to describe observations and anticipate outcomes.

5. The children planted pumpkin seeds in small containers, placed them on the windowsill, and observed them regularly for many days. The process of planting involved considerable talk. The regular observations were recorded by the teacher on a chart kept near the windowsill. The teacher read these aloud periodically, and the children discussed what they had observed and predicted what they might see in the future.

6. The children drew pictures of pumpkins, wrote about pumpkins, and shared their pumpkin stories with one another. (Although the children were not yet adept at encoding words in written form, the teacher encouraged them to use invented spellings, a process described in Chapter 8.) As they drew and wrote, they talked about what they were putting down on paper, making the acts of drawing and writing natural extensions of what they were expressing orally.

This sequence of activities illustrates ways in which meaningful talk can be made an integral part of a teaching unit that includes other language activities. The children had many opportunities to explore the attributes and functions of pumpkins. They were able to develop new understandings through exploratory talk. They saw some of their language recorded and read by the teacher and became attentive to written forms of language. They heard a story and interpreted that story through drama. They drew and wrote, expressing their ideas in ways that could be kept and shared with others. With each activity, in which their talk was a central feature, they refined and extended their language and learning abilities.

Similar sequences of activities may be planned on a variety of themes from kindergarten through the upper grades. The principles are the same at any grade level. Students are encouraged to talk for a variety of purposes. Their talk stems from and leads to other activities that may involve reading and writing as well as listening and viewing.

Talking Leads to Reading: Using Experience Stories

In all grades, students' talk can lead directly to the creation of materials that children can read. As students discuss, tell, dramatize, explain, or demonstrate, their words may be transcribed by the teacher. The resulting reading material is highly motivating to students, especially to those who are just learning to read. Seeing their own words recorded in print, students of all ages gain new awareness of the functions and effects of language. Talking has a special purpose when the object is to create something to read; reading takes on special meaning when the words are the students' own.

At times, the creation of student-dictated materials may be done simply to

Students' talk can lead directly to the creation of materials that children can read.

build young children's awareness of language in print. The activity is a first step in the process of learning to read. For instance, the kindergarten teacher in the last example listed words the children used in describing pumpkins. The main purpose of the activity was to observe and talk about pumpkins; the group spent relatively little time listing and reading the descriptive words. Creating the list simply helped children to reflect on the words they were using, to see their language recorded, and to notice how their words looked in print.

Other speaking activities described earlier in this chapter may also lead to the creation of materials that students can read. For instance, as was suggested, students may dictate and read portions of pattern stories. Children in notation groups are also engaged in dictating reflections to a listener-recorder. Their responses may be reread periodically as students examine the folders they maintain in this program. With such activities, the dictated materials are often read and enjoyed, but they are seldom used for actual instruction in reading. At other times, dictated materials may become the primary means for teaching reading.

When reading instruction is the objective, the talking-reading connection is readily made with the experience story, a key element in the Language Experience Approach to reading (LEA). Many variations of LEA have been developed, including those described by Ashton-Warner (1963), Veatch et al. (1973), Stauffer (1970, 1980), Allen (1976), and Fields and Lee (1987). Any of these related approaches may be used as the basic program in regular classrooms (Stauffer, 1980; Nessel and Jones, 1981). The approach also helps students for whom English is a second language (Dixon and Nessel, 1983). Typical steps in creating an experience story are these:

1. Teacher and students discuss an object or an event. Listening and speaking abilities grow refined as observations and opinions are exchanged. Concepts are developed as children talk things through and receive the teacher's help.
2. Students dictate to the teacher, and the teacher transcribes the dictation. Together, the students and the teacher create the instructional material.
3. Students read the dictated account several times, with the teacher helping as needed. With repeated readings, students gain confidence in their abilities as readers and begin to learn individual words from the story.
4. Reading and other language abilities are reinforced through teacher-designed activities that are related to the dictated account.
5. Students move from reading their own dictations to reading materials by other authors. At some point they can read trade books and school texts. Thus, they develop confidence and skill with reading.

The rationale for using the language experience approach is straightforward. Students see their own language recorded in print. Because they themselves composed the account, using their own words and language patterns, the written language is highly predictable. That is, the authors know what they said and use this knowledge to decode the message they see in front of them. Their first efforts are not like actual reading, of course; they must instead rely on their auditory memory of what they said. However, as children see that their words may be recorded and read back, they become aware of the basic purpose of written language and of the connections between the spoken and the written word. There is an ease to this natural approach that gives children a positive opportunity. Seeing and reading their very own words, they quickly "catch on" to what reading is and gain confidence in their ability to master the process eventually.

Let us examine more closely each of the steps in creating and using dictated stories. We can thereby see how reading instructional goals are accomplished as speaking abilities are refined.

Observation and Discussion

The teacher provides a stimulus that will encourage students to observe and discuss. Almost any object or experience will work well, from a carefully planned field trip to the analysis of a simple house plant brought in to the class. Typical daily activities (going to the cafeteria for lunch) or unusual occurrences (a violent storm) may both be used as the basis for discussion. Science experiments, creative dramas, or favorite folk tales may all be used to stimulate discussion that can lead to dictation. As students become familiar with procedures, they will be eager to suggest their own ideas for stimuli, and they should be encouraged to do so.

Discussions may be carried out with the whole class or with small groups. The teacher's role is to pose open-ended questions that encourage close observation, analytical thinking, and as much oral expression as possible. Students are urged to talk freely about the object or event. As they talk, the teacher observes, stepping in only to guide thinking or to influence oral language gently by introducing specialized terms or by modeling good patterns of usage.

Here is one illustration. The teacher provided a meat thermometer and a medical thermometer as stimuli for a class discussion. Several students immediately identified the objects, using the word *thermometer*. Others offered statements such as these: "The nurse at the doctor's office took my temperature with one of those," and "My mommy uses one of those when she cooks roast beef." The teacher's questions led to a discussion about the words *temperature, dial,* and *mercury*. Students also pointed out several ways in which the two thermometers were alike and different. The children were observing carefully, learning from each other and the teacher as they talked enthusiastically about their experiences with thermometers.

Several of these students were still using immature language. The teacher accordingly often tried to influence their usage by suggesting alternative language patterns as models. Instead of correcting the children directly, he would rephrase the students' contributions, using more mature or more precise wording. For example, when one boy said, in reference to the thermometers, "This here one ain't got no gray stuff," the teacher smiled, nodded, and remarked, "Steven says the meat thermometer doesn't have mercury." Steven was not criticized for his way of speaking. In fact, he was quite pleased that the teacher called attention to his observation in an approving manner. At the same time, the child heard his own statement refined; the interaction thus added to the student's growing awareness of language usage.

As students participate in such types of discussions, they are learning to observe, to think carefully, and to express various ideas about the topic at hand. The discussion is valuable in its own right, whether or not dictation is to follow. When dictation does follow, the discussion is like any good prewriting activity: it helps students collect their thoughts for use in composition.

Dictation

Most teachers prefer to have students dictate experience stories in relatively small groups (five to ten students). This arrangement enables all group members to have ample opportunities to contribute their ideas. Some children will fare well in larger groups, but others may need the support of very small dictating groups. Teachers will need to try different arrangements to determine the best situation for a given class. Teachers should also be aware of students' levels of readiness for reading instruction.

The teacher who conducted the discussion on thermometers knew his students well. He used a variety of dictating activities, each selected to match specific students' needs and abilities. After the discussion, he divided the class into four smaller groups, and he met with one group at a time. The first group was composed of immigrant children who had only a limited knowledge of English. Each child chose just one word to learn, and the teacher printed the word on a card and read it aloud with the student. Students then drew illustrations of their words and discussed their work with the other members of their group. The next two groups were composed of students who were more fluent speakers of English. Here the children dictated group stories; several children contributed ideas to these accounts, and then each group read its composition together. The final group was made up of children who were learning to read quite rapidly and easily; here each student dictated a brief, individual account.

Students in any class will vary in their abilities to express ideas orally in this kind of setting. Some will have only a few words to say, whereas others will be eager to contribute a great deal. A program based on students' dictation allows all students to participate in shared experiences. The children can benefit from talking and listening to each other while they progress in reading at their own rates. For example, two members of the same first-grade group dictated the following individual stories after the group discussed the antics of a pair of hamsters:

HAMSTERS

They spin around the wheel. They eat. They're furry. Sometimes boys say, "Fuzzy-wuzzy had no hair."

CHIPPER AND FLOWER

They have small teeth. They like to eat a lot. They like to dig holes in the soil. They like to play with each other and they like to climb up the tunnel.

These stories reflect different levels of oral language sophistication and different abilities with regard to maintaining continuity within a dictated account. Yet because both children thoroughly enjoyed the hamsters and the dictating and were able to read their own stories, both had positive experiences as speakers and readers.

No matter which dictation plan is used, children's contributions should be transcribed exactly as dictated. When it is time to take dictation, the teacher should listen and record. He or she should not try to influence or correct language usage. If reading skills are to be acquired smoothly through the use of dictated stories, there must be a perfect match between the written text and the words the student remembers saying. Thus, if a student dictates, "The thermometer ain't got no mercury," the teacher must be prepared to record the sentence as given. The alternative (recording a teacher-corrected version of the statement) will very likely confuse the child. If the child says, "The thermometer ain't got no mercury," but the teacher writes, "The thermometer doesn't have any mercury," the child, when reading the story, will invariably say, "ain't got no," when the teacher points to the words "doesn't have any." Wrong associations will thus be made between the printed words and the words the child says.

The teacher need not feel that accepting anomalous language in this situation somehow reinforces bad habits. Each dictated story is used for only a short period of time and has relatively little influence on children's oral language habits. By contrast, the teacher's daily modeling of mature language, the language of more mature classmates, varied oral and aural activities, and wide exposure to literature all have a much more significant influence on a child's usage of language. As students' oral language matures, helped along by other oral activities and direct instruction, the language of their dictated stories will also improve. Meanwhile, by accepting some immature or non-Standard English statements for dictated accounts, the teacher will prevent confusion as the children develop reading skills.

Reading the Dictation

Once a dictation is completed, the text becomes the instructional material. When a child dictates a word, the teacher should read it aloud several times, urging the child to join in. When the dictation consists of a sentence or a full story, the teacher should also read the text aloud several times with the students, sliding a pointer along the line to call attention to the words as they are spoken. This reading should be done with normal cadence and intonation that closely approximates fluent, mature oral reading. After reading with assistance from the teacher several times, students should then be given many opportunities to read their accounts to each other, to the teacher, and to classroom visitors. Many teachers also send copies of dictated stories home to be shared with the students' families.

Rereading makes the word order of the story become quite familiar. Students begin to learn individual words simply by encountering them over and over in a highly familiar context. They do tend to memorize the story, but this stage does not last long. Later steps in the process ensure solid development of sight vocabulary and word-recognition ability.

An example will illustrate the first steps in the reading of a dictated account. A group of first graders had read and discussed many wordless picture books and had developed good ability to follow these stories. They were now ready to compose a story to accompany such a book and to see their words in written form. The group first viewed and discussed the wordless picture book *Hiccup* by Mercer Mayer (Dial, 1976). Here, they followed a plan like the one used for the discussion about *April Fools* (see Chapter 2). Then they dictated the following story, which the teacher recorded on large chart paper. Note how the teacher gave each student credit for his or her contribution to the story:

Robert said, "Once upon a time a gentleman hippo and a lady hippo went on a picnic in a boat." Sue said, "The lady hippo started hiccuping and the boy hippo said let's go for a swim." Peter said, "He threw her so far she went to China. She flew back in an airplane and she still has the hiccups." Tao said, "And then the other person next to her didn't like her hiccups so he kicked her out the window."

The group enthusiastically read their story with the teacher several times, the teacher allowing her voice to drop out gradually on successive readings. Then each student had a chance to read the story (with the teacher's help) individually. Robert and Sue were able to read almost all the words easily, with very little assistance. Peter recognized several of the words without help, especially those that he had dictated. Tao recognized only his own name and a few of the words that were prominent and repeated often (hiccup, hippo). For each child, the reading and rereading of the story fostered word learning, and each met with a level of success as a reader.

The next day, the group recalled their discussion and again read the chart story together. Then the teacher handed out copies of the story, which students pasted in their individual storybooks. Each child had a chance to reread the story individually with the teacher. While she dealt with individual children, the students drew illustrations and underlined words they were sure they knew. As the teacher made the rounds, she noted which story details the children had included in their pictures and how well they had judged their knowledge of individual words.

Reinforcing Reading Skills

Success with the Language Experience Approach to reading requires that students repeatedly use the words they are learning. Use enables them to build sight vocabularies and develop other reading skills. The words learned from dictated stories are first written on word cards. These are filed alphabetically in sturdy containers known as *word banks*. Each child has a word bank of known words that is used for a variety of games and activities that foster skill development. Typical word bank activities include the following:

1. Categorizing words according to color, shape, size, or some other dimension (for instance, things that are edible or inedible, alive or not alive, etc.)

2. Composing sentences (or new stories) by arranging word cards on desk tops or flannel boards
3. Alphabetizing word cards that have been dumped in a pile on a desk
4. Playing games such as "Go Fish" with word cards
5. Finding words that start (or end) with the same sound.

In addition to planning practice activities with word banks, teachers can also use the stories themselves for meaningful instruction in word recognition and comprehension. Here are two examples of story-related skill activities.

A group of second graders dictated this account at the beginning of the school year:

JUDY'S FROG

Judy brought her frog in today. Mrs. McFadden got a box to put the frog in. Francis and Judy went out to get grass to put in the box. When they got the grass, the frog got out. Francis caught the frog. The frog is big. The frog is green and it has black on it. It is pretty. We like the frog.

The teacher decided to use this story to reinforce the group's knowledge of "*r* blends" (consonants followed by the letter *r*). First she wrote the words *frog* and *Francis* on the board and asked how they were alike. The children quickly noticed that both words started with the same sound, generated by the letters *fr*. The teacher repeated the procedure with the words *grass* and *green*. Then the group located all four words in the story as well as the additional "*r* blends" in *brought* and *pretty*. Next, the group named other "*r* blend" words and finally returned to their desks to look for examples in their word banks and in printed materials such as trade books and periodicals.

In a first-grade class, a group dictated this story after conducting a science experiment:

MAGNETS

Candida said, "Magnets can pick up paper clips." Bob said, "Magnets can pick up scissors." Lupe said, "Magnets can't pick up a penny." Ruth said, "Magnets can't pick up a ruler."

The teacher used this dictation to reinforce concepts from the science lesson. His questions led the group to discover that the dictation mentioned two categories of objects—things the magnet would pick up and things it wouldn't. He then gave each student a set of sentences from the story, printed on strips of paper. The children sorted their sentences into appropriate piles and then compared their results.

These two examples illustrate the kind of skill instruction that may be conducted when the experience story is used as a starting point. Appendix B describes the basic reading skills that should be included in such a program and suggests how those skills might be taught.

Reading Other-author Material

Dictated stories provide a natural bridge from oral language to written language. They enable beginning readers to learn to make sense out of print. These students are soon ready to handle other-author materials. The transition to other texts may be made in different ways. Some teachers use dictated stories as the sole vehicle for instruction until students are able to handle second- or third-grade level material comfortably. Others use experience stories to supplement another approach to reading instruction. Here are a few ways in which other-author materials may be integrated with students' own dictated accounts in an instructional program.

At very beginning levels of reading, students need to see words they are learning in a variety of contexts. For instance, if a group has dictated a story about spiders, the teacher will want to provide a collection of books and periodicals about spiders for students to browse through. The children will very likely find words they have just learned (e.g., *spider*) and will thereby take the first step toward reading other-author materials.

As students gain proficiency in reading, the teacher will have many chances to dovetail dictated stories with other reading materials. For instance, one teacher had students discuss and dictate material about fire safety before they read a textbook selection on the same subject. Here is the dictated account:

WHAT TO DO IF THERE'S A FIRE

Andre said, "I would get out of the house and I would go to my next door neighbor's house and ask if I could call the fire department." Phillip said, "If a fire happened I would get out of the house as fast as I can and if I caught on fire I would stop, drop, and roll." Sara said, "When you're in bed and you wake up and you see a fire, you roll over and get out." Jonathan said, "If a fire gets on you, you should stop, drop, and roll."

The textbook selection ("Fire," from *Inside My Hat,* Level 4, Ginn, 1982) is a story about two children and a mother who discover a fire and call for help. Thus, the group read two stories on the same topic and were able to compare the two accounts. Word learning was also reinforced, because twelve words from the published story happened to be used by the children in their dictated story: a, call, do, I, fire, said, see, the, to, on, what, and you.

Another group had a lively discussion about dolphins. The children dictated this story:

HOW DOLPHINS LEARN

If you see any dolphins you shouldn't go near because they can bite. Dolphins need air to breathe and they need their mothers to help to learn to swim. Dolphins need protection from sharks and when the baby dolphins are born they always stay with their mother. Dolphins are mammals and they always need air. When you see babies with their mother dolphin you should stay away. The mother teaches the baby dolphins how to swim.

After working with this story for several days, the group had little difficulty reading a dolphin story in their textbook; the story they read was "Ken and the Fish" (from *Fish and Not Fish,* Level 3, Ginn, 1982).

At the earliest levels of reading ability, students' own dictated stories are almost always more interesting and challenging to the readers than are many commercial, easy-to-read materials. As students gain more skill, however, published materials become preferable because they introduce youngsters to a much wider world of ideas and language than the students are able to create by dictating. As students grow in reading ability, a greater proportion of instructional time should accordingly be spent in reading other-author materials.

Students who are essentially beginning readers (average kindergarteners or first graders, older students who are making slow progress in reading, or students of any age who are just learning to speak and read English) probably can benefit from spending most of their time reading their own dictated stories. Trade books and texts should be used only as supplementary materials. As students make progress, other-author texts can become the basic materials; dictated stories may then be used to extend and refine concepts. Generally, when students have acquired a sight vocabulary (a word bank) of about two hundred words and are able to read their own dictated stories easily and fluently, they will be ready to handle many materials that are considered to be at the primer or first-reader level.

At this later point, students should be able to begin participating in Directed Reading-Thinking Activities (see Chapters 4 and 5), using different kinds of easy-to-read stories and books. Children should also be encouraged to read widely from a variety of trade books written for beginning readers. Books with highly predictable language are especially good choices for independent reading at this stage (Rhodes, 1981; Bridge, Winograd, and Haley, 1983). Children who have special problems may need to work with their own dictated stories for a longer period of time before making the transition to regular school texts and trade books.

Other Uses of Experience Stories

Although experience stories have usually been associated with beginning reading programs, student dictation may be used at any grade level to make the talking-reading connection. As mentioned earlier, dictated stories are ideal materials for students who are just learning to speak English or who have other special needs (Dixon and Nessel, 1983). In the upper grades, discussion and dictation may also be incorporated into lessons. Here is one example of such an application.

A seventh-grade class was studying the Panama Canal, using as a basic text a survey social science book that had only a few paragraphs describing the building of the canal. The text also contained one drawing of the lock system. Though the students had read the text, they still had only a very limited understanding of how ships actually went through the canal. Through group discussion of the book drawing and through the teacher's explanation, the class began to grasp the principles. As they talked, the teacher wrote notes on the board. At the end of the period, the group worked together to compose an explanation of how the canal locks worked. The teacher recorded this composition on the board. The next day, the teacher handed out copies of the group dictation, which the students reread, discussed, illustrated with their own drawings, and then placed in their notebooks. Talking and composing helped them learn the information to begin with; the dictated account served as a useful text for later review.

Discussion and dictation may be incorporated at any level, in any content area, as an aid to learning. When students try to explain new information in their own words, they are working to comprehend. As a guide and a recorder, the teacher is in an excellent position to help students state what they have learned clearly and to help them create an account that may be used as a record of that learning.

Listening, Viewing, and Speaking:
Some Conclusions

The oral and aural components of the language arts curriculum are as important as are those parts of the program devoted to developing skill in reading and writing. Oral language is the basis of communicating and learning in the early years. It is also the foundation on which students must build their knowledge of how to comprehend and use written language. The stronger the oral base, the more successful students will be as learners and, eventually, as readers and writers. For these reasons, good listening, viewing, and speaking activities are at the heart of an effective program.

In many schools today, however, there is an emphasis on paper-and-pencil activities, especially on those that accompany commercial language arts materials. It is believed that basic language skills are best taught and reinforced through these kinds of exercises. However, these exercises require little in the way of oral exchange among students or between students and teacher. Yet if students spend a great deal of time sitting quietly and completing workbook or ditto pages, they are being deprived of opportunities to develop the oral ability so critical to effective communication and learning. Though some of these structured exercises are useful for practicing certain skills, their use should not dominate the program. Students must be given many opportunities to listen, view, and talk for a variety of interesting purposes.

Indeed, oral exchanges in the classroom may affect students' learning more than any other facet of the program. The amount and kind of exchanges set the tone in the classroom and can make a big difference in the amount and kind of learning that goes on (Barnes, Britton, and Rosen, 1971). Torbe and Medway (1981) reflect on the importance of student talk, arguing that in general, the more students are allowed to talk about what they are doing, the better they learn. They describe how they developed this perspective:

> If what Vygotsky and Piaget, George Kelly and Sapir, D. W. Harding and Cassirer (and all the others) said was true, that we learn by talking, and that learning is an act of creation by which we make and shape the very world we inhabit, then that meant the *pupils* had to do the talking, not the teachers. Thus, teachers had to become listeners, paying attention to what their pupils were trying to do in talk, accepting their present understandings and building on them so that learners could make the information they were presented with into comprehended knowledge. (p. 9)

As this chapter has shown, there are many speaking activities that are interesting to students and that are extremely valuable for building language proficiency. Informal sharing, work in a notation group, creative dramatics, storytelling, discussion, and exploratory talk all afford good opportunities for students to use language to hypothesize, interpret, reflect, and learn. As students are encouraged to speak out (and as their efforts are valued), they will improve their fluency, their confidence, their skill, and their knowledge.

Equally important are the activities the teacher develops to help students be better listeners and viewers. The teacher must realize that there is more to good listening and viewing than being quiet and attentive enough to follow directions. Teachers must strive for active intellectual and emotional student involvement and must provide captivating material for students to hear and see.

Students also need many opportunities to make connections between listening, viewing, speaking, reading, and writing. Meaningful oral language experiences are not accomplished in isolation but are incorporated naturally with activities that draw students' attention to language in written form.

Suggested Activities

1. Read aloud a predictable storybook to two or three kindergarten or first-grade children. Encourage them to retell the story. Then have them dictate their own version. Help the children reread their dictated story.
2. Read aloud a story to a primary-school class. Choose a tale with which they are already familiar. Help a small group of volunteers to plan and enact the story or to produce a puppet show.
3. Locate a story that is similar in story line and content to one that a group of "slow" readers will be reading in their basal reader. Read the story aloud. Have the children retell it in their own words. Then have them dictate their version of the story. After they have reread their dictation, direct the reading of the story in the basal reader according to the instructions in the teacher's manual. Evaluate the children's responses to these activities.
4. Conduct the listening activity described on page 82 with a small group of students. Evaluate the children's ability to follow the rules you established. Evaluate your own performance in conducting the lesson.

References

Allen, R. V. *Language Experiences in Communication.* Boston: Houghton Mifflin, 1976.

Ashton-Warner, S. *Teacher.* New York: Simon and Schuster, 1963.

Barnes, D.; Britton, J.; and Rosen, H. *Language, the Learner, and the School Program.* London: Penguin, 1971.

Bridge, C. A.; Winograd, P. N.; and Haley, D. "Using Predictable Materials vs. Preprimers to Teach Beginning Sight Words." *The Reading Teacher* 36(May 1983):884–90.

Britton, J. *Language and Learning.* London: Penguin, 1970.

Bryant, S. C. *How to Tell Stories to Children.* Boston: Houghton Mifflin, 1924.

Cottrell, J. *Creative Drama in the Classroom, Grades 1–3.* Chicago: National Textbook, 1987.

—————. *Creative Drama in the Classroom, Grades 4–6.* Chicago: National Textbook, 1987.

Dixon, C. N., and Nessel, D. *The Language Experience Approach to Reading and Writing: LEA for ESL.* San Francisco: Alemany Press, 1983.

Farrell, C., and Nessel, D. *Word Weaving: A Teaching Sourcebook.* San Francisco: Zellerbach Family Fund, 1984.

Fields, M. V., and Lee, D. *Let's Begin Right: A Developmental Approach to Beginning Literacy.* Columbus, OH: Charles Merrill, 1987.

Kelley, E. *The Workshop Way of Learning.* New York: Harper and Brothers, 1951.

Landor, L. "The Study of Individual Culture: A Matter of Human Survival." Unpublished master's thesis. Sonoma State University, 1979.

—————. "Developing the Habit of Notation." Paper presented at the International Conference on Universal Education. Pomaia-Pisa, Italy: October 1982.

McCaslin, N. *Creative Dramatics in the Classroom*. New York: David McKay, 1968.

——————. *Creative Drama in the Classroom*. New York: Longman, 1984.

Morrow, L. M. "Reading and Retelling Stories: Strategies for Emergent Readers." *The Reading Teacher* 38(May 1985):870–75.

Nessel, D., and Jones, M. B. *The Language-Experience Approach to Reading: A Handbook for Teachers*. New York: Teachers College Press, 1981.

Pradl, G. "Learning How to Begin and End a Story." *Language Arts* 56(January 1979):21–25.

Rhodes, L. K. "I Can Read! Predictable Books as Resources for Reading and Writing Instruction." *The Reading Teacher* 34(February 1981):511–18.

Rowe, M. B. "Science, Silence and Sanctions." *Science and Children* 6(March 1969):11–13.

——————. "Wait Time: Slowing Down May Be a Way of Speeding Up." *Journal of Teacher Education* 37(January-February 1986):43–50.

Stanford, G., and Stanford, B. D. *Learning Discussion Skills Through Games*. New York: Citation Press, 1969.

Stauffer, R. G. *The Language-Experience Approach to the Teaching of Reading*. New York: Harper & Row, 1980.

Sticht, T. G.; Beck, L. V.; Hanke, R. N.; Kleiman, G. M.; and James, J. H. *Auding and Reading: A Developmental Model*. Alexandria, VA: Human Resources Research Organization, 1974.

Thomas, S., and Dinges, S. *Curtain I*. New York: Trillium Press, 1986.

——————. *Curtain II*. New York: Trillium Press, 1986.

Torbe, M., and Medway, P. *The Climate for Learning*. Montclair, NJ: Boynton/Cook, 1981.

Veatch, J.; Sawicki, F.; Elliott, G.; Barnette, E.; and Blakey, J. *Key Words to Reading: The Language Experience Approach Begins*. Columbus, OH: Charles Merrill, 1973.

Whaley, J. "Readers' Expectations for Story Structure." *Reading Research Quarterly* 17(Fall 1981):90–114.

Wright, L. "Creative Dramatics and the Development of Role-taking in the Elementary Classroom." *Elementary English* 51(January 1974):89–93.

Zimiles, H., and Kuhns, M. *A Developmental Study of the Retention of Narrative Material, Final Report* (Research Report 134, National Institute of Education). New York: Bank Street College of Education, 1976.

Suggested Readings

Cameron, J. R. "Accessibility to Literature through Oral Performance." *English Education* 13(February 1981):3–9.

Cazden, C. B.; John, V. P.; and Hymes, D. *Functions of Language in the Classroom*. New York: Teachers College Press, 1972.

Donaldson, M. *Children's Minds*. New York: W. W. Norton, 1979.

Fillion, B. "Let Me See You Learn." *Language Arts* 60(September 1983):702–10.

Hartley, R.; Frank, L. K.; and Goldenson, R. M. *Understanding Children's Play*. New York: Columbia University Press, 1964.

Jones, M. B., and Nessel, D. D. "Enhancing the Curriculum Through Experience Stories." *The Reading Teacher* 39(October 1985):18–22.

Kirkwood, W. G. "Storytelling and Self-Confrontation: Parables as Communication Strategies." *Quarterly Journal of Speech* 69(February 1983):58–74.

Lauritzen, C. "Oral Literature and the Teaching of Reading." *The Reading Teacher* 33(April 1980):787–90.

Lee, D. M., and Rubin, J. B. *Children and Language.* Belmont, CA: Wadsworth, 1979.

McClure, A. A. "Integrating Children's Fiction and Informational Literature in a Primary Reading Curriculum." *The Reading Teacher* 35(April 1982):784–89.

Pinnell, G. S. "Ways to Look at the Functions of Children's Language" in A. Jaggar and M. T. Smith-Burke, eds., *Observing the Language Learner.* Urbana, IL: National Council of Teachers of English/International Reading Association, 1985.

Purves, A., and Monson, D. *Experiencing Children's Literature.* Glenview, IL: Scott Foresman, 1984.

Rosen, H., and Rosen, C. *The Language of Primary School Children.* Harmondsworth, England: Penguin, 1973.

Rouse, J. *The Completed Gesture.* New Jersey: Skyline Books, 1978.

Siks, G. B. *Creative Dramatics: An Art for Children.* New York: Harper & Row, 1960.

Smith, E.; Goodman, K. S.; and Meredith, R. *Language and Thinking in the Classroom.* New York: Holt, Rinehart and Winston, 1976.

Taylor, L. E. *Storytelling and Dramatization.* Minneapolis: Burgess, 1965.

Tough, J. *Listening to Children Talking: A Guide to the Appraisal of Children's Use of Language.* Portsmouth, NH: Heinemann, 1976.

—————. *Talk for Teaching and Learning.* Portsmouth, NH: Heinemann, 1979.

Verriour, P. "Toward a Conscious Awareness of Language Through Drama." *Language Arts* 60(September 1983):731–36.

—————. "Drama, Distance, and the Language Process." *Language Arts* 62(April 1985):385–90.

Wells, G. (ed.) *Learning Through Interaction.* London: Cambridge University Press, 1981.

Active Involvement in Reading

If students become motivated to read and if they develop good comprehension abilities, they will greatly enhance their potential for learning. Children who are readers add to their firsthand experiences by entering other lives and worlds, real and fictional. They develop their vocabularies, learn concepts, encounter new ways of using language, and acquire a sense of how stories and informational texts are organized and written. These learnings, which accumulate gradually over time, have a strong positive influence on students' language and learning abilities. Furthermore, if students derive pleasure from books, they will be on their way to acquiring a lifetime habit of reading. This can bring them great intellectual and emotional satisfaction throughout their adult years and can make them lifelong students of language and the world.

The previous section described ways in which young children become aware of printed language through seeing familiar words recorded. They learn to recognize refrains from pattern stories or poems that they know well orally, and they learn to recognize words they have dictated themselves. These materials can be used to teach the process of reading to those children who are at the beginning reading stage. Children may also learn to read through use of a basal reading program (a carefully structured and graded set of materials that is designed expressly for teaching reading). After children learn to read, they inevitably progess to more and more difficult materials. Their eventual studies will include selections at the upper levels of a basal reading program, literature, subject matter texts (such as science or social studies books), reference materials, and periodicals. The way the teacher guides the reading of all these materials has a significant effect on students' comprehension abilities and, equally important, on their attitudes toward books and reading.

In all grades, language in print is often the core around which a variety of language activities are planned. For instance, a work of literature can serve as the basis for a number of speaking, listening, and writing activities. Or informational materials from social studies or science may be the central feature of a unit that involves many language activities. The way teachers guide the reading of such materials can influence students' interest in the text and their comprehension of it, both of which will affect students' ability to talk and write about what they have read.

For all these reasons, the language arts teacher needs to know how to develop comprehension and how to do so in a way that arouses interest in reading. The next two chapters explore these issues. Chapter 4 contains a discussion of the reading process and illustrates how that process is used with narrative materials. Chapter 5 examines how the reading process is used with informational materials that are usually expository in nature. The emphasis in these two chapters is on how to stimulate readers' active involvement with a variety of texts. Also emphasized are the ways in which reading is a thinking process. Connections between reading and the other language arts are also made here, as in other chapters.

Children who are readers add to their firsthand experiences by entering other lives and worlds, real and fictional. If students derive pleasure from books, they will be on their way to acquiring a life-long habit of reading.

Reading Narratives

This chapter explores the reading process as it is applied to narrative material—to stories from the world of literature, to basal reader selections, or to any other narratives, including novels. The teacher needs to guide the reading in such a way that students enjoy and appreciate the story while developing their ability to comprehend. Both comprehension and appreciation are enhanced by discussion; in fact, the heart of guided reading lies in the questions the teacher uses to promote discussion. The best questions encourage students to apply their prior knowledge and thinking abilities to respond to a story.

The Reading Process

Effective guidance of students' reading begins with an understanding of the reading process. The teacher must know what happens when a reader opens a book and sets out to make sense of it. This process has been of great interest to teachers and researchers for many years, and no one yet has all the answers. But there is general agreement on one point: No two readers will make exactly the same sense out of the same material.

Each person is an individual, different in at least some ways from all others. We have different personalities and temperaments, and we have led different lives. Though we may share many experiences with others, we will always see things in our own way, and thus we will always make our own sense of what we read, despite what the author may have intended. This is as true for children as it is for adults.

Children come to school each year with all their life experiences in tow. Their knowledge, attitudes, and expectations about the world have been acquired both in and out of school. Children's backgrounds affect their interpretation and understanding of what they read. There will always be some children who know very little of what others take for granted. A single classroom, for example, may be the group setting for all these different children:

- A child from a large, active family who is used to going camping and studying nature
- A child from a single parent home who has never been camping but is an avid reader
- A child who seldom reads but is an accomplished baseball player
- A child who has never played baseball but who can program a computer
- A child who vacations at the seashore but has never been in a large city
- A child who vacations in New York City but has never been to the seashore
- A child who has always lived in the same house
- A child who has had four different homes in the past eight months, having just arrived from a different culture
- A child who regularly visits grandparents on a farm
- A child whose grandparents are not living and who has never been on a farm.

Each of these individuals will respond in different ways to stories about camping, family life, sports, the seashore, city apartment living, moving, grandparents, farms, baking cookies, or any other topic. No matter how clear or explicit the text, each student will bring a different background of experience to it and will thus have a somewhat different understanding of it.

It is this recognition of the reader in the reading process that has led to the most recent descriptions of what reading is. Rosenblatt (1978), for example, stresses that in responding to literature one brings experiences and attitudes to the text; the text, in exchange, presents the writer's perspective. Working together, the reader and the text create meaning. Stein and Glenn (1979) also emphasize that the process of comprehension involves an interaction of reader and text. The text presents information, but one's prior knowledge affects one's interpretation of that information. Other scholars agree; they observe that effective reading is a process of integrating textual information with what one already knows (Anderson, Spiro, and Montague, 1977; Spiro, Bruce, and Brewer, 1980; Singer and Ruddell, 1985).

Yet many students have not learned to integrate what they read with what they know. They treat materials read in school as foreign and regard them as unconnected to their own knowledge and experience. Spiro (1977), for example, observes as follows:

> It has been for some time this writer's impression that students approach text in the same way as subjects in a memory experiment. They appear to compartmentalize new information, differentiating it from prior knowledge as much as possible. One has the feeling that students, in part because of the nature of the tests they anticipate, insufficiently integrate related knowledge acquired in school . . . and furthermore, treat most school material as unrelated to everything outside of school. (p. 162)

This may be because many teachers spend more time testing comprehension than teaching it (Durkin, 1978–79, 1981). Students are frequently asked to read and answer questions, either orally or in writing. This strategy of testing presumes that the text contains the meaning and that if the students read carefully enough, they will find it.

But as Anderson (1977) states, "text is gobbledygook unless the reader possesses an interpretive framework to breathe meaning into it" (p. 423). That is, effective readers do not passively *get* meaning so much as they actively *construct* meaning by using what they already know to make sense of new material. Anderson, Reynolds, Schallert, and Goetz (1977) demonstrated this constructive aspect of comprehension by giving college students an ambiguous passage about a man named Rocky who was in a difficult situation. These researchers found that the readers' backgrounds and experience strongly affected their interpretation of Rocky's predicament. Some students assumed Rocky to be a prison inmate planning to escape his cell. Those students who were physical education majors generally interpreted the passage as a description of a wrestler in the middle of a match. Subjects' different perspectives directly affected their comprehension of the material. Bransford (1979) cites similar research to show the vital influence that prior knowledge has on a person's ability to construct meanings from texts.

What the teacher does to foster use of prior knowledge to construct meaning is critical to the development of skillful readers. Stauffer (1969, 1975) recognized this and developed the Directed Reading-Thinking Activity (DR-TA) as a method for teaching and refining what he calls the reading-thinking process (see also Stauffer, Burrows, and Black, 1960).

Guiding Response to Narratives

The DR-TA may be used for guiding students who are reading the same story at the same time. The material may be a selection from a basal reader, a literature text, or any other narrative. The method is effective because it stimulates readers to use their prior knowledge and experience to comprehend. During a DR-TA, students become actively involved in hypothesizing, reflecting, and revising their thinking in light of the text. They construct meaning as they read and discuss, using the reading-thinking process to make sense of the material. The approach is purposeful and intellectually stimulating for both students and teacher, and in many ways it is radically different from the traditional way of guiding reading—the Directed Reading Activity (DRA). The differences between the DR-TA and the DRA will be highlighted later in this chapter. First we shall examine the DR-TA in detail, with examples to illustrate the steps of the process.

Thinking before Reading

At the beginning of a DR-TA with narrative material, students are given the first part of a story. They can then set purposes for reading by predicting the outcome of the story. Students, for example, might read the story title and then discuss what they think will happen in the story. Or they might read the first page (or a longer segment) and then predict what will happen next. A DR-TA begins with a bit of story information, accompanied by the question

• What do you think will happen (next)?

Predicting outcomes provokes natural curiosity, and curiosity can serve as strong motivation. Once people begin to wonder about something, they usually make an effort to find out about it. We take objects apart to find out how they work; we watch the next episode of a television mystery to discover who the villain is; we keep turning the pages of a good book. We may be just mildly

curious while waiting for the punch line of a joke; or we may be very determined to find something out, spending hours looking for a fact we just have to
know. Efforts are intensified when we seek to prove ourselves right; for instance,
we doggedly search official records to settle arguments about the outcomes of
past sporting events. When students predict outcomes, their natural curiosity is
aroused, too. They want to know whether or not they are right, and they will-
ingly and eagerly seek information (through reading) to see if their predictions
are accurate.

While asking for predictions, the teacher also requires students to justify
their ideas. The first question is, therefore, accompanied by an equally important second:

- What do you think will happen (next)?
- Why do you think so?

As students give reasons to support their first preditions, they will take into
account their own experiences. They will think about the story in light of what
they know. The initial information may remind them of a firsthand experience,
a different story they have read or heard, or perhaps a television program. As
students share ideas, their talk is not just a random sharing of anecdotes but a
pointed discussion, related to the story, that develops readiness for comprehension. The first interpretations that students make are based on their existing
knowledge, which is organized into sets of related concepts, called *schemata*
(Anderson, Spiro, and Montague, 1977; Rumelhart and Ortony, 1977; Rumelhart,
1980). As students continue reading, they assimilate textual information and
modify their schemata accordingly. The ongoing process of comprehension is
controlled not only by the contents of the text but also by the students' unique
interpretations of the contents (Tierney and Pearson, 1981; Collins, Brown, and
Larkin, 1977). As students make their predictions and discuss their reasons, they
use a range of complex thinking processes: hypothesizing, inferring, justifying,
and evaluating. Reading begins with thinking, a process that lays important
foundations for comprehension.

Predicting outcomes in a story involves anticipation of story events. A similar kind of word-by-word anticipation is at the heart of the psycholinguistic
model of reading that Goodman (1967) presents:

> Reading is a selective process. It involves partial use of available minimal language
> cues selected from perceptual input on the basis of the reader's expectation. As
> this partial information is processed, tentative decisions are made to be confirmed,
> rejected, or refined as reading progresses. (p. 127)

Oral knowledge of vocabulary and language structures guides listeners' expectations about which words will come next in spoken sentences. In a similar
fashion, experiential knowledge and an understanding of narrative structure

allow people to predict story events and outcomes as they read. Whaley (1981) found that elementary-grade students were able to predict the events of incomplete stories and could supply missing information. Her findings support recent theories that our intellectual schemas guide our interpretation and assimilation of story information (Mandler and Johnson, 1977; Stein and Glenn, 1979). Not surprisingly, Whaley found age differences in students' abilities to use what they know about stories to predict outcomes. These findings are consistent with Applebee's (1978) conclusions that "sense of story" (knowledge of how stories go) is a developmental phenomenon.

To illustrate the use of predictions in a DR-TA, here is a discussion that took place in a group of fifth-grade students who were about to read a story called "Danger in the Deep." The teacher had written the title on the board as the first piece of information for students to consider.

TEACHER: What do you think will happen in this story?

AL: Well, I'm not sure, but it could be about the ocean. Sometimes you call the ocean "the deep." Maybe someone drowns.

TEACHER: That's a good thought. We do call the ocean "the deep." What does anyone else think?

JANIE: It might be about someone falling down a well.

TEACHER: Why do you think so, Janie?

JANIE: We read a story last year about someone who fell down a well. It was a deep well, and it was really dangerous!

TEACHER: That's possible. This could be the same kind of story. Any more ideas?

JEFF: Maybe it's a space story.

TEACHER: Why do you think so?

JEFF: Well, sometimes on science fiction programs they talk about going deep into space.

TEACHER: And what might happen in this story?

JEFF: Maybe the crew gets lost in space.

Al's response was prompted by his vocabulary knowledge. Janie recalled a vivid story she had read before, and Jeff, with his interest in space and astronauts, saw yet another possibility. Other students in the group offered more predictions, all of which were stimulated both by the given information (the title) and by the students' previous experiences that affected their thinking in unique ways.

In a DR-TA, each prediction is as acceptable as every other. There are virtually no wrong answers, because several outcomes seem possible when the information is limited. Hence, students often feel more free to participate in this kind of discussion than they do in typical question-answer exchanges. Any sincere response is a good one. The teacher purposely values divergent thinking and avoids giving the group verbal or nonverbal clues about the actual outcome. In the example, the teacher praised astute comments and probed for specificity or explanation, giving each student a chance to contribute but not expecting responses that were right in terms of the story's outcome.

Not every student in the group must think of an original idea. At the beginning of some stories, only a few predictions may arise. In some groups, a few students will be reticent. But readers can be urged to accept other students' purposes as their own. It is the decision to set a purpose (to make a prediction) that is important, not the originality of the idea. When a few predictions have been made, and no other ideas seem forthcoming, the teacher may then ask students who have not yet responded which predictions they will use as their own. In this way, everyone will have a chance to participate and to set a purpose, whether or not everyone can think of an original idea.

Revising Thinking

After the first predictions have been made, students read the next part of the story (the teacher having decided previously on the stopping point). They gather evidence and then decide whether or not to change their predictions. Students repeat this process throughout the reading of the story. With each new segment, new information will require reconsideration of earlier predictions. The teacher uses questions like these in the continuing discussion:

- Were your predictions on target?
- Do you want to change a prediction?
- Now what do you think will happen?
- Why do you think so?

As students gather evidence, the teacher may ask them to read aloud the sentences from the story that support their ideas. Through discussion and rereading, students demonstrate their comprehension of the material by thoughtfully changing or maintaining their predictions as they receive new information.

Revising predictions in a DR-TA is a direct practical application of the reading process as it is described by Tierney and Pearson (1981):

> The reader's schemata drive text processing toward the refinement of a model or scenario that "matches" the text against the reader's world and that is complete, interconnected, and plausible. That is, the reader's schemata will be involved in the construction of a scenario to account for the elements and relationships within the text and the world as the reader sees it. If the reader's model seems tenable, then those schemata that comprise the model will be involved in further text processing. If the reader's model seems untenable, then schemata will drive the reexamination, reconstruction, or restructuring of elements in the text to build a new model. (p. 54)

The simplest way to illustrate this process is to provide an example. We will continue following the group reading of "Danger in the Deep." This is the first part of the story the students read:

DANGER IN THE DEEP
by Charles Coombs

Stan Holmes was tugging the straps of his rubber swim fins over his heels when he saw Doug Sanders coming down the bluff that overlooked Rocky Cove. There was no mistaking Doug's familiar light-blue trunks or his old gray sweat shirt with the big hole in the left elbow. Doug carried a fish spear over one shoulder. Dangling from it were his swim fins and a diving mask. In the other hand he carried an inflated inner tube with a gunny sack tied to it.

"Hi," said Doug as he dumped his diving gear on the sand beside Stan. "You down here alone today?"

"Guess it's too cold for the others," Stan said. "But I kind of like it this way."

"Me too," Doug said.

Stan wondered if the other boy's real reason for being here was the same as his own. Although Stan really liked to skin-dive, it was a summer sport. On a chilly September day like this he would much rather have been home reading a good book. But the season in which it was legal to catch lobsters was nearly over. Most of the commercial lobstermen had quit and gathered up their lobster pots. It was late in the season, and the lobsters seemed scarce.

Doug stripped off his sweat shirt and began to put on his diving gear. "I sure hope I can find some lobsters today," he said. "Not many around, though, I guess. The fish markets in Seaview are really paying a good price for lobsters. And I can use a little money. I've got a chance to get a paper route. But I've got to have a bike to do it. Bikes cost money."

Stan didn't mention how badly he, too, needed spending money. School was about to start again. What clothes he hadn't outworn during the summer, he had outgrown. At the age of thirteen he seemed to be growing faster than Iowa corn in July.

Any other year his parents would have bought school clothes for him. But since his father's accident at the factory, the family seemed to have just enough for food and rent. Later his father would be well and back to work. But right now things were pretty crucial in the Holmes household. Stan knew that it would relieve his parents of a big worry if he could earn enough money to buy his own school clothes this year.

"Well, I guess I'm set," Doug said. He left his spear stuck in the sand and picked up the inner tube with the sack. "Shall we go out together, Stan?" he asked.

Stan knew the rule that a skin-diver never should go out alone. A fellow never knew when something might go wrong and he'd need help. But he also knew Doug's reputation as one of the best young divers at the cove. If they went down together and there were any lobsters around, Doug would probably get them first.

"I—I guess not," Stan said "I'll follow you out in a few minutes. I want to try over on the other side of the point."

He felt Doug's eyes on him. "OK, Stan," Doug said. "But be careful. I hear there are quite a few moray eels hanging around those rocks. They can give you a nasty bite."

"I'll be careful," Stan said, thinking of some of the teeth marks other divers had on their hands and arms. Of course, if you didn't go reaching into places where you couldn't see, you didn't have much to worry about.

Doug waded out through the rolling surf and then swam out into the cove.

He pushed the rubber tube ahead of him. Stan watched him make a couple of dives, but both times Doug came back to the surface empty-handed.

"Boy, I hope I have better luck than that," Stan said to himself as he strapped his sheath knife to his leg. He slipped on his face mask. Carrying his own inner tube, and waddling like a duck because of the rubber fins on his feet, he took to the water.

Stan swam out past where Doug was diving. As Doug surfaced, he shook the water from his face. "Sure don't seem to be many lobsters down here," Doug said. "Saw a big one, but he was over the legal size. All the others seem to be too small."

Legal-sized lobsters were between ten and a half and sixteen inches. Smaller or larger than that, they had to be left alone or tossed back. The West Coast spiny lobster is actually a large sea crawfish. It has no dangerous pinchers like the Eastern lobsters. But when a fellow was ten or fifteen feet underwater, trying to wrestle one out of a rock crevice, he had a job on his hands—especially since the diver has only a short period of time to work before having to surface for air.

"I'm going to try off the point," Stan said. But he didn't ask the other boy to go with him. If Stan found any lobsters, he needed them for himself.

Arriving at his chosen spot, Stan let go of the inner tube. Taking a couple of deep breaths, he jackknifed his body and disappeared beneath the surface.

He was immediately thrilled by the beauty of the bluish-green underwater world. No matter how often Stan dove, he never got over the sights below the surface. Schools of small, brightly-colored fish swam leisurely around him. The seaweed swayed gently in the currents. The ocean bottom was covered with giant boulders that were encrusted with spiny sea urchins and all kinds of razor-sharp shells. Nothing there to bother a diver if he kept his feet off the bottom. A giant crab scurried into a crevice. To Stan's right, a large halibut fluttered across a patch of sand. But there were no lobsters.

Then, just as the breath was beginning to pound in his chest, Stan saw the dark form of a lobster duck into a shallow hole. Marking its location in his mind, Stan fluttered his swim fins and shot back to the surface.

Stan refilled his lungs several times. Then he nosed under for his next dive. Diving downward, he quickly spotted the lobster, which had come back out of its hole. Stan eased up to it and was just about to make his grab. Suddenly, from the corner of his eye, he saw the snakelike head of a large moray eel watching him from under the ledge. He knew that if he made a grab for the lobster, the vicious eel would make a grab for him. The rows of needlelike teeth in the eel's open mouth were anything but inviting.

"That's one lobster I don't want," Stan decided quickly. He shifted direction, following an undersea canyon through the rocks. Having made several dives at Rocky Cove and other inlets, Stan knew that he must be nearly twenty feet down, just about as deep as he had ever gone. Older, more experienced divers thought little of thirty- or even thirty-five-foot dives. But twenty feet was plenty deep for Stan.

Careful to keep his hands off the rocks, he threaded his way along the underwater canyon, pushing against the current. He had just decided to start back for the surface when a sudden flurry of motion directly ahead caught his attention. A cloud of sand fogged the water. But through it, Stan was able to make out the cause.

Lobsters! There were dozens of them. An entire colony, all sizes! The place was crawling with them.

Even through the murk, Stan saw that the ledge under which they scurried was shallow. They should be easy to catch. Making a quick mental note, he stroked back to the surface.

TEACHER: Were any of your predictions right so far?

AL: I was right. It is about the ocean.

TEACHER: Do you all agree? [All students nod or say "Yes, Al was right about that."]

TEACHER: What about the rest of your prediction, Al? You said someone might drown. Do you still think that will happen?

AL: It could. One of the boys could drown. But I don't think so.

MARGIE: I think Stan will go back and get lots of lobsters.

AL: I agree. He'll tell Doug, too. They'll both go together this time. And they won't drown.

JEFF: I don't think he'll tell Doug. Stan said before that he wanted them for himself, and I think he'll just get as many as he can alone.

TEACHER: What do the rest of you think?

LINDA: I agree with Jeff. I don't think he'll tell Doug. He'll go back down by himself. But I think he'll get in trouble with that eel. That's what the danger is.

HANK: I think that's what will happen, too. He'll get in a fight with the eel.

The students used the information from the first part of the story to revise their predictions. Some pointed out how much Stan needed money. Most agreed that even though it wouldn't be very nice, the desperate boy would not tell Doug. A few thought that Stan would relent and share the catch; these students pointed out that the other boy was just as needy. Everyone agreed that before anything else would happen, Stan would be attacked by the eel. But being optimists, they also predicted that Stan would not drown. The group was eager to get back to the story, sure that an exciting underwater struggle was about to take place. Here is the next part.

He came up twenty feet from his floating inner tube. He swam to get it and tow it directly over the spot where he had seen the lobsters.

"Any lobsters?" Doug called to him from fifty yards away.

Without answering, Stan held up his empty hands. Doug could figure it out for himself, he thought.

"I'm about to give up," Doug went on. There was no mistaking the disappointment in his voice. Stan wondered how Doug would get a new bike now. Newspaper routes were not easy to get. "Kind of hate to leave you out here alone, though," Doug said. "It's not a good idea. Besides, the tide's due to change before long."

"Oh, I'll be all right," Stan assured the other boy although he knew it was against all rules of the sport to be out in the water alone. "I'm only going to make a few more dives anyway."

"Then I'll stick around a while," Doug said. "We don't want anything to happen to a fellow skin-diver."

"Suit yourself," Stan called back. Then, anxious to get at the lobsters, he started back down. He was halfway to the bottom when a shadow suddenly passed above him. Stan looked up—straight into the face of a shark!

For an instant his blood chilled with terror. But, knowing that fear is a diver's worst enemy, Stan quickly calmed himself.

The shark was a fairly small one, about four feet long. It seemed just as wary of Stan as Stan was of it. Besides, no man-eating sharks of any size had ever been seen along this part of the coast, especially this close to shore.

Once again in full control of his nerve, Stan flailed out wildly. With a quick flip of its tail, the shark spurted away. It turned and watched from a safer distance.

Stan smiled confidently to himself and went on. Approaching the ledge from a blind angle, he reached down and grabbed a lobster before it or the others knew what had happened. It would probably measure about fourteen inches. A beauty.

Even as he grabbed it, Stan realized what a gold mine of sea food he had discovered. There were so many lobsters that getting his limit would be no problem. In fact, he could come back day after day until the season ended.

He swam back to the surface with the lobster clutched firmly in one hand. Stan felt well rewarded for coming to the cove when most other divers had quit for the season.

But Doug hadn't given up either. His flippers were once again disappearing as Stan reached the surface. Quickly, before the other boy came back up, Stan swam to his floating inner tube and dumped the lobster into the sack hanging beneath it.

Stan took a couple of deep breaths and went down for another lobster. He repeated the performance several times. Each time he came back up with a legal-sized lobster. And each time he managed to drop it into the floating sack while Doug wasn't looking.

Doug called over, "I think I'll call it quits. I've got two pretty good ones. But all of the others seem to have gone south for the winter or something. Let's go in. I'm getting cold. Tell you what. I'll give you one of mine. Then neither of us will be empty-handed."

"Th—thanks," Stan called, "but I think I'll stick around a little longer."

After all, he thought, it would be nice if Doug did go on home. If Doug wasn't on the beach, Stan wouldn't have to explain anything when he finally came in dragging his own heavy sack of lobsters. Yes, it would be better if Doug did go.

Doug seemed to shrug. He pushed his face mask up onto his forehead. Leaning on his inner tube and propelling himself with his rubber-flippered feet, he started easing toward shore.

It was then that a feeling which had been building up in Stan—almost without knowing it—boiled over.

Doug had always been a friend. Maybe not a close friend, but maybe that had been Stan's own fault. Doug had always been such a good athlete and diver that Stan just never felt in his class. Just like today, Stan thought. He hadn't wanted to dive with Doug because he had been afraid that the other boy might hog all the lobsters. And now Doug, who needed the lobsters as much as Stan did, maybe more, had offered to share his own two with Stan. While all the time, right down beneath Stan, there were plenty of lobsters for both of them.

"Hey, Doug," he called suddenly, "I've found a whole nest of them down here. Come on."

The other boy stopped and looked back. "OK, Stan," he said grinning. "If you don't want to be left alone, I'll stick around a few minutes longer. But snap it up, OK?"

It didn't help Stan's feeling of guilt much when he knew that Doug had been sticking around for the past twenty minutes just to be on hand if Stan needed help.

"No kidding, Doug," he called. "They're down here. Lots of them. Come and look in my sack." Stan reached down carefully, pulled one out, and held it up for Doug to see.

A strange look passed over Doug's face. Then, just as quickly, it was gone. "Wow!" he cried, swimming over to Stan. "Where'd that come from?"

Stan told him about his underwater discovery.

"Well, let's go down and have a look," Doug said. Then he peered closely at Stan. "You sure you want me to have some of them?"

"I—I wasn't sure a few minutes ago, Doug," Stan said honestly. "But, well, I am now. Besides, I don't own the ocean, do I?"

Doug smiled. "Come on, let's go down together."

They pulled their diving masks over their faces, filled their lungs, and started down. Stan led the way to the lobsters. Many of them had ducked into crevices. But there were still plenty to be had for the taking. Each boy picked off a good one and took it back up with him.

"Boy, you weren't just kidding, were you?" Doug said, grinning as he dropped his catch into his nearly empty sack. "How many more do you need for your limit?"

"Just one," Stan said. "I'll get it this trip and then wait for you to finish out yours." Without waiting for the other boy, Stan headed back down.

A small school of scarlet fish swam in front of him. They glistened brightly against the pastel green of the water. Rounding a rock, Stan startled a small octopus. Shooting a stream of ink, it pulled its eight tentacles together and propelled itself quickly out of reach. Since no octopus ever grew to any threatening size along this part of the coast, it was another sea creature that gave no fear to an experienced skin-diver.

Arriving once more at the underwater ledge, Stan was just in time to see a big lobster back quickly into a grotto. Stan hadn't noticed the cave before, but he imagined that it must be full of lobsters. Not considering how careless he was being, Stan poked his head and shoulders into the cave.

TEACHER: Were any of your predictions right so far?

LINDA: I was right at first. Stan did go down alone and he didn't tell Doug. But then he felt guilty and told him.

AL: I was right too. They went down together.

HANK: He didn't get in a fight with the eel yet, but I still think he will.

JANIE: I don't think the eel will come back. But I bet that shark's in the cave. The shark will come after him.

MARGIE: Maybe the mother octopus will come along.

TEACHER: What did you read that gave you that idea?

MARGIE: It says here, "Rounding a rock, Stan startled a small octopus." Maybe that's a baby and the mother will come back. But then it also says that they don't get very large around there, so maybe that's not really a baby. I don't know.

TEACHER: What do you think will happen?

MARGIE: I agree with Janie. I think the shark will come after him.

JEFF: I think Stan will get stuck in the cave. It said he put his head and shoulders in and that he was being careless.

AL: If he gets stuck, then he would run out of air. That could really be dangerous. He's been down for a long time holding his breath.

LINDA: That's what I think, too. He'll get stuck and then Doug will come and save him.

MARGIE: But Doug is diving in another place now. He won't be around to notice.

JEFF: No, Doug went down at the same place. Or at least he was going to. If Stan gets into trouble, he'll be there, and I think he'd help him.

HANK: I still think he'll be attacked, maybe by the shark or the eel. But he might get stuck, too.

The discussion continued along these lines. Each of the predictions was based on facts that had clearly been grasped (a shark and an octopus had been mentioned; the eel had been described as dangerous; Stan had gone down alone to swim into the cave) and on logical inferences (a small octopus could be a baby near a parent; Stan could be running out of air if he was being careless; he might be attacked by one of the sea creatures mentioned so far). The students were comprehending the story; the teacher was evaluating their understanding by noting which facts they brought up and how they made sense of them. But the group was doing more than getting the facts and making some inferences. They were *using* the evidence to modify their predictions. This is the key feature of the reading-thinking process: reasoning is based on the evidence found in the text. Students did not just recall that sharks and eels had been mentioned; they reasoned, logically, that Stan might be attacked by one of these creatures. They noted that Stan was being careless and concluded that he might get stuck in the cave.

As they read a story, students will find more and more information that actually supports or contradicts their predictions. Therefore, the teacher should also ask students to read aloud statements that prove points. The goal of this rereading is to give students more opportunities to cite evidence. Not all points need to be proved with oral reading, just as not all predictions need to be justified with oral reading. The momentum of read-predict-read need not be broken with lengthy sessions of oral reading.

The group read this segment next:

As he did so, a sudden surge of underwater current lifted him from beneath. A burst of air escaped his mouth as he felt his shoulders suddenly wedged into the V-shaped roof of the shallow cave.

A feeling of panic surged through Stan as he tried to wriggle free. Then he fought back the terror, realizing that panic was as big an enemy as the current which held him fast. He felt the coarse edge of the rocks scrape his skin. He waited, saving his breath, hoping and praying for the current to ease up.

TEACHER: Were any of your predictions on target?

JEFF: I was right. He *did* get stuck.

TEACHER: Can you prove it?

JEFF: It says here, "he felt his shoulders suddenly wedged into the V-shaped roof of the shallow cave" and it also says, "he tried to wriggle free."

TEACHER: Do you all agree? [Students nod or say, "Yes, he got stuck."]

AL: I was right, too. Well, almost. It says, "a burst of air escaped his lungs." That means he's lost some air, so he could run out soon.

The most important element of this exchange is not that Jeff was right but that he could find the evidence that proved he was right. Al, too, demonstrated good thinking, not by being right but by finding evidence to support his reasoning and recognizing that, although he did not yet have clear proof, he seemed to be on the right track. Students may take special pride in having anticipated actual outcomes; even more significant, however, is their ability to find clear proof for a point or to recognize when, in the absence of proof, the available evidence leads to a certain conclusion.

Sometimes students will be partially right; they can read aloud statements that show where they were right and where their predictions deviated from the story's events. Sometimes, of course, no one will be right, and the group may be citing evidence that proves them to have been wrong. But because anyone's ideas can be possible as predictions, students will not feel defeated if the story takes a different turn from the one they anticipated. The point of having students prove the accuracy of their anticipation is not to focus on the accuracy but to make them conscious of the process of recognizing proof (or lack of it) when they see it.

As students attempt to give proof, the teacher also asks the group to help make judgments. When one student reads aloud to support an idea or brings up evidence to make a point, the teacher will ask the others if they agree: Has the reader proved a point? Does the passage support the statement? Are there other possible interpretations? Is there more evidence to consider? It is important at these times to have the rest of the group *listen* rather than try to read along with the person who is citing textual evidence. If everyone is trying to follow the reader, the group can be distracted by looking for the passage and seeing if the reader is saying the words accurately. It is good practice to say, "Look up and listen" when one student is about to read. Students soon learn both to pay attention to other children's ideas and to make their own judgments about the validity and relevance of the evidence.

The teacher is careful to ask the group's opinion when the student is on

When one student reads aloud to support an idea or brings up evidence to make a point, the teacher will ask the others if they agree. The point of having students prove the accuracy of their anticipation is not to focus on the accuracy but on the process of recognizing proof (or lack of it) when they see it.

the right track, as well as when the student is mistaken. This is an especially important balance to maintain. Too often, teachers fall into the habit of asking a group to chime in only when a student is wrong; this calls attention to error. The point of asking the group if they agree is to encourage students to make their own judgments, not just to prove someone wrong. These exchanges will encourage students to make their own decisions; they will not just rely on the teacher to be the judge.

Once readers have made predictions, they are extremely reluctant to put aside the text until they know the actual outcome. You, too, have been predicting and reading along with the group; therefore, you must be at least mildly curious about the outcome of this story. Here is the ending. See if *you* were right.

> Then, numbly, Stan realized that there was little chance of the current changing. He had stayed out too long. The tide was coming in. It was the pressure of the tide that had pinned his shoulders so tightly to the roof of the cave.
>
> Stan's lungs were crying for air. Rockets were beginning to explode in his head when he felt something suddenly grasp his ankle.
>
> The first thought that flashed into Stan's mind was the shark. Maybe if it saw something struggling, it would become brave enough to attack. But then Stan realized that the grip had no teeth. He knew that it was two hands—Doug's two hands.

Stan's thoughts spun wildly. He realized that there was just time for one good effort. He braced his hands against the top of the cave. As he felt Doug's downward and outward pull, he shoved with all his waning strength.

And he came free!

Immediately he kicked upward. Numbly, he felt Doug shove him from beneath to help him surface faster. Up, up he went. Moments later, Stan was clinging weakly to his inner tube, and Doug's head broke the surface at his side. . . .

[The boys swim to shore, gather their catches, and go home together, friends.]

Extending Response

When students have finished a story, response can be extended in many ways with follow-up activities. The choice of activities will, of course, depend on the students' ages, needs, and interests, but whatever is done should add depth to the lesson. Students might, for example, discuss the author's use of language to describe a setting or create a mood. Students might also reflect on the characters and note changes in behavior and attitudes as the story progresses. Other activities might include reviewing interesting vocabulary, dramatizing a scene, or writing a personal opinion of the outcome of the story. Whatever is done should encourage students to refine their appreciation of the story.

Some activities may require rereading the story, but this should be done only when the rereading will provide enrichment. It is not necessary to cover points of the story that were not discussed during the reading. For instance, if a group does not mention an event or character while discussing predictions, they do not have to read the story again to prove that they noticed the information. Rereading can be of value, however, if the group is considering how an author created suspense or described a particular setting. Students might also return to the story to note how certain words are used or to review character traits or actions if they are planning to act out a scene. Any rereading should be purposeful and should allow students to achieve greater insight about some aspect of the story.

There are so many possibilities for post-story activities that all cannot be listed here. These few suggestions can be adapted to suit different groups:

1. Have students write in response to the story,
   a. composing a new ending
   b. continuing the story
   c. creating a new story in which the main character has other adventures
   d. telling about a firsthand situation similar to the one in the story
   e. composing a letter to a character in the story.
2. Have students enact a scene from the story, rereading the chosen part first to get information that can be used in the drama.
3. Discuss interesting vocabulary found in the story. Have the group think of synonyms or antonyms for key words, or have them create analogies to illustrate word meanings.

4. Use key story words to illustrate how to use various word-recognition skills that students are learning.

5. Use the story as a script for a read-aloud play. One student is the narrator, reading aloud the connecting lines between dialogue. Others are assigned character parts; these children read the dialogue, omitting words that indicate speakers (e.g., "Joe said"). Students may read the story aloud several times in this way, with different youngsters taking different parts. The activity helps to build oral-reading fluency and oral expression. It is particularly effective with short stories that contain a good deal of dialogue, the kind of story often found in the primary levels of basal readers.

Reading a Folktale: "The Giant Beet"

Here is another example of a DR-TA, this time involving a group of second-grade students. This illustration is included to provide another close look at the process and to show how students at the beginning levels of reading can participate actively in the reading-thinking process. Only parts of the group's discussion are quoted to show some of the children's responses. Some of the teacher's thoughts are reproduced in brackets to illustrate what the teacher was observing as the group read.

TEACHER: [I introduced the lesson by writing *Once upon a time* . . . on the board and asking, "What kind of story do you think we're going to read?" This group had had a good bit of experience with fairy tales, and I wanted to see if this typical story beginning was meaningful to them.]

TRACEY: It's a fairy story.

JASON: It happened long ago.

OTHERS: It's make-believe. It's not true.

TEACHER: Open your books to page 195, read the title, and look at the picture. Now, this is a fairy tale about a . . .

CHILDREN: Giant beet!

TEACHER: Read to the bottom of page 197 and see if you can guess what will happen next. [I want them to read the first three pages so they will have a good bit of information on which to base their predictions.]

THE GIANT BEET

Once upon a time, a poor woman planted some beet seeds. Only one of the seeds grew. But that beet grew so fast that the woman could see it get bigger. Soon it was as tall as a tree.

As the days went by, she watched the beet grow bigger and bigger. It got redder and redder. The beet was so big that the woman could not believe her eyes. It was indeed the biggest, finest beet the woman had ever seen.

"What can I do with a giant beet?" thought the woman. "I could never bring myself to sell a beet as grand as this. It's much too grand to be used as food. What terrible luck for a poor woman like me!"

Day and night the woman thought about her giant beet. At last, she had an idea.

"Why, I'll give it to the queen!" she said. "She should be pleased to have it. I'll put it in my wagon and take it to her castle."

The woman put the beet into her two-wheeled wagon. She climbed on top of her giant beet. Then the old wagon, pulled by her two old horses, went slowly up the path.

When the queen saw the beet, she stared at it, open-mouthed. Could it be real?

"This beet is much too grand for me," the woman said to the queen. "I will give it to you, for it is the finest beet in the world."

"Indeed it is," said the queen. "I am proud and happy to have it."

Then the queen stared at the good woman. How poor she looked! But here she was, giving away the finest thing she had.

TEACHER: What do you think will happen now?

TRACEY: The queen's going to give the old lady something.

MELISSA: She might give her food.

SEAN: Or the old woman might get money from the queen.

TEACHER: [With three pages of information, logical predictions came quickly and easily.] Good thoughts. But why do you think the queen will give her something?

TRACEY: She's poor. She needs something.

TOMMY: Maybe the queen will let her stay overnight.

TEACHER: Why do you think so?

TOMMY: To show her appreciation. So the poor old woman won't have to drive home in the dark.

TEACHER: [I didn't realize Tommy knew the word "appreciation"! He also made an interesting inference about how long it might take the woman to get home.] Good thinking, Tommy. What do you think, Jason?

JASON: I think the woman and the queen sit down to eat the beet.

TRACEY: It's too big to eat! The woman said so. Anyway, that wouldn't be a reward for the woman. [Tracey has already inferred that the queen wants to reward the old woman.]

JASON: But the old woman might think the queen was kind if she asked her to eat with her.

MELISSA: I have another idea. The queen will give the woman food and then she'll put the beet on exhibit for people to see.

TOMMY: I agree with Melissa. It's really a big beet.

TEACHER: You all seem to agree that the queen will do something for the old woman. Read to the bottom of page 199 and see if you're right.

The queen wished to thank the woman for being so kind and good. She wanted to be fair to her. So she gave the woman a new house and some rich land. She also gave her two strong horses to help with the farming.

Now it happened that the poor woman had a rich brother. He was not only rich but also very greedy. When he heard about his sister's good luck, he grew very angry.

"It isn't fair! Why should my sister have all the luck?" he said. "Just because she gave the queen a big old beet? I can think of better things than beets to give the queen. I'll give her my finest horse."

Tickled by this idea, he lost no time. He got into a fine wagon. It was pulled by two old horses. Then, with the best horse following, he hurried along the path to the queen's castle.

The queen took the horse, for it was indeed as fine a one as she had ever seen. She looked at the brother. "I can see you do not need money or land," said the queen. "But I do want to give you something. I have it! I'll give you something very fine."

TEACHER: How did your predictions work out?

TOMMY: I was partly right. The queen wanted to show her appreciation. Here it says, "The queen wished to thank the woman for being so kind and good."

TEACHER: What do the rest of you think? Is Tommy right?

SEAN: Tommy's right, but the queen didn't give her any of the things we said. She gave her land and horses. [I see the other children nodding in agreement with this; they understand this point.]

JASON: What happened to the beet? [Jason is well aware that all the elements of the story have not yet been brought together.]

MELISSA: I think the queen put it on exhibit. [Melissa is staying with her earlier idea.]

TEACHER: Perhaps you'll read more about the beet as you finish the story. What do you think? [I see some head shaking and some frowns; they are not sure.] How do you think the story will end?

TRACEY: Maybe the queen will give the brother the beet.

TEACHER: Why do you think so, Tracey?

TRACEY: The queen thought it was a fine beet, and it said she's going to give him something fine. [It's evident that Tracey has this story figured out; she's made the connection.]

TEACHER: That's an idea. What do the rest of you think?

MELISSA: The queen might give the brother land.

TEACHER: Why do you think so?

MELISSA: He needs land.

TEACHER: [Melissa has misread "need" for "not need."] Let's stop a minute. Everyone go back to page 199. Everyone read. See if you can find the lines that say the brother needed land.

TRACEY: I have it.

TEACHER: Lift your eyes and listen, everyone, while Tracey reads.

TRACEY: " 'I can see you do not need money or land,' said the queen."

TEACHER: Now what do you think?

CHILDREN: He doesn't need land.

MELISSA: I agree with Tracey. I think the queen will give him the beet.

TEACHER: [Melissa has understood and changed her prediction without my having to tell her she made a mistake.] OK, why?

MELISSA: Well, she liked the beet and thought it was a good present.

TEACHER: Tommy, how do you think the story will end?

TOMMY: I think he'll be glad to get the beet. He'll put it on exhibit and make a lot of money. [What an interesting combination of Melissa's earlier prediction and Tommy's grasp of the man's character!]

JASON: The man's greedy. I don't think he'll want the beet. He'll want money.

SEAN: I agree with Tommy. I think he'll get the beet and make a lot of money.

TEACHER: Anyone else? OK. Finish the story and see if you're right.

> The greedy brother was so happy he could not say a thing. He waited with his mouth open to see what she would give him.
>
> The queen went on, "Yes, I will give you a giant beet! There it is! You must see that no other beet is so fine. And thank you for the horse."
>
> The queen walked away with her new horse. And now the rich, greedy brother was very angry indeed. But there was only one thing to do. He put the big beet into the wagon and headed for home.
>
> "Alas," he thought. "It's so unfair! My sister has all the luck. This giant beet that made her rich has made me poor. Because of it, I have lost my very best horse."

TEACHER: [I see they are reading quickly, and their comments show their understanding: "Gee whiz!" "Now I know!" and "We were right!"] Were any of your predictions right?

JASON: I was right and so was Tracey.

TEACHER: How were you both right?

JASON: He was greedy and wanted land. That's what I said. And Tracey said the queen would give him the beet, and she did.

TOMMY: I was partly right, too. The stuff about getting the beet.

SEAN: I was right, too. But, you know, he really was mad about not getting any money.

MELISSA: Tommy said the man would put the beet on exhibit. It didn't say that, but he still could. Then he could still get money like he wants.

TEACHER: [I see they have tied up loose ends pretty well.] I'm wondering about one statement in the story. Read the last paragraph again. Do you agree with the brother when he says, "My sister has all the luck"? [This is a concept I want to develop with the children; I need to see what they know about "luck."]

TOMMY: Sure. Good luck. The lady had good luck.

TEACHER: What do you mean? Let's talk about luck.

TOMMY: The woman was lucky.

JASON: Some people have bad luck, and some people have good luck.

TRACEY: He was greedy, so he had bad luck.

TEACHER: Was it luck?

JASON: Well, you could say he had it coming to him.

TEACHER: What about the old woman? Did she have good luck coming to her?

SEAN: She was good and she got a reward. The brother was greedy and he got what was coming to him.

TEACHER: Was that luck?

SEAN: It's a kind of luck.

TEACHER: OK. That's enough for now. We'll talk about luck later. [I stopped here, recognizing the children's limited concept of luck. I decided to work on "luck" versus "effort" the next day.]

The Elements of Active Reading

The examples illustrate the key features of the DR-TA. It is an approach that can make response to narratives especially purposeful and interesting. Despite its effectiveness, however, the DR-TA is not a commonly used method. For many years, the Directed Reading Activity (DRA) has dominated classroom practice, an approach that has been used with selections from basal readers, literature texts, and other materials. But the DR-TA provides more opportunities for active reading, as a contrast between the two methods shows.

When the DRA was first advocated as an instructional method, it proved to be a significant improvement over existing practices. In the early years of the century, students had been expected to memorize and recite passages from literary works and classroom textbooks. Teachers gave meager attention to the extent to which students comprehended and appreciated the material. Then educators began to take a closer look at reading, and they recognized the complexity of the process. They saw the need for instruction that went beyond memorization and recitation. Basal readers grew in prominence and were accepted because they offered systematic plans for developing comprehension and appreciation. The DRA became the foundation of the lessons in these programs (Smith, 1967). This approach has since been used for years for lessons in basal readers and has also influenced the way teachers guide the reading of literature and content-area textbooks. Thus, the DRA has endured despite considerable advances in our understanding of the reading process.

The basic DRA procedure includes these steps:

1. Motivate students to read the story.
2. Give students specific purposes for reading.
3. After each story segment, or at the end of the story, ask students questions about their reading, to check their comprehension.
4. Provide follow-up skill instruction and enrichment activities.

At first glance, it would seem that there are no differences between the DRA and the DR-TA; indeed some educators claim that the two methods are essentially the same. In both types of lessons there is attention to motivation, to purposes, to comprehension, to skill development, and to enrichment. But the specific ways of attending to these important elements can make a critical difference in the kinds of readers they produce. Let us look at two major differences between the approaches—the way purposes are set for reading and the way comprehension is developed.

Setting Purposes

Purpose setting in a traditional DRA is largely the teacher's responsibility. For example, here are the guidelines for beginning a DRA with a story called "Robin and the Dog Sled Race." These suggested procedures come from the teacher's edition of a basal reader and are typical of what many such programs offer:

> Explain that the story pupils are going to read is about a sled dog race in Alaska. Ask pupils to share any information they may know about Alaska and sled dogs. You may wish to give pupils some of the information from the Background for this story. [The "Background" is provided in the manual for the teacher.] Tell pupils that as they read they will find out more about sled dogs and their training. Tell pupils that in this story Robin has entered her dog team in a race. Have them keep in mind the following question as they read: How important is winning the race to Robin?

It is the teacher who will do the purposeful thinking before reading. It is the teacher who will answer the key questions: What is this story about? What are we looking for? What must we pay attention to? Students are not given the chance to think on their own before they read the story. They will not anticipate what they might encounter; nor will they be prepared to understand what is before them.

In a DR-TA, the practice of asking students what might happen (instead of telling them what will happen) stimulates important prereading thinking that students need to do on their own. Through predicting, students are not only thinking (hypothesizing, anticipating); they are also making a commitment to comprehend. They will be able to say, "I think this will happen; I will read to find out if it does." Because the student does the thinking, the prediction is an especially effective purpose for reading.

In a traditional DRA, the teacher also helps students recall experiences that may help them understand some part of the story. In the example, the statement "Ask pupils to share any information they may know about Alaska and sled dogs" serves this purpose. Recalling related information is valuable preparation for reading, but asking for it in this way can produce negative results. When students start to tell about their experiences, they can easily be distracted from the task at hand. Students may enjoy such talk, but they do not necessarily make useful connections between what they know and what they are about to read. In fact, reminiscence at this time takes attention away from the story as students vie with each other to tell all sorts of amusing anecdotes. This sort of discussion introduces irrelevant material and moves the discussion in a different direction (Hammond, 1983, 1986; Nessel 1987). Though it can be great fun, such sharing should be reserved for another time in the school day, perhaps for a prewriting discussion.

In contrast, the DR-TA requires students to supply reasons for their predictions. Doing so, they will naturally recall what they know and what they have experienced. They will connect their prior knowledge about the world and stories directly to the text at hand. Instead of simply telling what they know, students will use what they know to help them make sense of what they read. There is a distinct difference between saying "I know about the beach. I went there last summer with my family . . ." and saying "I think in this story the boy will find a starfish on the beach. I think so because I went to the beach last summer and I found a starfish." The first remark is unfocused, idle reminiscence; the second is a purposeful, text-related use of experience.

Comprehension

In a traditional DRA, comprehension is assessed when the teacher asks specific questions to draw out main points, details, and implications that the students are expected to have grasped. This direct approach seems logical enough (if you want to know what students have comprehended, ask them). But the question-answer tactic subtly affects students' thinking and, over time, students' expectations of what it means to read. When the teacher asks direct questions (usually those suggested in the teacher's edition of the book), students are, in a sense, taking a comprehension test; they are not being helped to comprehend (Durkin, 1978–79, 1981). They either answer correctly and pass, or they give wrong answers and fail.

Some students become very uncomfortable in these circumstances, especially if they habitually fail. They learn to avoid eye contact with the teacher, making themselves inconspicuous as they pretend to think deeply; in reality they are hoping that someone else will answer and get them off the hook. They seldom learn how to read more effectively, though they may learn sophisticated strategies for avoiding participation. Knowing that postreading questions are inevitable can also affect students as they read. Some children may be so preoccupied with the thought of being put on the spot that they will be unable to give reasonable attention to the material.

In this same situation, of course, some students will shine. They always manage to remember the right things, so they can answer the teacher's questions easily. These children are the first to raise their hands. They enjoy reputations as good students and get lots of positive attention. But they may not be learning to refine their reading-thinking abilities. By simply doing what comes easily, they achieve better than their classmates, but there is no opportunity or reason for them to accept greater challenges.

A predetermined set of "comprehension" questions will not usually bring out evidence that students actually comprehend the story. Almost all students will have missed some points that the teacher (or the program) judges to be important. Some questions may have very little to do with the main story line, focusing as they do instead on extraneous details that may be neither interesting nor important to the readers. (Questions about the physical features of lobsters, eels, or sharks following the reading of "Danger in the Deep" would fall in this category, for example. Details about sea creatures are not as important as what is happening to the divers.) Students may be judged to be poor comprehenders if they miss such details, when, indeed, it could be considered good reading strategy to overlook them. Students may also have picked up information or made interpretations they are not asked about. An interesting word, a seemingly minor event, or a detail of characterization may turn out to be especially significant to certain individuals, affecting their interpretations of the story. Such unique reactions can be missed if the questions are set beforehand and if certain answers are expected.

This is not to say that asking students specific questions about their reading is a misguided activity. Pointed questions are sometimes useful and necessary. But when the predominant pattern is to read and then to answer questions, the lessons can become artificial reading situations—more like tests—and students can acquire odd and erroneous notions about what reading is. Consider that in nonschool life, people are seldom asked questions about what they read. (One adult does not say to another: Read this story carefully. I am going to ask you several questions when you finish.) The reading process for nonstudents is private and unsupervised. They may miss some details, pay special attention to a peripheral piece of information, or get the gist while overlooking some facts. People read with their own needs, their own backgrounds of experience, and their own attitudes toward the significance of the material. If lessons were more like this real-life reading, teachers could help students use the process to better advantage. Teachers' questioning should help students refine a natural process in which the reader interacts with the material by reading for self-generated purposes.

In a DR-TA, the guided discussion develops students' skill with the process of comprehension. As they evaluate and modify their predictions, they must use information from the story, even though each may use different details and make slightly different interpretations. It is the continual testing of hypotheses that leads to comprehension in a DR-TA. Making a prediction is only the first step. The reader must also examine his or her reasons for making that particular prediction, must keep the prediction in mind while reading, and must eventually decide whether or not the prediction was confirmed. This is the essence of comprehension—knowing what one is looking for and recognizing whether one has found it. It is not speculation alone that makes for good reading and thinking; everyone can make a guess. It is predicting and then *acting on the basis of that prediction* that is the key to effective reading and that is the critical feature of the DR-TA (Stauffer, 1975).

Story information becomes significant because it confirms the prediction or leads to a different idea, not because it is significant in some absolute sense or because the teacher says it is important and that the group had better pay attention to it. But during discussion, it will sometimes be obvious that students have missed key facts or misread some words. Usually, this results in disagreement among students about what might happen next or about which evidence supports an argument. At these times, the teacher will ask students to go back to the material to clear up disagreement. These directives come from the obvious need to reconsider the text. The purpose is not simply to test students.

In a DR-TA, students learn that they can make sense of what they are reading. They are not put in the embarrassing position of being unable to answer questions based on details they may have overlooked. Instead, each in his or her own way is able to offer ideas obtained from reading that are as good as his or her classmates'; each has a unique reader's perspective concerning the direction of the story. The collaborative efforts of the group will help each individual to understand; each student will have a part to play in the process. This collaboration is more useful for building comprehension and makes for more realistic reading than does the traditional question-answer session following reading. Students learn that comprehension is not usually an all-or-nothing circumstance (right or wrong answer) but rather a gradual process of gathering information, thinking about it, hearing what others have to say, putting the pieces together, and finally achieving understanding.

DR-TA participants also learn that information and answers are found in the text, not with the teacher. The teacher purposely maintains a neutral role in the process, asking questions, calling for evidence, seeking consensus, but rarely passing judgment. Rather than telling students that they are right or wrong, the teacher asks the following questions: Can you find proof in the story? What did you read that gave you that idea? Do you all agree? Why? Why not? The teacher is a guide, not a judge, and students soon learn to think for themselves instead of giving an answer and waiting for the teacher's praise or disapproval.

Besides building a sense of individual responsibility for learning, this role of the teacher also significantly improves group interaction as students become experienced with the process. Students begin to talk directly to each other instead of only to the teacher; this occurs because they are *listening* to each other. By staying neutral, the teacher encourages true discussion—an exchange among equals. Some experienced groups of students become so involved in discussion that the teacher has only to sit back and observe the active thinking. It is worthwhile for students to achieve this independence instead of learning by experience that *discussion* means addressing and getting response only from the teacher.

The critical differences between the DR-TA and the DRA have been described to emphasize the value of guiding reading as a thinking process. To summarize, here are the key features of the DR-TA that make the approach advantageous for developing skillful use of the reading-thinking process:

1. Students think before they read, actively using prior knowledge and experience to make predictions that become their purposes for reading.
2. Students think while they read, gathering evidence from the material to confirm or reject their predictions. Revising predictions results directly from their comprehension of the story.
3. Students learn to listen to each other during discussion. Anyone's perspective can help the group see the story in a new light. Peers' reasons are respected and considered.
4. Students learn that the answers are found in the text. The teacher plays a neutral role, insisting that students return to the story to clear up confusions or achieve greater insight.

Responding to Literature

Guiding reading as a thinking process is particularly important when students are responding to material of high literary quality. Such works, more than any other texts in the classroom, are used to stretch imaginations, to help children achieve greater insight about themselves and others, and to develop the beginnings of a lifelong appreciation for literature. The reading of these works needs to proceed not as a series of academic exercises in which there are certain right answers to be found, but as thoughtful, enjoyable excursions into the world of story.

Through the years, there has been a growing commitment to developing and refining students' first responses to a work of literature. The stress is no longer on "reading the text and answering the ten comprehension questions that follow it in the anthology" (Probst, 1981, p. 44). Response-based teaching encourages both emotional and intellectual reactions to the literature, allowing students to express their thoughts without fear of being judged wrong. At the start, all responses are considered equally acceptable, even if they would be thought naive by more sophisticated readers, and even if they would, on careful rereading, be found to be quite different from what the author almost certainly intended. Through discussion and rereading, students extend and refine their initial responses, gradually constructing meanings with the tolerant guidance of the teacher (Squire, 1968; Rosenblatt, 1978; Berthoff, 1981). This response-based approach is an application to literary works of the kind of reading-thinking that has just been described.

In the early grades, students can readily respond to a variety of enjoyable stories that the teacher reads aloud. Predictable books (those that have repetitive language or an easily perceived pattern of episodes) are especially valuable not only for building children's sense of story but also for encouraging participation in the oral reading. Kimmelman (1981) describes her work with such selections:

> when I would read books that had simple plots supported by rhythmic sentences and cumulative illustrations, even poor readers quickly grasped the flow of language and events. They would become so interested in the story's unfolding that they would insist on chiming in with the reading. Often the children could predict not only what would happen next, but also what the next word or phrase would be. Thus, children's books were able to do what worksheets alone could not do: launch children into an intimacy with good stories as well as an eager involvement in thinking. (pp. 441–42)

Such lively experiences with good children's books get young students in the habit of anticipating as they respond to the language and events of a story. This habit of thought can have a positive influence on their later reading of more sophisticated literary works that contain more complex characters and plots.

As students mature, they can apply the reading-thinking process to a variety of literary works. For instance, a novel such as *Charlotte's Web* by E. B. White (Harper & Row, 1952) can be read over a period of days or weeks, with pauses to speculate about coming events in light of how the story is developing. Such alternation of reading and discussing stimulates thinking and encourages close reading. Children obtain different perspectives on the characters and events as they anticipate outcomes together. The experience can heighten enjoyment and appreciation as well as deepen understanding. Follow-up activities to extend appreciation and enjoyment, such as creative drama or writing, will be highly meaningful if students have been given the chance to respond fully to the work as they read.

Older children can also be led to construct the meanings of a poem by using a response-based approach. Here, for example, is a brief summary of some of the responses of one group of middle-school readers to a poem that was revealed line by line (the poem was printed on a transparency and shown on an overhead projector). The title was not announced. As each line was revealed, the teacher asked the students what the words made them think of and what they thought the poet was describing:

He clasps the crag with crooked hands;

- It's a man on a mountain, like a mountain climber.
- If it's a man, it's an old man. His hands are crooked. Maybe they're all bent and twisted.
- Maybe it's a tree. The crooked hands could be roots.

Close to the sun in lonely lands,

- I can picture him way up high—close to the sun.
- No one else is around. It's in the wilderness. I think it's a tree.
- Now I picture a desert—close to the sun—with sand all around.
- The mountain climber is all the way to the top.

Ringed with the azure world he stands.

- Now I can see an island in the middle of the ocean. Blue water and blue sky all around.
- I still see the mountain climber all the way at the top.
- It could still be the desert—sand everywhere and a big blue sky up above.

The wrinkled sea beneath him crawls;

- Why does it say wrinkled sea?
- I think because he's so high up on the mountain that when he looks down at the sea it's all wrinkly.
- Now I don't think it's the desert. I think it's a diver now, one of those divers that dive from the cliffs. He's looking down at the water getting ready to dive.

He watches from his mountain walls,

- Why does it say *his* mountain walls? Does the mountain belong to him?
- He's watching, looking all around, at the sea and everything else.

And like a thunderbolt he falls.

- Oh! How could it be a mountain climber? They're careful. They don't fall.
- If it's a diver, why does it say falls? Just because that rhymes? But divers dive, they don't fall.

After some additional speculation, the teacher revealed the title: "The Eagle" (by Alfred, Lord Tennyson). Students were amazed since none had thought of this possibility. They reread the poem, now seeing different meanings in many of the words. The group discussed their previous ideas and compared them with the idea of an eagle perched on a cliff. These comparisons enriched their understanding of the poem; for instance, the fleeting images of an old man, a mountain climber, a tree, and a diver were all like the image of an eagle in certain respects. Students considered more carefully the poet's choice of words and the layers of meaning that those words suggested.

This kind of response-based reading and thinking is especially important to use with stories, novels, and poems because it is based on the notion that meanings are not necessarily obvious at first glance but can become clearer in the process of responding. Comprehension and appreciation of a work of literature do not emerge all at once but rather accumulate when readers share responses freely. As Britton (1982) points out:

> We do not, as we read, add word meaning to word meaning—like watching coaches come out of a tunnel; rather, it is like watching a photographic negative in a developing-dish, a shadowy outline that becomes etched in with more of the detail as we proceed. The finished picture represents a transformation, brought about by the text-as-we-have-interpreted-it—a transformation of our initial expectations. (p. 134)

Getting Started

As teachers use response-based DR-TAs in their own classes and discuss the procedures with colleagues, they realize the value of the approach. But, as they gain an understanding of the methods, they learn that not all students respond with alacrity when they are expected to think. Simply conducting a DR-TA will

Comprehension and appreciation of a work of literature do not come all at once but rather accumulate when students share responses freely with other readers.

not necessarily bring about noticeable results. Most students need experience with the method to reap the benefits. The first few times may be rough because all members of the group will be adjusting to new expectations. Here are a few suggestions for getting started.

1. DR-TAs may be conducted with very small groups or with whole classes, but medium-sized groups of five to ten students are often best. These numbers allow everyone a chance to participate but also ensure a variety of points of view. Ideal group size will depend to some extent on the material and the instructional purpose. Teachers might find it valuable to try DR-TAs with different kinds of materials in different situations to see how variations affect students' responses. For instance, stories in children's magazines, selections from literature texts, or novels for young readers may all be used with small groups or with the whole class to develop thoughtful responses to narratives.

2. All group members should be able to read the material comfortably. Ideally, students should be at about the same reading level, and the material should be geared to that level. However, a group ranging in reading abilities from second-grade through sixth-grade levels might all participate successfully in a DR-TA with material written at second-grade level; this is because all members should be able to read it. Sometimes such heterogeneous mixes have distinct advantages. The diversity of reading experience in the group will prob-

ably result in rather different perspectives on the story; these can add interest to the discussion.

Participants should also be able to read at approximately the same speed so that everyone finishes reading and is ready to continue the discussion at about the same time. Minor differences in pace can be accommodated if the teacher holds brief individual conferences with students who finish first. These whispered exchanges can focus on the ideas that the student will be presenting to the group in the next discussion.

Teachers may also choose to read aloud the first part of a story, elicit predictions, and then have students finish the story at their own pace. Such a combination of teacher-reading and student-reading can be especially helpful for those children who are easily discouraged at the thought of completing a long story or for those students of English as a second language who may read well but who are still reading very slowly.

3. Stopping points should be chosen thoughtfully. A group might be given a title, a paragraph, or several pages to read before making initial predictions. DR-TAs may include as many as six or seven stopping points or as few as one or two. The pattern of reading-discussing may be varied to suit the material or the need of the group. Time may also affect the choice of stopping points—the more stops for discussion, the longer the lesson. No matter how many stops are planned, however, the important principle is to stimulate thinking purposefully each time.

Some stories have titles that generate a variety of initial predictions. For instance, one entitled "Call the Police!"[1] stimulates a wide range of predictions because its name suggests several ideas. Students are almost always surprised and amused to find out that the story is actually about a raccoon who wanders into a house at night. If this same story were called "The Invading Raccoon," the title would not generate the same diversity of initial predictions and would not offer readers the same experience of a complete shift of expectations as they begin to read. Many stories offer similar possibilities for moving thinking in one direction and then requiring readers to revise their predictions substantially as they obtain new information.

The same story may be segmented in different ways to bring about different results. For instance, "The Beggar and the Gazelle" (Chapter 1) yields different initial predictions depending on whether readers are stopped when the peddler first comes on the scene or are stopped a bit later, after the gazelle speaks. When the peddler and the beggar first begin their conversation, the story seems to be a conventional one, and readers might think that the beggar will ask the peddler to help him find work or perhaps will beg the peddler for a few coins. But when the talking gazelle appears, the story takes on a decidedly fanciful, fairy-tale quality, and predictions are altered accordingly. There is no "right"

[1] From *People on Parade* (New York: Holt, Rinehart and Winston, 1960).

way to segment a story; there are only different ways that will generate different responses.

Selecting stopping points, the teacher should keep in mind what an experienced teacher once said: "You want to leave readers where the TV director leaves *you* just before a commercial, with several likely alternatives and a real desire to see that next scene." As the story progresses, students narrow the range of possible outcomes; fewer outcomes seem likely as the story draws to a conclusion. Thinking goes from the divergent to the convergent as story information is revealed (Stauffer, 1975).

Of course, even if there are eight or nine likely places to stop, only a few might be chosen. The story should not be overly fragmented to take advantage of every possible stopping point. Generally, three or four discussions to revise predictions are enough to generate effective thinking and reading. For a change of pace, students should be stopped more or less often than is the usual practice. The amount of text may easily vary between stopping points. For instance, in the example from "Danger in the Deep," students at times read several pages and once read less than a full page.

4. Students may at first be reluctant to make predictions. They may be confused or indifferent when asked, "What do you think will happen next?" and may well answer, "I don't know. I haven't read it yet." Hesitation to predict may stem from a fear of being wrong or from uneasiness about bringing up a potentially foolish point. Confidence can be strengthened through the teacher's encouragment and assurance; readers need to trust the teacher who says, "I know you don't know, but what do you think?" Some students may just be unfamiliar with this kind of thinking and may need more experience to gain skill. The more DR-TAs students participate in, the more able they will be to hypothesize confidently and easily.

If predictions are sparse or nonexistent, these strategies can help:

a. Suggest a few ideas to the group, making sure to mention outcomes that are logical but that are not necessarily what actually happens. Have students decide which of the ideas is most likely, given what they know so far. For instance, assume that a group has read the first part of "The Giant Beet"—the story used in a previous example—finishing with the following sentences:

> Then the queen stared at the good woman. How poor she looked! But here she was, giving away the finest thing she had.

If students have no predictions to make about the plot, the teacher might get them thinking by posing questions like these:

- Do you think the queen will throw the beet away?
- Do you think the queen will give the woman some food in return? Some money? A new wagon?

b. Have students put themselves in the place of the characters. Encourage them to decide how they would act if they shared the characters' circumstances. For instance, given the same stopping point for "The Giant Beet" as in the example just given, ask these questions:

- What would you do if you were the queen? Would you want to give the old woman something? What?
- What would you do with the beet if you were the queen? Why?

c. Provide more information. For instance, if students have not been able to predict the plot from the title alone, have them read further (a page or two more) to look for clues. As an alternative, have them examine all the illustrations and then make predictions.

Some groups catch on rather quickly when these strategies are used. Others may require more practice, more encouragement, and more help to think about a story. It is important not to get discouraged. Keep trying. The ultimate goal—developing thinking abilities—is worth the effort it may take to get there.

W. Dorsey Hammond relates an interesting story that confirms the success of this process. He was demonstrating these teaching methods to a group of educators. The students were disadvantaged, inner-city youngsters who had a history of poor achievement, negative attitudes toward school, and problems with reading. The students also were suspicious of being in the spotlight. After an initial struggle to overcome their reticence (he met with many "I don't know" responses) and lack of motivation (students slumped in their chairs), Hammond finally persuaded several students to make a few simple predictions. One idea stimulated another. Before long, the discussion became lively, and students were producing astute predictions and thoughtful supporting arguments. After the lesson, one of the observing teachers commented, "Wasn't that a group of kids from the gifted program?"

It must be realized that *all* students are capable of reasoning effectively and creatively. It is the teacher's responsibility to bring out these abilities; he or she can get results from an effective approach to guided reading.

5. Students may have difficulty using evidence from the story to revise predictions. They may overlook perfectly obvious information or be unable to decide if their initial predictions were confirmed or need to be rejected. It will sometimes seem as if students' predictions do not relate to their reading at all; some pupils will stick with a first idea no matter how clearly the story is taking a different direction. If students have this kind of trouble, the following strategies can help:

a. After the story is completed, have students reread it to look for clues to the final outcome. Such clues are often unmistakable once the ending is known. The group can work together to compile a list of clues; students should not be expected to do this individually. The next time they begin a story, remind them to read carefully for clues.

b. During discussion, raise issues that students have not considered. Be sure to mention some ideas that are not relevant to the final outcome, in addition to some that are. Students should not get the idea that only teacher-suggested information is relevant. They should simply be asked to think about points that have not been addressed.

6. To come up with the correct prediction, some students may at first try reading ahead during discussions. While others are thinking and discussing, these students will peek at the next page or begin reading the next segment. Of course, a group's effort will be diffused considerably if a student says, "I know what happens. I just read it!" The following techniques will help to discourage students from reading ahead:

a. Establish the rules before beginning: Reading ahead is not allowed.

b. Insist that students close their books during discussion. Peeking ahead will be easier to spot and control if students are not allowed to be reading.

c. Put the story on transparencies (for use on an overhead projector) to maintain complete control over when students read the material.

Occasionally at the start of a lesson, a student will announce, "I've read this before!" This declaration may at first seem to ruin the chances of conducting a good DR-TA. When this situation occurs, it is usually best simply to ask the student to follow the discussion carefully and to help the group keep track of their predictions. The student can thus participate meaningfully without giving away the outcome. Sometimes it will be discovered that a student has only mistaken a story for a similar one.

7. Most published stories are not specifically designed and printed for use in DR-TAs. Good stopping points will often occur in the middle of a page; this makes it difficult for students to stop reading at the right place. Sometimes a page will end in the middle of a sentence, making the direction "Read to the bottom of the page" awkward. These techniques can help to remedy this situation:

a. Clip a piece of construction paper to cover the portion of a page that follows a stopping point. Place the construction paper in each student's book. Tell students to read to the paper and stop.

b. Scribble a light pencil mark at the end of a segment to be read. Tell students to read to the mark and stop.

c. Type the story, divided into chosen segments, on a master copy. Make transparencies or other copies for each student. Have them refer to the illustrations in the book while reading, but use the newly reproduced story as the text material. Keep the masters on file for future use.

When students are first learning DR-TA procedures, they do not always respond well. Besides having problems such as those just described, they may also misread words, get confused about what is happening, or mix up characters. Sometimes it will be necessary to have students reread carefully to note the evidence that *is* there, not what they mistakenly *think* is there. Sometimes the teacher must challenge the group directly if they are overlooking important evidence or getting off the track. The teacher need not expect complete success with each lesson but rather should help students improve a bit more each time they meet to discuss a story. Their ability to think well about what they are reading will develop over time.

Reading and Thinking: Some Conclusions

In some schools, reading is taught as if it were simply a set of specific skills to be mastered. Skills are grouped into major categories, such as "comprehension" and "appreciation of literature." Constituent skills might include getting the main idea, making inferences, interpreting figurative language, or recalling a sequence of events. Systematic instruction is given; the goal is skill mastery, which is equated with reading maturity.

A different point of view has been presented here. We have stressed that thinking is the foundation of reading and that effective use of the reading-thinking process is the mark of a mature reader. A teacher who holds this point of view does not forgo skill instruction but places it in proper perspective as a supplement, not a prerequisite, to reasoning about a text. The teacher also realizes that just because students have learned many skills does not necessarily mean they will be able to comprehend virtually any text.

As we have seen, there is good evidence that the use of prior knowledge and expectations strongly influences how well a reader will make sense of a text (Mandler and Johnson, 1977; Stein and Glenn, 1979; Rumelhart and Ortony, 1977; Rumelhart, 1980). What students know affects what they learn; what they expect influences what they see. Prior knowledge is as important as skills when it comes to competent reading.

The current emphasis on readers' prior knowledge is not a new perspective. Bartlett (1932) observed that the process of remembering involves construction rather than reproduction. He wrote of the "schemas" that individuals use during learning that influence later recall of the material. Britton (1982) reminds us that, in 1936, I. A. Richards wrote of the "literary context" (the text) and the "determinative context" (the reader's experience), the interaction of which leads to interpretation of meaning. And Kelley (1947) stated that

> we can never really make a fact ours completely because [someone] says it is so. When we take it and fit it into our background, we take only the parts which we can make fit. It is then ours uniquely, and no longer his. We can of course learn from others, but we can only learn those parts of what others can offer which we can fit into *our* experience and purpose. (p. 62)

These views—of the past and of the present—guide the teacher in selecting teaching strategies. Students can sometimes be helped by specific skill lessons, but not all readers will derive the same meanings from a text simply through applying those skills. Instead, students must have many opportunities to use the reading-thinking process with a variety of narratives. In this way, they will learn to use their prior knowledge and expectations consciously and effectively to construct meanings while they read.

Hunt (1982), concerned with the teaching of literature, stresses the importance of making students aware of the process they use to make sense of text and advocates use of the DR-TA to foster this awareness. Granowsky and Botel (1974) point out that students need to realize that although each story has just one existing ending, there may be other possible endings. They favor discussing alternatives because this forces readers to think actively. Tierney and Pearson (1981) call for the use of teaching methods that directly follow from what is known about the process of reader-text interaction. These viewpoints, as well as those of other researchers cited earlier, suggest that using reading as a thinking process must be a priority and that specific skill instruction is important only to the extent that it enhances students' abilities to use that process.

Research on the use of the DR-TA suggests that this method is a preferred way to develop thinking readers. There is evidence that the DR-TA enhances the quantity, quality, and variety of student responses during a lesson (Petre, 1969; Speirs, 1984), that it leads to teachers asking more questions requiring interpretation and inference (Davidson, 1970), and that it creates an especially positive climate for learning (Grobler, 1971). Thus, besides following logically from current models of the reading process, the DR-TA has been shown to be an effective teaching strategy for several reasons.

Students in any grade can use the reasoning processes described here. Even before they can recognize words, they can discuss the sequence of action in wordless picture books, making predictions and judging whether or not their ideas are confirmed. At an early age, they can also exercise the same kind of thinking with stories they hear. Reasoning about a story is thus not something that needs to be delayed until students can read well on their own. Good language arts instruction will, from the start, encourage students to respond to stories in a way that will be refined and extended as they gain proficiency with reading.

When students are actively involved in responding to narratives, they will quite naturally need to use a variety of specific skills. Direct instruction and practice can help them to use those skills effectively so long as actual reading is the priority. The teacher who places skills in the proper perspective uses workbook exercises or skill sheets sparingly, recognizing that such paper-and-pencil practice is not as effective as the practice that naturally comes from reading and discussing. Such a teacher knows that the asking of probing and challenging questions during reading will do more to develop comprehension abilities than special follow-up exercises labeled "comprehension" or "appreciation" can do. Such a teacher will also give students many opportunities to read books of their own choosing (which the group may not always discuss), to plan plays and skits based on stories they read, to write about the characters and events they meet in stories, and in other ways to respond thoughtfully and creatively to narrative works. Such a teacher will develop effective, thinking readers.

Suggested Activities

1. Examine a teacher's manual for a basal reader. Compare the directions for guiding the reading and the suggested questions with the directions and questions that are used in a DR-TA.
2. Team with a peer. Each of you should select a story for a DR-TA that might help a child deal with a handicap. Identify the handicap and justify your story choices. Individually plan the direction of your DR-TAs. Compare your plans.
3. Select a story for a DR-TA with a group of academically talented students. List interesting vocabulary words that can be explored for multiple meanings or shades of meaning. Identify concepts you might develop in follow-up activities. Plan a follow-up activity that will provide an opportunity for purposeful oral reading.
4. Conduct the DR-TA planned in activity 3 with a small group of children. Record the lesson on tape. Review the tape to evaluate the students' performance. Analyze your own performance. How could the lesson be improved?

References

Anderson, R. C. "The Notion of Schemata and the Educational Enterprise" in R. C. Anderson; R. J. Spiro; and W. E. Montague, eds., *Schooling and the Acquisition of Knowledge.* Hillsdale, NJ: Erlbaum, 1977.

——————; Reynolds, R. E.; Schallert, D. L.; and Goetz, E. T. "Frameworks for Comprehending Discourse." *American Educational Research Journal* 14(Fall 1977):367–81.

——————; Spiro, R. J.; and Montague, W. E. (eds.) *Schooling and the Acquisition of Knowledge.* Hillsdale, NJ: Erlbaum, 1977.

Applebee, A. *The Child's Concept of Story: Ages Two to Seventeen.* Chicago: University of Chicago Press, 1978.

Bartlett, F. C. *Remembering: A Study in Experimental and Social Psychology.* London: Cambridge University Press, 1967 (First edition, 1932).

Beck, I. L.; McKeown, M. G.; McCaslin, E. S.; and Burkes, A. M. *Instructional Dimensions That May Affect Reading Comprehension.* Pittsburgh: Learning Research and Development Center/University of Pittsburgh, 1979.

Berthoff, A. E. *The Making of Meaning*. Montclair, NJ: Boynton/Cook, 1981.

Bransford, J. D. *Human Cognition: Learning, Understanding and Remembering*. Belmont, CA: Wadsworth, 1979.

Britton, J. "A Reader's Expectations" in G. Pradl, ed., *Prospect and Retrospect: Selected Essays of James Britton*. Montclair, NJ: Boynton/Cook, 1982.

Collins, A.; Brown, J. S.; and Larkin, K. M. *Inference in Text Understanding* (Technical Report No. 40). Urbana, IL: Center for the Study of Reading/University of Illinois, 1977.

Davidson, J. L. "Quantity, Quality and Variety of Teachers' Questions and Pupils' Responses during an Open Communication Structured Group Directed Reading-Thinking Activity and a Closed Communication Group Directed Reading Activity." Unpublished doctoral dissertation. University of Michigan, 1970.

Durkin, D. "What Classroom Observations Reveal About Reading Comprehension Instruction." *Reading Research Quarterly* 14(No. 4, 1978–79):481–533.

——————. "Reading Comprehension in Five Basal Series." *Reading Research Quarterly* 16(No. 4, 1981):515–44.

Goodman, K. S. "Reading: A Psycholinguistic Guessing Game." *Journal of the Reading Specialist* 6(May 1967):126–35.

Granowsky, A., and Botel, M. "Creative Thinking, Reading, and Writing in the Classroom." *Elementary English* 51(May 1974):653–54.

Grobler, C. "Methodology in Reading Instruction as a Controlled Variable in the Constructive or Destructive Channeling of Aggression." Unpublished doctoral dissertation. University of Delaware, 1971.

Hammond, W. D. "How Your Students Can Predict Their Way to Reading Comprehension." *Learning* 12(November 1983):62–64.

——————. "Common Questions on Reading Comprehension." *Learning* 14(January 1986):49–51.

Hunt, R. A. "Toward a Process-Intervention Model in Literature Teaching." *College English* 44(April 1982):345–57.

Kelley, E. *Education for What is Real*. New York: Harper & Brothers, 1947.

Kimmelman, L. "Literary Ways Toward Enjoyable Thinking." *Language Arts* 58(April 1981):441–47.

Mandler, J. M., and Johnson, N. S. "Remembrance of Things Parsed: Story Structure and Recall." *Cognitive Psychology* 9(January 1977):111–51.

Nessel, D. "The New Face of Comprehension Instruction: A Closer Look at Questions." *The Reading Teacher* 40(March 1987):604–06.

Petre, R. M. "Quantity, Quality and Variety of Pupil Responses during an Open Communication Structured Group Directed Reading-Thinking Activity and a Closed Communication Structured Group Directed Reading Activity." Unpublished doctoral dissertation. University of Delaware, 1969.

Probst, R. E. "Response-Based Teaching of Literature." *English Journal* 70(November 1981):43–47.

Rosenblatt, L. M. *The Reader, The Text, The Poem: The Transactional Theory of Literary Work*. Carbondale, IL: Southern Illinois University Press, 1978.

Rumelhart, D. E. "Schemata: The Building Blocks of Cognition" in R. J. Spiro et al., eds., *Theoretical Issues in Reading Comprehension*. Hillsdale, NJ: Erlbaum, 1980.

——————, and Ortony, A. "The Representation of Knowledge in Memory" in R. C.

Anderson et al., eds., *Schooling and the Acquisition of Knowledge.* Hillsdale, NJ: Erlbaum, 1977.

Singer, H., and Ruddell, R. *Theoretical Models and Processes of Reading.* Newark, DE: International Reading Association, 1985.

Smith, N. B. *American Reading Instruction.* Newark, DE: International Reading Association, 1967.

Speirs, H. "Directing Reading-Thinking Activities in a High School Composition Class." Unpublished master's thesis. University of California at Santa Barbara, 1984.

Spiro, R. J. "Remembering Information from Text" in R. C. Anderson et al., eds., *Schooling and the Acquisition of Knowledge.* Hillsdale, NJ: Erlbaum, 1977.

—————; Bruce, B.; and Brewer, W. (eds.) *Theoretical Issues in Reading Comprehension.* Hillsdale, NJ: Erlbaum, 1980.

Squire, J. (ed.) *Response to Literature.* Champaign, IL: National Council of Teachers of English, 1968.

Stauffer, R. G. *Teaching Reading as a Thinking Process.* New York: Harper & Row, 1969.

—————. *Directing the Reading-Thinking Process.* New York: Harper & Row, 1975.

—————; Burrows, A. T.; and Black, M. H. *Winston Basic Readers Communication Program.* New York: Holt, Rinehart and Winston, 1960.

Stein, N. L., and Glenn, C. G. "An Analysis of Story Comprehension in Elementary School Children" in R. O. Freedle, ed., *Advances in Discourse Processes, Vol. II: New Directions in Discourse Procession.* Norwood, NJ: Ablex, 1979.

Tierney, R., and Pearson, P. D. "Learning to Learn from Text: Improving Classroom Practice" in E. K. Dishner et al., eds., *Reading in the Content Areas.* Dubuque, IA: Kendall Hunt, 1981.

Whaley, J. F. "Readers' Expectations for Story Structure." *Reading Research Quarterly* 17(Fall 1981):90–114.

Suggested Readings

Anderson, R. C., and Biddle, W. B. "On Asking People Questions about What They Are Reading" in G. Bower, ed., *Psychology of Learning and Motivation* (Vol. 9). New York: Academic Press, 1975.

Anderson, R. C.; Hiebert, E. H.; Scott, J. A.; and Wilkinson, I. A. G. *Becoming a Nation of Readers: A Report of the Commission on Reading.* Washington, D. C.: National Institute of Education, 1984.

Bransford, J. D., and Nitsch, K. E. "Coming to Understand Things We Could Not Previously Understand" in J. F. Kavanagh and W. Strange, eds., *Speech and Language in the Laboratory, School, and Clinic.* Cambridge: MIT Press, 1978.

Bruner, J. S. *The Process of Education.* Cambridge: Harvard University Press, 1960.

California State Department of Education. *Handbook for Planning an Effective Literature Program.* Sacramento: California State Department of Education, 1987.

Carroll, J. B., and Freedle, R. O. (eds.) *Language Comprehension and the Acquisition of Knowledge.* Washington, D.C.: V. H. Winston, 1972.

Cook, D. *Guide to Curriculum Planning in Reading.* Madison: Wisconsin Department of Public Instruction, 1987.

Cooper, J. D. *Improving Reading Comprehension.* Boston: Houghton Mifflin, 1986.

Dewey, J. *Experience and Education.* New York: Macmillan, 1938.

Gitzlaff, L. *Teaching Reading Comprehension* (Telecourse and Book of Selected Readings). Bloomington, IN: Agency for Instructional Technology, 1987.

Goodman, Y., and Burke, C. *Reading Strategies: Focus on Comprehension.* New York: Holt, Rinehart and Winston, 1980.

Jennings, F. G. *This is Reading.* New York: Teachers College Press, 1965.

Langer, J., and Smith-Burke, M. T. (eds.) *Reader Meets Author: Bridging the Gap.* Newark, DE: International Reading Association, 1982.

Mason, J., and Au, K. *Reading Instruction for Today.* Glenview, IL: Scott, Foresman, 1986.

Nessel, D. "Reading Comprehension: Asking the Right Questions." *Phi Delta Kappan* 68(February 1987):442–45.

Norman, D. A., and Rumelhart, D. E. *Explorations in Cognition.* San Francisco: W. H. Freeman, 1975.

Osborn, J.; Wilson, P. T.; and Anderson, R. C. (eds.) *Reading Education: Foundations for a Literate America.* Lexington, MA: Lexington Books/D. C. Heath, 1985.

Pearson, P. D. "Changing the Face of Reading Comprehension Instruction." *The Reading Teacher.* 38(April 1985):724–38.

————, and Johnson, D. *Teaching Reading Comprehension.* New York: Holt, Rinehart and Winston, 1978.

Richards, I. A. *How to Read a Page.* New York: W. W. Norton, 1942.

Wolf, M.; McQuillan, M.; and Radwin, E. (eds.) *Thought and Language/Language and Reading.* (Harvard Educational Review Reprint Series No. 14). Cambridge: Harvard Educational Review, 1980.

As predictions are made, students get ideas from one another that help them refine their own thinking. As many share, they learn from each other and generate new ideas as a group.

5 Reading Expository Text

When students respond to narrative material, they are reading, interpreting, and enjoying a story while using the reading-thinking process. Factual information may be learned incidentally, but the retention of facts is usually not a major goal. However, when students read assigned expository material, they encounter concepts, facts, or other information that is important to learn, evaluate critically, and remember. For example, students are often required to study textbooks in science, social studies, or other content-area subjects. Students also encounter informational material in basal readers, in periodicals, and in nonfiction books of all sorts. Such materials may serve as well to help students learn to read expository text effectively.

This chapter explores the reading process as it is applied to informational texts. Activities based on these kinds of materials stem from specific content objectives as well as from reading-thinking process objectives. The methods that are described may be used in reading/language arts classes or in content-area classes where language processes are applied to the learning of information that is part of a subject curriculum. In either situation, students need to use their prior knowledge to comprehend the text. As Anderson et al. (1977) point out, "the principal determinant of knowledge a person can acquire from reading is the knowledge s/he already possesses" (p. 378).

Setting Purposes

The first step in a lesson with informational material is to determine the content objectives. The teacher must decide which factual information should be emphasized and which vocabulary and concepts are the most important. Who? What? Where? When? How? and Why? will be key questions to consider when planning the lesson. Once these objectives are set, the teacher needs to decide how students will make predictions about the key points that will be addressed in the text. Other process objectives should also be selected at this point. An example will illustrate.

A fourth-grade teacher planned a lesson on North Atlantic fishing communities, based on an article in a textbook. The teacher's content objectives were as follows:

1. To develop the students' understanding of life in the Maritime Provinces. The class would discover
   a. that many people fish for a living.
   b. that the sea can be a friend or an enemy.
   c. how the people learn to fish.
2. To help students gain an understanding of the term *self-sufficient*.

The teacher selected these objectives because of their suitability for this group's level of knowledge and because of the information the students would learn from reading and discussion.

Process objectives included the following:

1. To use the children's prior knowledge to prepare them to learn the information presented in the text.
2. To have the students make predictions by letting them respond to prereading questions about the content objectives.
3. To discuss key information in light of original predictions.
4. To write sentences illustrating the concept *self-sufficient.*

On a map of North America, the class located Maine, Nova Scotia, and the other Maritime provinces. The group discussed the terms *coast line* and *islands,* both of which the students understood. They also noted how far some of these areas were from large cities. Then the teacher posed objectives-based questions to get students to predict what they might learn.

First, the teacher asked, "What do you think these people do for a living?" Students immediately replied that fishing, skiing or sailing were likely pursuits. To probe further, the teacher asked, "Why do you think so?" These were some of the expanded responses:

If they live so close to the coast, they probably can make a living at fishing. I know there are a lot of people in Maine who catch Maine lobsters.

Maybe they go sailing just to catch fish. It's probably cold up there, so probably not too many people go around in sailboats just for fun.

But they might try out sailboats in the cold water to see if they can build better ones.

Maybe they do a lot of skiing because of the mountains you can see on the map. If it's cold there, there is probably snow, and the skiing would be good.

Students continued to make predictions, based on what they knew or on what they surmised about this part of the world. Responses were recorded on the chalkboard. At the end of the discussion, the notes looked like this:

What do they do for a living?

fish   test sailboats
sail   ski

How could the sea be a friend to these people?

- people know it (know the sea like a friend)
- gives people food (fish, crabs, clams, lobsters)

How could the sea be an enemy to the people?

- tidal waves (could kill people)
- people drown when there's a storm
- strong tides take boats off course

How do these people learn to be fishermen?

- from books
- from other people (friends, family)
- by accident (like something surprised them)

After these predictions were recorded, the teacher went over them, one at a time, having the students decide which ones were best. Because the discussion had been rather thorough, some who made the first predictions changed their minds and adopted new ideas.

As predictions are made, students become influenced by ideas from other members of their groups. These ideas help them refine their own thinking. Each student comes with a unique background of knowledge and experience. As many share, they learn from each other and generate new ideas as a group. Because everyone is speculating before reading, a change of mind is quite acceptable. In the group discussed in the example, several students at first thought that the people sailed for a living, but the discussion swayed their minds. At the end, no one thought that the people just sailed or tested sailboats. Most thought that the residents fished (or fished and sailed) or perhaps owned ski resorts. Similarly, at first several students thought that people would learn to fish by reading books. By the end of the discussion, however, most of the group thought that there would not be too many books in such remote areas and that people would probably best learn to fish if they were taught by others.

Gathering Evidence

Students turned to their readers to find the selection, "The Sea's Special Breed" (from *Person to Person,* Level 15, Allyn and Bacon, 1978). The teacher instructed, "Read to see what you can find out. Check the board if you need to, to keep in mind what you are looking for." Students read silently. When they finished, the teacher began the discussion.

TEACHER: Did we find any answers?

FRANK: We found out about the fishing. It said the men went out in boats and fished for lobsters.

MELANIE: Yes, they used special traps. They put the bait in and then put a stone on the trap so it will go down to the bottom.

SAM: They even go out in the storms because they have to make their living at it.

TEACHER: What about skiing and sailing?

KEN: Well, it didn't say anything about skiing at all. Maybe they ski some, but it sounds like they spend a lot of time fishing.

LINDA: You know they have to know how to sail because they go out in the boats every day.

BETH: And it said if they're not careful, they'll get into trouble at sea, so you know they must be good sailors.

The discussion continued in this manner until the group had reviewed all the questions and had decided which predictions had been the best, given the evidence they had found from reading. The teacher kept the notes on the board, erasing predictions the group now rejected and adding to accurate ones as the students talked. Because the prereading discussion had been extensive, students had little difficulty staying with their purposes, finding answers, and discussing the material knowledgeably. The teacher had not expected them to learn everything presented in the article. The aim had been for them first to notice and then to remember points related to their specific purposes.

Extending Learning

The predictions and the first reading of the article were only the first steps in developing the concepts that were the objectives of this lesson. Right after the discussion, the teacher directed attention to the vocabulary of the story, first asking students for words they wanted to discuss and then bringing up terms that related to the objectives. Several students wondered about the term *artisans,* so that was discussed first. Then the teacher listed the following words and phrases on the board, having the students return to the text, where they found the terms in context and discuss their meaning:

- neither for the soft nor the cowardly
- hit off your rocker
- sea's special breed
- weather-beaten
- float (multiple meanings)
- perched
- headland
- self-sufficient
- handy

The next day, the teacher brought up the term *self-sufficient,* one of the original concepts the students were to develop from the lesson. The students found the word, which had been briefly discussed the day before, in the text. The teacher asked, "What does it mean?" Answers varied but the responses showed that the students were understanding the term:

to fix something	be dependable
take care of yourself	be self-reliant
take blame	know what you're doing

To enlarge the concept, the teacher then asked students to find lines in the story to illustrate that the people in the text were self-sufficient. Three students responded:

KIM: They go out to sea, usually alone, in their small boats.
MARK: I built my own boat and I built my own home.
MINDY: Now if Charlie has some trouble, he knows he can count on me to come over and help him.

Finally, the teacher wrote the following framed paragraph on the board, with slots for modifiers:

_____ lobstermen are _____ self-sufficient because they _____. _____ they go out in _____ weather to _____. We say they are _____.

The class completed the first sentence as a group, the teacher writing alternate word choices on the board:

Brave		very
All	lobstermen are quite self-sufficient	
Maine		really

usually fish alone.
because they go out in little boats.
can ride out a storm.

Students completed the paragraph independently. Here are two of their papers:

All lobstermen are really self-sufficient because they usually fish alone. Often they go out in cold weather to look at their floats. We say they are independent.

   Maine lobstermen are very self-sufficient because they always go out in little boats. Most of the time they go out in good weather to fish. We say they are brave because the ocean can be dangerous.

When everyone had finished writing, students took turns reading their work aloud to partners. Reading the work later, the teacher could see how well different students had grasped the concept. Understanding was developing because students were working with the concept in a meaningful context.

This example demonstrates some basic principles of teaching a lesson in which informational learning is the goal. It illustrates how content objectives and reading-thinking process objectives can be met in a coordinated way. Predicting before reading establishes a solid base. Reading and discussing clarify key points. Further discussion and writing reinforce learning.

Content-area Applications

Here are summaries of two other lessons that illustrate how reading-thinking abilities can be developed at different grade levels with different kinds of content-area materials.

The first example is from a two-day lesson that was conducted in a middle school health class, in which there were many students for whom English was a second language. The teacher's health objectives were to increase understanding of the term *fast food,* to foster nutritional awareness when students selected foods, and to encourage better eating habits. The teacher also wanted to encourage students to express themselves in English by talking about some foods that were familiar to them. The lesson was designed to provide good opportunities for oral language exchanges.

The teacher conducted an extensive prereading discussion, using these props to stimulate talk: a pizza box, a cup and bag from a local fast-food restaurant, a cheeseburger, and a soft drink. The class talked about the types of restaurants that serve these foods, decided on a tentative definition for fast food, and discussed how it may or may not differ from junk food (the subject of a previous lesson).

Then the teacher elicited predictions from the title of an article the students were about to read: "How Good Are Fast Foods?" Even after the previous discussion, students thought in terms of taste rather than nutrition as they considered the "goodness" of fast foods. Predictions fell into two categories: "very good" (delicious) and "terrible" (taste very bad).

In the next phase of the lesson, done on the second day, the teacher started with the title and its subheading ("They're cheap, filling, a hit with kids and tasty. But are they nutritious?"). This title led the group to discuss the word *nutrition,* a term that they were able to relate to the previous day's distinction between fast food and junk food. A vigorous debate ensued, with the class about equally divided between those who believed fast foods must all be bad and those who thought these foods were nutritionally sound. There were no middle-ground positions. The teacher then asked three more specific questions and recorded the following predictions on the board:

Which restaurants might be mentioned in the article?

McDonalds   Pizza Hut
Taco Bell   Shakeys

Which fast foods do you think are nutritionally good?

Egg McMuffin   milk shake
hamburger   fishwich
chicken

Which do you think are nutritionally poor?

hot fruit pie   soda
French fries   pizza

Finally, the teacher asked each student to plan a menu for a fast food meal that might be nutritionally sound. Then the group read the article:

HOW GOOD ARE FAST FOODS?
THEY'RE CHEAP, FILLING, A HIT WITH KIDS AND TASTY.
BUT ARE THEY NUTRITIOUS?
by Jane E. Brody

Meals around the family table are less common today than in the past. As a result of smaller families, working wives, and increased discretionary income and time, more than half of all Americans eat more than half their meals away from home. The main beneficiaries of this new pattern of American eating are the fast food chains, where edibles roll out like car parts on an assembly line. The fast food industry has been growing at a rate of about 15 percent a year, pizza has become a staple, and the burger—billions sold annually—has replaced the hot dog as the national dish.

In addition to pizza, burgers, and franks, American appetites are regularly whetted by such fast foods as fried fish and chicken, tacos, French fries, onion rings, soft drinks and shakes. Many of these foods have been attacked by nutritionists and public-health physicians because they are high in fats and/or sugar, and overly laden with calories for the amount of essential nutrients they provide. Fairly or not, fast foods have been singled out as symbolic of what's wrong with nutrition in the United States today.

But no matter what is said about them by health professionals, the 140,000 fast-food establishments sprinkled across the country like salt on fries are likely to continue to prosper and multiply. The reasons: they're fast, filling, inexpensive, attractive to youngsters and—let's be honest—millions like the taste of what's dished up. Since the chains are here to stay, here are some facts and guidelines to help you choose wisely from fast-food fare.

The main problems with most fast-food meals is that they're not nutritionally balanced. Those of pizza, chicken or beef usually contain more than enough protein for a child or adult for one meal. But for the number of calories they provide—generally more than a third of an adult's daily requirements—they tend to over-supply you with fats and salt and undersupply you with vitamins A and C, several B vitamins and iron. While pizza is one of the better-balanced fast foods—with plenty of protein and less fat than other types of meals—it is especially high in salt content, a negative factor for those predisposed to developing high blood pressure. Fast-food meals are also sadly deficient in vegetables (except potatoes) and fruit. Thus a good rule of thumb is to eat salad, vegetables and fruit at your other meals on the days when you eat fast food.

Selecting a nutritious drink at a fast-food restaurant is often difficult. Milk and fruit juice (not a fruit drink), if on the menu, are probably the best choices. Regular soda provides no nutrients besides a hundred or more calories of sugar, and diet sodas contain saccharin, which causes cancer in laboratory animals. Shakes are high in fat (usually cholesterol-raising saturated fats), sugar and calories.

Another pitfall is French fried potatoes. As they come from the ground, potatoes are a nutritional bargain—low in fat, high in desirable complex carbohydrates. But when fried in deep fat, potatoes become a high-fat, high-calorie food. A typical fast-food serving of fries contains 200 or more calories, too many of them fat calories.

Finally, if you're watching salt intake, skip the pickles on your burger!

After reading, students compared their group's predictions with the data mentioned in a chart that was included with the article (see Table 5.1). The comparisons raised several issues, involving such matters as the value given to the amount of protein in a hamburger versus the amount of fat and sodium. The students concluded that there was no absolute answer and that the terms *good* or *bad* could be applied only in the context of a person's food intake for a day or a week. The class went back to the text of the article, too, to confirm their reasoning. They reread the advice on how to balance a fast-food meal with different foods at other meals.

Then the teacher asked students to use the information from the article to evaluate the menus they had planned earlier. One student had originally planned a menu that included a Whopper, French fries, and a vanilla shake. He consequently reevaluated his choices:

This meal has plenty of protein. It is bad because it has too much fat, too many calories, and too much salt. It could be a better meal by eating a taco or drinking milk or juice instead of the shake.

This exercise allowed the teacher to evaluate the success of his original objectives and to plan for an extension of the concepts during the rest of the nutrition unit.

TABLE 5.1   Caloric and Nutritional Content* of Popular Fast Foods

Item	Calories	Protein (gm.)	Carbohydrates (gm.)	Fat (gm.)	Sodium (mg.)
Hamburgers					
Burger King Whopper	630	26	50	36	990
McDonald's Big Mac	541	26	39	31	962
Burger Chef Hamburger	258	11	24	13	393
Fish					
Arthur Treacher's Fish Sandwich	440	16	39	24	836
McDonald's Filet-O-Fish	402	15	34	23	709
Long John Silver's Fish (2 pcs)	409	24	24	24	N.A.
Chicken					
Kentucky Fried Original Recipe Three-Piece Dinner	830	52	56	46	2285
Kentucky Fried Extra-Crispy Three-Piece Dinner	950	52	63	54	1915
Other Entrees					
Pizza Hut Thin 'n Crispy Cheese Pizza (half of 13″ pie)	340	19	42	11	approx. 900
Pizza Hut Thick 'n Chewy Pepperoni Pizza (half of 10″ pie)	450	25	52	16	approx. 900
McDonald's Egg McMuffin	352	18	26	20	914
Taco Bell Taco	186	15	14	8	79
Dairy Queen Brazier Hot Dog	270	11	23	15	868
Side Dishes					
Burger King French Fries	210	3	25	11	230
Dairy Queen Onion Rings	300	6	33	17	N.A.
Burger King Vanilla Shake	340	8	52	11	320
McDonald's Chocolate Shake	364	11	60	9	329
McDonald's Apple Pie	300	2	31	19	414

*Data supplied by companies   N.A. = not available

This next example—a lesson with fourth graders—shows how an activity emphasizing facts can be planned around a selection in the narrative mode. The story that the class read, about landing an airplane in bad weather, could have been handled as a DR-TA with narrative material, with predictions and discussion based on the story line. Instead, the teacher used the selection to help the class develop an understanding of the concept of an instrument landing.

The teacher first showed a picture of an airport control tower, surrounded by runways glistening in the rain. Students used prior knowledge about airports and weather as they discussed what they might learn from reading:

TEACHER: We will be reading about this today [showing picture]. What do you think it is?

CHARITY: Maybe it's an airport.

TOM: I think it is. Maybe we'll read about men who work radar.

LEE: It looks foggy. Maybe planes will have to land without seeing.

CHARITY: The runway is shiny. Maybe it's icy.

RICK: If it's icy, it'll be hard to land.

LEE: It's hard to land in the fog, too.

TEACHER: What is meant by an instrument landing?

TOM: It's like a crash landing.

LEE: Buttons inside the plane help the pilot land.

TEACHER: Any other ideas? [Students shake their heads. They do not know any more about it than this.] How do you think the men in the tower help the pilot?

CHARITY: He talks on the radio and they talk back.

MARGY: They turn on the runway lights.

LEE: They turn on the radio and talk.

TEACHER: How do you think the pilot knows he's close to the airport?

TOM: He sees the flashing lights.

RICK: He sees other planes.

LEE: The person in the tower tells him.

MARGY: A light in the plane flashes.

Students thought creatively and analytically about several different ideas, based on what they knew. They recalled films and television programs they had seen about air travel. Those who had flown and landed in bad weather offered predictions that reflected their experiences. As students predicted, the teacher compiled a list of ideas on the board. This kept the discussion on target and stimulated additional thinking. After a number of possibilities had been listed, the teacher returned to each original question and had each student decide individually which prediction seemed most likely.

Before reading, each student knew what to look for and had tentatively decided which answers were the right ones. Although the teacher had set the direction with selected objectives and specific questions, it was the students who set purposes by making predictions. Listening to their responses, the teacher was able to judge how much the students actually knew before reading and therefore how well they would be able to assimilate the new material. This group had few ideas about instrument landings. They had some knowledge, but their concepts were limited and fuzzy.

When students turned to their copies of the selection, the teacher said, "Read to see if you are right. Check the board if you forget a question." As they read, several of the children looked up to review the questions. Some said, "Oh, I get it" as they came to relevant information. Here is the selection that the students read:

THE HARD WAY
by Seymour Reit

Night closes in around the big airport. With it comes fog. The runway lights shine brightly. The tower beacons turn and flash, turn and flash. But the fog is rolling in low, and visibility is getting poor.

In the tower, the flight control officer glances at his clock. The plane from Shannon Airport should be reporting at any moment. Bringing a big jet in through this fog won't be easy.

Suddenly the loudspeaker crackles:

"Kennedy tower . . . this is TWA Flight 33 from Shannon . . . how do you hear me?"

The control officer answers quickly:

"TWA 33 . . . I hear you loud and clear . . . come in, 33."

"Kennedy tower . . . this is TWA 33 . . . 50 miles north of the airport . . . altitude 5000 feet . . . request weather and landing information."

"Kennedy to TWA 33 . . . wind two-five/zero degrees . . . altimeter setting 29.5 . . . visibility 1200 yards . . . ceiling 600 feet . . . use runway two . . . repeat, runway two."

On board Flight 33, the passengers fasten their seat belts. They watch the fog and wait. The great plane's landing gear is down and locked. The pilot and co-pilot check and recheck their instruments.

Five miles from the end of the runway, the jet passes the Outer Marker of the airport. The Outer Marker is a radio beacon that sends a signal straight up into the air. When the plane passes this point, the radio beam triggers a light on the pilot's instrument panel. It tells him that he has only five miles to go.

Still the fog rolls in.

On the ground, a GCA operator studies the radar screen. GCA stands for Ground Control Approach. On the radar, Flight 33 appears as a bright, greenish-yellow dot. At a 90 degree angle, a second plane appears on the screen. The GCA operator watches both dots carefully. His job is to keep the two planes clear of each other, and to take Flight 33 in for a landing.

The pilot, unable to see through the fog, is using an ILS approach. ILS, which means Instrument Landing System, gives him an extra set of "eyes." Two invisible radio paths—a Localizer Beam and a Glide Slope Beam—will help to guide him down.

But the pilot also needs the GCA operator. The radar operator is tense, but he keeps his voice calm.

"Flight 33 . . . adjust left . . . hold your course at 180 degrees."

The pilot peers out of the cockpit window—but there is nothing to see except fog. He listens carefully to the cool voice coming over his earphones.

"... you are now 250 feet over the runway ... improve your rate of descent to correspond ..."

Somewhere overhead the huge jet is hurtling along, but the GCA operator never raises his eyes from the radar screen.

"... now you are just right ... just right ... take over by sight ... and report to control."

Flight 33 is at a critical point. Outside the cockpit windows there is nothing but fog. Thick fog, which the plane must break through. If the pilot fails to see the runway lights, he will have to open his throttle wide and pull the plane up fast.

The jet rushes through the night. The GCA operator keeps his eye on the tiny dot. Everything is touch and go.

Suddenly Flight 33 is through the fog, and the runway lights shine below like a string of twinkling pearls!

Now the jet is almost on the runway. Wing flaps have helped to cut its speed. The wheels touch. They bump once. And the plane is down at last. It speeds along the runway. There is a low whining sound as the pilot applies his brakes and reverses engines to slow the plane further.

He taxis to the exit ramp. The passengers relax. They open their seat belts and begin to collect their belongings. Flight 33 has made it on schedule. The hard way.

When students finished reading, the teacher called their attention to their first predictions, listed on the board, and began the discussion.

TEACHER: Are either of our first predictions correct?

TOM: Not really. The pilot has two invisible radio paths and he glides down on two light beams.

TEACHER: Is that right, class? [Some students nod; some shake their heads. This point has caused confusion.] Go back to the passage, Tom, and find the lines that tell what an instrument landing is. [Tom reads aloud the few sentences that tell about the ILS and the radio beams.]

TEACHER: Were you right?

TOM: Yes. He slides down on light beams.

TEACHER: Do you all agree? [Some nod; some shake their heads. There is still no agreement.] Let's all look at the lines Tom read. Do you see the dash after paths and the dash after beam? Those dashes mean we can take those words out of the sentence. Tom, read it again without those words.

TOM: "Two invisible radio paths will help guide him down."

TEACHER: Now, what is an instrument landing?

CHARITY: It's using his buttons on his instrument panel and following the invisible radio paths.

TOM: He doesn't really slide down. The tower sends him radio messages, and he follows with his own radio.

TEACHER: Do you all agree? [Students nod.]

The teacher erased the incorrect prediction from the board and added to the partially correct one, using Tom's words. Then the group went over the other points, discussing and rereading until it seemed that everyone understood. At the end of the lesson, the original questions, with their expanded and corrected answers, remained on the board.

The postreading discussion allowed the teacher to clarify and expand key concepts. It was necessary to take time to reread and restate, sharing ideas and interpretations until everyone achieved greater understanding. Tom's first response could have been accepted; it was close to the actual answer. But his statement was not really clear, and others in the class were puzzled. The teacher stayed with the point until everyone seemed to get it. (But teachers can never be absolutely sure of the level at which students grasp concepts and must adjust expectations to match students' ages and backgrounds. This teacher went as far as she thought appropriate for these fourth graders.) Comprehension was developed through the use of prior knowledge, from reading to gather information, and from revising first thoughts in light of what was in the text.

Follow-up activities included discussing vocabulary from the selection, viewing a filmstrip about airport control towers, and writing a summary of what was learned.

Planning for Active Reading

To foster active involvement in the learning of factual material, teachers need to plan lessons carefully. The first step is to decide on the content objectives—that is, the major concepts or pieces of information that are to be learned. It is best to choose only a few key points. The more selective the teacher can be, the more easily the students will be able to achieve understanding. The reading selection will seldom match the objectives exactly, so it is not wise to aim for mastery of everything that is presented in a text. The material will probably contain some very important information for students to retain. Other information can be judged less important. For example, there may be material that, although interesting, does not relate directly to the lesson's goals, or there may be simply too much for a group to handle in the allotted time. The text must be examined to see how it matches the objectives and to discover which parts are most important.

Once these decisions are made, the teacher should consider the following issues:

- Given the objectives, which questions should guide reading?
- Where will students find relevant information?
- Which facts should they note?
- Will they need to make inferences, draw conclusions?
- Is some information presented graphically?

Teachers may put themselves in the students' place, asking prereading questions and seeing where and how the answers might be found. Knowing what students will be looking for, a teacher can see where the facts may be discovered. (Students may not be able to find all the information in the text; in such cases, the teacher will need to plan other learning activities.)

The next step is to phrase the prereading discussion questions so as to stimulate predictions about key points. It may seem simpler just to tell students, "Read to find out ———." But making predictions is a vital step in the reading-thinking process. When students speculate before they read, they are using prior knowledge and establishing a base on which to build new knowledge. They begin to organize their thoughts around the key concepts. In this way they are preparing to assimilate what they are about to read. The topic of the day becomes a series of interesting questions, and students are encouraged to discover the answers. Predictions, based on teachers' questions, become students' purposes for reading. The predictions are significant because students make a commitment to understand the material before they start to read.

The prereading discussion also serves other valuable purposes. Students pool their knowledge and learn from each other. One prediction stimulates another, so that ideas are refined and expanded as the thoughts of many participants are considered. Because students do not need to worry about being right at this early point, the discussion can be lively and free. The result is a stimulating atmosphere for learning. As students suggest ideas, the teacher gains opportunities to note their levels of knowledge about the topic; he or she can judge how well students will be able to handle the material. Giving students a chance to display what they already know, teachers achieve new perspectives on the children's background. The insights will usually be surprising; students will reveal unanticipated depths of knowledge or, sometimes, almost total lack of it. Either way, the information is significant.

Henderson (1969) has a good example of how useful prereading discussion can be, to students and to the teacher who wants to assess students' reasoning ability and background of experience and information. A group was preparing to read about the invention of the automobile. The teacher's goals were to have students learn when the first cars were made, and to be aware of the problems the inventors faced.

Students predicted that the first cars appeared somewhere between 1870 and 1890; they reasoned that no cars were around during the Civil War and that the Wright brothers were flying at the turn of the century. Students decided, sensibly, that autos would have been invented at some point in between. Then the group responded to the teacher's question: What problems had to be solved in order to build the first car? Here there was considerable fuzzy thinking. Some students thought the problem was to design a steam engine (they remembered something about steam boats in the nineteenth century); others were convinced that steam could never be used to power a car. Many declared that a gasoline engine was essential, but these students had few arguments to support this notion. One student said, knowingly, "The main problem was the differential." When questioned further, this boy admitted that he didn't really know what a differential did but that it must be an important element because he had read about it somewhere. Henderson stresses the value of "pressing for rigorous hypotheses" to identify areas where "verbalism" rather than solid knowledge leads to predictions. Recognizing one's fuzzy thinking is the first step toward learning. When these students read, they learned more about invention problems than they did about dates. Whereas they only obtained confirmation of their predictions about the beginning of the automobile era, they acquired new information about the problems the inventors faced.

The recording of predictions as they are made gives students a visual aid that is useful when they start to read. Some students need this more than others, and the extent of board notes can be adjusted to suit students' needs. If notes are kept, however, it is important to record all the main ideas that students suggest. Students need to know that their thoughts are valued and that the discussion at this point is the first step to learning, not just a way of filling time. They also need to see how their thinking is affected by what they read. As Britton (1970) notes, reading becomes meaningful to the extent that readers can confirm or refute what they expected to discover. Predictions need to be reviewed after the reading of the text so that concepts can be revised in light of it; initial ideas can be forgotten if they are not recorded. Also, if students are expected to take notes themselves, the final record, modified after reading and discussion, will be an excellent model for them to follow and a good summary for them to review.

Reading and developing concepts through discussion is the "meat" of the lesson, for which students prepare by setting purposes. When they have clear purposes in mind, students can usually find answers rather easily in the text. They can often demonstrate comprehension while reading by saying, "Oh, *That's* what it is!" when they come to relevant information. Postreading discussion modifies initial thinking and continues to develop concepts. Follow-up activities cement learning so that later reading on the same topic will be meaningful.

Planning effective lessons with informational material requires careful attention to strategies of prediction and reinforcement. The examples have illustrated different approaches to each. Now we will explore both phases of the lesson further.

Prediction Strategies

Posing specific questions before the students read is only one way to stimulate purposeful predictions. Other strategies may also be used, for a change of pace and to exercise students' thinking in different ways. Two alternatives are 1) to use anticipation guides, and 2) to predict with key words from the reading selection.

Anticipation Guides An anticipation guide provides a relatively formal approach to prereading prediction. The method is suitable for older students who are faced with more lengthy and complex reading assignments and yet who still need help in setting meaningful, motivating purposes for reading. Responding to an anticipation guide, students must use prior knowledge and reasoning ability to speculate. The teacher constructs the guide, basing the items on important concepts and facts that are presented in the text.

Here is an outline of one possible lesson, based on a chapter entitled "Energy Alternatives" in the textbook *Accent on Science* (Merrill, 1985). The lesson is intended for use in a sixth-grade classroom.

Before students read, the teacher briefly explains the concept of *energy alternatives* (a source of energy that is not based on consumption of fossil fuels) and then gives students a guide to complete individually. Here is a sample guide:

ANTICIPATION GUIDE
ENERGY ALTERNATIVES

Here are some statements about different kinds of energy alternatives. In column A, put a T if you think the statement is true and an F if you think the statement is false.

A	B	
_____	_____	1. Wind can be used to produce electricity in any community.
_____	_____	2. Using the wind to make electricity creates pollution.
_____	_____	3. Rivers are a better source of water energy than lakes.
_____	_____	4. Ocean tides can be used to make electricity at over 100 locations around the world.
_____	_____	5. Geothermal energy is energy that comes from the earth's underground heat.
_____	_____	6. Using nuclear energy to make electricity produces dangerous wastes.
_____	_____	7. The sun produces energy by nuclear fusion.
_____	_____	8. Solar collectors are made of glass and metal.

(Other teachers using this text might choose to include different items; this example is designed to illustrate the kind of guide rather than to suggest which concepts from this text ought to be emphasized.)

Students then meet in small groups to discuss their responses. Differences of opinion come out at this point, stimulating careful reasoning based on what students already know or on what seems plausible. Some students may decide to change their answers; others may become more firmly committed to what they initially thought. Then the whole class discusses the items, allowing each individual to hear an even wider range of opinions and reasons. During these discussions, the teacher serves as moderator, asking students to explain their reasoning but being careful not to give away answers. In fact, the teacher encourages disagreements (sometimes playing devil's advocate) to encourage rigorous thinking and stimulate curiosity. Students are also encouraged to raise questions about any of the stated ideas or any of the words used. (The teacher does not assume that students will have a full grasp of the basic concepts at this point.) Students are then given the material to read.

In the chapter on energy alternatives, students encounter the following information that relates to the issues they discussed:

- Using wind energy is practical only in communities where there are rather constant, strong winds.
- Wind energy does not create pollution.
- The energy released by falling water can be used to create electricity. Modern hydroelectric power plants are like early mills. They need to be built on rivers, which are usually dammed to create the necessary waterfall.
- According to scientists, there are approximately twenty-five locations in the world that would be feasible sites for tidal power plants.
- Geothermal energy refers to energy obtained from extremely hot water and rocks below the surface of the earth.
- Nuclear energy may involve nuclear fission or nuclear fusion. The process of fission, a current source of nuclear power, produces dangerous wastes. The process of fusion, though not mastered for commercial use today, does not produce dangerous wastes.
- The sun produces energy through the process of nuclear fusion.
- Solar collectors are made of dark metal covered with a layer of glass or plastic.

After having read the account, students return to the anticipation guide, this time marking their responses in column B. This is best done in small groups to encourage additional discussion and rereading as students reconsider the items. Discussion at this point is especially important if some of the items cannot be marked true or false as stated. For instance, item 6 in the example really should be qualified before it is judged; students should have discovered from reading that not all nuclear energy creates dangerous wastes, although nuclear fission does. Finally, through whole-class discussion students review the items in the guide, consider other issues presented in the text, and raise questions that will lead to further reading and research.

For additional information on the use of anticipation guides, see Herber (1978), Readence, Bean, and Baldwin (1981), and Vacca and Vacca (1986).

Prediction with Key Words   Hammond (1983, 1986) describes the reading-thinking process as one that involves three stages: action, interaction, and reflection. Accordingly, Hammond developed this next prediction strategy, which stimulates action (active thinking) before reading, enhances students' interaction with the text, and refines their skill at reflecting on the meanings they construct while reading.

The teacher first reviews the text and selects key words or phrases. These are put on the board in random order before the students have seen the text. Students are told that all the items have something to do with the topic. They work together to group them, using their prior knowledge and their reasoning ability to make plausible matches. Here is an example based on a section entitled "Pioneer Life" in the textbook *Our United States* (Follett, 1983). The text is intended for use in a fifth-grade classroom.

PIONEER LIFE

All of these words have something to do with pioneer life in the United States. Which ones do you think go together and why?

sugar   corduroy
            Conestoga wagons
                                      eggs
        schooners
                        plank
                                      springhouse
    log cabin   general store
            butter   salt

    greased paper   Natchez Trace

Trying out different combinations of items raises questions and provokes thought. For instance, could butter, eggs, salt, and sugar all be bought at a general store? If so, those five items might go together. Or did sugar have to be shipped in from overseas (on schooners) and then delivered by Conestoga wagon to the pioneers? Maybe greased paper was used for wrapping butter. Or did the paper have something to do with a springhouse? Was Natchez Trace the site of a springhouse? Or was that the name of a person who owned a springhouse? (What is a springhouse, anyway?) Conestoga wagons were covered with some kind of cloth, weren't they? Maybe it was corduroy. Or was corduroy another of the things sold in the general store? Maybe plank and log cabin should go together. Didn't log cabins have wooden floors?

Trying to match up items requires careful reasoning that can be exercised even in the absence of students' detailed prior knowledge. For instance, students might not know a great deal about Conestoga wagons or log cabins, but they will have some idea about wagons and cabins in general, which will allow them to form some hypotheses. As students share ideas, discussion will be lively; there is sure to be some disagreement.

Prediction strategies promote active involvement in subject learning by stimulating curiosity and helping students read purposefully. Equally important is postreading attention to developing and reinforcing the concepts that are the key elements in any subject lesson.

In the textbook section on "Pioneer Life," students encounter the following information that relates to the items in the set:

- Conestoga wagons were shaped like boats, leading many people to refer to them as "prairie schooners."
- Log cabins seldom had glass windows. More often, pioneers used greased paper or animal skins to cover the windows.
- The Natchez Trace was an early dirt road used by pioneers. Travel was made easier when corduroy roads and plank roads were built in later years. (Descriptions of both kinds of roads, along with a diagram, are provided in the text.)
- Springhouses, which were ample holes dug in the ground, were used for storing butter, eggs, and other foods that needed to be kept cool.
- The general store sold many necessities that pioneers could not easily produce themselves, such as sugar and salt.

After reading, students are asked to group the items again, applying what they learned from reading. Discussion and rereading at this point help them to review key concepts, go over other interesting information that was presented, and raise questions to guide further study.

Besides having the result of stimulating predictions, this activity contains other advantages. Students are required to make sense of the array of details, and their reasoning processes, as they work on the items, provide good information about the way individuals think and influence each other. Listening in on small-group discussions will give the teacher valuable information about students' abilities to make inferences, draw conclusions, and form hypotheses. Also, because the teacher controls the items in the array, certain concepts or vocabulary (judged to be particularly important by the teacher) may be included in the set. Prereading discussion will stimulate interest in these words, and the words will then stand out to students when they read. Finally, it is almost certain that some students will try to justify very odd combinations of items; this in itself will generate a healthy spirit of merriment in the group and will make the reading that much more fun.

Reinforcement Strategies

Prediction strategies promote active involvement in subject learning by stimulating curiosity and helping students read purposefully. Equally important is postreading attention to the developing and reinforcing of the concepts that are the key elements in any subject lesson. The examples in this chapter have illustrated several ways to reinforce learning. Here the process is explored further.

Reviewing Predictions   After reading, students should always review their predictions, considering them in light of what they have read. It is through confirming or rejecting predictions that students reveal their comprehension—to the teacher and, equally important, to themselves.

The postreading activity will depend on how the predictions were made. If the teacher posed questions, then students should go over these, deciding if their predicted answers were on target or if their reading led them to change their minds. If students grouped key words before reading, they should regroup them after reading. If they worked with an anticipation guide, they should make use of that guide to review learning. The force of any prediction strategy is enhanced considerably when, after reading, students look again at their original purposes. Coming back full circle allows them to achieve closure and to recognize what they have learned.

This may seem so obvious a point as to not even be worth mentioning. But all teachers are subject to getting off the track when they teach; sometimes they neglect to keep their original objectives in mind. It is not uncommon for a teacher to begin a lesson with one set of purposes and, perhaps without even realizing it, to wind up emphasizing something altogether different. For instance, a teacher might begin a lesson on covered wagons and, being eager to move ahead quickly after students have read the text, might begin talking about how railroads superseded wagon travel in the nineteenth century. The connections will be quite clear to the teacher, who knows the material well, but the students may be left puzzled, because they had been attending to a lesson about covered wagons as a means of transportation. Learning will be most solid when original purposes are kept clear, both during and after reading.

Additional follow-up can reinforce and extend learning by requiring students to reorganize and reflect on what they have learned. Several different strategies may be used for this purpose. A few are described here.

Semantic Mapping   Semantic mapping gives students the chance to organize graphically what they know about a concept or a topic of study. Semantic maps may take different forms. An example is shown in Figure 3. Johnson, Pittelman, and Heimlich (1986) suggest the following steps for generating a semantic map:

1. The teacher selects a key concept from the unit of study and writes this word on the board.
2. Students brainstorm words that are related to the term on the board. The teacher writes these on the board in categories.
3. Students work individually or in small groups to think of additional words related to the key term, listing these in categories.
4. Lists are shared with the whole class, the teacher adding the categorized terms to the board map.
5. Students decide on labels for the different categories they have created.
6. The class discusses the items on the map to enhance understanding of familiar terms, review meanings of new terms, and see relationships among the various concepts included.

A semantic map may be created at the beginning of a unit of study and may be revised periodically as students gather more information. Similarly, a map may be generated at the end of a unit to review information that has been learned. As students work together to organize and display what they know, they will be using vocabulary and discussing relationships that will help to cement learning. Such a map may also be used by individuals to help them organize their ideas before they write (see Chapter 7). For more detailed information on this strategy, see Hanf (1971) and Johnson and Pearson (1984).

Writing to Reinforce Learning   A variety of writing activities may be used to reinforce learning. For instance, students may complete paragraphs structured by the teacher (see, for example, the one used at the end of the lesson on the Maritime Provinces). They might also compose stories, news accounts, make-believe diary entries, letters, poems, or plays, using what they learned as a basis for the writing.

A particularly useful strategy is *student summary writing* (Cunningham and Cunningham, 1983). Students devote a few minutes at the end of a class session to writing a summary of what they have learned. The teacher may collect and

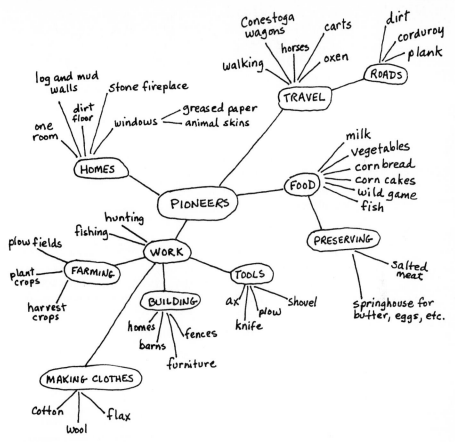

FIGURE 3   An example of a semantic map

read the papers to judge how well students seem to have understood the lesson, but some variety in the follow-up is often more practical and enjoyable. Instead of always submitting their summaries, students may be allowed to choose a number from a hat to determine the fate of their papers each day. Procedures could vary to include the following: 1) The teacher collects and reads the papers; 2) students exchange papers with partners and read aloud each other's papers; 3) three students volunteer or are selected to read their papers aloud to the class; 4) students simply keep their papers; no further handling is required.

Thelen (1986) advocates the use of student summary writing, pointing out that students' comprehension is enhanced when they write new concepts in their own words. Through writing, students make new use of information and vocabulary that were highlighted in the lesson. They approach the material from a different perspective, and this allows them to reorganize information and to recall and state facts and concepts in their own words. If students read their finished work aloud, each will hear how others use the same information; all will benefit from the additional review. Writing about their learning can also help students gain confidence in their ability to handle the writing process (see Chapter 7).

As an alternative to writing, students may dictate to the teacher. This activity, too, will help them rethink and restate what they have learned. Students may be gathered in small groups to discuss and compose a group account, with the teacher serving as moderator and recorder. The dictation may be reproduced so that each student has the account to use for later study. Such dictation following learning is especially useful for young children who are not yet writing fluently, for older children who have severe difficulties with writing, or for children who are in the process of mastering English as a second language and who are usually able to share their ideas orally more easily than in writing.

Referential Questioning   Wood, Readence, and Mateja (1982) describe an interesting sequence of activities for developing concepts. They stress the importance of promoting reader-text interaction through carefully structured *referential* questions—questions that require students to relate their own knowledge to the newly learned concept. Their suggested questions include these types (presented with our examples):

1. Morphemic/Semantic Questions.

    Have students compare and contrast the newly learned concept with what they already know. For instance, if students are learning about telecommunications, they could be asked to think of related known words such as *telephone, telegraph, communicate,* or *talk.* Each would be explored by seeing how it relates to the key concept.

2. Direct Metaphor/Analogy Questions.

    Have students think of the concept in terms of analogies and metaphors. For instance, if students are learning about expansion, the teacher might say, "Think of something you know that expands. What is expansion like? What about something that doesn't expand? What is expansion not like?" Students might reply as follows:

    • A balloon expands when you blow it up. Expansion is like a balloon.
    • It's not like this wood ruler. The ruler doesn't expand.
    • It's like when you spill water on the floor. The water sort of expands. It flows all over.
    • A brick stays put. It can break, but it doesn't expand.
    • Expansion is like a fire, where the smoke goes up and away.

3. Personal Metaphor/Analogy Questions.

    Have students think of themselves as the concept, creating idiosyncratic metaphors. For instance, if students are learning about aerodynamic thrust, the teacher might say, "Imagine you are powered by thrust. How would you feel?" Students may respond with these possible answers:

- I'm zooming!
- I feel like a jet engine. Vroom! Vroom!
- When I sneeze, it's like thrust.
- I'm Superman.

These kinds of personal associations can help students grasp the essentials of a concept. Rather than memorizing the textbook meanings or dictionary definitions of terms, students will be connecting the new concept to what they know in personally meaningful ways.

Experimentation/Demonstration   Some concepts can be developed best through experiments or demonstrations. For instance, in a second-grade class one day, the children were clustered around a basin of water with an assortment of objects on a nearby table. The group had just completed a DR-TA in science period, and they had been introduced to the concepts of floating and sinking. The teacher set up the experiment to develop these concepts further. The children took turns dropping one object at a time into the tank, observing whether the item sank under the water or floated on top. Rubber balls, nails, pencils, scrap paper, rocks, marbles, toy boats, and many other objects were put to the test. The group listed each item in the FLOAT or SINK column on the board as they observed what happened to it. When the testing was finished, the group then drew some conclusions: The heavy things went to the bottom; the light things stayed on top. Then the teacher brought out a new box with different objects. She handed them around, one at a time, and had the children predict whether each would sink or float. Each of their predictions was then tested. Rather than relying on a verbal explanation alone, this teacher was developing the concepts through having the children demonstrate active thinking and doing.

Holt (1964) describes another example of concept development through experimentation. His students regularly worked with a balance beam, starting with a weight at one end of the locked beam. The students then had to predict where a second weight would have to be placed to make the beam balance. His description of individuals' efforts emphasizes how important such activities can be. When faced with an imminent, objective test of their knowledge, students grew uncertain, even anxious. They might have been able to give a satisfactory verbal explanation of the concept, but they needed concrete activities if they were to be able to attach meaning to the words.

Dramatization   Many concepts can be developed through dramatization. Putting themselves into the act, students get a unique perspective on the concept being studied. For instance, when studying the westward travels of early pioneers, one third-grade class went out to the school yard to improvise a drama of typical travelers' struggles. Some pretended to be wagon drivers with imaginary wagons; others led imaginary mules loaded with personal belongings. Having read and talked about the pioneers' adventures and hardships, the group was able to recreate a good scene extemporaneously. Some complained of being tired and thirsty; some scouted for Indians; some conversed about what they missed in their "home towns," and some revealed their expectations of a prosperous new life. It was a hot, sunny day, and before long the travelers began to experience genuine thirst. The slightly hilly yard also soon turned spritely walking into trudging. Several children sat down to rest, while the more energetic urged them on, saying "We've got to do fifteen miles today! Come on!" Later, in the classroom, the children revealed better understanding of the concepts of pioneers, western expansion, hardship, and perseverance.

Reinforcement after reading is as important as prediction before reading. The more students have a chance to use what they glean from reading, the better their chances of retaining the concepts and information they have learned. As Dale (1969) wrote:

> Many studies show that additional time spent on reflection, on thinking about what we have read, heard, seen or done is highly profitable. Hence the importance of that knowledge which helps us organize, classify, pattern, structure, rearrange, reconstruct, synthesize, conceptualize what we know.... Instead of always trying to learn more information, we might better learn how to rearrange, reconstruct or systematize what we already have. Indeed, we might well test a person not only on what he "knows" but also on how skillfully and critically he files, retrieves, and uses what he already possesses. In short, we must try to discover how well a person thinks. (p. 2)

Reading and Thinking: Some Conclusions

When teachers begin to use DR-TAs with factual material, such as textbooks, they often ask these questions:

- Doesn't this approach encourage students to skip over text information? If they are reading only to find some facts, won't they miss a lot?
- Doesn't all the time it takes for predicting take time away from *learning*?
- How can I cover all the material in the book if I focus on a few purposes in this way?

It is true that the approach of using selected objectives encourages students to pay more attention to some parts of the text than to others. The readers will generally attend to purpose-relevant material. This is not a disadvantage, however. The alternative is broad coverage of the text (with the general purpose of reading all of it carefully), a process that does not guarantee greater understanding. It is more sensible to aim for students to gain thorough comprehension of selected material. If there is a great deal to be learned from a text, then the material can be reread with new purposes. The methods described here do not foster careless reading; rather, students are encouraged to read with greater care and attention than they do ordinarily.

Predicting before reading does take time, but this step is extremely important for calling up prior knowledge, stimulating curiosity, and building readiness to understand. Predictions are not frills. Hypothesizing is an essential part of active reading; it is an act that is important for students to do and that is equally important for teachers to monitor. When planning a lesson, teachers are always in danger of assuming that students know more (or less) than they actually do. Even if educators are well organized, they can be ineffective if they don't know what students' prior knowledge is. In asking for predictions, teachers come to know their students better and can help them prepare to read purposefully.

A good purpose-setting discussion can also affect learning in surprisingly beneficial ways. Many groups become so interested in finding answers that they later claim the facts almost leaped out at them from the page. For instance, a teacher once worked with a group of academically advanced middle schoolers, using a reading selection that was dry and terse—a brief, fact-filled account of the life of Francis Scott Key, lyricist of "The Star-Spangled Banner." A short discussion established that the students knew only that Key wrote the words while he was on board a ship, watching a battle. Students were asked, "What was he doing there?" Predications included:

- He was a soldier in the war.
- He was captain of the ship.
- He operated the ship's cannon.
- He was a spy.
- He was an arms dealer.

No one knew for sure, but each child soon became fervently committed to one of these ideas. Individuals backed their predictions with well-reasoned arguments. Factions formed, and friendly rivalries developed as each group sought to convince the others that they were right. The "spy" advocates, for example, described an adventurous and romantic scenario in which Key was the central figure; these students viewed Key as an early version of James Bond. Additional discussion centered on the following topics:

1. The particular war during which the song was composed.

   Predictions ranged from the Revolutionary War to World War I. Different factions formed on this issue. Some began singing the national anthem to analyze the vocabulary and language for clues to the era in which it was written.

2. When it became a national anthem.

Some decided that it was adopted early in the nineteenth century; others believed it was the early twentieth century.

3. Where the music came from.

Most thought the melody was a military tune. One fellow said he had heard it was a drinking song, and he was confronted with stares of disbelief from the rest of the class.

The discussion was lively; thinking was active; interaction was excellent. When the group was finally shown the material, they tore into it with alacrity, never even noticing that the language did not produce the most interesting prose treatment of the subject. Cries of satisfaction or groans of despair told when individuals had found information that proved them right or wrong. A few months later, students from that class were able to answer the original questions immediately. They would not forget those facts for a long time.

This same level of active involvement and excitement to find out can occur in groups of all ages. Not all prereading discussion will be filled with creative thought, and not all groups become so motivated as to practically beg for the reading selection. This *does* happen occasionally when group dynamics and individual personalities add a special energy to the discussion. But always, students will want to find the answers once they have decided that a particular prediction is the right one. Rather than taking time away from learning, predicting enhances learning by creating in students the urge to know.

Teachers who are faced with thick curriculum guides and expectations that they must cover a certain amount of material may have the most difficult time accepting this approach to reading and learning. A teacher in a seventh-grade social studies class once used these principles to begin a lesson on the Dust Bowl and its effect on midwesterners who lived in the 1930s. The lesson was one of many in a history unit on that era. At the start, students told what they thought the Dust Bowl was. Answers ranged from the extremely literal (a bowl of dust) to a somewhat broader concept (an area filled with dust and dirt). Then they discussed what they knew about farming life during the Great Depression. These late twentieth-century East Coast students had very little understanding of farming in the Midwest, of social conditions in the 1930s, or of how drastic climatic changes might have affected communities many miles and years away. In forty-five minutes, the group determined what they knew and, by examining text pictures, discovered some information about the Dust Bowl. Students were attentive, cooperative, and thoughtful. But the teacher realized how little the students knew even though the group had discussed relevant material previously. The lesson covered only the first part of a long chapter—a chapter that was, according to the curriculum guide, to be covered in three days, and yet the group had hardly begun.

And that is the dilemma that most teachers face—enormous gaps in student knowledge versus great quantities of concepts and reading material that must be covered. There are no easy answers to the questions raised by the dilemma, but most teachers would agree that it is probably better for students to learn a few important things well rather than touch lightly on (and soon forget) much larger amounts of information. If students are to learn anything, they should learn it well. This may mean that curriculum schedules cannot always be maintained and that careful, thoughtful learning of a small amount of information will have to replace "covering" the book. Active reading-thinking, as described here, seems to be the most effective way of directing learning of factual material. This approach is both purposeful and thorough.

Suggested Activities

1. Choose a reading selection from a social studies or science text. Determine teaching objectives and write questions that could be used as a basis for predictions and for postreading discussion. How would you change your plan if you were teaching a group of students who might have difficulty reading the text on their own?
2. Prepare an anticipation guide for a reading selection in a content-area textbook. Ask two students at the appropriate grade level to complete the guide. Discuss their responses with them. Then have them read the text and review the guide to confirm or change their original answers. Evaluate the students' responses to the activities.
3. Using a unit, or a partial unit, from a social studies or science text, design three activities to reinforce learning. Prepare one for average students, one for accelerated students, and one for students who have only limited reading abilities.
4. Select a unit in either a social studies or a science textbook. Prepare a bibliography of ten books, both fiction and nonfiction, which children might read to extend their knowledge of the concepts in the unit.

References

Anderson, R. C.; Reynolds, R. E.; Schallert, D. L.; and Goetz, E. T. "Frameworks for Comprehending Discourse." *American Educational Research Journal* 14(Fall 1977):367–81.

Britton, J. *Language and Learning.* London: Penguin, 1970.

Cunningham, P. M., and Cunningham, J. W. "SSW—Better Content Writing." *The Clearing House* (January 1983):237–38.

Dale, E. "What Knowledge is of Most Worth?" *The News Letter* 35(October 1969):1–4.

Hammond, W. D. "How Your Students Can Predict Their Way to Reading Comprehension." *Learning* 12(November 1983):62–64.

──────. "Common Questions on Reading Comprehension." *Learning* 14(January 1986):49–51.

Hanf, M. B. "Mapping: A Technique for Translating Reading into Thinking." *Journal of Reading* 14(January 1971):225–30+.

Henderson, E. H. "Directed Reading-Thinking Activity for Content Material—Group Types." Unpublished course handout. Newark, DE: University of Delaware, 1969.

Herber, H. *Teaching Reading in the Content Areas.* Englewood Cliffs, NJ: Prentice-Hall, 1978.

Holt, J. *How Children Fail.* New York: Dell, 1964.

Johnson, D. D., and Pearson, P. D. *Teaching Reading Vocabulary.* New York: Holt, Rinehart and Winston, 1984.

Johnson, D. D.; Pittelman, S. D.; and Heimlich, J. E. "Semantic Mapping." *The Reading Teacher* 39(April 1986):778–83.

Readence, J. E.; Bean, T. W.; and Baldwin, R. S. *Content-Area Reading: An Integrated Approach.* Dubuque, IA: Kendall-Hunt, 1981.

Thelen, J. "Vocabulary Instruction and Meaningful Learning." *Journal of Reading* 29(April 1986):603–09.

Vacca, R. T., and Vacca, J. *Content Area Reading.* Boston: Little, Brown, 1986.

Wood, K. D.; Readence, J. E.; and Mateja, J. A. "Referential Questioning: A Strategy for Enhancing the Reader-Text Interaction." *Reading Horizons* (Summer 1982):263–67.

Suggested Readings

Ausubel, D. P. *The Psychology of Meaningful Verbal Learning.* New York: Grune and Stratton, 1963.

Bruner, J. S. *The Process of Education.* Cambridge, MA: Harvard University Press, 1960.

Cheyney, A. B. *Teaching Reading Skills Through the Newspaper.* Newark, DE: International Reading Association, 1984.

Dale, E., and O'Rourke, J. *Techniques of Teaching Vocabulary.* Palo Alto, CA: Field Educational, 1971.

Dupuis, M. M. *Reading in the Content Areas: Research for Teachers.* Newark, DE: International Reading Association and ERIC/RCS, 1983.

Eeds, M. "What To Do When They Don't Understand What They Read—Research-Based Strategies for Teaching Reading Comprehension." *The Reading Teacher* 34(February 1981):565–71.

Elkind, D., and Flavell, J. H. (eds.) *Studies in Cognitive Development: Essays in Honor of Jean Piaget.* New York: Oxford University Press, 1969.

Flood, J. *Understanding Reading Comprehension: Cognition, Language, and the Structure of Prose.* Newark, DE: International Reading Association, 1983.

Gitzlaff, L. *Teaching Reading Comprehension* (Telecourse and Book of Selected Readings). Bloomington, IN: Agency for Instructional Technology, 1987.

Graham, K. G., and Robinson, H. A. *Study Skills Handbook: A Guide for All Teachers.* Newark, DE: International Reading Association and ERIC/RCS, 1984.

Hayes, D. A., and Tierney, R. J. "Developing Readers' Knowledge Through Analogy." *Reading Research Quarterly* 17(No. 2, 1982):256–79.

Moore, D. W.; Readence, J. E.; and Rickelman, R. J. *Prereading Activities for Content Area Reading and Learning.* Newark, DE: International Reading Association, 1982.

Palincsar, A. S., and Brown, A. L. "Interactive Teaching to Promote Independent Learning from Text." *The Reading Teacher* 39(April 1986):771–77.

Thelen, J. *Improving Reading in Science.* Newark, DE: International Reading Association, 1984.

—————. (ed.) *Ignite! A New Program to Build Higher Level Thinking Skills.* New York: Newsweek/International Reading Association, 1987.

Torbe, M., and Medway, P. *The Climate for Learning.* Montclair, NJ: Boynton/Cook, 1981.

Vacca, R. T.; Vacca, J.; and Gove, M. K. *Reading and Learning to Read.* Boston: Little, Brown, 1987.

Active Involvement in Writing

Many pre-school children play at writing as they play in general. Scribbles, rudimentary drawings, and other pseudowriting satisfy the young child's interest in exploring the uses of pencils and paper as toys. As children become more aware of the communicative function of written language, their writing play becomes more focused and more purposeful. They may write "messages" or "stories" and show these proudly to playmates or parents. These early experiences with writing are generally pleasurable and rewarding. Children write because they enjoy doing so; their efforts are recognized and praised by parents and others around them.

When children enter school, teachers need to build on these early satisfying experiences by encouraging continued exploration and by providing the recognition and praise that will maintain the children's positive attitudes toward writing. At the same time, teachers must gradually introduce a variety of writing experiences that will help children develop greater facility with written expression. In the chapters that follow, we examine the means to these two ends. Chapter 6 is concerned with writing done for the student's own use (e.g., jottings, notes, journals). This type of writing is not destined to receive a grade or to be shared, except perhaps informally. Experiences with private writing build writing fluency and encourage nonthreatening exploration with written language. Chapter 7 discusses public writing that is intended to be shared with an audience. Public writing requires that the writer pay attention to such features as clarity and mechanical accuracy. This type of writing is refined by successive revision. Experiences with public writing encourage students to attend carefully to their purpose for writing and to the audience who will respond to their words.

Either private or public writing may be in any of several modes (e.g., narrative, expository, poetic) or may include a combination of modes. Many students find writing easier and more enjoyable when they can make up a story or write a personal narrative, such as an account of a firsthand experience. Hence, there is good reason to encourage this kind of writing in the classroom. However, students also need experience with exposition, because they will probably use that mode more than any other when they leave school. Mature writers often write letters, reports, memoranda, or other kinds of explanatory prose related to their work and personal lives, and the audiences for these communications generally expect the writing to be clear and polished. A good writing program will maintain a balance among different modes of expression to help students gain confidence and skill with a wide variety of writing tasks.

In these chapters, the teaching of writing is examined with particular attention to the ways in which writing is a thinking process. Different kinds of writing demand different kinds of thinking. The thought that goes into the creation of an original story is different from the thought that underlies an orderly presentation of a body of information that one would find in a report. Describing an event in one's private journal involves a different kind of thinking than is expected in describing the same event for a wider audience. When students respond to other students' work, there are also many opportunities for careful thought about how the writer's work affects the audience.

In addition to emphasizing writing as a thinking process, these chapters stress the value of integrating writing with other language activities. Writing is best and most easily accomplished when it stems from and leads to reading, listening, and discussion. With such a focus on integration, writing can proceed as a natural adjunct to other forms of communication.

Private writing—unrevised, unevaluated work—can give students needed experience and can help them become comfortable with the process.

6

Private Writing

Most students spend very little time writing for their own, private purposes. A few keep diaries at home; even fewer compose stories or poems or write about their studies just because they want to. The great majority write only when they are called upon to complete an assignment. It is not surprising, then, that most students lack practice, confidence, and an understanding of the writing process. Private writing—unrevised, unevaluated work—can give students needed experience and can help them become comfortable with the process.

Three kinds of private writing are described here: journals, learning logs, and writing that stems directly from reading and talking. Any of these, or a combination of the three, may be included regularly in the language arts program or may be tied to one or more other curriculum areas, including science, mathematics, or social studies. These activities build positive attitudes toward writing and help students see that writing is a meaningful form of communication. In the process, students can develop fluency in writing. They will also have the chance to practice mechanics such as spelling without feeling pressured to achieve perfect accuracy.

Journals

Inexperienced writers sometimes have great trouble thinking of a topic and writing about it fluently and naturally. Professional writers have these difficulties too. The difference between these two types of writers is in the commitment of the professionals to *write*—they do not give up in despair. They often use journals for practice and reflection or for developing ideas that later will become finished works. A journal is simply a notebook of private writing—it is a collection of notes, observations, and other fragments that may later be used in finished pieces or that may simply be kept as a record of thoughts and experiences. As writers scribble, dream, and experiment in their journals, they also achieve insights about themselves that can make their lives more satisfying and their published works richer and fresher. As Huyghe (1981) points out:

> Writers often mention that journal keeping provides them with subject matter and helps them develop a natural style. Most often, however, journal writing is cited by practitioners for its cathartic function. The journal is, and has been throughout history, a tool for self-understanding. (p. 101)

A journal can be equally as useful for the inexperienced writers who are students. The journal allows students to explore knowledge and attitudes through "expressive writing" (Britton, 1970; Britton et al., 1975). Journals can also generate new ideas and perspectives; students may discover what they want to say as they write (Elbow, 1973).

Writing-for-self has been recognized as vital for building effective writing ability. Some years ago, Moffett (1968) identified the journal as an important element in an effective language arts program. More recently Botel (1977) accorded "sustained writing" particular significance as a major feature of a state plan for communication arts instruction. Robertson (1975) and Robinson (1985), in extensive reviews of the literature, stress the increasing value that teachers are discovering in students' journals. Both researchers emphasize the usefulness of the journal for fostering expressive abilities and for improving students' skill with the writing process. Many teachers now recognize that regular writing in a private journal should be accorded some time every day, or as often as possible, in school. From first graders to high school seniors, all students can benefit from keeping a journal. They may have some trouble getting started; they may not all respond in the same manner. But they will gain different perspectives on themselves and on writing if they are encouraged.

Journal entries are not corrected for spelling, punctuation, or language usage, and students are not required to revise or rewrite journal material. Without the pressure of having to write correctly, students can attend to what they want to say without having to worry simultaneously about properly encoding their thoughts. Freedom from strict evaluation of form and accuracy gives students invaluable experience as real writers.

Getting started with journals first requires a commitment on the teacher's part. Students may resist at first (What is this for? Why should we do this if we don't get a grade?), and the teacher may not see immediate benefits. But the activity is worth the first awkward times, and the teacher must be persistent in expecting students to keep writing. Here are some suggestions for getting the students started:

1. Have students select notebooks to use solely for their journals. Encourage them to choose special books—spiral-bound books in their favorite colors or with unusual covers, or perhaps bound books containing blank pages.
2. Set aside a time every day, or several times a week, for journal writing. A regular time is best at first. Students may do best at a time such as just after lunch or at the beginning of a class period.
3. Establish the rules. During journal-writing times, students may not study, talk, or work on anything else. They must write in their journals.
4. The first journal-writing sessions should last no longer than three to five minutes. Most students will still be writing when the time is up. The time span can be increased gradually as students become more comfortable and involved with this type of writing.
5. Give students ideas of what they might want to write about. Make suggestions, not requirements. Many stimuli will work; here are some examples:

   - tell what you are doing today
   - write how you feel
   - begin a letter to someone
   - describe the weather

- tell what you believe
- describe a friend or family member
- write about a book you are reading
- begin a story
- write a poem
- explain how to do something
- draw a picture and tell about it
- write a dialogue between you and a friend
- tell some jokes

Suggestions for journal entries may also stem from curriculum-related topics. Questions about selections from literature that are being studied in class, or about other subject matters, may give students ideas to write about. Macrorie (1970) also suggests showing students examples of journal entries, especially from famous journal keepers, to present possible topics for their own journals.

6. Explain to students why they are expected to write journal entries. Tell them of the pleasure that journals can bring, of their function in clarifying thought, and of their value as expressive writing.
7. Be a model for the class. Write in your own journal.

Most students will adjust to the routine in a few weeks. Many will come to value the quiet, private time with their own thoughts that the journal brings. Some will become so involved that they will continue working on their journals at home.

Milz (1980) made journal keeping a regular activity for first-grade students. She gave the children 8½″ × 11″ notebooks the first week of school, explaining that they could write in the books as they wished. Students wrote whenever they wanted to during the day. Milz read the entries daily, frequently writing responses and messages but not correcting spelling or language use. In the margins, she also wrote "adult" observations on the children's efforts; the students ignored these comments. Many children at first scrawled only their names and a few other words. But soon most were writing sentences, short accounts, stories, and records of personal experiences. They also invented narratives starring favorite characters from the stories they heard in class. When a child filled one notebook, it was sent home to be shared proudly with his or her family. Parents read the "adult" notes and better understood how their children were moving toward literacy. As the year progressed, children's entries increased in fluency, showed improved control over the conventions of spelling and punctuation, and reflected the students' growing sense of writing as communication. There was great excitement when a book was almost filled; a child's writing increased markedly at those times.

The journals were only one element of the rich communication environment this teacher created. Students also had mailboxes in the room for receiving messages from the teacher and their peers. Parents were encouraged to enclose notes in their children's lunch boxes. The students had pen pals (older students in the school and education majors at a local university). Because of this teacher's commitment to presenting writing as a natural act of self-expression and communication, these students wrote easily and fluently. Their journals were a concrete record of their growing proficiency with writing skills.

Other teachers have devised different strategies for encouraging journal keeping. Fader and Shaevitz (1966) worked with adolescents and required a certain amount of paper to be "covered." Students could write what they wished as long as they wrote the set amount. This arbitrary rule, along with the teacher's acceptance of any sort of content, helped poor achievers overcome their resistance toward writing and, over time, they developed fluency. Schlenz (1983) also encouraged writing about almost anything but made a point of suggesting topics daily, "cleverly selected to surreptitiously address a major theme" of the literature being studied in class. Whatever the strategy, the teacher must provide time, must encourage participation, and must avoid correction of these private writings.

Although journal entries are not corrected or graded, the act of writing can be evaluated, and content may be assessed informally. Some teachers circulate as students write, conspicuously placing a check in the grade book to show students that they are being credited for writing even if their pieces are not graded. Other teachers verify that students have filled the required number of pages of their notebooks. Still others ask students for written self-evaluations of journal keeping. Different procedures can be devised to suit the class. The principle is to credit participation, not to grade the product.

Although many teachers respect students' privacy and do not read journals, others do read entries periodically, writing margin notes about the content alone and sometimes writing full responses (Gambrell, 1985). Either approach is acceptable, but if the teacher intends to read the journals, students should know this fact beforehand so that their privacy is not inadvertently invaded. Informal response by the teacher may encourage more writing, because a teacher's comments and praise can stimulate students to elaborate and extend their entries. Also, through reading journals, the teacher gains regular opportunities to evaluate progress. Over time, students' written expressions will improve, and the gains will show in their journals.

As students accumulate journal material, their entries can serve as a source of ideas for public writing assignments. Many assignments based on journal entries are possible. Here are a few:

- Read a journal entry to a partner. Discuss additions, alterations, improvements. Revise and polish.

- Rewrite an entry as a dialogue (a letter, a narrative, an essay).

- Describe a person, place, or event in detail, using journal material as a first draft.

- Rewrite an entry from another person's perspective (a teacher's, a parent's, a friend's).

- Turn an entry into a front-page newspaper story.

As a record of day-to-day thinking, observing, and feeling, journals do more than give students practice with writing; indeed, journals freeze time. At the end of the year, students will have an accumulation of material that was interesting enough to write about at certain points in their lives. Only those who have kept a journal can understand the unique pleasure of reading entries that were made months before. The writer is surprised and delighted to be reminded of a funny incident, is amazed at earlier feelings, and is intrigued by words that were written, forgotten, and now recaptured. The journal is worth keeping and treasuring as a part of oneself.

Writing in a journal is like reading for pleasure. Teachers know that it is important to allow students time to browse in the library, to have quiet recreational reading time in class, and to explore the world of books without fear of being questioned or tested on the contents. Few teachers doubt the importance of free reading for developing positive attitudes toward reading and for giving students the chance to practice skills with books they truly enjoy. Just so, journal writing provides the chance to write—for the *pleasure* of it.

Learning Logs

Private writing can also be a direct aid to learning in all subjects (Martin et al., 1976; Geeslin, 1977; Beyer and Brostoff, 1979; Draper, 1979; Giroux, 1979). Emig (1977) stresses that the process of writing is similar to other successful learning strategies in that it requires active, personal involvement and focused attention to the topic, all of which aid learning. A most useful device is the learning log (Platt, 1975; Healy, 1979), a journal based on the course of study. To keep a learning log, students write, after a lesson, about the concepts that were covered. They record what they have learned, what they are unsure of, and what questions or comments they have about the lesson. Kept regularly, learning logs significantly improve content learning and concept clarity (Weiss and Walters, 1979). Like personal journals, learning logs also give practice with writing and help to demystify the process.

Learning logs, like journals, are not graded. They function as informal records of learning, not as quizzes. Students are free to write whatever they can to review concepts in their own words. Spelling and sentence structure may not be polished, but students will be responding to course material in meaningful ways. The following examples show the diversity of expression and thinking that this kind of writing can stimulate.

A sixth-grade class spent a session learning about the work of volunteer firefighters. The lesson was part of a week's activities on fire prevention. The following entries were written impromptu at the end of the period:

We learned that firemen have to wear a cloth to cover their ears so the heat won't bother them. Volunteer firefighters don't get paid for doing their work. They have other jobs that they get paid for. When there is a fire, they have a transmitter to tell them where the fire is. They also have a walkie talkie in case they need help in the house or apartment. They can just call in for help or if they need more men. They have a thing that looks like a stretcher and they need that for getting people that are hurt. If the firefighters can't bring a person up, they need the fireladder.

Today I learned all about the kind of equipment firemen use when they fight a fire. I also learned that volunteer firemen carry radios, and that whenever they go into a fire they have an oxygen tank. I didn't realize how many fires there are and how close they are. I also didn't know that they use burned down buildings for practice and that the hoses have to be dry before they are used.

Today I learned that you have to know a lot about fire to fight it. I also learned that you have to wear fireproof pants and jackets and steel toe boots, so if you step on something sharp it won't hurt you. Also you have to wear a plastic hat with a face protector. They give you an oxygen mask so if you breathe in harmful gases, you won't pass out. I learned that gases are very harmful, and if you don't wear a gas mask or stay low, you'll pass out. It takes a lot of hard work to fight a fire. You have to be ready to go in less than a minute. It takes about 30 seconds to get your clothes on. I learned that firemen can't see in the fire and they have to hold onto each other. And if you hold on to the wall with the inner part of your hand, you will get an electrical shock.

It doesn't take firemen and ladies on the fire company long to put on the protection they need. When they go to a fire fight, the hoses get wet, and when they do it takes 10 hours to dry them. They go in two at a time and talk to each other. When a fire is put out, they tear a piece of wood out of the wall to see if any fire is left going. Firefighters have a pocket transmitter, and a radio they communicate with if anyone gets hurt. About every 30 seconds a fire is reported in the United States.

I learned this period all about how firemen dress and what other equipment they use. We had a fire two houses down, up at my grandmother's. (The house was just sitting there. No one lived in it.) At one o'clock in the morning, I heard sirens. Then the lady next door came racing out of her house screaming "Wanda, quick get out of your house." (Wanda is my grandmother's name.) It was so funny, she was pulling her hair and screaming. My best friend lived right next door to that house.

There's a lot more that happened about that story but I don't have enough time. The next morning the house's picture was in the paper. It looked like a haunted house. In the paper it also told about the fireman that the roof fell on. When the ambulance went by, I caught a glimpse of his face. Man, was that awful!

A fourth-grade class spent two days studying forms of matter. On the first day, they did some simple experiments and talked about molecules. On the second day, they read a selection about how water behaves in its different states. Here are some of their log entries:

Day 1

Today I learned about molecules. You can not see them. Everything is made of molecules, tables, books, chairs, water, and rocks.

Today I learned more about molecules than I did know. I learned stuff about liquid, solids, and gas. Put it this way. I learned a lot.

You cannot see molecules because they are invisible. Particles are made out of molecules. When we poured sugar into water, we thought it disappeared. It didn't. It dissolved, but the molecules were still there. We could taste the sugar. And when Mrs. Jones sprayed lysol we could tell it was still there because we could smell it. The molecules just spread out in the air.

Day 2

I learned that when water freezes it expands, and I got to read a new story about breaking a cannon ball. They filled it with water and it froze overnight.

When water molecules freeze, they get bigger. If water gets into the cracks in the highway and freezes the highway cracks. That's how we get pot holes. The water in the cannonball expanded and got bigger. The cannonball blew up.

I learned that water molecules don't go away, they just change. Like when you freeze water it makes ice. Ice is bigger. If you melt the ice till it boils it makes steam. Gas and steam are about the same thing.

Another fourth-grade class spent a week studying insects. Here are two log entries, each written at the end of the week:

All insects have six legs and three body parts which are head, thorax, abdoman. There are two sages they are called Medimorepheses it is a long word to remember. A complete medimorepheses has four stages they are eggs, larva, pupa, and adult. Bees are so amazing the queen bee is choosey for a clean honey comb to lay her eggs. The insects have their skeleton on the outside. The insects breathe out of little holes called sparticalls.

I've learned alot about bees. There is only one queen bee of a hive and she's the only bee who lays the eggs. The drone bee does not have a sting. The queen bee only uses her sting to kill other queen bees. The drone always stays in the hive and makes with the queen. The worker bees collect pollen and necter for honey and beebread for the baby bees and also feed the larvas. And they build new cells and repair old ones for new babys all that time the drone makes with the queen. The worker bees are not just males they are females also.

These entries all reveal students' depth of understanding of the lessons. The sixth graders grasped the material on firefighters quite well. They were able to write rather a lot in a short period of time, and they recalled and explained clearly a number of specific facts. Because the lesson was based on concrete information and familiar phenomena, students' levels of learning were relatively high. (One student had such a memorable experience with an actual fire that his entry focused on that rather than lesson content. As this example shows, log entries may not always reflect the lesson directly. This student's firsthand experience was too vivid to be ignored when the class learned about fires. The writing thus reinforced learning in a different way, by stimulating a second look at a personal experience.)

The fourth graders' entries on matter and molecules are shorter and reveal less depth of understanding. This is not surprising, given their ages and the relative difficulty of the material. However, individuals had clear concepts about certain things: Molecules were there even when the sugar dissolved; water expands when it freezes, causing pavements to crack. The children who wrote about insects showed a good grasp of the basic concepts presented. Use of precise vocabulary shows that they were beginning to understand these terms, even though new words were not yet well established in their vocabularies ("Medimorepheses it is a long word to remember.").

There are distinct advantages to using learning logs. Because their writing follows a lesson, with stimulating material as a base, students are usually able to write easily. They experience the pleasure of fluency instead of the frustration of writer's block. This is good for building up confidence in writing. Also, students must think about the material, recalling facts, vocabulary, and key concepts. The material becomes more meaningful; as they write, they reor-

The value of learning logs is cumulative. As students make entries regularly, they acquire the habit of writing. Writing becomes a natural thing to do, not a chore.

ganize ideas and express in their own words what they have comprehended. By producing their own explanations, they can see for themselves where they lack understanding about processes or terms. Their writing reflects and stimulates their thinking, and they discover that writing is a way of learning.

The value of learning logs is cumulative. As students make entries regularly, they acquire the habit of writing. Writing becomes a natural thing to do, not a chore; the process seems easier. Their logs are soon filled with personal reactions and unique comments; the children learn to speak naturally in print. Also, as students write often about their studies, they will refer to key ideas again and again, repeatedly reinforcing learning as they think about and use new words and concepts in different contexts. For some examples, here are successive entries from science learning logs of elementary-grade students:

STUDENT 1

March 6

Lots of leeches on rocks. Animals in our pond. Rock, moss, and soil specimeins. Erosion on the rocks. Salamanders and snails like each other. The bridge is broken there's a big gap right smack dab in the middle of it.

March 21

Today we had a flash-flood. It will be written in the paper. The Brandywine was flooded and the creek near my house was also flooded. Our 3rd pond is in sedimentation. Today we had part of a water cycle today. It was raining. Alot of soil washed away.

April 4

Yesterday I went to the Philadelphia zoo. It had a pond just like ours except they have waterbugs not fish. I could bring in some waterbugs if I could catch them. The space shuttle Challenger took off at 1:30. We have had 9 days off. It has been 14 days since I have written in this book.

April 14

Mrs. Bradley brought 20 guppies. I brought in waterbugs and a baby snail. The temperature is 63. I hope the Great White snails won't eat the guppies. We are going to the science park. I can't wait. I hope somebody has an extra pair of boots.

April 15

I had to borrow Debbies boots. They wern't waterproof so I couldn't go in the water. I found a lot of clay. I also found some rocks that could possibly be graphite which can be pressed under certain pressure and turn into a genuine diamond. Graphite is made out of carbon materials. From the evidence I can see so far there was once a cave with a little stream running through. I am thinking of taking records of what I see and see what there was about one-million years ago or longer. I have found a small staigmite.

STUDENT 2

March 15

We put huge snails in our pond. We colected soil, water, clay, and other interesting plants. We put salamanders in the pond too. We got a bigger tank for our class. There was a lot of sedimentation in our pond. Now most of the water is clear.

March 21

We are having flash floods today. A lot of the roads are flooded. The water cycle was really working today. It is not raining right now. Michele brought in a lima bean that sprouted. We are putting the snails in the big tank. Mrs. Dougherty is getting more snails.

March 24

I think the reason all of our fish are dying is because we don't have a lid on ours. I had fish once and we didn't put a lid on ours and they croaked. We don't have salamanders in our tank. Correction we just put one in our tank. We need more snails in our tank to clean it. We put more plants in our tank to give the fish more oxygen. The snails are eating the dead fish. One of the two fish are eating the minerals from the rocks. One of the snails layed eggs and they hatched. We have only two fish in our tank. We have four snails and a few baby ones. I just put in more little blue mineral rocks. I think they will help.

April 4

We had a week off from school. We didn't give the fish anything and they are still living. They are eating the plants and the dead fish that was in the tank. The spaceship Challenger was launched at 1:30 today. We have minnows in our tank.

April 14

We got twenty guppies today. We are praying that the great white snails don't eat them alive. I don't think they will make it. The high today is 63°. We are going to the science park. Thanks to Miss Bradley we now have life in our pond! And off we go! "Whew," we are back from the science park. It was fun. Mrs. Dougherty gave us a speech as we were walking across the bridge with planks. We got some flowers with roots to plant in the classroom. Skunk cabbage was everywhere. We walked in the stream. Chris had boots that went up to his waist.

STUDENT 3

March 16

Our pond has four big snails, a couple salamanders, rocks, and plants in it. We also put on a lid. Mrs. Dougherty put up a chart for the temperature in March. Mrs. Locke is coming in we are wating for her right now. She is going to show us how to make a micro slide. We also found out that some jerks broke the bridge.

March 18

Today in Science we talked about the chart. Some people are going to jot down the highs in March. We also talked about Mrs. Dougherty's classes pond. We didn't add any animals to our pond.

March 22

Our snails in our pond had eggs. The eggs are stuck on the glass. We saw an egg being layed. We added fish to our pond also.

April 5

We are going to keep our calendar going for April. We had a one week vacation and our ponds stayed alive without anyone taking care of it. It had enough water, food, and air for it to stay alive. I think that's amazing! I might make a pond at home myself if I have enough time. We are going to the science park tomorrow. I can't wait. I think I already brought in my boots. The water in the pond doesn't evaporate because we have a lid on it. I hope the bridge is fixed.

April 6

We went out to the science park. Heather got some mud. Chris caught 3 skeeders. I saw some clay, but I didn't want to pick it up. Kelly wore my boots and I wore Kelly's boots. The bridge was broken so we had to walk across one side. It looked like this (drawing). That's all I have time for. See you.

These entries reveal a good grasp of terms that were introduced (*erosion, sedimentation, evaporate*). Students were making these words meaningful as they used them to describe firsthand experiences ("There was a lot of sedimentation in our pond. Now most of the water is clear."). But the writing goes beyond simply reviewing facts, and the entries reveal original thinking. Conclusions are drawn: "Salamanders and snails like each other." Deductive reasoning is exercised: "From the evidence I can see so far there was once a cave with a little stream running through." Hypotheses are formed: "I think the reason all our fish are dying is because we don't have a lid on ours." Purposes are set for future learning: "I am thinking of taking records of what I see and see what there was about one-million years ago or longer." The writing also reflects interesting reactions related to course material—for example, excitement about a field trip and concern for a neighborhood bridge that had been vandalized. There is even attention to the act of writing: "It has been 14 days since I have written in this book." The entries are personal, fluent, and clear. These students were actively involved in thinking, writing, and learning.

The more often students write in their logs, the more useful the activity will be. Entries should be made daily, or at least several times a week, if at all possible. Writing may follow lectures, demonstrations, discussions, reading assignments, films, or field trips. A separate notebook or folder can be used to keep notes in order and in one place. Entries should be dated for future reference. Directions can be simple: Write what you have learned (observed) today. Write about whatever was most interesting (unusual, confusing, important).

Once students establish the habit and are comfortable with keeping logs, the entries can be used to extend learning in several ways:

1. The teacher may collect logs periodically, reading the entries to see how well students are learning the material. This immediate, direct type of response can help the teacher modify future lessons to review difficult concepts. Correction of language usage and mechanics is unnecessary because entries are not revised or graded, but the teacher may want to write marginal notes to students, praising good explanations or clearing up minor confusions. Informal response from the teacher can help students see that their day-to-day learning is as significant as their test performance.
2. Students may work in groups to read aloud their logs. What one has missed, another will have grasped. Group members can help each other clarify their understanding of concepts through reading and discussion.
3. Students may work in groups to compose new explanations of basic concepts, using their log entries as first drafts. Through discussion and group composition, each group can prepare notes or summaries that will be useful for later reviews of the material.
4. Fulwiler (1980) tells how teachers in various disciplines use learning logs. Here are some examples:
   a. A history teacher has students write from their experiences about the topic of the day. For instance, when the class is studying railroad development, students write what they know about trains and so become more personally involved in the topic.
   b. Before the class begins a unit, a natural science teacher has students write what they know about a concept such as conservation. After study, students write again. They and the teacher see how knowledge has increased.
   c. A political science teacher has students record their opinions of current world events.
   d. Fulwiler asks literature students to write daily. In these papers, students might tell their interpretation of a line of poetry, give their reaction to an essay, or write their own opinions about a poem or a chapter in a novel.

These teachers encourage students to read their entries aloud in class, to use them as the basis for short papers, and to reread them to reflect on what they have been learning. The result is active, rather than passive, learning.

Read-Talk-Write

Another form of private writing stems from a reading-talking experience. Based on the principles outlined by Botel (1977), this exercise includes three steps:

1. Students read self-selected materials silently for five to ten minutes. The classroom library or collections of magazines and newspapers can be used as the reading material. Students are told to choose something that looks interesting and to spend a few minutes reading it. They are not expected to finish reading the piece. The teacher times the reading session, stopping the group after a short period.
2. Students work in pairs, taking turns speaking. Each must talk (uninterrupted by the other) about the just-read material. Listeners must be attentive to talkers but should give minimal verbal response; sustained talking, not conversation, is the goal. On the teacher's signal, each first talker begins (all talking at once, but each talking only to a partner). Again on signal, after three or four minutes, students reverse roles.
3. Students write what they just covered orally, each writing for four or five minutes (or longer) until stopped by the teacher.

Reading provides a topic; talking stimulates and organizes thinking. The writing that emerges is fluent and fresh. As an exercise, this three-step process integrates all the language arts and allows for considerable individualization in exercising language skills. Students derive pleasure from dipping into reading; those few minutes spent with the material may stimulate them to finish it later. All have an opportunity to tell, informally, what they read and to hear about what someone else has read. Most important, perhaps, is the great ease that students will have with writing, having just expressed orally what they will then say in print.

At least one reluctant writer has discovered the unique value of this exercise. Ms. Sayer is an intelligent, articulate college graduate. Seeking a career change from science to education, she was working on her teaching certificate and so enrolled in a university course to learn about the teaching of language arts. On one occasion she described to the class her most memorable school experience: a writing class that was completely frustrating to her. As youngsters, she and her classmates had been required to write a theme a week. Errors in their papers were strictly marked, first by the teacher and then by a team of outside readers. Students were required to correct their papers each week, carefully eliminating all the errors that had been noted by all the evaluators. As she described the experience, she said, "I was paralyzed. I hated writing, and I still do!"

The education students wrote learning log entries at the end of each class session. Here is the entry this young woman wrote the day the class participated in a reading-talking-writing exercise like the one just described:

Today I found that writing does not have to be the pure torture that I knew it to be. The read-talk-write exercise showed me that if you have a topic that you have just read about—no matter how trivial—you can still talk about either it or its relationship to you or your ideas. And once having talked about it, writing a short passage (although still not enjoyable or fun because of the hatred I have for writing) can be made easier and less arduous.

Had I had that three times a week every week in seventh grade, I may actually have come to like writing. I do know the only writing I like is writing to my boyfriend when I have so much to say to him I don't know where to start. When I was in the hospital, it was a joy to write to him. I loved to write to him. I could have gotten to like writing if it had not been such a painful experience. This class today was worth the time and money I expended to take it for this experience alone.

I don't think I will ever like to write, but now I can at least understand someone who does like to write. I can understand how they can get the ideas flowing and the words flowing. I have shied away from finishing my Ph.D. because I do not like writing. I had a terrible time doing term papers in college. I did anything not to write. I have even turned in papers in outline form, rough drafts, stapled on quotations. My physics and math teachers would go to the English teacher and plead that I should be allowed to pass because I could read and I did understand.

Ms. Sayer's entry is used with her permission. In the years since she took the graduate class, she has been writing more, for her own purposes, and happily claims that she is slowly overcoming her long-standing aversion to writing.

Private Writing: Some Conclusions

Private writing that is linked to literature study and subject learning can enhance students' appreciation and understanding of the contents of those studies. Responding through private writing, students have the chance to use new concepts and to express their opinions in a natural, easy way. The writing is a form of reflection on what they read or hear, and it allows them to think through new ideas while knowing that they will not be judged on the form and organization of those first thoughts.

Private writing also does much to develop students' fluency. Writing freely and often, they get used to putting their thoughts on paper and begin to feel comfortable with the act of writing. Journals, learning logs, and read-talk-write sessions are enjoyable endeavors that help students to maintain positive attitudes toward writing. Writing in these ways, knowing that their errors will be overlooked, students can develop the confidence that they will need to undertake writing for an audience.

Suggested Activities

1. Keep a journal for three weeks. Write an entry every day. Evaluate the experience. Did you notice any changes in your writing or in your attitude toward writing?
2. Team with a peer. Each of you should read a magazine or a book for five minutes. Then, take turns explaining what you read. After talking, write a summary of what you read. Discuss how the reading and the talking influenced your writing.
3. Plan a content-area lesson that includes writing about a key concept before the instruction is given and after the lesson is completed. Teach the lesson. Compare students' understanding of the concept as revealed in the two written responses.
4. Teach a group of children the prewriting technique of mapping by helping them map memories of first-hand experiences.

References

Beyer, B. K., and Brostoff, A. "Writing to Learn in Social Studies." *Social Education* 43(March 1979):176–77.

Botel, M. *A Comprehensive Reading/Communication Arts Plan.* Harrisburg, PA: Pennsylvania Department of Education, 1977.

Britton, J. *Language and Learning.* London: Penguin, 1970.

——————; Burgess, T.; Martin, N.; McLeod, A.; and Rosen, H. *The Development of Writing Abilities 11–18.* London: Macmillan, 1975.

Draper, V. *Formative Writing to Assist Learning in All Subject Areas.* Berkeley, CA: Bay Area Writing Project/University of California, 1979.

Elbow, P. *Writing Without Teachers.* London: Oxford University Press, 1973.

Emig, J. "Writing as a Mode of Learning." *College Composition and Communication* 28(May 1977):122–27.

Fader, D., and Shaevitz, M. H. *Hooked on Books.* New York: Berkley, 1966.

Fulwiler, T. "Journals Across the Disciplines." *English Journal* 69(December 1980):14–19.

Gambrell, L. B. "Dialogue Journals: Reading-Writing Interaction." *The Reading Teacher* 38(February 1985):512–15.

Geeslin, W. E. "Using Writing About Mathematics as a Teaching Technique." *Mathematics Teacher* 70(February 1977):112–15.

Giroux, H. A. "Teaching Content and Thinking Through Writing." *Social Education* 43(March 1979):190–93.

Healy, M. K. "Learning Logs." Convention presentation. San Francisco: National Council of Teachers of English, 1979.

Huyghe, P. "Diary Writing Turns a New Leaf." *New York Times Magazine* (November 8, 1981):98–108.

Macrorie, K. *Telling Writing.* Rochelle Park, NJ: Hayden, 1970.

Martin, N.; D'Arcy, P.; Newton, B.; and Parker, R. *Writing and Learning Across the Curriculum 11–16.* London: Ward Lock Educational, 1976.

Milz, V. E. "First Graders Can Write: Focus on Communication." *Theory into Practice* 19(Summer 1980):179–85.

Moffett, J. *Teaching the Universe of Discourse.* Boston: Houghton Mifflin, 1968.

Platt, M. D. "Writing Journals in Courses." *College English* 37(December 1975):408–11.

Robertson, P. E. "Psychological and Pedagogical Rationale and Process for the Teaching of Expressive Writing." Unpublished doctoral dissertation. University of Texas at Austin, 1975.

Robinson, J. "Case Studies of the Journal Writing Process: Three Eleventh Grade Journal Writers." Unpublished doctoral dissertation. New York University, 1985.

Schlenz, M. "An Outline for a Classroom Journal and Composition Program." Presentation to the South Coast Writing Project. Santa Barbara, CA: University of California at Santa Barbara, 1983.

Weiss, R. H., and Walters, S. A. "Research on Writing and Learning: Some Effects of Learning-Centered Writing in Five Subject Areas." Presentation to the National Council of Teachers of English. San Francisco, 1979. ERIC Documents No. ED 191 073.

Suggested Readings

Calkins, L. M. *Lessons from a Child.* Portsmouth, NH: Heinemann, 1983.

Cramer, R. L. *Children's Writing and Language Growth.* Columbus, OH: Charles Merrill, 1977.

Graves, D. *Balance the Basics: Let Them Write.* New York: Ford Foundation, 1978.

Haley-James, S. (ed.) *Perspectives on Writing in Grades 1–8.* Urbana, IL: National Council of Teachers of English, 1981.

Hipple, M. L. "Journal Writing in Kindergarten." *Language Arts* 62(March 1985):255–61.

Holdaway, D. *The Foundations of Literacy.* Sydney, Australia: Ashton Scholastic, 1979.

Jaggar, A., and Smith-Burke, M. T. (eds.) *Observing the Language Learner.* Urbana, IL: National Council of Teachers of English and the International Reading Association, 1985.

As students gain fluency and confidence with private writing, they also need experiences with public writing. This type of writing encourages them to consider a variety of audiences and purposes.

7

Public Writing

As students gain fluency and confidence with private writing, they also need varied experiences with public writing—that is, with writing for an audience. Public writing requires students to attend to certain aspects of their work more carefully than when they write only for their own, private purposes. Students must consider if a public piece is organized effectively, if meanings are clear, if words are well chosen and spelled correctly, and if the work achieves its overall purpose. These are some of the issues of public writing—writing that will receive outside response and that is accordingly presented to the best of the writer's ability.

This chapter begins with an overview of the public writing process and goes on to suggest how this process may be used with different forms of discourse. Then imitation writing is described to show how this strategy can lead students to explore many different modes of expression. Finally, there are some specific suggestions for helping students revise and polish their work. Throughout the chapter, particular attention is given to the ways in which writing is a thinking process and to ways of coordinating writing activities with activities involving the other language arts. The relationship between writing and reading is noted throughout and is highlighted at the end of the chapter.

The Process of Public Writing

Ongoing developments in the area of writing instruction have enlarged our views of how public writing may be effected in the classroom. Traditionally, a student's purpose for writing has been set by the teacher, and the teacher has served as the sole audience for the student's work. This situation has made classroom writing rather artificial—an exercise that serves mainly to satisfy the teacher's requirements. Thoughtful teachers now realize that students must learn to define their own writing purposes and that children should write for their classmates and other audiences as well as for the teacher. That is, students must learn to use the process of public writing in more realistic ways, as it is used by those who write for their own purposes and audiences outside of school.

The process of public writing includes prewriting efforts to define topic, purpose, and audience; creation of one or more drafts to shape the work; revision of the drafts to refine the statement of ideas; and editing of the final piece to polish such mechanics as spelling and punctuation. These various steps require effort over time. That is, a writer will seldom compose a satisfactory final draft in one sitting but must be prepared to work to achieve the intended purpose. Also, each stage requires both individual and collaborative efforts. That is, writing involves not just the solitary act of putting words on paper but also discussing the work in progress with others, acting as a responder for other writers, and giving and receiving editorial help. The way students adjust to this multifaceted process is as important as the final products they turn out.

Each step in the process has its own purposes and emphases. For instance, in the early stages a writer organizes and shapes ideas. At this point, the composition need not be mechanically perfect, because the purpose is to develop a train of thought. A first draft is a kind of private writing that may remain in its initial rough form unless the writer decides to present the work to an audience. Revising successive drafts, the writer needs to clarify, elaborate, and in other ways improve the content of a piece rather than simply correct mechanical errors. Finally, when the writer has revised content and wording, the emphasis shifts to details of form and mechanics, such as spelling.

The extent to which students can be encouraged to make full use of this process depends heavily on the purposes that guide their efforts. Students will be more likely to sustain enthusiasm and concentration if they are writing about something that truly interests them, if they feel they have something important to say, and if they know a receptive audience will respond to their work. Thus, important groundwork must be laid for any public writing activity.

Adequate time must be given to the prewriting stage, when children are deciding what they wish to write about and what they might have to say once they have an idea in mind. Almost any stimuli can serve as a starting point. For instance, the teacher may read a story or show a film that will spark discussion and lead to writing. Content-area units of study or interesting occurrences at home or school may also provide children with ideas to share and thus give them a reason to write. In the early grades, children may simply talk informally for several minutes until they decide what they want to write about. In the later grades, prewriting preparation may take longer and may include more extensive discussion and perhaps some preliminary notes. No matter what the stimuli or mode of preparation, however, time is needed at this point for thinking and talking.

As students begin to write, they need to realize that their initial work will be considered a draft, subject to revision, and that they will have several opportunities to receive help with that revision. Concerns about mechanical accuracy should be minimal as students put their first thoughts in writing. When these drafts have been completed, students need to meet with each other and with the teacher to consider how they might revise their work. In the early grades, such revision may involve simply adding a thought or two to the piece. In later grades, students may consider aspects of organization, emphasis, or coherence. In the final stages of revision, students need to fix up spelling and other mechanical details. No matter how simple or extensive the revisions and editing, students will benefit from sharing works in progress and using the response they get to consider what they have accomplished by writing. The ongoing process of writing, sharing, and rewriting helps students see that they have an interested audience for their work and that their efforts are valued.

Although this ongoing process lends considerable credibility to classroom writing activities, students' reasons for writing are still somewhat artificial if the writing never leaves the confines of the classroom. As often as possible, students should have the pleasurable experience of sharing their work with a wider audience. Parents, of course, are natural audiences, and students will enjoy taking some revised and polished pieces home. More extended audiences include readers of a school newspaper or a school district's literary magazine. In some schools, children bind some of their works in book form and display these at a young authors' book festival or donate them to the school library. Submissions to local newspapers or children's magazines provide still other outlets for student writing. These various forms of publication give children especially meaningful reasons for writing and enhance students' pride in their work.

Public writing can take many forms. Among these forms are essays, stories, letters, scripts, poems, letters, and instructions. The different types are not all discussed in this chapter. Rather, a few have been selected for emphasis in order to make certain points about writing for an audience. Whatever form public writing takes, the goals are essentially the same: to develop students' confidence and skill with the process of sharing their ideas in writing.

Expressive Writing

As Britton (1982) points out, expressive speech or writing is an intimate form of communication that provides "information about the speaker as well as conveying his message about the world; revealing, for example, the speaker's attitude towards his message, towards his listener and towards his present state of mind. . . ." (p. 124). Britton contrasts expressive language with "transactional" and "poetic" language, both of which involve greater distance between the speaker or writer and the audience. Thus, there is a greater degree of formality in the way language is used. Britton goes on to stress that "expressive writing might be seen as a beginner's all-purpose instrument; and 'learning to write' would involve the progressive evolution both of the other two forms, transactional and poetic, and of the mature forms of expressive writing that we continue to use in personal letters and the like" (p. 124).

In other words, children will develop facility with writing to the extent that they are allowed to write as if they were talking directly to their audience. Their writing will thus closely reflect the speech that they use so easily and naturally for communication. As they extend their experiences with language and with the world, and as their command of oral language is extended and improved, they will gradually be able to use language in other, more formal, ways to deal with more unfamiliar topics and to address audiences who are relatively distant.

Expressive writing may be encouraged through the use of journals and other private writings, as described in Chapter 6. However, the expressive mode should also be encouraged in writing that children wish to share with an audience. As mentioned earlier, many children find it easiest and most enjoyable to write from firsthand experience. In the early grades, especially, children's activities at home and in school provide excellent material that can be shaped into simple, personal narratives or descriptive pieces in the expressive mode. For instance, here is an account from a primary-grade child about her pet. This is the first-draft form, before the child attempted revision and editing.

You would like my dog. His name is rusty. He is a tereer. He ate a bone last night and on Wen. he almost killed a squeel. Dering the summing he run across the road and almost got hit. If I am doing my homework and he wants me to play with him he bits me.

The advantage of this kind of writing is that students are dealing with subjects that are important to them and about which they have something significant to say. Such personal interest and involvement with the topic makes ideas relatively easy to generate and leads naturally to the use of expressive language. Once this child decided to write about her dog, several ideas readily occurred to her. She discussed these briefly with a small group of classmates and composed her first draft with little difficulty, writing her ideas as she had expressed them orally. When she read her account to another group of classmates, their questions encouraged her to add more information. Again, she was easily able to elaborate because she was drawing on firsthand experience and had discussed possible additions with her peers. Here is her second draft:

You would like my dog. His name is rusty. He is a tereer. He ate a bone last night. We gave him the bone after diner. He went ovr to the rug and chooed and chooed. On Wen. he almost killed a squeel. He chasd the squeel all around the yard and then he jumped at it. But the squeel got away. If I am doing my homework and he wants me to play with him he bits me.

In later grades, firsthand experiences continue to provide a wealth of material for young writers. Older students will be ready to shape their experiences into somewhat more sophisticated form, but their writing will still be grounded in what they know well and will reflect their unique perspectives and modes of expression. Here, for example, is a first draft composed by a fifth-grade girl that resulted from a group discussion of surprising or perplexing incidents in the children's lives:

THERE ARE NO SUCH THINGS AS GHOSTS

One day I had to go to a camp for a week in the summer. While I was away my friend Mary Beth was going to have a welcome back party for me. She decided that she was going to try to give me a real scare, too. She had planned to throw the party the day after I got back.

So I came home from camp and I find that all my chairs were gone and my desk and even some of my clothes. She had nerve, real nerve. So I ran down to my mom to ask her where all my stuff had gone. Mary Beth had told her all about her plan. So my mom said that she didn't know what happened. "You don't think there's a ghost, do you?" she said.

"No! There's no such things as ghosts!" I said.

Then she said, "It will all probably be there in the morning. Just go to bed." So I did.

The next morning it wasn't there. I was really scared now. Then the phone rang. At least it was still there. It was Mary Beth. "Want to come on over? I got something to show you," she said.

"Sure," I said. "Nothing's going for me here."

As soon as I got there she opened the door and everyone yelled surprise. I looked up and saw a sign that said WELCOME HOME. Then I saw all my stuff that was missing.

"Did I scare you?" she asked.

"You sure did," I said. Then I thought, just wait till Halloween, Mary Beth, just wait.

Reading this first draft to a small group of peers, the writer received positive response for describing an amusing incident and for bringing the event to life with her use of realistic dialogue. Encouraged by this response, she eagerly accepted suggestions for revision and continued working on the piece.

Placing too much emphasis on a "right" way to write in the early grades usually intimidates youngsters and prevents them from fully developing their own expressive voices as writers. This type of pressure hampers the development of the confidence and skill they will need if they are to write with growing strength and versatility as they mature. Rather than requiring students to write certain forms of discourse or to use certain sentence structures or organizational patterns in their work, the teacher needs to encourage children to write about what they know in their own language. From these efforts, the children's unique voices and viewpoints will emerge. As this raw material is shaped and refined through collaborative revision, students will develop confidence as writers and will gradually improve their skill with written language.

Reports

The report is a traditional school writing assignment that requires a writer to find information about a topic, to organize the material, and to prepare a written account that reflects attention to correct form and mechanics. In some schools, primary-grade children are expected to learn the basics of report writing. In almost all schools, by the time children reach the third or fourth grade, they must write reports regularly. Report writing continues in high school and college, culminating in term papers and theses. Although school reports may include some original ideas, almost all require the synthesizing of material that others said or wrote.

The report is difficult for many students, especially for those in elementary school, because they are just beginning to write this kind of project. The typical report requires persistent library work. Sources must be perused, notes kept in order, and all put together coherently and properly. It is no wonder that students spend inordinate amounts of time producing maps, illustrations, charts, and elaborate covers. Completing those tasks is not as difficult as trying to understand new concepts and writing to meet teachers' standards of quality. Moffett (1979) questions the authenticity of such writing, pointing out that it involves "minimal authorship" (p. 277). Indeed, most papers of this sort reflect only determined, even desperate, efforts to finish the assignment. There is little effort to communicate something interesting or meaningful.

As it is usually handled, the report does not provide the best way to occupy a student's time and energy. However, reports are firmly entrenched as school tasks, and the assignments do reflect typical demands of the nonschool world in that they often require writing that is not done out of personal choice. Thus, this kind of writing needs to be learned. This being the situation, report assignments should be handled as intelligently and thoughtfully as possible.

First we must consider what the report is. It is, essentially, a piece of writing that is assigned so that students will learn to take a body of material, interpret and summarize it, give it a personal perspective, and present it in acceptable form. The more remote the body of material is from a student's experience and knowledge, the more difficult it will be for the student to interpret it, summarize it, and give it a personal perspective. This is evident to anyone who has had to prepare a report on an unfamiliar subject. The less interesting the topic is to the writer, the more forced and artificial the report will be. This phenomenon is evident to anyone who has been stuck with the last topic on an assigned list because everyone else quickly volunteered to write about the others. The keys to well-written reports include having some familiarity with the subject, and having reasonable, if not considerable, interest in the topic.

Those who agree with this point of view will see the logic of the following suggested activities. These projects reflect the belief that students should mainly write reports based on firsthand experience. Students should then move gradually and only occasionally into reports that require vicarious experience (e.g., reading about the subject). The best topics are those that students suggest themselves or that they may at least select from a wide range of choices.

Saturation Reports

Saturation reporting or "reporter-at-large" writing (Moffett, 1968) is based on the writer's immersion in a firsthand experience. Students produce a completely original piece that stems from their careful observations of a self-selected occasion, place, or group of people. This approach to reporting is advocated by the National Writing Project[1] as a stimulating experience of observing, thinking, and writing. Teachers who use the activity regularly have slightly different approaches, depending on the particular students they work with. What follows is a typical sequence of activities.

Students select a place of interest. In school they might choose the cafeteria, the library, the principal's office, or a locker room. Out of school they may decide on the beach, a market, a busy local street, or a farm yard. The target might also be a group of people (movie-goers, restaurant diners, a soccer team) or a special occasion (a parade, a concert, a Super Bowl). Students first observe, "saturating" themselves with the sights, sounds, and atmosphere of the subject. They may remain unobtrusive, only looking and listening, or they may interview people and take part in events. They get a feel for the subject, and they record details while observing and experiencing. Children may gather data individually or with partners.

Students examine their notes and reflect on the experience to define the general impression they perceived and want to convey in writing. A visit to a playground may have impressed them with the gleeful, charming liveliness of preschoolers. The local fire house may have had an atmosphere of alert preparedness. The Little League game may have revealed the concentrated effort of sport. Class discussions at this time can help students identify and convey different general impressions. Reading selections may be introduced so that students can note how other authors created certain effects; saturation reports from former classes can be read and discussed.

Students begin to select details from their notes that best illustrate their overall impressions. They start to form a cohesive whole of the bits of information that have been gathered. Conversations, facial expressions, objects, weather, and incidents are all reexamined and assessed. Students could also consider that the small segment of society they observed may in some way reflect key elements of the larger society. For example, the local police station may present a microcosm of the criminal justice system. Such an observation may be developed along with a portrayal of the essence of the subject if students seem able to handle the notion of a theme. In any case, the primary object of the saturation report is to describe the experience so vividly that readers feel as if they have actually gone through it themselves.

Students also consider the audience to whom they will address their reports. Will they be writing to peers who will understand certain things with little explanation? To young children who will want to be entertained? To adults who need to be convinced? As students think about an intended audience, they must decide what background the readers probably have, what would interest

---

[1] The National Writing Project is a consortium of teacher training projects modeled after the Bay Area Writing Project (University of California at Berkeley).

them, and what kind of language would be appropriate. Raw material is again assessed as students select the best information to engage their audience.

Students write first drafts of their reports, using the selected details to create the overall impression and/or to develop the chosen theme. They write with the intended audience in mind. Then students revise and polish their works, working both in small groups and individually to rewrite, edit, and correct their work. (See Revising and Polishing, Chapter 7, for suggestions on helping students work together.)

Students submit final drafts to the teacher for evaluation. Their papers are also shared publicly in some way. They may be duplicated and bound together so that each student receives a booklet containing all the reports, or students may read their papers aloud to the whole class.

Saturation reports require firsthand observation and original composition based on the writers' perspectives of the subjects. The unit activities develop thinking-writing abilities to a high degree as students organize their material to create the intended impression, evaluate works in progress, and produce a piece that reflects creative effort. Students usually become intensely involved in their reports because they are writing from their own experience for their own purposes. Working together, and with the teacher's guidance, they learn a variety of effective writing techniques: creating a mood, selecting the best vocabulary, incorporating dialogue, organizing details effectively, and bringing the

Saturation reports require firsthand observation and original composition based on the writers' perspectives of the subjects.

piece to a good conclusion. These are not learned as isolated exercises but are approached within the context of the need to create a paper that "works."

Here is an example of a finished report that shows what one student reporter produced. This was written by a fourth grader.

OUR HOUSE

My sister is getting ready to do dishes and my mom and dad are watching t.v. Little Bits is chirping happily. My mom is in the rocking chair and my dad is on the floor. Patches, our dog, is trying to sleep. I can hear the t.v. well. Charley is chirping back to Little Bits. Corky is sitting on his perch. It's quiet except for the t.v. and the birds. My mom is rocking back and forth. My mom is enjoying the show. It's bright because of the lights. The show is sad. Patches is looking for a comfortable position. My research cube is swinging (I swing it a lot). My dad is watching "Eye on L.A." right now and my sister, Becky, is doing her homework. She is talking her problems out loud. It sounds funny. I think she's doing math.

I guess she's finished because she's starting to do ice trays and now she's doing dishes. My dad is smoking. I can hear Becky doing dishes. Becky is washing dishes and I can hear the water. It is loud. My mom and dad are laughing. It is a funny show. My mom is still smiling. I can hear the silverware. My sister keeps peeping in. My mom laughed again. My mom just said, "Are you O.K.?"

I said, "Who me?"

My sister asked, "What are we going to watch?"

Becky and Dad are talking. I can hear dripping and a bang! I can hear the drain and some water. My sister just walked by. My sister is watching t.v. right now. My mom just screamed. They are watching "Battle of the Network Stars." My sister is eating pie. They are having a swimming competition. There are fireworks on t.v. Now it's parachuting. I can hear Becky's fork banging. The t.v. is playing music. They are telling about stars and their shows. I can hear a glass tapping. Dad is still smoking. Becky is talking about the show. I can hear the birds. The t.v. is loud. Dad is sitting in the rocking chair now. Becky is on the floor. Sherry somebody is talking. Dad is smoking again. A commercial for video games was just on. My sister just laughed. They are talking about the score. They are talking about the stars' football game. Their game is going on now. That's a live report from my house.

Students who write saturation reports have a solid, meaningful purpose for writing. Their aims are to tell what they have experienced firsthand and to share their perspective with others. Because their own observations are the source of information, they write in their own voice. The reports have a fresh, straightforward tone.

As with any activity, saturation reporting requires experience and practice to reach high standards of quality. As children progress through the grades, their vocabulary and sentence structure will become more mature. With more experience, they will also be able to draw insightful conclusions about their observations, and their reports will show their growing ability to interpret as well as describe events. In any grade, however, even students' first attempts with this assignment will result in writing that is quite good in comparison with the usual reports that students produce.

The teacher's experience with the process is as important as the students'. Some teachers have tried the activity once, were disappointed with the results, and gave up, convinced that the method does not work. And it *may* not work the first time. Each teacher will need to try different techniques to get young writers reporting well. Here are a few suggestions for making things go smoothly:

1. Bring in examples of good firsthand accounts for students to hear or read. Use current newspaper feature stories or interviews, articles from magazines such as *National Geographic, Sports Illustrated,* or *Ranger Rick,* and other relevant examples. Discuss these with students. Help them note techniques of using vivid descriptions, dialogue, and anything else that is interesting and age-appropriate. Give them good models to follow, as they begin the unit and as they work on their own reports.

2. Take time to suggest how students might make their own observations. Give them ideas of what to look and listen for: colors, conversation, background noise, weather, objects people use, clothes they wear. Encourage them to observe fully and to write, following journal-style, as soon as possible after they have made their observations. Stress that good observation and full notes will help them when they write.

3. Maintain clear priorities as students begin to write. Help them with content and organization first, stressing the importance of full descriptions and over-all coherence. Save suggestions about spelling, punctuation, and other aspects of form and convention until the report is ready for the final draft.

4. Give students help in working together to revise their writing. (See Revising and Polishing, Chapter 7, for suggested procedures.) Offer your own ideas, but make sure students suggest improvements to each other as often as they listen to what you have to say.

5. Be enthusiastic about the work. Give students something to look forward to. Enable them to work for goals other than a grade. Class publication of the reports takes only a little extra effort at the duplicating machine, and everyone will be glad to have a personal copy of all the papers. Widespread publication might also be possible. The engaging *Foxfire* books, based on this kind of student reporting, have brought much pleasure to the writers and their many readers (Wigginton, 1972).

This reporting process gives students needed practice in examining a body of material, interpreting it, synthesizing it, and presenting it from a personal perspective. Subsequent reporting involving book research will be easier and more meaningful if students learn to select details and to see relationships in the context of concrete, personal experience. But student reporters should not just be preparing to do research-from-books writing. Firsthand saturation reporting is valuable in its own right and is one of the best kinds of writing for students to do because it is original and so clearly communicative.

Reports Based on Reading

A book, bound and official, can be intimidating. The words are fixed—the "authority" wrote them—and the author's particular phrasing may really be the only way to make a statement on the subject. So students think. Aren't they praised most of the time for recalling exactly what the text said? Yet, reports based on book research require students to turn those very words into their own as they write. This process is perplexing and difficult. The body of information is remote and hard to synthesize. As a result, student reports are too often only awkwardly arranged, thinly disguised statements from books.

Encyclopedia language, as this type of writing might be called, is easy to spot. Vocabulary and sentence structure are remarkably precise and sophisticated, not at all typical of the language the student ordinarily uses in speech or writing. For example, here are portions of two reports, completed by fifth-grade children, both of which clearly illustrate encyclopedia language:

LIFE OF THE INDIANS

Each family lived in a section on a raised platform running around the walls. Each was separated from the others by knee-high partitions, some of boards, some of matting. In one or two of the families, possessions were arranged in an orderly fashion or out of sight in chests.

The women made baskets, dog hair blankets, and cedar mats. The women working with bark wore shell in their ears, and their dark faces were streaked with darker paint and tatoo lines. Some wore cedar bark skirts, others merely waistbands, and their bare skin glistened in the dim firelight.

THE OCTOPUS

An octopus has eight arms to help it catch food, which consists chiefly of crabs. It paralyzes a crab by injecting a poison into its body. The crabs are eaten in little pieces. When an octopus crawls, it goes on its arms, moving by a kind of jet propulsion. Like its relatives, the squids, an octopus swims by shooting itself backwards.

Many teachers will experience mixed feelings at receiving such reports. They will feel pleasure at the show of effort but discomfort at the inappropriate language. In high schools and colleges, where students are expected to have acquired scholarly ethics, encyclopedia language is severely frowned upon as plagiarism. At any level, this kind of writing is usually not part of an intentional effort to pass off someone else's work as one's own. Rather, it involves simply an ineffective, naive attempt to complete the assignment.

Some teachers make special efforts to have students use their own words in one paper, only to find source language in the next. Others will overlook the problem altogether, hoping that students will have at least learned something from the assignment. Many teachers simply feel helpless when faced with this recurring problem and do little except urge students to avoid the practice.

Before working on the problem, it is important to determine why students use encyclopedia language. There are several possible reasons:

- They understand only partially, or not at all, what they are reading, and so they copy anything that has something to do with the topic. They do not learn; they transfer words from the books to their papers.

- They are not interested in the topic but must complete the assignment. They fill in the required number of pages to finish a tedious task quickly.

- They do not have clear purposes to guide them. They do not know what they are looking for, and so they copy everything in hopes of covering the essentials.

- They do not know there is anything wrong with encyclopedia language.

- They think changing a word here and there or rearranging sentences is the same as using their own words.

These reasons, in different combinations for different students, account for the awkward, poorly written reports that are turned in to fulfill the requirements of the assignment. Students are not working with their own meaningful observations. They start with someone else's observations on an unfamiliar topic in different language patterns, which they pursue with fuzzy purposes and little understanding. Assigning more and more reports will neither ameliorate these conditions nor improve the writing. What is needed is a different approach, one that is purposeful and meaningful.

The I-Search Paper   One way to get students comfortably into research is to use the I-Search assignment (Macrorie, 1976). This assignment is based on the premise that students should conduct a personal and subjective ("I") examination ("Search") of material that *they* want to pursue. Students start their work with questions or problems that are of current concern to them. One child, for example, may have received an aquarium as a birthday present and is eager to know all about tropical fish. Another may be preoccupied with how to build a bird feeder. A third may be engrossed in the intricacies of computer programming.

Before beginning research, students reflect on what they already know about the chosen area. They write and discuss at this point, determining exactly what it is they want to learn, making predictions as to what they might find out, and thinking of possible information sources. Then, their purposes guide the search. They soon develop specific questions that they want to answer. They consult books and periodicals, but they also interview people and use other sources of information, like films and television. They are involved in an absorbing hunt for information that is important to them; they are not just reading books on a topic.

When students write this kind of paper, they adopt a very personal tone. Papers may begin with statements like these: "I wanted to find out what happened to the dinosaurs," or "My bike broke and I needed to fix it," or "I'm going camping with my family in Canada this summer, and I wondered what it is really like there." They tell what they were looking for, where they found information, and what they learned. They do not write as if they were a detached author of an encyclopedia article: "The principal foods of a cardinal are. . . ." Instead, they write to tell about their search: "I found out that cardinals like sunflower seeds, so I bought some of those to put in my feeder. Sure enough, the cardinals loved them."

The process of writing an I-Search paper is the same as the one used for writing saturation reports. Models are again needed to show students how their reports might be written. Class discussion and instruction give the necessary background for locating and using information and for writing from a personal perspective. Students work together to revise and polish their work. The finished papers are displayed, "published," or read aloud to provide a wide audience for student efforts.

The primary advantage of the I-Search paper is that students are doing meaningful research to answer meaningful questions. They are not juggling books and magazines and encyclopedias to fill a required number of pages. Their purpose is to find something out, not to write a research paper. They know just what they are looking for, and they actually want to know the answers to their questions. Furthermore, they are encouraged to make their reports personal rather than third-person, passive-voice objective. Their purposes and their approach have profound effects on the writing. A girl writes about her visit to a laboratory at an aerodynamics research center; she informs her audience about what she found out when she saw a wind tunnel experiment. A boy tells about what he learned when he spent a Saturday afternoon interviewing the director of the local SPCA. Although students will also include information that they learned from reading, they are not likely to insert sentences or paragraphs from books. They will quite naturally write in their own words because they have something of their very own to say.

The I-Search paper helps students use printed sources by demonstrating what a "source" is: Students learn that people have information; television has information; books have information. *Doing research* becomes a meaningful concept, tied directly to students' urges to know something specific. Regular experience with I-Search papers makes the research process understandable. This understanding will be reflected in students' use of sources, their writing, their attitude about the assignment, and their concept of what it is they are doing. This last is perhaps most significant. When asked what they are trying to achieve, students will say, "I'm trying to find out how a steam locomotive works" or "I want to know how they write videogame programs." By contrast, students' usual perceptions abut their aims for a research-paper unit are these: "I'm writing a ten-page paper on Scotland" or "I'm doing a paper that has to have at least five sources."

The research process must be perceived as a search for information, not just a perplexing assignment involving footnotes. Sources must be regarded as the places to go to find information; they are not just the list of books at the end of the paper. Students also need to learn that including others' ideas and words is sometimes necessary and is always legitimate when done properly. I-Search gives students the right kinds of perceptions of the process so that when it is time to talk about footnotes, direct quotations, and bibliographies, students will have a solid understanding of how those things really apply to writing.

Using Printed Sources   With saturation reports and I-Search paper experience, students will be learning the process of writing research reports. The design of these activities does not give much occasion or reason for using encyclopedia language. But as students write more sophisticated papers that require the use of a number of books and periodicals and a more detached writing style, they may well run into difficulty and may resort to copying source material. They will awkwardly fit together paragraphs from different books and magazines. Even with a good sense of what research is, students may still have difficulty dealing with unfamiliar topics presented in books.

The following strategy can help students use printed sources effectively. Most important, this sequence can in a small way make this kind of writing a process of learning rather than a tedious exercise in word transfer.

First, students need to set clear purposes for a report based on extensive reading. They must know what to search for when they open a book or magazine so that they will not be overwhelmed. Before doing any reading, students should talk about the topic, exploring what they already know and what they might find out. Several class periods should be devoted to recalling known information, to raising questions, and to setting directions for study. The important goals are to focus thinking and to set purposes for doing the research. This preliminary thinking is probably the most important part of the process.

If students rush to the library before they have given careful thought to what they will be looking for, their reports will illustrate the problems described earlier—awkward use of information characterized by heavy reliance on encyclopedia language.

Students should then make one list of what they already know about the topic and another list of what they need (want) to find out. Once they have done this a few times with the teacher's help, they can do it on their own or in small groups. At first, the teacher needs to guide, by raising questions and stimulating the students' curiosity. For instance, fifth-grade Sally was preparing to do a report on raccoons. The teacher helped her make one list by asking her to think of all she knew about raccoons:

WHAT I KNOW

have a mask and striped tail
long fingers
live in trees
come out at night
wash their food

As Sally mentioned these ideas, the teacher guided her by asking related questions. Discovering things she did not know, Sally compiled a second list:

WHAT I WILL FIND OUT

Why don't we see them in the day?
Why do they wash their food?
What do they like to eat?
How large do they get?
How many babies do they have?

Sally had focused her thinking and gained valuable practice posing questions to guide her learning. The teacher also had her predict answers to her own questions; Sally added these to the question list. This step, too, helped the child think before she set out to find information. Working in groups, students can help each other think of known facts, suggest questions to each other, and make predictions as to what they might find out.

When students have set their purposes, they should next decide where to look for information. The class should discuss many possible sources. Much material can be found in the library, but other places should not be overlooked. Special agencies may publish informative pamphlets; relevant filmstrips may be available; knowledgeable people may be contacted by mail or telephone. Students should have several clear ideas of where they might find good information.

The next concern is for students to comprehend what they read. Good comprehension will determine to a large extent how well written the report will be. The first step to comprehension is to let the purposes guide the research. This means that students should first look for answers to the questions they raised. They will probably need to consult several sources before finding relevant material. At this early point, they should skim materials, making notes only of where key information is located. These notes can be kept on the original question sheet, with source names and page numbers placed next to each question. This survey is important not only to teach useful previewing skills but also to keep students from opening a book and copying the first information they see. Of course, the survey may also suggest other areas for students to include in the report. Students can make notes about these ideas and their sources after the initial purposes have been covered.

After the survey, students will be ready to begin studying the information. This stage is probably the most important step in the process for ensuring final results that reflect good comprehension. Students should follow four steps repeatedly as they go back to each source:

1. Read the relevant information.
2. Close the book.
3. Explain the information aloud to a partner.
4. Write down what was explained orally.

This sequence is useful because when books are closed and students tell someone else what they read, they will seldom repeat the exact wording of the source. They will, instead, explain the ideas in their own words. When they write, they will be more likely to use their own words.

Some students will be able to follow these steps easily; others will have difficulty. When students are first learning this technique, the teacher should listen to their explanations to make sure that they are on the right track. The teacher may need to say, "Now just tell it in your own words," or "Well, what does that actually mean?" If the material contains many unfamiliar words or concepts, students may try to recall the exact textual language. That is, if they cannot understand the text, they will not be able to paraphrase it easily. The teacher can spot areas of confusion and can help at that immediate point.

This process is time-consuming, but its value cannot be overestimated. Through closing the book and explaining its contents aloud, students can demonstrate their degree of understanding. The extra effort devoted to this step will, over time, result in better reports that reflect comprehension of the information that was found in books. Once students learn the process, they can work in pairs or small groups to read and talk before they write.

Here are some portions of reports from the same group of fifth graders whose encyclopedia language papers were used for illustrations earlier in this chapter. The teacher followed the suggested procedures, and the students' writing shows marked improvement over the previous efforts. Here, the students' language and organization reveal their comprehension.

HOW INDIANS MADE TOOLS

To make a hammer an Indian looked for a smooth and rounded stone in a creek. Then he made a groove in the middle. He did this by pulling wet rawhide dipped in sand back and forth. This took a long time. For the handle the Indian found a piece of hard wood with a fork in it. Then he fitted the grooved stone into the fork and tied the wet rawhide around the stone. When the rawhide dried, it tightened the two pieces of the hammer together.

INDIAN SIGN LANGUAGE

The Plains Indians had six different languages. The Indian language was very difficult, but many people believed it was very simple. Sometimes members of a tribe had trouble talking to members of another tribe. I bet you are thinking how did they find sign language! Perhaps it started when members of several tribes were on a buffalo hunt. They could not talk to one another so they tried sign language.

HOW INDIANS GREW CROPS

Indians did a lot of farming. They got water to their crops in different ways. Some built irrigation canals and others prayed for rain. Some Indians knew how to grow good crops of corn. They used curved sticks for hoes. The women did most of the work while the men went hunting.

HOW INDIANS MADE PIPES

Some Indian pipes were made of clay and some were made of wood. To make a wood one, they took a stick of wood and slit it. Then they hollowed it out. Then they carved another hunk of wood and hollowed it out with a hole on top. They stuck the carved hunk on the stick. The way they made it stick together was to use some sap from a tree.

Students will be reinforcing reading comprehension skills as they read, talk, and write their way through sources. They must rephrase ideas, identify facts that relate to their purposes, understand and use new vocabulary, and make necessary inferences. They may not cover as much material by stopping to explain orally and then write, but what they cover, they will read with solid understanding. Here, for example, is a second-grade reading selection and the summary one student composed after reading, talking, and then writing. The article was accompanied by illustrations, which are not reproduced here.

U.S.S. FISH

When is a fish not a fish? When it is a submarine! Many of the submarines of the United States Navy are named after fish. Because of this, and because of the way in which they move under water, these ships are sometimes called "fish." Men can work, eat, and sleep on a submarine for many days at a time.

Sometimes, the submarine rides the ocean waves. Sometimes, it races along right below the water. And sometimes, it goes deep, deep down to the floor of the ocean. As you can see, submarines look like big, long fish.

Some submarines have a tall conning tower near one end. The conning tower is the place from which the ship is run when it comes to the top of the water. The conning tower is also the place from which the periscope is used.

The periscope can be moved up and down. When the submarine goes below the water, the periscope is moved up. The top of the periscope is then above the water. By looking into one end of the periscope, the men below can see anything that is above the ocean waves.

Each United States Navy submarine has a name and number. Only the number is painted on the sides of a ship. So when a Navy man looks at a submarine, he sees only the number. But because he has learned both the name and the number, he knows the name of the ship, too.

A Navy man says "port" for "left." He says "starboard" for "right." If he is facing left, he says he is facing "port." If he faces right, he says he is facing "starboard." The number of the ship is painted port and starboard.

If you look below, you can learn the names and numbers of some of the Navy's submarines. On the starboard side of each name, you see the number the Navy uses for that ship. On the port side of each name, you see the letters U.S.S. These letters stand for United States Ship.

U.S.S. Bream—243	U.S.S. Blackfin—322
U.S.S. Perch—313	U.S.S. Dogfish—350

SUBMARINES

by Marc

Submarines look like a fish so it is given fish names like U.S.S. Blackfin 322. It can go on top of the water, on the ocean floor, it can work right under the water. When it is on top of the water the men on the submarine work in the conning tower. The submarine uses a periscope to see when it is under water to see things around it. The left side is the port side, the right side is the starboard side.

Marc was able to reorganize the information in his own way, clearly using his own words to write his summary. His work shows the interdependence of reading and writing. Reading and discussing made possible Marc's comprehension of the material; the written account is clear and well written because he had been actively involved in reading before he attempted to write.

Notes that are written while students study sources can be jotted down on one side of the paper. Space should be left between main points. Ideas may also be recorded on note cards, one item per card. Older students may be encouraged to take more extensive notes, perhaps including direct quotations from sources. Quotation is useful in some circumstances, when paraphrases are not adequate, but its use should never dominate. (If used, these instances should be marked clearly so that they can be set off properly in the final report.) Most important is that students take and organize notes in an orderly fashion so that the notes will be useful when the final paper is prepared.

When it is time to write the full report, pages of notes can be cut apart (or cards can be reshuffled) as the student puts related ideas together and decides how to organize the information. This step also reinforces comprehension by requiring students to see relationships among facts and to determine the main points that will be made. It is at this time that an organizational scheme can be created. Once students have information, it will be relatively easy for them to categorize it, and they can then make outlines to guide them with the final draft.

Several kinds of outlines are useful for organizing information, and the teacher may prefer one over others. For most students, a simple format is best. One approach that works well is illustrated in Figure 4. Often called mapping (Hanf, 1971) or clustering (Rico and Clagget, 1980), this scheme makes relationships among ideas easy to see. Students can then decide from their diagrams how ideas should be organized in the report. This scheme is also useful for students who may be learning formal outline form. When ideas are grouped graphically, students can see how to indicate the relationships in a formal outline.

When the ideas are organized, the writing of the report itself can begin with firm foundations. Students will use their original notes, written in their own words. The cluster or map outline helps them to sequence the information. Some children will need help with transitions, with introductions and conclusions, and with other aspects of the form of the report. Older students, who use direct quotations, will need help to set these off properly from the rest of their statements. As they work, the teacher will be assured that students have

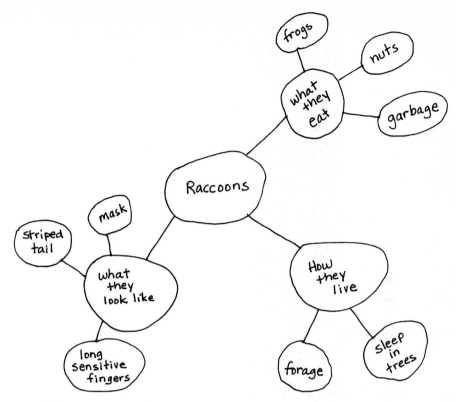

FIGURE 4 A simple cluster outline for a report on raccoons

been encouraged and been shown how to write reports that reflect learning, not copying.

During draft stages, students should work together, giving each other help with organization, wording, and so on. Students need to do at least one draft, preferably more, and they can benefit from several responders who can suggest improvements. (See Revising and Polishing, Chapter 7, for suggested procedures.)

Additional sharing after students have completed the last draft is also valuable, for students derive pleasure from seeing their work recognized. The teacher can do some of the following things: display reports on bulletin boards or in the library; bind them in special classroom books; have them read aloud to the rest of the class; arrange for their publication in the school newspaper; and/or lend them to other classes for reading and discussing. Students should know that the report is not a task done only to receive a grade or to prepare for stiffer report requirements in the next school year. Properly handled, the report that is based on reading will increase the author's knowledge and unearth information that will interest others in the class and school.

Even with careful help from the teacher, students may continue to have difficulty putting ideas into their own words and organizing information from multiple sources. Several exercises are useful for reinforcing these skills:

1. *Learning Logs.*   Regular writing in learning logs provides an excellent way to help students learn to write simply and clearly about what they read. Keeping a learning log gives them regular practice in writing about newly learned material. This practice makes it easier for students to write well when they prepare special reports.

2. *The Group Paraphrase.*   Give each member of a group a copy of a short selection, perhaps a one hundred–two hundred word segment from a social science text, a basal reader, or a magazine article. Tell the group they will work together to rewrite the information as if it were to be part of a report.

Have students read the material silently once or twice. Then ask someone to explain the first main point. If the student starts to use source language patterns and vocabulary, ask someone else to try. Avoid criticizing students' attempts; maintain a light tone, as if the class were playing a game. Urge students to use synonyms and to state the ideas in their own ways. When someone provides a good paraphrase of the first point, write the statement on the board and have students note how the student's language differs from the original and thus why the statement is in the student's own words. Then go on to the next idea. Work through the selection in this way until all points have been rewritten. Make copies of the group composition and have students attach these to the original for later reference as an example of correctly paraphrased information.

This exercise takes time, but it is extremely valuable and, if handled with good humor, can be fun as well. A group of seventh graders once took forty-five minutes to paraphrase three paragraphs in their social studies textbook. It was slow going; they had a very difficult time breaking away from the exact wording of the text, but they kept at it, laughing at their difficulties, until they caught on. The teacher helped by suggesting how they might start different sentences (to help them avoid using the textbook's language patterns), by pointing out where synonyms could be used, and by saying repeatedly, "But what does that sentence really mean?" Most in the group finally saw what "own words" meant. They needed many such sessions to learn the skill well enough for them to use it independently.

3. *Reorganizing Exercise.*   Give each member of a group the same paragraph, cut into individual sentences. Have each rearrange the sentences into a satisfying order and then compare their results with the other students' responses and with the original. Discuss why some arrangements are better than others. The same exercise can also be done with large sentence strips that will attach to the chalkboard. The group will work together to reorganize, discussing their thinking as they go.

4. *Outlining Exercise.*   Write a number of different words or facts relating to one topic on large cards. Arrange the cards randomly on the board. Have the group work together to decide which words or facts go together; rearrange the cards accordingly. When the group is satisfied with an arrangement, have them label the clusters to indicate the several main points. This exercise can also be done as an independent activity, with facts (words) on small cards to be arranged on desk tops.

5. Other good exercises for helping students avoid copying and improve organizing skills are described by Suid (1979) and McKenzie (1979). They include the following:

    a. Revising a source explanation
    b. Simplifying source material for a younger audience
    c. Comparing two sources on the same topic
    d. Adapting source material to a new form (for example, writing a story based on an encyclopedia article)
    e. Constructing data charts for organizing information from several sources

A Single Question   Writing from book research requires experience and practice. One long report, such as a term paper that requires an entire semester to complete, is usually not as valuable as several shorter reports, assigned periodically and tempered with other kinds of writing activities. Several short reports allow students to apply basic research skills to a variety of topics and sources of information. These reports help them develop greater flexibility with this kind of writing. A series of short assignments also helps them to maintain interest and motivation. Chesney (1982), for example, suggests using one-page research reports. This is a slightly modified version of his procedure:

1. Make up a collection of specific questions for which students probably do not have answers. Phrase them in such a way that they will stimulate curiosity. For instance, note the following questions:

- How do they get the nests for birds' nest soup?
- What is a Yorkshire dale?
- Why did Louis XIV put Fouquet in prison for building a palace?
- How did they discover the cause of yellow fever?
- Who built the very first automobile?

Do not limit the list to material you know. Students should not feel that they are scrambling to get answers you already have. Even if you do have some of the answers, do not let them know, or the fun of the search will be lost.

2. Give students the list and have each choose a question to answer. It is a good idea to include more questions than there are students so that no one is stuck with a question he or she really has no interest in.

3. Send them to the library. Have them keep track of all the sources they consult, even if the material turns out to be unfruitful. You may want to set certain standards; for instance, Chesney stipulates that only one encyclopedia article may be used as a reference. At this stage, students should read and talk before they write.

4. Have students write up their findings in one page or less and list their sources on a second page. This part of the assignment involves the usual public writing process; several drafts may be needed before the final paper is ready to be turned in, and response groups can help with the drafting process.

5. Give students a good grade if they 1) find the answer and state it in their own words, or 2) have consulted a good number of relevant sources but still have been unable to find the answer.

Chesney developed this plan in his high school class, but it is workable at any level. Questions can be geared to students' ages, interests, and abilities. Requirements can also be altered to suit different groups.

The exercise gives students good practice in searching for information in books and in writing up findings without intimidating students by such requirements as minimum numbers of pages. Longer research reports may have their place, but short, single-question research teaches the same basic skills and can entail a great deal of fun besides. These almost off-hand questions become extremely interesting to students, as does anything that is perceived to be outside the usual routine. Students will doggedly search for answers simply because the oddity of a question stimulates their curiosity. Of course, students might contribute questions too, and when they do, the exercise becomes even more interesting and meaningful.

Reporting: Some Conclusions

The overall goal of a report based on reading should be to have students express in writing what they have learned from the books they consulted. If students have not understood what they have read, their writing will most certainly reflect their confusion. Good reports follow from good prewriting activities. These prewriting activities include clearly identifying purposes, reading to satisfy those purposes, and discussing information to cement learning. Only when students have read and thought will they be able to write well. In fact, report writing is one extension of the reading-thinking process described earlier—it is not just a test of reading but the result of purposeful learning. For elaborations of this point of view, see Tierney and Pearson (1983), Wittrock (1983), and Stein (1983).

A report based on reading is only one type of report. It is not necessarily the best or most interesting to write or read. Saturation reports and I-Search reports give students just as much practice in writing and just as much experience in using sources as do the formal research papers that are more typically assigned. Thus, when students do write reports, it seems most sensible to have them mainly write reports based on first-hand experience. They can then move gradually into reports that require solely vicarious experience (reading about the subject). If students are expected to write research papers, then purposeful prewriting and reading must be the foundation of these assignments.

Balancing the Report with Other Writing

Reports should not dominate student writing. There are many other types of writing that can build expressive abilities and give students a sense of pride in their growing skill. There are essays, plays, haiku, letters to pen pals, jokes, petitions, autobiographies, and many other possibilities. It is beyond the scope of this chapter to consider all the possible writing activities. Instead of considering what might be done with many different forms, we shall examine one such form and then look at the process of imitation writing.

Writing Stories

With a little encouragement, most students will be able to compose a reasonable story and have a good time doing it. Getting started requires freeing students' imaginations and establishing enough understanding of story elements so that students can construct a tale. Almost all students have the basics of these two requirements. They *know* about stories (Applebee, 1978; Mandler and Johnson, 1977; Stein and Glenn, 1979) and they *can* think creatively. Teachers must tease the knowledge and ability out of them. Here is a method of doing so.

1. Engage the class in a discussion about a particularly good story—one from a book, a magazine, or a television program. Have students tell why they liked the story, why it held their interest. Elicit comments about characters, setting, key events, and any other features worth noting. List all responses on the board for reference as the group continues.

2. Give students the beginning of a story they do not know. Make copies for all or read aloud the first segment. Or, have the group compose the first part of a story, establishing characters and setting.

3. Have each student write a next part to this story. Give them plenty of time over several class periods. Suggest that they use the same kinds of elements they mentioned during their first discussion. Students should not finish the story; they should just write the next part.

4. Divide students into groups of three. Have each read the parts the other two wrote. Readers must predict what will happen next in each partially completed story. Discussion should pinpoint why the readers made certain predictions. Which events seemed to suggest a particular story direction? What was it about the characters that led to predictions about their behavior? Groups should also discuss what they liked about each story so far.

5. Have students finish their stories individually and read them aloud to the whole class.

This process gets students thinking actively and involved quickly in story composition. The prewriting discussion helps them to recall what it is that makes for a good story. The story's beginning or the initial group composition gives them a place to start; commencing in this manner is easier than beginning from scratch. Peer response is helpful to students as they write; they may get new ideas to use. They will also see how their first attempts strike at least two readers, and they might decide to revise the first segments in light of that response. Sharing their stories with the whole class provides a wide audience for the completed work. Students will find this sharing quite interesting because each pupil will have concocted a different story based on the beginning that all have in common.

This approach does not guarantee immediate results. At first stories may be inadequately developed or may show little sense of style. Readers may not initially be able to make insightful predictions. The overall effect of the activity may not seem very worthwhile the first or second time. But students will gradually improve their skills. They will become more attentive to techniques of characterization, to establishing settings and motives, and to moving the action forward. Of course, the more good stories they hear, read, and discuss, the more experienced they will become and the easier it will be for them to write stories.

Group response helps students evaluate their work in progress. As writers become more skilled, predictions will be easier for responders to make; students will learn that good predictions can be made only if there is good, detailed material to start with. Perhaps most important, students must think, read, and talk as they write. They must be actively involved in the process. Ultimately, they will not need such story starters. They will be ready and able to compose their own, original stories.

Selected anecdotes from realistic children's literature may also be used to stimulate narrative writing. Here, the teacher chooses a good scene from a book to read aloud (the more typical of children's lives the better) and then asks students to recall their own similar experiences. Discussion will stimulate ideas, and students will be encouraged to write from their own firsthand experiences. (Many young writers do not realize that their own lives provide excellent material for written anecdotes and stories; they often believe that in order to write interesting stories they must invent exotic fantasies.)

One example will illustrate. The teacher read the first few pages of Betsy Byar's *After the Goat Man* (Viking, 1974), which describes three children playing Monopoly on a hot summer day. The students enjoyed the descriptions and laughed at the character whose mind was concentrated wonderfully because he was deeply in debt to the other players. When the teacher finished, the children were eager to tell of their own Monopoly games, remembering when boards were upset, when players tried to cheat, and when especially clever deals were made. In telling their own stories, they realized they had much to write and were eager to get started. When first drafts were finished, response groups suggested how each student's paper might be made more vivid with details and dialogue. Revisions were made, and final drafts were read aloud to the whole class. It was an enjoyable occasion for all.

Imitation Writing

All students have something to say. They have strong opinions that can become essays; they have perceptions and feelings and ideas that can become poetry, plays, and much more. But most students haven't acquired the knack of using various forms to express their thoughts. Imitation writing helps students build skill in using patterns and forms by providing a model as a guide. Original composition is the goal; imitation is the means to achieve the end.

Bates (1979) argues that, far from being a passive behavior, imitation is an active process that is basic to cognitive development and language learning. She suggests that imitation will be used especially when the learner is acquiring a new or difficult behavior. In such cases, the imitation serves partially as a means to get the individual to understand and learn. Students may imitate a language structure, for instance, without necessarily understanding it fully, and, in the process, will come to learn it and use it spontaneously to communicate. Imitation appears to be a common, natural process of learning, and it has implications for the teaching of writing as it relates to reading.

Imitation writing is advocated by numerous theoreticians and practitioners, including Moffett (1968), Odegaard and May (1972), Cramer and Cramer (1975), Healey (1978), Myers (1978), May (1980), and Moffett and Wagner (1983). All of these researchers stress the value of helping students write their own ideas effectively by giving the students good models to follow.

Dunning (1983) suggests a four-step sequence:

1. Read.

> So, laughing, the Tsar went on his way, knowing that the girl had outwitted him.
> FROM **"The Maiden Wiser than the Tsar," a Serbian folktale in I. Shah,**
> ***World Tales*** **(Harcourt Brace Jovanovich, 1979)**

2. Copy.
   Reproduce the original in writing.
3. Change.

> So, chuckling, the king went on his way, seeing that the girl had fooled him.

4. Imitate.

> So, muttering, the driver accelerated slowly, realizing that the traffic cop was watching his next move.

In reading and copying, students note the form of the original. In changing through the substitution of synonyms, students begin to make use of the form and understand the pattern. In imitating, they fit original ideas into the same pattern, generating new content while retaining the form. This sequence may first be used with single sentences. Dunning uses the same process with paragraphs and much longer segments of text as well.

Noyce and Christie (1981) outline an effective program of sentence imitation for primary students that is based on children's literature. Students first listen to stories in which a particular structure is repeated throughout (for instance, "If I were a ...") and then speak the structure repeatedly in oral language games. Next, students write their own stories, using the structure to express their ideas. Books of these stories, bound and illustrated, are placed in the classroom library as recreational reading material. Over several lessons, the teacher stresses the value of staying with a given form; he or she uses a variety of different books based on a given structure. Noyce and Christie recommend that the teacher personally write some simple stories if collections of coordinated books are inaccessible. Their program makes purposeful use of the linguistic patterns that are the basis of some of the most popular and entertaining children's books.

Many teachers use this type of literature-modeling approach to composing in the primary grades. Here are some storybook models and children's imitations from one teacher's classroom.

A hill is a house for an ant, an ant.
A hive is a house for a bee.
A hole is a house for a mole or a mouse,
And a house is a house for me.
FROM **Mary Ann Hoberman, *A House is a House for Me***
(Puffin Books, 1982)

Here are some of the children's imitations (each sentence from a different student):

A head is a house for a brain.

A spaceship is a house for E.T.

A uniform is a house for a baseball player.

A is for the zoo. Why? Because *a*nimals live in the zoo.
FROM **Mary Elting and Michael Folsom, *Q is for Duck* (Clarion Books, 1980)**

The children's imitations:

P is for Susie. Why? Because she loves *p*oetry.

Y is for Ricardo. Why? Because he loves to *y*ak on the phone.

K is for Stephen. Why? Because he loves *K*nott's Berry Farm.

Appendix B lists a number of books that can be used as models for this kind of imitation writing.

Teacher-composed sentences may also be used as models. Here are some examples:

- When I saw the moon, it was gold and full.
- If I had a sled, I could slide in the snow.
- She was an old woman who had a gray cat.

Older students might be given figurative language, teacher-generated or from literary selections, that requires attention not only to syntactic form but also to the relationships of concepts and the power of images:

- The hikers paused, wilting in the heat like thirsty plants.
- He was a mouse in her trap.

> The next morning I saw dawn for the first time. It began not as the gorgeous fanfare over the ocean I had expected, but as a strange gray thing, like sunshine seen through burlap.
>
> FROM **John Knowles'** *A Separate Peace*

> And soon Victoria left; she disappeared around a corner, a few blocks up the street, handsomely and gradually as a sailboat.
>
> FROM **James Agee's** *A Death in the Family*

As students become accustomed to the process of imitation from working with sentences, longer passages may be used as models. Here, for example, is a middle-school student's extended imitation based on Byrd Baylor's *Guess Who My Favorite Person Is* (Macmillan, 1985):

Favorite color: My favorite color is the lilac shade that is painted in sunsets only found in Manhattan Beach.

Favorite smell: On highway 41 on the way to Yosemite, there is a scent of cedar and sugar pines that brings back memories. This smell can be captured in late June when wildflowers are still scattered about.

Favorite taste: In Del Amo Fashion square in Torrance, California, there is a restaurant called The Magic Pan. At this restaurant, I tried a spinach crepe that I will never forget!

Favorite sound: My favorite sound remains trapped in the Grand Canyon from April of 1981. The sound is an echo, which my best friend and I experienced on a strenuous hike.

Something weird about myself: I have always enjoyed making a fool out of myself. For example, I walk on the highway wearing a trenchcoat and hiking boots while waving at the cars that pass. I also like to find sea slugs and smear their purple ink all over my body.

Favorite thing to do: I love to sit around a comfortable, warm campfire and tell stories with my friends. While sitting, I often look up at the stars and watch some of their twinkling lights fall and then vanish into the darkness.

The length of an imitation does not have to be determined by students' ages. Even primary-grade children can compose extended imitations of materials they have understood and enjoyed. For example, a group of second graders composed a fine story after using a model for a starting point. Everyone in the group had read *Nate the Great* by Marjorie Weinman Sharmat (Dell, 1972). It is a story about a boy who, identifying with a no-nonsense, clear-thinking detective, solves mysteries in his neighborhood. With the help of the teacher, the students discussed the book, reviewing elements of style that they had noticed. They generated this list of stylistic features:

1. Told in the first person—"I."
2. Talks about himself. Brags a lot. Always says "I, Nate the Great."
3. Repeats words, like pancakes ("I had just eaten breakfast. It was a good breakfast. Pancakes, juice, pancakes, milk, and pancakes. I like pancakes.")
4. Funny things happen.
5. Simple, short sentences.
6. Sentences begin with "I" a lot.

The group then decided to dictate their own version of *Nate the Great*. Working together, using what they had discussed and learned, they composed the following delightful story, which was transcribed by their teacher. The children contributed illustrations to the final, typed copy, which was "published" for the rest of the class to enjoy.

NATE THE GREAT AND THE GREAT QUACK CAPER

I, Nate the Great, woke up. I put on my robe and slippers. I made my bed. My pillow fell on the floor twice. I kicked the pillow to the front of the staircase. I tripped over the pillow. I tumbled down the stairs. I, Nate the Great, hate pillows.

I stomped into the kitchen. I went to the cupboard and got out a box of cereal. It was Cheerios, of course. Low sugar, lots of protein. I, Nate the Great, need energy.

I walked very carefully to the refrigerator. Fast but easy, I opened the door. An egg fell from the container on the side of the door. It fell on my head. I, Nate the Great, had to take a bath.

I took a fast glance at the tub. I, Nate the Great, knew something was missing. It was my rubber ducky, Webster. I put on my bathrobe and slippers again. I went for my notepad and pencil. This was a tragic case. It was time to interview myself.

Q. What color is Webster?

A. Yellow with orange feet. He is wearing a green detective hat that I, Nate the Great, painted myself.

Q. When was Webster last seen?

A. A week ago on Friday, May 27.

Q. Where was it last seen?

A. At the movies.

Q. What was it doing at the movies?

A. It was watching a double feature: "Sherlock Duck and the Star Quacks."

I, Nate the Great, had a clue. I ran to Cinema Three. I gave a dollar for a ticket to the lady. I told her to keep the change. The ticket lady told me, "A dollar is not enough."

I told her, "I, Nate the Great, am on an important case—the Great Quack Caper." She looked at my head. She wondered if a duck had laid an egg on my head. While she was thinking about it, I, Nate the Great, dashed in.

I walked into the theater. It was very dark. I needed time to think. By now the egg was in my ear. I, Nate the Great, ignored it. After all, this was the Great Quack Caper. I had brought some Cheerios to munch on. I found a seat and sat down to munch and think.

Suddenly I heard a squeak. I thought it was the chair. I sat down again and heard a louder squeak. The person next to me told me to keep it down. I checked my seat and found Webster, my rubber ducky.

I walked home. I took my bath with Webster. I, Nate the Great, washed the egg off my face. I got dressed. I went back to the kitchen and finally I got to eat my Cheerios. The Great Quack Caper was solved.

As readers of the original *Nate the Great* will recognize, the children's story is faithful to the elements of style and the essence of Nate's character. These children worked within a clear structure that required careful attention to language, characterization, description, and plot structure. But the details and incidents are original. Following a model stimulated not only excellent thinking and composing achievements but also substantial creative effort.

The book *Fortunately* by Remy Charlip (Parents Magazine Press, 1964) is a string of amusing incidents connected by the words *fortunately* and *unfortunately*. This pattern stimulates lively extended imitation writing. Here is one third grader's version:

BIG PROBLEMS

Fortunately I went to Europe. Unfortunately there was an automatic pilot that blew up.

Fortunately there were enough parachutes for everyone. Unfortunately they would not shoot out.

Fortunately there was enough trees for everyone to land on. Unfortunately all of them fell on one of them and the tree fell over.

Fortunately there was a basket of fruit. They fell in it. Unfortunately it broke.

Fortunately it wasn't very far down. Believe me! Unfortunately we weren't in Europe and I mean it.

Fortunately there was a plane stopping at one o'clock in the morning. Unfortunately it was ten o'clock in the morning and we had no money.

Fortunately we snuck in to the airplane. Unfortunately the airplane was scheduled for Europe and not America.

This is a popular book, and students enjoy creating their own series of events with first positive and then negative perspectives. They will often string a story out, inventing one outrageous incident after another just for the fun of it. All this requires creative thought, selection of incidents that work in the structure, and the making of transitions from one event to the next. These features all develop writing-thinking skills.

A group of primary students had listened to the story *The Velveteen Rabbit* by Marjorie Williams (Doran, 1922). This is a story of a boy and his beloved stuffed rabbit. The rabbit is told by Skin Horse, another toy, that playthings become real when their owners love them dearly. The rabbit longs for the time when he can become real, but all seems lost when the boy is sick and the doctor insists that all the playthings be burned to destroy germs. Nana, the housekeeper, reluctantly sends the rabbit to the trash heap. The rabbit is saved, in the end, by a fairy godmother who makes him real.

After discussing the story, the group dictated a puppet play that was their own version of the tale:

ACT I

Skin Horse said, "When you are real your thread will break."
"Okay!" said the Velveteen Rabbit.
Boy said to the Velveteen Rabbit, "I will make you a little place to sit when I'm gone."
The two bunnies laughed at the Velveteen Rabbit and said, "Do you have hind legs?"
Just then Nana came outside and said, "Get away from the bunny and leave him alone!" Then the two rabbits ran away.

ACT II

The doctor said, "Burn the rabbit at once!"
"But the boy likes the rabbit," cried Nana.
The boy yelled, "Don't burn the rabbit or I'll burn you!"
Just then the fairy came into the room and made the boy much better. "I'll make animals and people small if they're going into my home."
He made the boy and the Velveteen Rabbit small and took them into his flower home. He saved them both!

In their script, the children included the characters and incidents that were most memorable to them. Interestingly, they changed the fairy godmother to a godfather and invented an entirely new ending to the story. This writing activity started with imitation and ended with originality.

Pradl (1979) describes a poetry-writing exercise that is based on the principles of imitation. This is his suggested sequence, given with a different example from the one he uses.

1. Choose a poem. Omit several key words and put these on a list. Give students the list and have them write the first word they think of when they read each item.

a. weeping   _____
b. laughter   _____
c. love   _____
d. portion   _____
e. gate   _____
f. roses   _____
g. misty   _____
h. path   _____
i. closes   _____
j. dream   _____

2. Have students use their words to fill in the blanks that are marked in the original poem.

> They are not long, the (a) _____ and the (b) _____,
> (c) _____ and desire and hate;
> I think they have no (d) _____ in us after
> We pass the (e) _____.
> They are not long, the days of wine and (f) _____;
> Out of a (g) _____ dream
> Our (h) _____ emerges for a while, then (i) _____
> Within a (j) _____.

3. Have students read their poems and change any words they wish to in order to create a meaningful, interesting piece.

4. Have students share their poems with one another in small groups, comparing their efforts for the different effects they create.

5. Have students compare their poems with the original. (The poem on which the example is based is Ernest Dowson's "Vitae Summa Brevis Nos Vetat Inchoare Longam," written in 1896.)

The poems selected as a base should be age/grade appropriate so that students will understand the words on the original list and will be able to work with the language of the poem as they make their revisions. As an exercise, this activity will help students see how different words convey different moods and images. The task will give them some experience in playing with poetic language.

Imitation exercises also develop children's vocabulary and reading comprehension. Even if students only alter a passage, they must select synonyms; choosing the best word becomes important. As they change or imitate literary passages, the original author's meaning becomes clearer. Students pay particular attention to models, rereading with greater appreciation for the author's choice of words and with deeper understanding of the meaning. Students read and write, write and read, developing and refining skill in both areas. In fact, these writing exercises are particularly effective when they are directly coordinated with a literature program (Moffett, 1968; Stotsky, 1975; Hennings, 1978; Moffett and Wagner, 1983).

The benefit to the development of language and cognitive skills becomes evident in students' responses to these writing tasks. They must see relationships, generate ideas, and convey their meaning accurately. The first grader who wrote "A head is a house for a brain" formulated a concept and expressed it in precise terms. The child who wrote "*K* is for Stephen. Why? Because he loves *K*nott's Berry Farm" was aware of a spelling idiosyncracy and turned it into a clever visual joke. The student who wrote "My favorite color is the lilac shade that is painted in sunsets only found in Manhattan Beach" expressed a perception in clear, vivid language.

As Loban (1963) demonstrated in his study of children's language, it is "not [the] pattern but what is done to achieve flexibility within the pattern [that] proves to be a measure of effectiveness and control of language at this level of language development" (p. 84). The activities suggested here are more than writing drills. They are exercises in language and thinking that help students gain control over their written expression of original ideas.

It must be emphasized that imitation is practice. It is not the same as writing well independently. But it is excellent practice. Students begin to acquire skill in writing by actually producing their own ideas in well-formed sentences. In following models, they are like beginning painters trying to imitate Van Gogh's brush strokes or novice pianists playing along with a Horowitz recording. They are apprentices, constructing effective prose and poetry, learning by doing. As they change, imitate, manipulate, and create, they master a wide range of language forms and conventions. Eventually, they will not need the models and exercises; they will write well on their own.

Revising and Polishing

A significant feature of public writing is that the work, intended for an audience other than the writer, needs to be free of confusing wording and careless errors. Because we seldom write a first draft with clarity and precision, we must revise and polish to communicate effectively. Reworking a draft may include rewriting sentences, reorganizing the sequence of ideas, elaborating points, deleting or changing words, and editing the copy to check spelling and punctuation. Revision involves fussing with the work, which requires disciplined attention to meaning and form. Judgments must be made about relatively simple matters such as spelling or punctuation and about more elusive matters such as overall effect or tone.

The revision stage of the writing process, perhaps more than any other, involves high-level thinking. The writer must reexamine the piece critically to see if, indeed, it conveys the intended meaning. The writer must, in effect, become the audience. Graves and Hodge (1979) advise

> that whenever anyone sits down to write he should imagine a crowd of his prospective readers (rather than a grammarian in cap and gown) looking over his shoulder. They will be asking such questions as: 'What does this sentence mean?' 'Why do you trouble to tell me that again?' 'Why have you chosen such a ridiculous metaphor?' 'Must I really read this long, limping sentence?' 'Haven't you got your ideas muddled here?' By anticipating and listing as many questions of this sort as possible, the writer will discover certain tests of intelligibility to which he may regularly submit his work. . . . (p. 19)

A significant feature of public writing is that the work, intended for an audience other than the writer, needs to be revised and polished to communicate effectively. When students share their work regularly, writing becomes a real act of communication.

The advice is intended for adult writers, but even immature writers can learn to attend to fabricated readers over their shoulders. In fact, the basic process of revision is the same whether a first grader decides to add a single adjective to a description of her cat or whether an adult decides to reorder an argument so that it will be more forceful. In both instances, the writers—at different levels of sophistication—are anticipating, reflecting, evaluating, and making decisions. In short, these writers are thinking.

Sometimes it is easy to spot needed changes, as when writers realize that they have left out important details or have not described something accurately. At other times, it is not clear how much revision is necessary. Even accomplished writers confess that rewriting involves a certain amount of intuition. Antonia Fraser, a British author, was once asked how she knew that a work of hers was finished. She replied by comparing a piece of writing to a kitchen sponge. There comes a time, she said, when you look at a well-used sponge and just know that it is time to throw it out; similarly, there comes a time when you examine a piece of worked-over writing and just know that you are through with it.

To develop their own revision abilities and intuitions, students need to realize that rewriting is an integral part of public writing, not just something the teacher requires. Many will resist because they do not see how their work might be improved. Some will claim they "don't care" and would rather not put more effort into their papers. Resistance and indifference may take time to overcome because these feelings usually result from a general sense of ineptitude with writing. The feelings of incompetency may have developed over a period of years. Students need support and encouragement as *writers* if they are to be convinced that *rewriting* is a worthwhile activity.

To develop confidence, students most of all need audiences for their public writing. Someone besides the teacher must read their work. Other adults—in school, at home, and in the larger community—may all serve as audiences. Students may write to companies for information, send letters to newspaper editors or public figures, communicate concerns to the principal or to government officials, and in other ways write about real issues to people outside the classroom. Such audiences can give students compelling reasons to revise and polish their work and can bolster confidence, even if responses are delayed or never come at all.

Peer response is also extremely valuable, not only because peers serve as audiences but also because the response is immediate. When students share their work regularly, writing becomes a real act of communication rather than an artificial assignment. Peer response also shows students that rewriting is desirable, even necessary. As Moffett and Wagner (1983) point out, when students read each other's work, they act both as responders and coaches. The need to revise follows naturally as the writer considers how the audience has responded. For these reasons, one of the best ways to help students revise and polish is to let them help each other.

In the primary grades, peer response can take very simple forms. Children might read their papers aloud and make a few comments about what they especially liked. They may also help each other with spelling, punctuation, and capitalization. As they mature, students may work together on other elements such as organization, sentence structure, and word choice. One-to-one peer conferences are useful, and writing response groups of three or four are also valuable (Moffett and Wagner, 1983; Healy, 1980; Crowhurst, 1979). As students work with each other on their first drafts and on later rewrites, their collaborative efforts will be extremely useful in helping them achieve their writing purposes.

Students may read one another's work or, in a group conference, may take turns reading their work aloud and listening to responses. They discuss papers in a workshop environment, recognizing that the goal is not just to find errors but also to help each other communicate clearly and effectively. Because each student acts as both writer and responder, different techniques of writing and responding will be demonstrated in the group. All will learn to improve their abilities in both areas. Perhaps most important, students learn that their writing is of interest and of value to an audience other than that provided by the teacher. The emphasis is on writing as communication rather than on writing to earn grades.

It is useful to establish a classroom routine for taking public writings through several drafts with the help of peers and teacher. In one elementary classroom, for example, this list of steps in the public writing process was posted on the bulletin board:

The Writing Process

1. Get a story idea.
2. Talk about your idea with a classmate.
3. Write a first draft.
4. Have a conference with a classmate.
5. Revise and write a second draft.
6. Have a group conference.
7. Revise again.
8. Choices:
   a. If satisfied, edit for mechanics.
   b. If not satisfied, return to Step 4.
9. Have a conference with a classmate.
10. Make final changes and corrections.
11. Have an editing conference with the teacher.
12. Publish your work.

Early in the school year, the teacher had explained each step and had guided the children through the process several times, explaining the value of writing successive drafts based on the audience's response. At first students were hesitant about discussing their work with each other, and they often turned to the teacher to ask what to say and do. The teacher gave them many suggestions and often sat in on peer conferences to model the kind of responses that students could learn to do on their own. As the year progressed, the students needed less and less teacher direction and help as they learned how to discuss their work and gained confidence in their own judgments.

Throughout the year, the teacher repeatedly stressed the value of revision, not only by expecting students to follow the steps on the list but also by praising students for their work on successive drafts. Students, indeed, received as much praise for these as for their final, published products. The teacher maintained a relaxed, workshop atmosphere in the room; this attitude also encouraged the children to devote time and attention to revision. Students did not hurry to produce a final draft. They eagerly sought advice about how they might improve their first efforts.

In this classroom, students learned from experience that writing is a gradual process of reshaping initial ideas into final, published works. They learned that developing an idea is the first order of business and that editing to correct spelling and other mechanical details comes only with the preparation of final drafts. They learned that discussing their work is an integral part of the process and that peer response is as important as the teacher's response. In fact, students came to rely on one another to revise and polish their work—more than they relied on the teacher.

Some groups will need more guidance than others to learn to work together productively. If students have had little experience in responding to each other's writing, they may need to begin with a rather structured approach. Writing response guides are useful tools for this purpose. Students use these forms as a basis for their discussions of other students' work. A guide should stimulate critical and creative thought about the writing while encouraging students to make positive comments. Here is one version:

Writing Response Guide

1. This is what I thought when you finished _____.
2. This is what I think you are trying to say _____.
3. These details were most vivid to me _____.
4. I didn't understand _____.
5. I'd like to know more about _____.
6. I thought of these words when I was listening: _____.
7. I liked _____ best because _____.
8. Here's an idea for a title _____.

As peers respond, the writer gets interesting, useful feedback. If the guide is used in a group conference, group members hear diverse responses; each learns new ways of talking about writing. All hear several papers that have different styles and techniques; students pick up ideas to use in their own work. Response guides also promote use of a variety of thinking processes. Students must evaluate, interpret, summarize, determine the need for elaboration, and respond creatively. With active thinking, talking, reading, and listening, peer-response sessions become lively and productive. As students become more practiced, they will have less need for response guides. They will have their own ideas about what to say.

Questions inevitably arise as students discuss a paper: What do you mean here? How does this relate to that? Could you say more about this? But what happened when...? What did that look like? What did you say when...? Elaborating, specifying, and clarifying result; better writing appears. Responders also listen critically for the purpose of helping a peer write more clearly. Response groups develop listening skills as surely as they develop writing skills.

Here is an example of a response-group session that took place in a sixth-grade class. Four children had put their names on the board under the heading of Group Conference. This meant that each one had a work in progress and had had brief conferences with one or two other children and perhaps with the teacher at the first-draft stage. Having done some revising, all four now felt the need to read their pieces to a group. The teacher decided to sit in on this group conference, as these four children still needed some help in discussing their works.

After a child read his or her paper, at least one other person summarized the piece. These summaries helped the writers to see if they had achieved their intended order and emphasis. The responders, in turn, gained practice in listening attentively and restating the main points of the pieces. After summarizing, the group asked questions; this helped the writer decide how the work might be revised. The teacher took notes for the writers so that each could concentrate on the responses and yet would have a record of what was discussed.

TEACHER: Martin, what is your piece about?

MARTIN: My summer at the beach.

TEACHER: Did you spend the whole summer there?

MARTIN: My whole family always does. My Dad owns a store, and we all work in it.

TEACHER: That sounds very interesting. Let's hear your paper.

MARTIN: In the summers I go to the beach. I mostly work in my dad's store and it is called Surf's Up. My dad bought it in 1983. That summer I worked some of the time as a busboy, washing tables. I got 20 dollars a week. Last year and this year I did the French fries and I got 75 dollars a week. I really like to work in the store.

In my spare time I go to the beach. With the money I have I bought a Boogie Board that cost $104 with leash, fins and handle. A Boogie Board is something you ride in the water. It is something like surfing but you lay on it. I also bought 45 dollar flippers. You need flippers when you go Boogie Boarding so you can catch the wave.

So when I go to the beach I have lots of fun. We live in a condo called the Firefire Meadow.

My dad bought another store about 5 miles away from Surf's Up. That store is called Surf's Up Too. I will be working in Surf's Up Too making pizza.

TEACHER: Let me summarize your piece, Martin. Let's see, you spend your days at the beach working in your Dad's store where your job is to fry French fries. And with the money you made you bought a Boogie Board and flippers. Now your father has a new store called Surf's Up Too and you're going to be the pizza man. Did I miss anything?

MARTIN: You forgot that we live at Firefire Meadow and that we go to the beach.

TEACHER: That's right, I did. All right, questions from anyone?

ERIN: Is your dad's store a restaurant?

MARTIN: Yeah, it's pretty neat.

ERIN: Does everybody in your family work in the restaurant? [Erin knows that Martin is one of six children.]

MARTIN: All but the two youngest. They're too irresponsible.

TEACHER: [wanting to encourage questions that will help Martin see he needs to focus his account] Martin, what is the most interesting part of your piece to you?

MARTIN: [after a pause] Working in the store.

TEACHER: You really like to work in the store.

MARTIN: Yeah. I like making French fries. They're the best. My dad doesn't buy the cheap ones, you know, the thin ones. He buys the medium and I fry them just right.

BEN: Did anything funny ever happen when you were frying French fries?

MARTIN: Well, one time I dumped the fries into the pan where we keep the cooked ones only somebody had washed the pan and hadn't put it back. Boy, was that a mess! All over the counter! Then sometimes I forget I'm cooking them and I let them burn. One man walked out.

BEN: Why did he walk out?

MARTIN: Because I burned his fries and he didn't want to wait while I cooked some more.

SANDY: How long do they take to cook?

MARTIN: About three minutes.

TEACHER: Martin, do you want to write about this?

MARTIN: Yes.

TEACHER: Find the place you think it should go and write a 1. [On a separate piece of paper the teacher writes the following: 1. French fries, cooked, spilled, sometimes burned.]

BEN: You said you're going to make pizza. Will your dad teach you?

MARTIN: Nope. I already know how.

BEN: You know how to twirl dough?

MARTIN: Sure! It's easy!

BEN: I think that would be a good thing to put in your story.

MARTIN: Yeah. I think so too.

TEACHER: Find the place and put a 2. [On the separate page the teacher writes the following: 2. How I make pizza.] Any more questions for Martin? No? All right, Martin, what do you think you want to do with your paper now?

MARTIN: I think I'll write more about cooking, I mean cooking at the beach. I think I'll leave out the stuff about the condo and the Boogie Board.

The teacher saw that Martin had several stories to tell about his summer at the beach. By asking Martin about what was most interesting to him, the teacher helped him focus on one aspect of his experience and identify a central point for this paper. The other students asked questions that showed Martin what they were interested in. The exercise helped him to realize how much else he had to write about on the topic of cooking. The group continued.

TEACHER: Who's next? Ben? Let's hear your piece.

BEN: One day in the winter of 1981, my brother Willie and I were playing out in the snow. When we got cold we went inside. My mother made us some hot chocolate, but she forgot to turn the burner off on the stove. Nobody noticed it. Willie and I were playing a board game and I won. We decided to get some blankets in the den, because we were still cold. We had to go through the kitchen to get to the den. When we got the blankets we started to wrestle. Willie ran out of the den and into the kitchen. I ran after him. He was right next to the stove and we didn't notice the burner was on. I ran at him and gave him a push. He tripped over a little stool next to the stove and his elbow landed on the hot burner. The burner gave him a second degree burn. We didn't have to go to the hospital because my mother is a nurse. Willie was too busy crying to be mad at me, but after he stopped crying, he blamed the whole thing on me. But it was both our faults. My mother took Willie's side and I had to go to my room for the rest of the day. When my father came home he sort of took my side. He said, "It was both Willie's and Ben's fault." I got out of staying in my room all day. We usually don't wrestle around the stove anymore.

TEACHER: Who would like to summarize Ben's story?

SANDY: Once when you were little, you and your brother were playing in the snow. When you went in the house, your mother made you hot chocolate, but she forgot to turn off the stove. Then when you and your brother were rough-housing, he got burned. You got blamed until your dad came home and said it wasn't all your fault. Did I miss anything?

BEN: No.

SANDY: How big was your brother's burn?

BEN: This big. [He makes a circle with his fingers.]

TEACHER: Would you say as big as a quarter?

BEN: No, as big as two quarters.

SANDY: You could put that in your story.

BEN: Yeah. I think I'll say as big as an egg yolk.

TEACHER: Find the place you think it should go and write a 1. [The teacher starts a page of notes for Ben, writing the following: 1. burn as big as an egg yolk.]

MARTIN: You said your mother is a nurse. What did she do?

BEN: She grabbed Willie. He was screaming. And she shoved his elbow under the spigot, under cold water. Then she squeezed some greasy stuff out of a tube all over it. She knew what to do because she's a nurse.

MARTIN: Are you going to put that in your story?

BEN: Yeah, I think I will.

TEACHER: Find the place and write a 2. [On the page of notes the teacher writes the following: 2. shoved elbow under cold water, squeezed greasy stuff out of a tube.]

TEACHER: Ben, when you got the blankets, did you wrap up in them?

BEN: No, we were just carrying them from the den to the living room. They were big and Willie was dragging his. I had mine all balled up under my arm. That's why I could shove him. And he got his feet and the blanket and the stool all mixed up.

SANDY: You could put that in your story.

BEN: Do you think it would be good?

SANDY: Sure. I didn't think you still had the blankets when you were at the stove. Telling about the blankets would show more about how it happened. About how Willie tripped and everything.

BEN: OK. [Ben puts a 3 on his paper while the teacher writes the following: 3. Blankets. Willie got feet, blanket, stool all mixed up.]

ERIN: How did you feel when your dad got home?

BEN: Scared at first, but then I felt better when he said it was both our faults. He really yelled at my mother, though. He said she didn't dare forget a hot stove burner.

ERIN: Do you want to put that in your story?

BEN: Maybe. I'll think about it. [He writes a 4 on his paper while the teacher writes the following: 4. Dad came home. I was scared. Dad yelled at Mom.]

TEACHER: I think you've had some good questions, Ben. Here are your notes. What do you think you want to do with your piece?

BEN: Well, I think I'll tell about how big the burn was and what my mom did. And I'll tell more about the blankets, too. And maybe I'll put in more about how I felt when my dad got home and what he said and all.

Ben had a well-focused account, but as the listeners asked questions, he realized that he had left out some important and interesting details. The group helped him determine which points to elaborate.

In both conferences, the teacher, though guiding and participating in the discussion, tried not to dominate. As much as possible, she encouraged the children to talk to each other rather than listen to her. Also, she purposely avoided becoming involved with every detail that she noticed. For instance, when Ben was describing how his mother gave first aid to Willie, he said that she "squeezed greasy stuff out of a tube." The teacher was tempted to suggest that perhaps a more precise word was needed here (e.g., salve, ointment), but she decided that the development of Ben's story line took precedence at this stage. She wrote Ben's own words on the separate page, knowing that she could talk about vocabulary with him at a later teacher conference if Ben or another child did not take up this matter.

Though peer response is extremely valuable to the young writer, the teacher also has an important role to play. The teacher monitors groups closely and is there, with a greater store of knowledge about writing, to help students refine their responses and look more closely at their work. Tactful guidance is necessary, of course. The goal is not to shape the work into the teacher's ideal but to help the groups improve their responding techniques and to help the writers make their own decisions about what they might wish to revise.

Besides guiding response groups, the teacher may sometimes plan special problem-solving sessions, based on needs that both the groups and the teacher have observed. For instance, if students are writing rather monotonous strings of simple, declarative sentences, some practice in sentence combining (see Chapter 9) may be in order. Then when students return to their revising, they may be encouraged to try sentence combining as they polish their work. Objectives for such sessions should be specific and limited, so as not to overwhelm students with negative attention to the immaturities in their work. Rather, students should learn that they have choices when they write—they should find out about alternate ways of stating their ideas, some of which are more vivid, clear, and precise than others.

Problem-solving sessions are most effective when the group has a specific bit of writing to consider—perhaps a sentence or two, or a paragraph. Samples may be taken from students' papers or from other pieces of writing, such as articles from periodicals or even the teacher's own work. The writing may be put on the board or an overhead transparency, or each student may be given a copy. The following kinds of problems can be tackled through discussion and group rewriting:

- Awkward sentences
- Sentences with ambiguous referents
- Wordy sentences in need of pruning
- Sentences that might be combined
- Paragraphs needing more development
- Vocabulary that could be more precise
- Elements of mechanics such as punctuation

The goals for revising and polishing are two-fold: to give students real audiences for their work (and thus a real need to rewrite), and to help them sharpen writing skills with well-timed lessons that address what they are ready to learn. For further reading on revising and polishing, see Petty and Bowen (1967), Moffett (1968), Moffett and Wagner (1983), Caplan and Keech (1980), Britton (1982), Graves (1983), and Calkins (1986).

Writing and Reading

Becoming an effective writer is a process that is inextricably linked to that of becoming an effective reader. However, it seems that reading and writing are often separated, in the minds of educators and in the curricula that they design and that guide their work. It is not uncommon to see a writing curriculum and a reading curriculum written by different committees, placed under separate covers, and perhaps even taught by different teachers. Yet educators do not think of dividing school time into addition class and subtraction class; they do not have a multiplication curriculum and a division curriculum. Certainly, teachers want students to practice and to use each mathematical operation skillfully, so they work on one or the other separately, to build specific skills. But they think of this as teaching mathematics, and they stress the underlying numerical relationships that they want students to grasp. In the same way, reading and writing are not separate subjects. Both are facets of communication through language. The more skilled students become in one, the more skilled they become in the other.

This chapter has included many examples of lessons that make conscious use of the inherent relationship between reading and writing. The approach is based on basic similarities between these two processes:

- *Reading and writing both require active thinking.* We cannot read idly and read well. We must anticipate, reflect, interpret, and judge, whether we follow a narrative sequence, look for particular facts, evaluate an essayist's point of view, or recreate the images that a poet has put into words. Similarly, writing requires effort and attention, whether we are constructing a story, presenting a body of information, stating our own point of view, or putting images into words in a poem. Both processes stem from the same kind of intellectual involvement—an active construction of meaning.
- *Writing and reading are purposeful actions.* The clearer the purpose, the better the action. The purpose for reading may be a determined effort to comprehend a complex technical manual or a lazy excursion into a fantasy world. In every case, the reader must know that purpose to accomplish it well. The same is true for writing. When we put words on paper, we must have some purpose in mind—to persuade, convince, inform, entertain, instruct, or describe, to name only a few. We need to have a clear sense of what we are about when we write or read so that we will perform well.
- *Reading and writing are both forms of dialogue.* An author speaks; a reader listens and responds. Effective writers are concerned about their readers; they choose words and arrange statements so that the reader will sit up and take notice. Much of writing is, in fact, putting oneself in the place of the unseen and unknown audience, reading the piece over and over to see if it holds together properly and creates the intended effect. Similarly, astute readers enter into a dialogue with the absent author. When we laugh, cry, muse, or hurl the book across the room in a rage, we are quite surely communicating with the writer.
- *Writing and reading are language dependent.* The more extensive our vocabularies, our sentence sense, and our rhetorical skill, the more easily we will be able to process text and put our own ideas into words. As language-based skills, reading and writing are equally dependent on our accumulated store of language knowledge. The beginning reader or writer who has a good command of oral language will be better able to receive and express language in print than one who has a limited oral background. The advanced reader or writer is no less dependent on general language ability; we read and write well to the extent that we understand and can use the language.
- *Reading and writing reinforce each other.* Whatever we read becomes a model for our own writing, whether or not we are conscious of the model as such. We may imitate a particular style directly, to practice and learn, or we may simply admire a certain kind of written expression and find our own work coming closer and closer to our ideal. Our writing also affects our

reading. Other authors stimulate our thinking, give us facts and opinions that shape our own perspectives, and make us want to have our own say in the matter. We often turn to books when we write because, as authors ourselves, we have a particular interest in what other authors have done with words and ideas.

Shaughnessy (1977), Applebee (1977), Hunt (1982), Oliver (1982), Smith (1983), Squire (1983), Tierney and Pearson (1983), and Pearson (1985), among others, stress the common elements that reading and writing share. They find a reciprocity inherent in the development of the two abilities.

Just as the "operations" of reading and writing are clearly related, so are the conditions under which these behaviors are developed most effectively. The best writing is purposeful writing, stemming from the desire to communicate. Similarly, the best reading is purposeful reading, growing from the desire to know. Students must act on their own intentions when they open a book or pick up a pencil. Without active, purposeful student involvement, educators might as well be holding forth in an empty room. As Kelley (1951) stated:

> Most of the time that is wasted in education is wasted when the individual proceeds on the dictum of someone else to do something that is devoid of meaning to him. By doing this, it is possible to get into so-called "production" sooner, and to turn out more volume of "product," but we mistake the shadows for the substance if we judge growth on the basis of volume of material produced. (p. 28)

Teachers can say, with no preliminaries, a statement such as "Read Chapter 4 for tomorrow," and they can assign writing topics from a list. Both practices may get students busy faster and may cover more ground. But the reading will be mechanistic and superficial, and the writing will be forced and awkward. Students must not just cover pages, trying to follow a structure that exists only in a teacher's head. What students read and write must reflect their purposes as learners and communicators. Effective reading and writing require thinking, talking, rereading, reflecting, and responding, all of which take time and which may disturb a tight schedule. However, these are the elements of learning that are vital to the development of literacy.

Suggested Activities

1. Guide a group of three to five children through the process of preparing a saturation report. Keep a log of your activities with the group.
2. Write an "I-Search" report that you could show to students as an example when you teach them how to write this kind of report.
3. Role play a writing conference with three peers. One should be the teacher; the others should be the students. The group should discuss

one or more first drafts. Analyze the experience. How could the conference have been more helpful to the writers?

4. Try out a word processing program that is designed for children. Teach a child how to use the program. Evaluate the program from your (a teacher's) point of view and analyze the child's reactions.

References

Applebee, A. "Writing and Reading." *Journal of Reading* 20(March 1977):534–37.
——————. *The Child's Concept of Story: Ages Two to Seventeen.* Chicago: University of Chicago Press, 1978.

Bates, E. *Emergence of Symbols: Cognition and Communication in Infancy.* New York: Academic Press, 1979.

Britton, J. "Notes on a Working Hypothesis about Writing" in G. Pradl, ed., *Prospect and Retrospect: Selected Essays of James Britton.* Montclair, NJ: Boynton/Cook, 1982.

Calkins, L. *The Art of Teaching Writing.* Portsmouth, NH: Heinemann, 1986.

Caplan R., and Keech, C. *Showing-Writing: A Training Program to Help Students Be Specific.* Berkeley, CA: Bay Area Writing Project/University of California, 1980.

Chesney, B. "In the Question was the Answer: A Study in Trivia." *English Journal* 71(December 1982):41–42.

Cramer, R., and Cramer, B. "Writing by Imitating Models." *Language Arts* 52(October 1975):1011–14+.

Crowhurst, M. "The Writing Workshop: An Experiment in Peer Response to Writing." *Language Arts* 56(October 1979):757–62.

Dunning, S. "Imitation Writing." Presentation to the South Coast Writing Project. Santa Barbara: University of California at Santa Barbara, 1983.

Graves, D. M. *Writing: Teachers and Children at Work.* Portsmouth, NH: Heinemann, 1983.

Graves, R., and Hodge, A. *The Reader Over Your Shoulder: A Handbook for Writers of English Prose.* New York: Vintage Books, 1979.

Hanf, M. B. "Mapping: A Technique for Translating Reading into Thinking." *Journal of Reading* 14(January 1971):225–30+.

Healey, J. *Teaching Writing K Through 8.* Berkeley, CA: Instructional Laboratory, University of California, 1978.

Healy, M. K. *Using Student Writing Response Groups in the Classroom.* Berkeley, CA: Bay Area Writing Project/University of California, 1980.

Hennings, D. G. *Communication in Action.* Chicago: Rand McNally, 1986.

Hunt, R. A. "Toward a Process-Intervention Model in Literature Teaching." *College English* 44(April 1982):345–57.

Kelley, E. *The Workshop Way of Learning.* New York: Harper and Brothers, 1951.

Loban, W. *The Language of Elementary School Children* (Research Report No. 1). Urbana, IL: National Council of Teachers of English, 1963.

McKenzie, G. R. "Data Charts: A Crutch for Helping Pupils Organize Reports. *Language Arts* 56(October 1979):784–88.

Macrorie, K. *Searching Writing.* Rochelle Park, NJ: Hayden, 1976.

Mandler, J. M., and Johnson, N. S. "Remembrance of Things Parsed: Story Structure and Recall." *Cognitive Psychology* 9(January 1977):111–51.

May, F. *To Help Children Communicate*. Columbus, OH: Charles Merrill, 1980.

Moffett, J. *A Student-Centered Language Arts Curriculum, Grades K–13: A Handbook for Teachers*. Boston: Houghton Mifflin, 1968.

————. "Integrity in the Teaching of Writing." *Phi Delta Kappan* 61(December 1979):276–79.

————, and Wagner, B. *A Student-Centered Language Arts Curriculum, Grades K–13*. Boston: Houghton Mifflin, 1983.

Myers, M. "Five Approaches to the Teaching of Writing." *Learning* 6(April 1978):38–41.

Noyce, R. M., and Christie, J. F. "Using Literature to Develop Children's Grasp of Syntax." *The Reading Teacher* 35(December 1981):298–304.

Odegaard, J. M., and May, F. "Creative Grammar and the Writing of Third Graders." *Elementary School Journal* 73(September 1972):156–61.

Oliver, L. J. "Helping Students Overcome Writer's Block." *Journal of Reading* 26(November 1982):162–69.

Pearson, P. D. "Changing the Face of Reading Comprehension Instruction." *The Reading Teacher* 38(April 1985):724–38.

Petty, W., and Bowen, M. *Slithery Snakes and Other Aids to Children's Writing*. Englewood Cliffs, NJ: Prentice-Hall, 1967.

Pradl, G. *Expectation and Cohesion*. Berkeley, CA: Bay Area Writing Project/University of California, 1979.

Rico, G. L., and Clagget, M. F. *Balancing the Hemispheres: Brain Research and the Teaching of Writing*. Berkeley, CA: Bay Area Writing Project/University of California, 1980.

Shaughnessy, M. *Errors and Expectations: A Guide for the Teacher of Basic Writing*. New York: Oxford University Press, 1977.

Smith, F. "Reading Like a Writer." *Language Arts* 60(May 1983):558–67.

Squire, J. R. "Composing and Comprehending: Two Sides of the Same Basic Process." *Language Arts* 60(May 1983):581–89.

Stein, N. L. "Methodological and Conceptual Issues in Writing Research." *Elementary School Journal* 84(September 1983):70–80.

————, and Glenn, C. G. "An Analysis of Story Comprehension in Elementary School Children" in R. O. Freedle, ed., *Advances in Discourse Processes. Vol. II: New Directions in Discourse Procession*. Norwood, NJ: Ablex, 1979.

Stotsky, S. L. "Sentence-Combining as a Curricular Activity: Its Effect on Written Language Development and Reading Comprehension." *Research in the Teaching of English* 9(Spring 1975):30–71.

Suid, M. "How to Take Copying out of Report Writing." *Learning* 8(November 1979):46+.

Tierney, R. J., and Pearson, P. D. "Toward a Composing Model of Reading." *Language Arts* 60(May 1983):568–80.

Wigginton, E. (ed.) *The Foxfire Book I*. Garden City, NY: Anchor Press/Doubleday, 1972.

Wittrock, M. C. "Writing and the Teaching of Reading." *Language Arts* 60(May 1983):600–06.

Suggested Readings

Atwell, N. *In the Middle: Writing, Reading, and Learning with Adolescents.* Portsmouth, NH: Heinemann, 1987.

Birnbaum, J. C. "The Reading and Composing Behavior of Selected Fourth and Seventh Grade Students." *Research in the Teaching of English* 16 (October 1982):241–60.

Boiarsky, C., and Johnson, C. "The Excellence in Education Report: Connecting Reading, Writing, and Thinking." *Curriculum Review* (December 1983):37–40.

Calkins, L. *Lessons from a Child.* Portsmouth, NH: Heinemann, 1983.

Donovan, T. R., and McClelland, B. W. (eds.) *Eight Approaches to Teaching Composition.* Urbana, IL: National Council of Teachers of English, 1979.

Emig, J. *The Composing Processes of Twelfth Graders.* Urbana, IL: National Council of Teachers of English, 1971.

Foster, D. *A Primer for Writing Teachers: Theories, Theorists, Issues, Problems.* Montclair, NJ: Boynton/Cook, 1983.

Gregg, L., and Steinberg, E. R. (eds.) *Cognitive Processes in Writing.* Hillsdale, NJ: Erlbaum, 1980.

Hansen, J.; Newkirk, T.; and Graves, D. M. *Breaking Ground: Teachers Relate Reading and Writing.* Portsmouth, NH: Heinemann, 1985.

Koch, K. *Wishes, Lies, and Dreams: Teaching Children to Write Poetry.* New York: Chelsea House, 1970.

Murray, D. M. *A Writer Teaches Writing: A Practical Method of Teaching Composition.* Boston: Houghton Mifflin, 1968.

Myers, M. *A Model for the Composing Process.* Berkeley, CA: Bay Area Writing Project/University of California, 1980.

Nessel, D. D. "Let's Start with the Conclusion." *Journal of Reading* 28(May 1985):744–45.

Nystrand, M. (ed.) *What Writers Know: The Language Process and Structure of Written Discourse.* New York: Academic Press, 1982.

Ponsot, M., and Deen, R. *Beat Not the Poor Desk (Writing: What to Teach, How to Teach It, and Why).* Montclair, NJ: Boynton/Cook, 1982.

Smith, F. *Writing and the Writer.* New York: Holt, Rinehart & Winston, 1981.

Tierney, R. J., and Leys, M. *What is the Value of Connecting Reading and Writing?* (Reading Education Report No. 55). Urbana, IL: Center for the Study of Reading/University of Illinois, 1984.

Wood, P. *You and Aunt Arie.* Kennebunk, ME: Star Press, 1975.

Zinsser, W. *On Writing Well.* New York: Harper & Row, 1985.

IV

Refining Expressive Abilities

As students develop abilities in oral and written expression, they need to learn the conventions of spelling, handwriting, grammar, and usage. Although these areas of study involve different emphases, they are alike in that they all demand attention to precision in communication. The value of precision lies not simply in adhering to language conventions because they exist but in consciously using them to make meanings clear to others. Mature speakers and writers know that carelessness will detract from a message, perhaps leaving the audience confused about the meaning or even making them doubt that either the message or the one who presents it deserves serious consideration. Concern for clarity is a mark of thinking individuals who are not satisfied with just getting the general idea across. Such people strive for exactness.

Precision is a worthy goal. Nonetheless, consistently correct spelling or usage, excellent handwriting, and detailed knowledge of grammar are not prerequisites for writing and speaking. Young children may be imprecise in many ways as they speak and write, and yet they still may communicate adequately. However, as children grow, they need gradually to gain control over language conventions so that they may speak and

247

write with ever greater maturity and effectiveness. Students who have a command of the language will be able to hold their own in oral and written discourse. They will gain the respect of listeners and readers, and they will develop a well-deserved sense of confidence that they will be successful in the adult world.

This section examines approaches to helping students refine their oral and written expressive abilities by learning to use language conventions skillfully. Chapter 8 includes discussions of spelling and handwriting. Chapter 9 presents some basic principles for teaching grammar and usage. Although each of these areas of study may be divided into a number of specific skills that can be taught and practiced, there should not be an emphasis on teaching skills in isolation, as if the end goal were simply the mastery of those skills. The teacher should always maintain a balance between giving specific skill instruction and providing opportunities for purposeful communication. As James Britton has suggested, "these skills of language are best acquired when made incidental to the achievement of a desired performance,"[1] such performances being, for example, the writing of stories or the enacting of creative dramas.

To achieve a good balance, the teacher must understand how knowledge of these conventions develops and what kinds of instruction are most effective for improving students' abilities.

[1] James Britton, "Take It From—Where?" in J. Britton, *Prospect and Retrospect.* G. Pradl, ed. Montclair, NJ: Boynton/Cook, 1982.

When writing is taught as a form of communication, children come to recognize the importance of spelling and handwriting as aids to that goal.

Spelling and Handwriting

When children first begin to write, usually before they come to school, they experiment with language in the same way that they experimented when they learned to talk. Their early writing efforts are more a kind of play with language than a concerted attempt to address an audience and receive a response. Gradually, children come to recognize writing as a form of communication. They become attentive to the writing of others, by seeing how adults use writing and by noting how written language appears in books. As children gain this new awareness, they become more attentive to the form of their own words on paper. They develop a new concern about how their writing looks because they want their writing to be read.

It is at this time, which usually occurs in the primary grades, that children can profit from instruction that will improve their ability to use conventional spelling. They also need to learn to form letters and words in a way that is clear and pleasing to the eye. Instruction in spelling and handwriting is best when it closely relates to what children experience and learn about language. The instructor can take advantage of students' natural desire to use writing to communicate. This chapter describes some approaches to teaching both spelling and handwriting.

Spelling

As little as three hundred years ago, there was no such thing as correct spelling. Variant spellings were used by writers and were readily accepted by readers. If a word could be deciphered, it was right. However, in our society, correct spelling is a mark of education. Indeed, it is assumed that literate people do not make spelling errors. Writers who want their work taken seriously are thus attentive to spelling. Besides not wanting to appear foolish, conscientious writers also want to be understood. They do not want the distraction of misspelled words to interfere with communication. As Graves (1983) points out, proper spelling is also a matter of good manners; it is the writer's way of being considerate of the reader. Taught from that perspective, spelling skill is an important element of writing ability. However, it is not a skill that young writers master easily in a short period of time.

Some people claim that English spelling is difficult because the written language is highly irregular; that is, many words are spelled in ways that do not correspond directly to their pronunciation. It is true that many words deviate from typical patterns. However, Anderson (1985) points out that English spelling is more regular than it seems when one considers that words are spelled according to meaning as well as according to sound (see also Follett, 1966; Mencken, 1980; and Templeton, 1983). Becker, Dixon, and Anderson (1980) analyzed 26,000 frequently-used English words and found that although sound governs the spelling of many, the meaning dictates the spelling of considerably more. Meaning rather than sound is reflected in the following spellings, for example: know, once, straight, sacrilege. Thus, learning to spell in English is rather difficult, not because the written language is unpredictable but because it is predictable in subtle ways that take time and experience to discover. Spelling involves more than simply learning sound-letter correspondence rules and memorizing the exceptions. Mature spelling is dependent as much on an understanding of word meanings and etymology as it is on knowing how to represent the sounds of the language. Spelling is actually a "highly complex intellectual accomplishment" (Hodges, 1981).

Learning to spell is probably best considered as a problem-solving process that extends over several years. The process is influenced by children's cognitive development and by their varied experiences with written language. In these ways, learning to spell is similar to acquiring oral language. Children learn to speak by listening to and interacting with others. Using a problem-solving approach, they test their understandings each time they speak, trying out different ways of using words that they retain or reject, depending on the kind of response they get (Chomsky, 1969; Brown, 1973; Menyuk, 1977). Children's sense of the rules of oral language is refined as they mature.

Researchers have observed that children employ a similar process as they learn to write (Read, 1971; Templeton, 1980; Gentry, 1981; Wood, 1982; Graves, 1983). Even before children come to school, they imitate the act of writing, usually by scribbling or drawing. Then, as they encounter books and learn to read, they want their own work to be intelligible, and they begin to refine their concepts of how written language looks. If they are encouraged to write freely, they repeatedly test these concepts through experimentation. They invent different ways of spelling words that they revise and refine as they assimilate information about sound patterns and meaning patterns. The experimentation, which yields much unconventional spelling, is an integral part of the development of a child's spelling knowledge and skill. This development occurs gradually and goes through predictable stages.

Stages of Spelling Development

Beginning with the studies of Read (1971) and Chomsky (1971), researchers have observed the stages of learning to spell by looking at samples of children's writing. They have analyzed the strategies that the children have used to encode words. Although young writers' products may seem almost meaningless to many adults at first glance, a closer look reveals that the children work quite thoughtfully and purposefully to communicate, using the best knowledge they have acquired about what writing is and about how written language should look.

First attempts at writing usually involve unrecognizable combinations of lines, rudimentary pictures, and any letters or numbers the child can produce. This scribbling, called "garble" by McDonell and Osburn (1980), is akin to the babbling stage of babies, who imitate speech sounds and rhythms before saying actual words. Young writers at the earliest stage are imitating the physical act of writing more than anything else, although they also realize to some extent that a paper with marks is a form of communication. They eagerly show their work to others.

Children move to the next stage of development when they begin to realize that print is composed largely of letters. At this stage, children write much less garble and begin to produce many more recognizable letters. However, they have not yet acquired a concept of what a "word" is, and they do not yet realize that letters can stand for sounds. Thus, their pseudowriting does not "work" and is often unintelligible even to themselves (Clay, 1975; Hall and Hall, 1984). Gentry (1981) refers to this pseudowriting as the *deviant spelling stage.*

Next, children acquire the concept of "word." Henderson (1985) identifies this point as the first critical step in the growth toward literacy. As children realize what *word* means, they also come to realize that letters can represent sounds in words. At this point, they become attentive to the sounds that they hear in words, and they begin to invent spellings as they write. Gentry (1981) labels children's early inventive efforts the *prephonemic stage* and observes that letter-sound correspondences are usually incomplete or inconsistent; only one or two letters may represent each word. For instance, the word *Christmas* might now be written as *Krms.* Wood (1982) observes that children at this stage attempt to represent sounds as closely as possible. Even though they may write only one letter to stand for a word, that letter will usually reflect the dominant sound the child hears in the word (for instance, *S* for *Santa* or *R* for *market*). Significantly, children will often reinvent the spelling of a word each time they write it; several different spellings of the same word may occur in a single piece of writing (Henderson, 1985).

As they continue to write, children match letters to sounds with ever greater thoroughness. Their invented and reinvented spellings represent in print almost all the sounds they hear in words. Gentry calls this next level the *phonetic stage.* Many words are still spelled unconventionally, with letter names often matched to sounds (for instance, *eighty* might be written *ade*). Some highly familiar words (frequently encountered in print) are sometimes spelled conventionally. At this stage, writers are gaining confidence in their abilities to encode whatever ideas they have. With encouragement, they can write fluently on myriad topics, and the work can be readily deciphered. Here are some examples from children in the primary grades:

Tuwday is a spchl day. Tuwday is Krismosday. Tuwday I em goag tuw gat mi thegs. Mi thegs our ioc skts and a slad and snuw skes.

I like scrglys and for the wintr the scrglys gathr nuts and put the nuts in the tree for the long wintr. I lik to weth the scrglys jmp frm won brach to a nater. Sume play gams weth ball. The balls are barys. I like to weth the scrglys chas ech uter.

> I like playgrowns becaues ther are sweing sets and sliting boods and juglojim to jlgol on and muce bars to muce on and gras and thats why playgrwns are so fun. They hav wut you need to play weth.
>
> I jus got a bulet in bord yester day. My mother hes a bulet in bord. My big brthrs don have a bulet in bord. I got it for my imporin paprs. My imporin paprs are my reprt cords.

Gradually, as phonetic spellers become more proficient with reading, they move to what Gentry calls a *transitional stage*. Many familiar words are now spelled correctly, although invented, phonetic spellings continue to occur. Children now include vowels or silent letters to mark vowels in each syllable, and words now include commonly occurring clusters of letters (however, the wrong clusters may be used in some words). Because children are now reading, they have a good idea of the way many words are spelled conventionally. They also have developed a refined sense of audience and want their writing to be readable. This child's story about birds is a good example of transitional stage spelling:

> I saw a woodpecker the smoring peching on my windoe. On Saturday my brother cawt a roben. My grandfather is a student all about birds.

After this transitional stage, according to Gentry, children move to the *standard spelling stage*. Most words are now spelled correctly.

Henderson (1985) integrated the research findings of Bissex (1980), Gentry (1981), and others to offer a comprehensive stage theory of spelling development. He suggests that skill develops from the early years, when young writers become attentive to the phonetic elements of written language, well into adulthood, when learners are ever more aware of the ways in which etymology and meaning account for certain spellings. Henderson's work is summarized in Table 8.1. Note how he relates spelling stages to stages of development in reading.

Here is a summary of Henderson's stages, some of his examples, and the implications for instruction. Most children enter the first stage before they go to school. Succeeding stages are reached at different chronological ages, depending on children's cognitive maturity (see Table 8.1 for age ranges).

Stage 1: Preliterate Word Knowledge   At this stage, similar to Gentry's deviant stage, children are acquiring oral language and are becoming aware of language in print. As they look at books and have many opportunities to scribble, draw, and "write," they begin to acquire a sense of how written language looks. They grasp the concept of what a word is.

Children need to be aware of words as concrete objects before they are

TABLE 8.1 Stages of Spelling Development

Age 1–7	Age 5–9	Age 6–12	Age 8–18	Age 10–100
Stage 1 *Preliterate*	Stage 2 *Letter name*	Stage 3 *Within Word Pattern*	Stage 4 *Syllable Juncture*	Stage 5 *Derivational Constancies*
Scribbles Identifies pictures Draws Imitates writing Learns letters	Most sight words spelled correctly Invented spelling by letter name	Most sight words spelled correctly Invented spellings honor short vowels and long vowel markers	Sight words may or *may not* be transferred to spelling performance Invented-spelling errors occur at juncture and schwa positions	Sight words may or *may not* transfer Invented spellings "most frequently misspelled"
Episode 1 **(Concept of Word)**		**Episode 2** **(Silent Reading)**		**Episode 3** **(Abstract Thought)**
Readiness	*Beginning Reading*	*Early Reading*	*Toward Maturity in Reading*	
Talks Listens to stories Requests stories Identifies symbols Recites to print	Steady acquisition of sight vocabulary Support for reading necessary Oral reading Word-by-word reading: prosodic form delayed Basic story form used functionally	Semantic support sufficient Silent reading established Prosodic oral reading Rapid word acquisition Predictions accurate for simple stories and expository material	Functional vocabulary mastered Common plot complexities mastered Basic discipline mastered	Classical vocabulary expands rapidly Metalinguistic reasoning applied to form and content

Edmund Henderson, *Teaching Spelling*, p. 41. Copyright © 1985 by Houghton Mifflin Company. Used by permission.

ready to examine words and letters within words systematically. Some children grasp this concept intuitively if they have had wide and meaningful experience with print. Parents who read to children and who point out words in the environment provide excellent information to help their youngsters develop word awareness. In a language-experience classroom in school, where children regularly dictate stories to the teacher, the students readily see the relationship between their spoken words and the words the teacher writes. Students also note how white spaces separate words. Words become concrete, familiar entities, and students begin to develop a sense of how language is encoded in print. Thus, beginning reading activities at home and in school help to develop prerequisites for their later development of spelling skills.

Stage 2: Letter-name Spelling At this stage, children are aware that letters can represent sounds, and they begin to spell alphabetically. They invent spellings according to the sounds they hear, making direct letter-to-sound matches. Their spellings are inconsistent because each time a word is spelled, it is reinvented. *Letter* may be written as *latr* or *ladr; water* may be *wootr* or *witr,* and the same word may be spelled different ways in the same piece of writing. Other typical characteristics of this stage include substituting letter names for short vowels and omitting *m* and *n* before a final consonant (*wet* for *went*). Children at this stage almost always omit silent letters and spell long vowel sounds by writing out letter names. For example, *baby* may be written *babe.*

At this stage, children need to write freely. They should not be expected to spell conventionally. Encouraged to write often and to invent spellings, children will explore the nature of written language eagerly and confidently. While writing frequently, children also need to read widely. Immersion in print at this stage gives children valuable models of written language, from which they gradually acquire a sense of certain common spelling conventions. Phonics instruction at this stage enhances children's growing awareness of sound-letter relationships. This awareness is reflected in their invented spellings.

In the latter part of this stage, two major developments occur. First, children start to use a silent "marking" vowel in words like *rain, peep,* and *mine,* writing, for example, *rane, pepe,* and *mian.* Second, children begin to spell short vowel sounds correctly. Also, they begin to encode blends (br, gr, sl, etc.) with greater accuracy, and they begin to include the *m* and *n* before a final consonant. At this point, their writing looks more conventional. They are moving away from rudimentary alphabetic spelling, where letters are matched directly to sounds, and are beginning to realize that clusters of letters often represent the sounds within words. Students are now ready to explore "within-word" letter patterns.

Stage 3: Within-Word Patterns As children continue to write freely, spelling many words conventionally and inventing spellings for others, they acquire the understanding that some letter groups work as units in relation to syllables and that certain letter patterns are related to the distinguishable sounds in words.

The word study of beginning reading helps children discover the pattern principle. The important knowledge obtained is that there is a logical separation between the beginning consonant(s), the vowel, and whatever elements follow. Practice in auditory discrimination (see Appendix B) develops the concepts of beginning and final consonants, blends, and medial vowels by involving children in active problem solving. After they have acquired the concept that words are made up of these parts, they are ready to study vowel patterns. Again they need to take a problem-solving approach, making discriminations among patterns of letters that represent elements of sound until the patterns are internalized.

As children learn about these common letter patterns, they also need to attend to how meaning affects spelling. Students start with simple concepts such as inflectional endings (e.g., -s, -ed, -ing) and common prefixes and suffixes (un-, -ness). Once they have a few models in their sight vocabularies, children can deduce certain principles. For example, they will soon learn that adding *s* at the end of certain words means *plural* (mother/mothers) or that adding *un* to the beginning of others means a reversal of action (tie/untie).

Other meaning-influenced spelling conventions may also be studied at this stage. In particular, homonyms and words that are related in meaning may be examined for children to see how meaning dictates spelling. Children will be ready to learn that homonyms usually have different spellings because the words have different meanings (meat/meet, here/hear, pair/pear, rain/rein/reign) whereas words that are related in meaning often show spelling similarities (bomb/bombard, local/locality). The concept of stress (accented syllables) may also be introduced at this point to show how stress affects pronunciation (e.g., the *a* in local vs. locality). Children need to see how meaning, rather than sound, determines the spelling of many related words that have different stress patterns.

Summarizing the characteristics of spelling instruction at Stage 3, Henderson writes that children must learn that sounds alone do not give reliable clues to spelling and that meaning must also be considered. He suggests using sorting (categorizing) exercises to help children be attentive to sound and meaning as these factors affect spelling. For instance, sound patterns might be explored with words such as boy, bone, boil, toe, spoil, join, and toy. Children would put the words into two groups, according to the vowel sound, and then discuss how the same sound is spelled differently. Meaning patterns might be studied with items such as coin, cooperate, coexist, covet, coax, and copilot. Children would discuss how the *co* at the beginning of some words is a prefix meaning *joint* or *together,* whereas the *co* at the beginning of others does not signal a prefix. Categorizing tasks like these involve children in active thinking about the various patterns that exist within words.

Stage 4: Syllable Juncture   At this stage, children spell many familiar sight words accurately and show good ability to use basic vowel patterns correctly. They still invent spellings for some words, but their inventions show different characteristics. Usually, students deviate from conventional spelling when they attempt to encode polysyllabic words and unfamiliar words with schwa sounds (*imporin* for *important, roben* for *robin*).

In addition to their continued study of the influence of word meaning on spelling, children are now ready to study doubling consonants. The principle of syllable juncture (providing a break between syllables) can first be introduced with words in which the inflectional endings of -*ed* and -*ing* are added to one-syllable words (pet/petted, run/running). Children may categorize words that include both exemplars and exceptions and then deduce the doubling principle. They will discover that if a first syllable ends with a consonant and has a short vowel in the inflected form, then the consonant is doubled. This principle does not hold for all words, but it occurs with enough regularity so as to be worth learning.

Stage 5: Derivational Principles   After children have passed through the first four spelling stages and have also reached the point at which they can think abstractly, they are ready to explore the logic behind the spelling of polysyllabic words. They need to recognize that many polysyllabic English words have been borrowed from other languages, notably from Latin and Greek, and that the spelling of these words is directly tied to their meaning. Mature spellers learn that English spelling is decidedly regular when meaning is considered; for example, *critic* and *criticism* are both spelled with an *i;* the *a* in *hilarity* also appears in *exhilarate; visionary, revise,* and *television* all contain the root *vis.*

By understanding the stages of spelling development, teachers can guide and strengthen a natural learning process. Perhaps most important to young writers at each stage is the freedom to experiment. Students need to invent spellings and thereby apply what they have discovered about written language. Their attempts will often deviate from conventional spelling, but these deviations are evidence of the children's purposeful thinking. At the earliest levels, children reason logically that letters can be matched directly with sounds. Later on, they discover and apply pattern principles. Still later, they draw semantic analogies as they learn that words that are derived from the same root often have certain spelling similarities. As Anderson (1985) observes, mature spellers often draw analogies that are based on sound patterns. When writing an unfamiliar word, they will think of one they know and spell the unfamiliar word accordingly; for example, knowing the spelling of *gratitude* may help the writer spell *latitude.* At all levels, students can make use of a combination of spelling strategies based on their linguistic knowledge and their ability to use such high-level thinking processes as generalizing and drawing analogies. A good spelling program will provide meaningful activities, geared to children's needs, that encourage students to become actively involved in problem-solving approaches to spelling.

Components of a Good Spelling Program

Certain features of a good language arts program also make for a good spelling program. One of these features is wide reading. When children read often, dipping into a variety of books, they see many words again and again, and these words become quite familiar visually. When a word is well known, it is usually easy to recall and to reproduce correctly in writing. This reliance on sight vocabulary as an aid to spelling is an especially prominent characteristic in the early grades, when children are reading simple texts and are especially attentive to individual words.

In later grades, wide reading continues to influence spelling, although as children become more proficient readers, they pay less attention to individual words and more to phrases or idea units. Also, advanced readers may encounter many words only a few times in books—often enough for them to be able to recognize the words again in print but not often enough to enable them to reproduce the words accurately in writing. However, students who frequently read will be familiar enough with many words to be able to recognize when, as writers, they themselves have produced a word that just doesn't "look right." Although wide reading does not teach children to spell, frequent contact with written language gives children at all levels a good sense of how words are spelled.

Instruction in word recognition and in the study of word meanings also helps children develop spelling ability. Learning letter-sound relationships, common vowel patterns, and other phonetic features of words can make children attentive to sound patterns. Learning structural analysis (syllables, roots, and affixes) can make students attentive to meaning patterns. Discussion of word meanings, as well as instruction and practice in using the dictionary to look up word meanings, also contribute to children's spelling ability. Thus, instruction aimed at specific word study is an important component of a spelling program.

Besides giving children opportunities to read widely and helping them be attentive to patterns within words, a spelling program should include three additional components:

1. It should encourage extensive writing.
2. It should develop students' independence in proofreading and in using the dictionary to find word spellings.
3. It should provide for the regular learning of high-frequency words.

Extensive Writing   If children are given many opportunities to write, they will be able to apply what they have learned about written language. They will have derived this knowledge from reading and from specific instruction in sound and meaning patterns. Regular writing brings into play the reinforcing relationship between writing and spelling. Children's spelling improves as they write and revise their work; they also gain confidence and skill with writing as their spelling improves.

Rule's study (1982) of one young writer's growth in spelling ability illustrates the way writing and spelling reinforce one another. Rule describes a student named Brian who moved gradually toward conventional spelling as he regularly wrote and revised his work. Although Brian studied and learned the weekly lists of spelling words his teacher assigned, he did not immediately apply these new learnings to his writing. Instead, he solved spelling problems in his own way. Brian's strategy was first to get his ideas down, spelling words phonetically. He said, "When I write, I don't think about what they look like. I don't do this [correcting] while I'm writing but after I see what they look like." Brian was eager to write because his teacher encouraged this strategy. Motivated by pride in his work, he gradually came to spell more and more words conventionally. In the autumn of third grade, he misspelled 23 percent of the words in first drafts and 16 percent in final drafts, but by the spring of fourth grade, he misspelled only 5 percent of the words in first drafts and less than 1 percent in final drafts.

If Brian had had teachers who expected accuracy in his early drafts, he might not have accomplished this self-motivated growth in spelling. As many children do, he might have limited his writing vocabulary to words he knew how to spell, fearing to risk making an error even on the first draft. When children are afraid of making errors, they do not put to use all they know, and their anxiety about mistakes can limit their confidence in their abilities. Also, risk-free writing, though correct, is usually stiff and stilted, conveying no sense of the writer's unique voice. But children who are encouraged to take spelling risks compose lively accounts and develop considerable confidence as writers. They find that they have much to say, and in using words freely, they also freely use the knowledge they acquire gradually about sound and meaning patterns.

Some teachers believe that they should always correct children's misspelled words because not doing so will only reinforce "bad habits." However, as previously noted, children who write freely constantly experiment and reinvent spellings as they write. The trial and error is a learning process, not one that cements bad habits. In fact, teachers' corrections of misspelled words often serve mainly to reinforce the need to use well-known words, not to increase spelling skills. Taylor and Hoedt (1966) and Gee (1972) found that if teachers provided frequent writing opportunities but abstained from correcting the papers, the children wrote more, were more creative in their use of language, and enjoyed writing more. Such an encouraging environment can do much to promote eagerness to write. The children, experiencing the thrill of writing, will have good reasons and opportunities to increase their spelling skill, as Brian did.

The wise teacher will maintain a sensitive balance between encouraging written expression and attending to accuracy. The first aim must be the priority in the early grades, so that children will want to write and will do so regularly with enthusiasm. Calkins (1986) tells of a group of five-year-old students whose teacher told them they were going to be spellers. Gathering the children around the chalkboard, the teacher asked for words the group might spell together. The children suggested *spaghetti, Tyrannosaurus Rex,* and *hippopotamus.* As the children called out each word, the teacher wrote on the board, saying, "Watch my hand and see if you can say the word as slowly as my hand goes." She urged them to prolong the pronunciation of the word and listen for the sounds they were producing. Asking which sounds they heard, she recorded their guesses on the chalkboard, including incorrect letters. In this way, the teacher demonstrated the process of inventing spelling, and she also showed that not knowing the exact spelling does not have to inhibit writing.

Older children, too, need to spell as best they can when they write early drafts. If they worry too much about spelling correctly, their pace becomes so tortuously slow that they have difficulty remembering what it is they meant to write. They need to realize that there will be plenty of time to correct their work when they edit a last draft. The teacher needs to encourage invented spellings in early drafts and to save correcting for the right time—when the piece is ready for a final editing.

Developing Independence in Proofreading and Dictionary Use   As children write freely in an encouraging environment, they also need to develop two skills of spelling independence: recognizing misspelled words when they see them and learning to find correct spellings on their own, especially in the dictionary. These skills allow children to edit their final drafts successfully. Both skills can be taught, but the teaching must include meaningful practice if children are to learn well. Some students will catch on more quickly than others, but neither skill can be learned well after one lesson or even, necessarily, after a year's worth of periodic instruction. If children have not yet learned, they simply need more help and practice, no matter which grade they are in.

Recognizing Misspelled Words. The first step in editing for spelling is to identify words that are misspelled. The writer must have a sensitivity to error that might be called *spelling consciousness.* Such consciousness develops as children gain competence in reading and begin to notice how words appear. For a while, they will be satisfied with their invented spellings, but as words become more and more familiar visually, the children will want their own spelling to be conventional. Spelling consciousness is also bolstered by the pride that young writers take in their work.

As children become more aware of how words look, they begin to ask how various words are spelled. Students usually ask questions about spelling when they are about to write an unfamiliar word. It is tempting for the teacher to assist at that point because the children are so eager to know. However, providing immediate help fosters dependence on the teacher and can lead to severe reductions in time spent on writing. Children will literally line up at the teacher's desk, clamoring for spelling help, instead of recording their ideas. At this stage, children must learn to concentrate on what they have to say rather than worrying about correctly encoding their ideas (Rule, 1982). If children are assured of opportunities to revise and are given help in correcting, they will be encouraged to keep concentrating on what they have to say when they write their first drafts.

When the piece is finished, and before they ask the teacher for help, children first should underline any words that do not look right. (This critical appraisal of their own work is an important step for writers to take. The habit of careful rereading will be useful for many different revising and editing purposes as children mature.) Sometimes, just highlighting a word will be enough; the child will see what needs to be changed and can make corrections easily. With other words, the student will be puzzled, realizing that something is wrong but not knowing what to do about it. After underlining words, the writer may meet with a peer for a second checking. (Many teachers encourage such peer support because the joint efforts are mutually useful and because dependence on the teacher is lessened.) Eventually, the writer will need to schedule an editing conference with the teacher.

Meeting with a child to edit for spelling, the teacher should first commend the writer for recognizing troublesome words and for making any corrections. Then, the teacher may simply cross out misspelled words and write them correctly for the child. For some words, a moment of teaching may be in order. For instance, if the misspelled word is *become,* the teacher may write *be* and *come,* may pronounce each, may combine them in saying the word, and may point out how the letter order of this combination differs from the child's arrangement.

Simply recognizing misspelled words and making some attempts at self-correction are reasonable expectations for primary-grade students. Their spelling will improve gradually as they continue to read, write, and study words. But by the time children reach the middle grades, they need to go a step further toward independence, learning how to find the conventional spelling for a word that does not look right.

Using the Dictionary for Spelling. Early on in school, most children learn to arrange words in alphabetical order and to find words in picture dictionaries. By the third or fourth grade, most understand and can use guide words. They come to think of the dictionary as an aid to finding word meanings, but they reject the idea that the dictionary is a spelling aid, and they wonder how they can find words in a dictionary if they don't know how to spell them. The following lesson illustrates how one fourth-grade teacher demonstrated this new use of a dictionary to his students.

In this teacher's class, children were writing daily—drafting, revising, holding conferences, and editing. Their responsibility for correct spelling had been limited to locating and underlining suspicious words, and they corrected only those words that needed a careful second evaluation. The teacher knew the students cared about correctness in a finished piece, and he also felt that they were secure enough with their writing for him to add another expectation—finding correct spellings in the dictionary.

First he paired the children so that each would have a partner to talk things over with. Children then chose a first draft from their writing folders and underlined suspicious words. Next, they were told to select one underlined word and copy it in the margin, thereby isolating it for careful examination.

After dictionaries were distributed to all, one child volunteered to write her spelling of *aluminum* on the board: She wrote *aluminmm*. Using this word as an example, the teacher demonstrated, by thinking aloud, the steps to finding the correct spelling: "Let's see. Aluminum. The first part looks right. It's the ending I'm not sure of. I'll find the page where there are words that start *a-l-u-m*. Let's look together. Here. *A-l-u-m* would probably be on this page, between the guide words *alterable* and *alyssum*. Have you found the page? Now, I'll look for *a-l-u-m* and keep looking until I find aluminum. Here it is! Do you see it? It's the fifth word that starts with *a-l-u-m*. How is the spelling different from what we have on the board? Right. We need a *u* instead of the extra *m*."

The teacher drew a line through the original word and wrote the correct spelling above it. Using the same procedure, he located and discussed the spelling of *toboggan*. This time, the writer was uncertain of the first vowel. She had spelled the word *taboggan*. The teacher first led the group to the *ta* words; the students saw that this led to a dead end. Then, reasoning aloud, the teacher suggested trying the *te* section. When that also turned out to be fruitless, one of the children, catching on, suggested trying *to*. Soon everyone had located *toboggan,* and the teacher wrote the correct spelling on the board.

The teacher suggested that when children were not sure of the first vowel in a word that they write *A E I O U (Y)* at the top of their papers. Then, as they checked vowels, they could cross out the ones that did not apply. The teacher reminded the class how they had followed this procedure with *toboggan,* and he showed them how the vowels *A, E,* and *O* would have been crossed out in that instance.

Then the children turned to their own writing to make corrections. Most found immediate success as they looked up underlined words. One child had a problem, though. The word she wanted was *tried;* her spelling: *treid*. The word was not in the dictionary under any spelling she could imagine. What should she do?

The teacher stopped everyone and wrote *treid* on the board. After reviewing the problem, he wrote *PRESENT* and *PAST* on the board. Then he asked, "If Tina says, 'I tried to lock the door,' when did she try to do it? In the present or in the past?" The class agreed it was the past, and the teacher wrote *treid* under *PAST.* Then he asked, "What word would she have used if it were the present?" The children replied, "try," which he wrote under *PRESENT.* Then he sent the class to their dictionaries to find *try,* and they found *tried* on the line immediately following.

To reinforce this strategy for verbs, the teacher dictated while the children wrote the words *stung, skipped,* and *taught.* After the children had looked up the present tenses of these verbs, the group discussed their findings, which the teacher summarized on the board:

Present	*Past*
try	tried
sting	stung
skip	skipped
teach	taught

(This strategy will not work with all dictionaries. In some, the past tense is entered as a separate word, unlike the dictionaries of this class, which listed the past tense with the present tense. However, in most dictionaries, students will find at least some variant verb forms listed with the present tense, or they will be referred to the infinitive.)

At the end of the lesson, the teacher suggested that the group summarize the strategies they had learned. He recorded their responses on the board and later made a chart for easy reference:

Use the Dictionary

1. Write *A E I O U (Y)* at the top of your page.
2. Decide which part of the word looks wrong.
3. Look up the first two or three letters you hear.
4. If you can't find the word, try the next best vowel.
5. If the word is a verb, look up the present tense.

Over the year, the teacher conducted short practice activities. These sessions indicated immediately if the children were right or wrong, and helped students to increase their speed at searching through the dictionary for correct spellings. Most important, the children refined their ability to figure out how to spell words with the help of the dictionary. These were some of the practice activities:

1. The teacher dictated three words the children probably could not spell. Children wrote the words as best they could and then checked the dictionary, writing the correct spelling next to their first effort. A few children

volunteered to copy their original and corrected versions on the board and explain the thinking, sounding out, and searching strategies they used.

2. The teacher dictated three words with tricky vowel sounds, for instance, *business, opportunity, bloom.* He reminded children of the vowel check-off strategy and had them go to work.

3. The teacher dictated variant forms of three verbs, for instance, *rode, jogged, traveled,* or *riding, jogging, traveling.* He reminded children of the verb strategy, had them try to spell the words correctly and then check the dictionary.

Some spellings at the beginnings of words are unusual and will pose special problems. One way to call attention to these words is to compose a list on a large wall chart. As children meet these spellings in their reading, or as such words occur in their writing, the words can be recorded. Part of a chart might look like this:

Sound	*Spelling*	
	REGULAR	IRREGULAR
r	run	wrong
		wrestle
z	zero	czar
n	no	knife
f	fish	phrase
		Philip
		phantom
s	say	sword
		cent

The fourth-grade students became increasingly proficient at using the dictionary for making spelling corrections. They also became more confident about word choice in their writing, because they knew they could find many spellings on their own when it came time to edit their work. Even though they were not expected to check the dictionary for every word they were unsure of, they were developing good strategies for finding almost any word they wanted to use. The teaching techniques are excellent for middle-grade students. Variations of these may be used at other grade levels.

Regular Learning of High-Frequency Words While children are writing extensively, becoming aware of sound and meaning patterns, and developing independence in editing their work, they can also profit from regular learning of high-frequency words—those words that are used over and over in speech and writing. Learning to spell high-frequency words is extremely useful for young writers who are becoming conscious of conventional spelling and who are confident enough about their writing to concentrate purposefully on learning to spell certain words. By the second grade, many children will be ready for regular learning of high-frequency words.

This section explains in detail how to select words for regular learning, how to group students according to their spelling levels, how to help students study words, and how to organize the overall program. The emphasis on details here is not to suggest that this aspect of the program is the most important, but rather to help teachers conduct this kind of work efficiently. Once a program for mastering high-frequency words is organized and underway, it will require minimal time in the language arts program, and it will allow considerable time for writing, reading, and other language activities.

Word studies suggest that about 3,000 words will provide children with 95 percent of the words they will use in writing (Horn, 1927; Rinsland, 1945). Hillerich (1977) refers to these 3,000 words as a basic security list that all children eventually need to master. Because, by definition, high-frequency words appear so often in print, wide reading will reinforce spelling instruction with these words.

Systematic learning is most profitable when children are learning those words that they will probably use most often in their writing. One high-frequency list that is useful for deciding which words children might learn at different grade levels is *The New Iowa Spelling Scale* (Greene, 1977). Table 8.2 provides an excerpt from this list. The Iowa Scale contains the 5,507 words children in the research sample used most often in their writing. Each word is coded by the percentage of children at each grade level, two through eight, who spelled it correctly. For example, *abandon* was spelled correctly by 2 percent of the second graders and by 49 percent of the eighth graders who wrote it.

At any grade level, however, there will be differences in spelling abilities. Some children will be capable spellers, and others will make much slower progress. Usually, the older the group, the greater the variance. In a second-grade class, there may be two or three levels of spelling ability. In a fourth- or fifth-grade class, there may be as many as four or five different levels. To learn well, each child in a given class needs to be learning words that he or she can master successfully.

High-frequency lists can be accommodated to the different levels in a class. For example, to make classroom lists from *The New Iowa Spelling Scale,* a teacher would decide on cut-off points. A list for very able fourth graders might include those words spelled correctly by 10 percent or fewer of the fourth graders in the research sample. Words for able students might include those spelled correctly by 11 percent to 30 percent; words for average students could be chosen from those falling in the 31 percent to 70 percent range; words for poor students from those in the 71 percent to 100 percent range. The following partial list for a fifth-grade class was compiled in this way with the words from Table 8.2:

Very Able	*Average*
absolutely	abroad
acceptable	absent
accommodate	abuse
accomplish	account
accurate	acre
admiration	act
admission	action
	active
	addition
Able	address
	adjust
abandon	admire
ability	admit
absence	
absolute	
abstract	*Poor*
abundant	
accept	able
accidents	about
accord	above
actual	across
additional	added
adjust	
adopt	

Although this procedure works very well for a school-wide spelling program for which several people work on developing lists, it can be quite an undertaking for an individual teacher. The Iowa Scale, with an example of how to use it, has been included here, however, because this illustrates so well what is meant by using a high-frequency spelling list.

For some classroom teachers, a more practical source for words may be either a list from a published spelling series or one such as is found in *Teaching Spelling* (Thomas, 1979). Thomas's list, which is comparable to others based on the Horn and Rinsland studies, was developed for Canadian students. Although a few words on this list could be omitted (e.g., *Saskatchewan*), the list is otherwise quite suitable for students in the United States. Each word on the list is given a grade-level designation, for example *but (2), are (2), before (3), ever (3), soon (3)*. Constructing weekly spelling lists from this master list is a reasonable task, even for an individual teacher. Lists can be developed for grades two through eight. Teachers can accommodate to ability differences by pretesting for placement with different grade-level lists (see the next section).

While they learn selected words from a list, children may also be given the chance to learn some words that are especially interesting to them. There was a time, for instance, when many youngsters were writing stories abut the Incredible Hulk, a popular television character. Of course, they wanted to know how to spell *incredible* and *hulk,* words that ordinarily would not appear on a

TABLE 8.2 Excerpt from the New Iowa Spelling Scale

Word	Grade Level						
	2	3	4	5	6	7	8
abandon	2	3	10	18	34	43	49
ability	1	2	6	19	30	57	71
able	2	21	56	76	86	95	97
about	9	51	78	91	97	97	99
above	4	29	59	76	84	94	97
abroad	0	10	13	37	54	69	86
absence	0	4	6	14	28	49	50
absent	0	4	35	67	74	77	84
absolute	1	2	6	13	25	41	56
absolutely	0	1	2	3	11	16	41
abstract	0	3	8	16	34	55	76
abundant	0	3	4	14	20	34	47
abuse	1	7	27	40	56	68	80
acceptable	0	0	3	5	21	39	48
accidents	0	1	8	14	41	54	66
accommodate	1	2	3	4	5	11	24
accompanied	0	1	1	6	14	32	42
accomplish	0	2	3	7	25	44	71
accord	0	3	7	16	26	53	73
account	0	3	5	32	46	73	81
accurate	0	0	1	3	15	42	57
acre	1	2	7	31	58	58	76
across	6	26	56	72	83	90	91
act	3	13	41	62	79	82	89
action	2	4	16	44	67	89	94
active	0	6	17	50	65	83	93
actual	0	6	4	12	27	55	78
added	6	47	71	74	93	93	97
addition	0	3	15	31	49	77	85
additional	2	2	3	12	25	49	62
address	1	8	39	62	78	86	91
adequate	0	0	1	5	6	9	22
adjust	2	5	13	24	44	47	76
admiration	0	1	4	10	21	36	59
admire	1	4	19	38	54	81	82
admission	0	1	3	9	33	53	69
admit	8	8	27	40	47	68	74
adopt	3	9	18	29	44	63	74

From Greene, 1977.

high-frequency list for children. A basic spelling list may also be augmented occasionally with one or two words from content-area studies that students use often in their writing.

Placing Students: The Spelling Inventory. A spelling inventory is used to determine the level at which a child should be placed for learning high-frequency words. Proper placement assures steady growth in skill. The child who is assigned activities at the right level will be challenged but not frustrated.

To construct a spelling inventory, select twenty words at random from each level of a graded spelling list, such as one prepared according to the previous suggestions. Start testing at one grade level below the child's reading level. Before giving the test, do not show the child the words nor allow study time. The placement inventory is for ascertaining where to start instruction, not for measuring how well the child can learn words.

The proper instructional level for spelling study is the highest level at which a child spells 70–80 percent of the words on a given list correctly. During testing, if the child scores below 70 percent, administer the next lower list; if a child scores above 80 percent, administer the next higher list. Continue testing (no more than one list a day) until an instructional level has been reached for each child. Children may easily be tested in groups; those whose levels have been determined may simply be excused from the next round.

Some children, especially in the upper grades, will "ceiling out" on such a spelling inventory, scoring 95–100 percent at each level, up to and including the highest level. These particularly good spellers may not need regular work with the high-frequency lists that are prepared for the rest of the class. Instead, they might concentrate on words with which they have consistent difficulty or that they particularly wish to learn to spell. These students may be encouraged to compile their own spelling lists, which may be augmented by the teacher as misspelled words occur in their writing.

Study Procedures. The generally accepted procedure for studying words, called *test-study-test with self-correction,* has been validated by several researchers (Blumberg and Block, 1975; Hinrichs, 1975; Hillerich, 1977). This is how to use the procedure:

1. *Pretest.* Dictate the week's list of twenty words as a pretest, before children have seen the words.
2. *Self-correction.* Have children check their own tests, writing the correct spelling beside each misspelled word.
3. *Study.* Have children study the words they misspelled. (See "Study Method for Spelling," later in this chapter.)
4. *Posttest.* At the end of the week, dictate the list again as a posttest.
5. *Self-correction.* Have children again check their own tests and again study any misspelled words.

The test-study-test technique with self-correction is justifiable because about 95 percent of all learning occurs when children correct their own spelling pretests (Horn, 1947). Furthermore, the persons most interested in the results are the spellers. By correcting their own tests, children get immediate feedback, seeing which words were correct, what kinds of errors they made, and how the correct spelling should look.

As they correct their tests, children need to have the accurate spellings in front of them. Teachers can write the words on the board or on an overhead transparency. Even better, they can give each child a copy of the test list. (Checking a paper is much easier and more exact if the key is right in front of the checker.) After children make corrections on their pretests, teachers should be sure to check the work because the misspelled (now corrected) words become the study list for the week.

If children are appropriately placed, a week's study list will not exceed six words out of a total of twenty. If children are consistently missing more than that each week (or getting 100 percent on their pretests), they need to be placed at a lower (or higher) level. Given the way this kind of program is organized, it is a simple matter to move children to new levels, and such adjustments should be made whenever several test results suggest that the words at a given level are either too easy or too difficult for a child.

Study Method for Spelling. Horn (1919) introduced a method that continues to be a very effective way to learn the spelling of words. Try the procedure yourself to see how visual, auditory, and kinesthetic modalities are all involved, reinforcing one another.

1. Look at the word and say it to yourself.
2. Close your eyes. Visualize the word letter by letter.
3. Look at the word again to see if you were right. (If not, repeat steps 1 and 2.)
4. Cover the word and write it.
5. Compare the two words to see if you were right. (If not, return to step 1.)
6. Repeat steps 4 and 5 two more times. This means you write the word correctly three times in a row.

A way to demonstrate the usefulness of this procedure to children is to have them conduct an experiment. First, dictate a list of five words, including some that the children probably cannot spell. Provide correct spellings and have children check their own work. Each child writes the correct spellings beside any misspelled words and records the number that were written correctly. Then children study the words they missed, following the six steps. Dictate the word list again. Have children correct their own papers and compare pretest and posttest scores. Discuss results.

Children may need supervised practice to learn the study method. It is a good idea to explain the steps, demonstrate them, and then have children practice in class. It might also be useful to send a letter to parents explaining the steps and asking them to help their children use them at home. Spelling study is a reasonable homework assignment, and most parents would be happy to learn about a specific study method that will help their children learn to spell better.

Scheduling and Record-keeping. Learning spelling words illustrates the need for regular practice. Words are quickly forgotten if students are simply given a list to study at the beginning of the week and then are tested at the end of the week. Continuous review and use must occur if children are to retain what they learn. If students work with a set of words one week, move on to other words in subsequent weeks, have a review period every five or six weeks, and all the while write regularly and participate in spelling activities, the probability of retention is high. Both students and teacher may keep records of progress from one week to the next.

Here is an efficient plan for working with a single list in one week. Each day requires minimal teacher-directed time. Students may perform many of the activities independently.

1. *Day 1.*   First, the teacher dictates pretest words. In most classes, there will be several spelling groups. Dictation can be applied to multilevels if the teacher assigns each group a number and dictates words in order—for example: "First word. Group 1, *snow;* Group 2, *kitchen;* Group 3, *memory.*" After children become used to the procedure, dictation can be shortened to "First word. *Snow. Kitchen. Memory.*" Children quickly learn to listen for their words.

For two reasons, words do not need to be used in sentences. First, when the teacher pronounces a word, reads a sentence, and pronounces the word again, students' attention is diverted from the word itself. The sentences are actually distracting to the students who are trying to concentrate on spelling the one word they are being tested on. Second, because children are placed at their proper levels and are dealing with familiar, high-frequency words, a sentence is not necessary for identifying the word, except when the word is a homonym. When dictating homonyms, the teacher should just explain briefly which word he or she means.

After dictating the pretest words, the teacher should give children the correct spellings and have them check their own papers. Students should write each misspelled word correctly next to the original effort. Because these corrections will be used for study throughout the week, the teacher will need to look them over, which he or she can easily do by circulating among the students to check their papers.

2. *Day 2.*   Children study the words using the six-step study method. This is the most effective procedure, in school or at home. Just having them write a word ten times, for instance, is not very useful. In fact, dogged, nonthinking repetition of this sort may even block the memory mechanisms that are needed if students are to learn and remember the word (Henderson, 1985). Unless there is thinking between each spelling attempt, children are apt to perpetuate misspellings.

3. *Day 3 and Day 4.*   There are several options for these days. Some teachers like to administer a trial test, a repetition of the first day's pretest. Others dictate review words for practice. Different spelling activities may also be introduced to give children further practice in attending to letter order. Special activities might include some of these:

a. Sorting words according to pattern.
   Give children models of a sound or meaning pattern. For instance, if they have been making distinctions between words that have the long or short vowel sound of *e,* examples might include *met, meet,* and *beat.*

Children could have a list of twenty words to sort according to one of these patterns. For variation and challenge, exceptions such as *head* could be included in the list. Children might also search through books and magazines to find words for each category. Henderson (1985) suggests that teachers may wish to label cookie tins by letter pattern, filling them with word cards for sorting. Sorting tasks can vary in difficulty, depending on the choice and number of pattern categories.

b. Making bubblegrams.

A bubblegram is like a crossword puzzle, easy to construct because the letters need only spell words in one direction. This convention permits a wide range of word choice, making the bubblegram a good spelling reinforcement task.

Give students a word such as *notice* for a stem. Students then supply bubbles for letters to make a word intersect with each letter on the stem. Each supplied word is then numbered and given a "clue." (See Figure 5 for an example of a bubblegram and clues made from words in a seventh-grade list.)

Children gain the most from constructing the bubblegram. To make one requires careful attention to letter order. Students may also enjoy exchanging bubblegrams and solving each other's puzzles.

c. Creating sentences for words.

Have children make up sentences in which words are ordered according to their first letter. First-letter order must match the letter

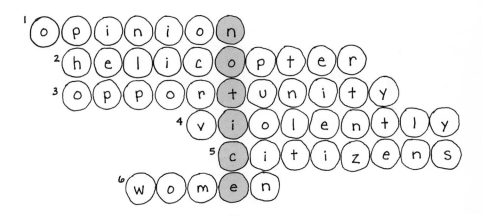

1. An _____ is the opposite of a fact.
2. This is sometimes called a chopper.
3. Chance is a synonym for this word.
4. An earthquake can cause buildings to shake _____.
5. CB is the nickname for _____ band radio.
6. _____ are the equals of men.

FIGURE 5   A bubblegram made with spelling words

order of a given spelling word. For example, the word *magic* suggests
the sentence *Mike and George inched closer.*

   d. Playing games.

      Some commercial games, such as Scrabble, Boggle, and Probe are
enjoyable ways to reinforce spelling knowledge. The game of Hangman,
played with pencil and paper, also gives pleasant practice in spelling.
Any such games may be used in the classroom, and parents may be
advised of the educational value of playing them at home.

   The criterion for a good spelling activity is that the task requires children
to attend to letter order, patterns, or meanings of roots and affixes. Sources for
appropriate activities include Thomas (1979), Hodges (1981), and Swisher
(1984).

   4. *Day 5.*   Dictate the posttest as you did the pretest. Have children correct
their own papers and record their scores.

   Accurate record keeping is important for both teachers and students. Children need to note their progress, and if they keep their own records they will also develop a sense of responsibility about their own learning. Records do not have to be elaborate to be useful. For example, students might simply maintain bar graphs on the backs of their spelling notebooks, recording their test scores weekly.

   Teachers need to observe progress and also will want to note which words are being studied from pretests and which words are being missed on posttests. One teacher uses envelopes, two per spelling group, to hold lists of words. Each week, any words missed in a group on the pretest go into one envelope, and any missed on the posttest go into the other. When it is time for the six-week review, she plans activities using problem pretest words. When she constructs review tests, she always includes words missed on posttests. In this way, she tailors review to children's specific needs and helps them continue to strive for mastery.

Summary

Knowing the stages of spelling development helps the teacher assess student needs and plan instruction to suit students' developmental levels. In the very early school years, students do not really need formal spelling instruction. Rather, they need opportunities to read and write freely so as to develop a sense of written language as meaningful communcation. As they write, they need to experiment with spelling. Invented spelling, a natural outcome of children's growing awareness of written language, should not only be allowed but should be encouraged. As students mature, they need regular practice with high-frequency words at the proper instructional level (using a test-study-test method), and they need continued extensive writing to apply learned spelling

As students work to improve spelling skills, they will benefit from studying common spelling patterns and from learning how word structure and meaning, as well as sound, affect spelling.

skills. They will also benefit from studying common spelling patterns and from learning how word structure and meaning, as well as sound, affect spelling. Students also need to develop independence as spellers, learning to recognize misspelled words in their writing and to use the dictionary to find correct spellings. Although they need to become more capable of correcting their own errors, they also need to suspend concern for accuracy until they are ready to edit a piece of writing at the final draft stage.

Handwriting

Handwriting began with pictures drawn on cave walls. These drawings were early attempts to capture the essence of an event in more lasting form and to share it with other people who were not available for oral reporting. These early writers faced the same problem writers must face today—ambiguity of interpretation. In an attempt to limit that ambiguity, the system of written communication gradually evolved through the development of consistent symbols or ideograms that represented whole words or events. This led to a more flexible system depicting word syllables and finally to an alphabetic system.

Given the artistic origins of writing, it is not surprising that much of handwriting instruction has been presented from the art-for-art's-sake perspective. Until very recently, school children often spent hours practicing perfect coils or spirals in the belief that this would produce better handwriting. Unfortunately, for many children this practice for the sake of practice was often a waste of time. They failed to understand its intent and were bored and frustrated. As a result, the carry-over to real writing situations was often minimal.

In recent years, increased attention to the writing process has also led to a revised view of the role of handwriting instruction. As with the shift in spelling instruction, emphasis has swung away from considering good handwriting as an end in and of itself, toward the view that regards legible handwriting as a necessary skill that will further the goal of successful written communication. The changed perspective is summarized by Graves' (1983) statement that "handwriting is a vehicle carrying information on its way to a destination" (p. 171).

This view of handwriting has enormous implications for instruction. When legibility becomes the primary criterion for handwriting, "the best way of helping children achieve greater legibility is making sure they care, because they have something to say to an audience they have chosen" (Goodman, 1986, p. 73). The goal of the language arts teacher is to provide appropriate instruction in the mechanics of handwriting within the framework of a total writing program where the emphasis is on communication.

Readiness for Formal Handwriting Instruction

Children come to the classroom with a wide range of experiences and abilities in handwriting skills. Many, like the little girl whose writing appears in Figure 6, come with a solid base of already well-practiced skills that have been developed at home. Other children have almost no experience with producing written language (Figures 7 and 8). Instruction that begins too early or that places inappropriate emphasis on correctness of formation too soon can actually cause writing disabilities. Children must come to writing instruction with appropriate physical and cognitive skills.

Physical Readiness

1. *Eyesight.*   Farsightedness is a common problem in young children (Flood and Lapp, 1981). Many do not have the necessary eye muscle development to focus on something close at hand for long periods of time. Copying from the chalkboard or wall charts poses particular problems for these children, because of the constant refocusing required as they look up to the faraway model and down to the paper in front of them. Children experiencing these problems will usually provide evidence of their discomfort by rubbing their eyes, squinting, tilting their heads, or complaining that their eyes or heads hurt. Refocusing difficulties can be minimized (although not completely eliminated)

FIGURE 6 One child's developing skill at writing her name (numbers indicate her age in years and months)

by providing model alphabet strips for each desk so that when reference is needed for a letter, children will have it close at hand.

2. *Adequate Muscle Control.* Children vary greatly in the development of small muscle coordination, as a result of different rates of maturation and different amount of experience with activities like sewing, model building, puz-

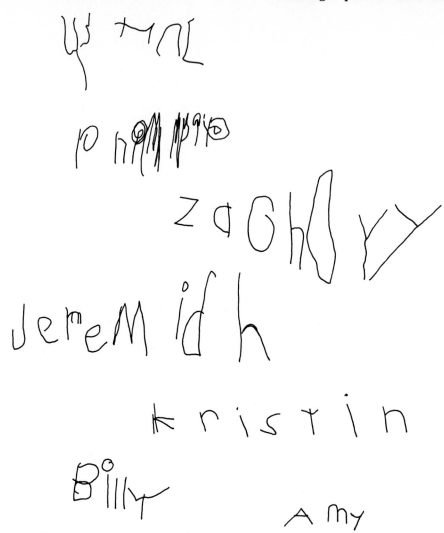

FIGURE 7 Range of skill at writing names (kindergartners at the beginning of the school year)

zle completion, and drawing. These activities develop small muscle control and eye-hand coordination. Observing children using crayons and scissors, copying simple shapes, working with clay, and practicing play or pseudowriting will make it possible to identify children who are ready for formal handwriting instruction. Children's pseudowriting is a concrete demonstration of their understanding of how written language works. Once the pseudowriting shows a grasp of the principles of directionality, generativity (a limited number of signs

FIGURE 8 Range of skill at writing the word *summer* (kindergartners at the beginning of the school year)

arranged in a variety of combinations), flexibility (a limited number of signs that can be made in a limited number of ways), and recurrence (writing uses the same shapes over and over), they have attained the basis to profit from instruction (Temple, Nathan, and Burris, 1982).

    3. *Established Hand Dominance.* Most children will have developed *handedness* by the time they reach school. Careful observation will help the teacher to identify those children who favor their right or left hands and those children who need more time to develop consistent dominance.

FIGURE 9   Sample of writing that illustrates inconsistency with size and spacing of letters and words

Cognitive Readiness

    1. *Awareness of Written Language.*   Before one can successfully learn to write, one must understand that the written code serves a function akin to that of oral language. To become a sophisticated user of written language, the child must also recognize that written language is not a perfect match for oral language. Young writers frequently attempt to reproduce oral language too closely, before they have a fully developed understanding of the importance of consistency of size, spacing, and spelling (Figure 9).

    2. *Interest and Desire.*   Children who are ready to receive formal handwriting instruction will already be doing a great deal of pseudowriting and will usually also be asking for specific help. Their requests will resemble these: "How do you make a B?" "Write my name on this."

    3. *Left-Right Progression.*   Instruction in written English requires students to coordinate left-right movements between hand and eye. It also requires them to understand that conventional written English follows that format. Confusions in left-right progression as evidenced by reversals of whole words (Figure 10) or by letters within words (Figure 11) are normally seen in the writing of young children until they reach the ages of eight or nine. After that time, the presence of a significant number of reversals may signal the need for special assistance.

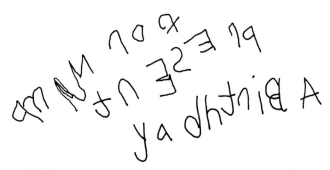

FIGURE 10   Sample of writing that illustrates reversals of words

FIGURE 11   Sample of writing that illustrates reversals of letters within words

Developing Handwriting Skills

Most handwriting programs in this country now begin with manuscript, or printed, letter production (Figure 12). The traditional form of manuscript letter formation was introduced in this country in 1922 (Dehaven, 1983). More recently, some schools have begun to teach a modified form of manuscript called D'Nealian (Figure 13). D'Nealian letters have a more oval shape and are slightly slanted. The features may make the letters easier to form, and may facilitate the later transition to cursive (or connected) writing (Figures 14 and 15). Published handwriting programs differ slightly on instructions for the formation of specific letters. However, there is general agreement that legibility depends on con-

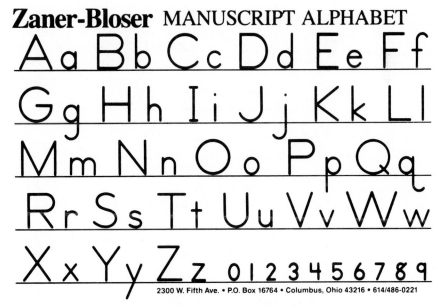

2300 W. Fifth Ave. • P.O. Box 16764 • Columbus, Ohio 43216 • 614/486-0221

FIGURE 12   Alphabet in manuscript form (Zaner-Bloser)

D'Nealian™ Manuscript Alphabet

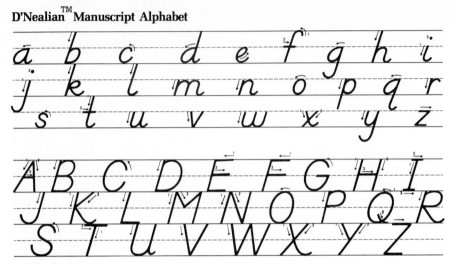

FIGURE 13   Alphabet in manuscript form (D'Nealian)

sistency of letter size, shape, spacing, alignment and slant, and evenness of pressure. To achieve those goals, teachers must first develop a writing program that encourages children to write freely. At that point, assistance with the mechanics of production is useful.

Zaner-Bloser CURSIVE ALPHABET

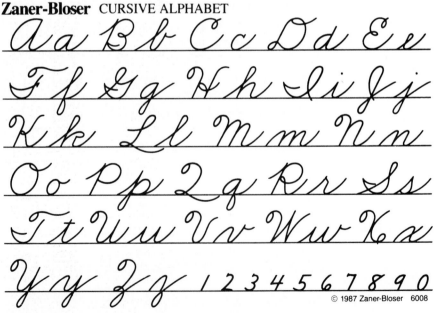

© 1987 Zaner-Bloser 6008

FIGURE 14   Alphabet in cursive form (Zaner-Bloser)

D'Nealian™ Cursive Alphabet

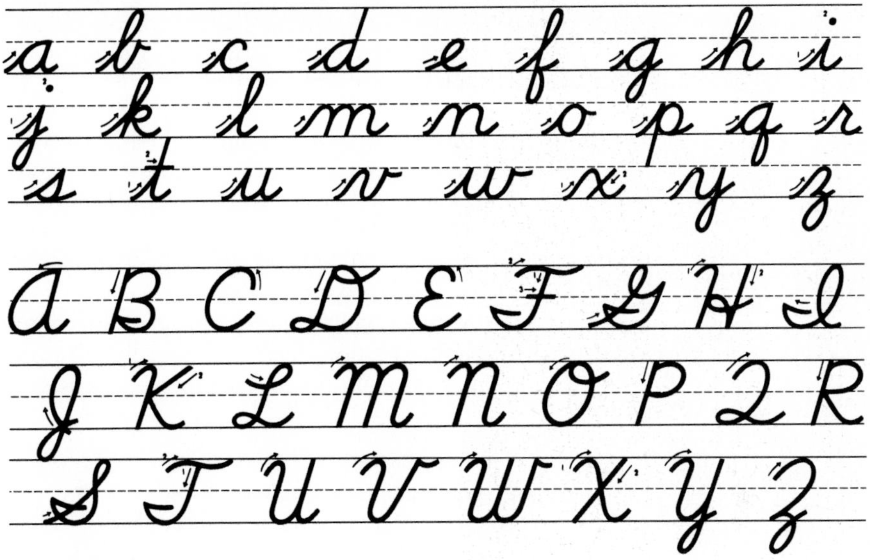

FIGURE 15 Alphabet in cursive form (D'Nealian)

Early writing activities should allow children to experiment with a variety of writing instruments (thick pencils, regular pencils, crayons, pens, felt markers) and both lined and unlined paper. Generally, initial writing instruction should encourage children to use the type of instrument and paper that they find most comfortable. Over time, as each child becomes proficient at letter formation and at the conventions of writing, uniformity of expectations for published writing (for example, using ink on lined paper) can be introduced. The physical act of producing written language remains very difficult for some children, and they resist the idea of revising their laboriously produced efforts. For such children, the word processor may provide a welcome solution because writing and rewriting on a word processor is physically easier than writing with pencil or pen.

In her work describing young children learning to write, Clay (1975) compared schools that provided formal handwriting instruction with schools that did not. She noted the following:

> Many of the schools in which observations were made did not place much emphasis on separate lessons in how to print during the first year of formal schooling. The creative urge of the child to write down his own ideas was considered by teachers to be the important thing to be fostered in written language. How did children learn to print? They
>
> - drew pictures as the teacher wrote dictated captions
> - traced over the teacher's script

- copied captions
- copied words around the room
- remembered word forms, and wrote them independently
- invented (generated) word forms, often correctly
- got a written copy of unknown words from the teacher

The teacher gave an occasional group lesson in letter formation, perhaps once a week, and gave daily individual guidance in letter formation.

    In schools that did have lessons on forming letters and printed words in addition to daily draw-a-picture and write-a-story activities the pupils did not appear to differ significantly from those in other schools in the skills they gained. (p. 1)

When handwriting is taught within a program that emphasizes it as a vehicle to be used in communication, the teacher's role is to provide a series of appropriate and timely models. Initially this involves assistance with the following:

1. Paper placement (for right-handers, slightly to the right of the body midline and at approximately a 45° angle).
2. Arm and wrist placement (resting comfortably on a flat writing surface that is approximately waist height or slightly above it).
3. Finger placement (a coordinated equal-pressure grip of thumb, index and middle finger, approximately 1½" from the point of the writing instrument, and held at approximately a 45° angle to the paper). Children can be assisted in finding the correct grip placement by wrapping a rubber band or piece of tape around their pen or pencil at the appropriate spot.

Children should be encouraged to practice their writing skills while seated comfortably at appropriate desks or tables, in chairs that provide support. They should not be lying on the floor or perched on stools because these positions will make the physical act of writing more difficult. When children have learned to sit properly and when they can control writing materials comfortably, they may profit from modeling of letter formation.

    There is no generally agreed-upon order in which letters must be taught. Generally, instruction will be facilitated by grouping together those letters that have similarities in construction (*i, l, t* or *o, c, e*). However, the development of appropriate handwriting skills requires both awareness and control of production for the distinctive features of letters as well as for their generalities. That awareness and control develops gradually over a considerable period of time and only with considerable practice, as can be seen in the illustration of the mastery of the capital letter *B* in Figure 6. The purpose of teacher modeling is not to promote drill on endless pages of isolated letters. Rather, it is to provide information about the correct formation of letters, in order to facilitate the business of communication. Isolated practice of letter formation will be beneficial only so long as the child sees it as a means to writing fluently. Students who are having an unusual amount of difficulty regulating the size of their letters or the spacing between words may benefit from writing, for a time, on paper that has been ruled into appropriately sized squares rather than lines. As they write, they can practice filling the entire square with the letter and also leaving one or two squares between words. This will help them to develop their control and sense of proper proportions. Appropriate letter formation will be encouraged most effectively through writing activities that require the writer to be very clear about the purpose and intent of the message for a real reader. The writer can then concentrate on the physical production task. A classroom that provides at least twenty minutes a day of uninterrupted writing time will need very little, if any, additional time for drill in individual letter formation.

Teaching the Left-handed Writer   Pity the poor left-hander! *Not* because there is anything wrong with being left-handed, but rather because there is even less agreement on how to teach left-handers to write than there is on teaching right-handed students. Helpful hints for instructing left-handers, available in current language arts texts, include variations of such statements as: Angle the paper more sharply than for a right-hander. Keep the paper straighter than for a right-hander. Place the paper perpendicular to the body and parallel to the desk edges for both right and left-handers. Allow the hand to hook slightly so the child can see the letters being formed. Don't allow the hand to hook at all so that the writer can see the letters being formed.

Generally speaking, it is somewhat more difficult for left-handers to learn to write comfortably and legibly because 1) they are less likely to see a number of adult role models in the act of writing, 2) they are pulling their hand and arm toward their body during the act of writing instead of pushing it away, and 3) even with the best writing posture it is somewhat more difficult for them to see what they have written because the empty space on the page recedes toward the eye, rather than retreating from it.

Nevertheless, the typical elementary classroom will contain at least two or three children with well-established left-hand dominance. The teacher should never attempt to change that preference. Instead, the left-hander should be shown and encouraged to use finger-grip, hand and arm, and paper positions that are approximately the reverse of those used by a right-handed child. As with right-handers, each left-handed child should be allowed to select the writing implement, type of paper, and variation of position that are most comfortable.

Developing a Handwriting Conscience

Caring about the legibility of one's handwriting is crucial to the production of a better product. Having something that one wants to say, and having a variety of audiences try to read what one has written are the ultimate incentives to improving handwriting. Children can be assisted in developing the ability to judge the legibility of their efforts in several ways.

1. Discussions of handwriting samples can help them identify the source of problems such as letter formation, spacing, and mixed slant.
2. Tools such as transparent overlays, or cards with holes punched in them, can be used to help judge consistency of size and spacing.
3. Techniques such as drawing vertical lines through the center of letters can help students develop consistency of slant.
4. Many opportunities to receive feedback from readers about the legibility of their efforts can be found.

Finally, the following query should be kept in mind:

> Do children come to school with an aversion to writing? Evidence proves quite the contrary. Most children enter school eager and ready to learn to write; some have even taught themselves to write their own names or have teased the grown-ups in their families into teaching them well before they start school. What happens, then, that dulls so many children's interest in mastering a much-anticipated skill?

> **Scott, Foresman & Company**
> **Teacher's Edition**
> **D'Nealian Handwriting, 1981**

When handwriting is taught as a necessary tool to facilitate communication, and children are involved in an active, problem-solving approach to its improvement, they remain enthusiastic.

Suggested Activities

1. Examine a published handwriting instructional program. Be able to discuss the kinds of learning activities provided for students. Would this program be suitable for all learners? Why or why not?
2. Teach a child how to use the dictionary to find the spelling of a word he or she cannot spell. Analyze the child's performance.
3. Teach a child to use the test-study-test method for learning to spell a word. Evaluate the child's performance.
4. From a middle-school student, obtain a sample of writing that contains several spelling errors. Examine the misspelled words. Do you see any patterns in the errors? To what extent do the errors show evidence of spelling sense (such as attention to the way the word sounds)?

References

Anderson, K. "The Development of Spelling Ability and Linguistic Strategies." *The Reading Teacher* 39(November 1985):140–47.

Becker, W.; Dixon, R.; and Anderson, L. "Morphographic and Root Word Analysis of 26,000 High Frequency Words." Eugene, OR: University of Oregon, 1980.

Bissex, G. *GNYS AT WRK: A Child Learns to Write and Read.* Cambridge: Harvard University Press, 1980.

Blumberg, P., and Block, K. "The Effects of Attempting Spelling before Feedback on Spelling Acquisition and Retention." Presentation to the American Educational Research Association. Washington, D.C., 1975. ERIC Documents No. ED 103 885.

Brown, R. *A First Language: The Early Stages.* Cambridge: Harvard University Press, 1973.

Calkins, L. *The Art of Teaching Writing.* Portsmouth, NH: Heinemann, 1986.

Chomsky, C. *The Acquisition of Syntax in Children from 5 to 10.* Cambridge: MIT Press, 1969.

——————. "Write First, Read Later." *Childhood Education* 47(March 1971):296–99.

Clay, M. *What Did I Write?* Portsmouth, NH: Heinemann, 1975.

Dehaven, E. *Teaching and Learning the Language Arts.* Boston: Little, Brown, 1983.

Flood, J., and Lapp, D. *Language/Reading Instruction for the Young Child.* New York: Macmillan, 1981.

Follett, W. "Spelling" in Follett, W., *Modern American Usage.* New York: Hill and Wang, 1966.

Gee, T. C. "Students' Response to Teacher Comments." *Research in the Teaching of English* 6(Fall 1972):212–21.

Gentry, J. R. "Learning to Spell Developmentally." *The Reading Teacher* 34(January 1981):378–811.

Goodall, J., and Levine, R. "The Grammar of Action: Sequence and Syntax in Children's Copying." *Cognitive Psychology* 4(1973):82–98.

Graves, D. *Writing: Teachers and Children at Work.* Portsmouth, NH: Heinemann, 1983.

Greene, H. A. *The New Iowa Spelling Scale* (revised by Bradley Loomer). Iowa City: State University of Iowa, 1977.

Hall, S., and Hall, C. "It Takes a Lot of Letters to Spell 'Erz.'." *Language Arts* 61(December 1984):822–27.

Henderson, E. *Teaching Spelling.* Boston: Houghton Mifflin, 1985.

Hillerich, R. "Let's Teach Spelling—Not Phonetic Misspelling." *Language Arts* 54(March 1977):301–07.

Hinrichs, R. "An Old But Valid Procedure." *Elementary English* 52(February 1975):249–52.

Hodges, R. *Learning to Spell.* Urbana, IL: National Council of Teachers of English, 1981.

Horn, E. "Principles of Method in Teaching Spelling as Derived from Scientific Investigation" in *Eighteenth Yearbook* (Part II, Chaper II). National Society for the Study of Education: Public School Publishing Co., 1919.

——————. *The Basic Writing Vocabulary.* Iowa City: University of Iowa, 1927.

Horn, T. D. "The Effect of the Corrected Test on Learning to Spell." *Elementary School Journal* 47(January 1947):277–85.

McDonell, G., and Osburn, E. B. "Beginning Writing: Watching It Develop." *Language Arts* 57(March 1980):310–14.

Mencken, H. L. "American Spelling" in H. L. Mencken, *The American Language.* New York: Alfred Knopf, 1980.

Menyuk, P. *Language and Maturation.* Cambridge: MIT Press, 1977.

Read, C. "Preschool Children's Knowledge of English Phonology." *Harvard Educational Review* 41(February 1971):1–34.

Rinsland, H. *A Basic Vocabulary of Elementary School Children.* New York: Macmillan, 1945.

Rule, R. "The Spelling Process: A Look at Strategies." *Language Arts* 59(April 1982):379–84.

Swisher, K. "Increasing Word Power Through Spelling Activities." *The Reading Teacher* 37(April 1984):706–10.

Taylor, W., and Hoedt, K. "The Effect of Praise Upon the Quality and Quantity of Creative Writing." *Journal of Educational Research* 60(October 1966):80–83.

Temple, C.; Nathan, R.; and Burris, N. *The Beginnings of Writing.* Boston: Allyn & Bacon, 1982.

Templeton, S. "Young Children Invent Words: Developing Concepts of Word-ness." *The Reading Teacher* 33(January 1980):454–59.

———————. "The Spelling-Meaning Connection and the Development of Word Knowledge in Older Students." *Journal of Reading* 27(October 1983):8–14.

Thomas, V. *Teaching Spelling.* Toronto: Gage Publishing Co., 1979.

Wood, M. "Invented Spelling." *Language Arts* 59(October 1982):707–17.

Suggested Readings

Beers, J. W., and Beers, C. S. "Vowel Spelling Strategies Among First and Second Graders: A Growing Awareness of Written Words." *Language Arts* 57(February 1980):166–72.

Giacobbe, M. E. "Kids Can Write the First Week of School." *Learning* 10(September 1981):132–33.

Goodman, K. *What's Whole in Whole Language?* Portsmouth, NH: Heinemann, 1986.

Goodman, Y.; Haussler, M.; and Strickland, D. (eds.). *Oral and Written Language Development Research: Impact on the Schools.* Urbana, IL: National Council of Teachers of English, 1982.

Henderson, E., and Templeton, S. "A Developmental Perspective of Formal Spelling Instruction through Alphabet, Pattern, and Meaning." *Elementary School Journal* 86(January 1986):305–16.

Hodges, R. E. "Research Update: On the Development of Spelling Ability." *Language Arts* 59(March 1982):282–90.

A Language for Life. Report of the Committee of Inquiry appointed by the Secretary of State for Education and Science under the Chairmanship of Sir Alan Bullock FBA. London: H.M.S.O., 1975.

Paul, R. "Invented Spelling in Kindergarten." *Young Children* 31(March 1976):195–200.

Teaching the Basics. NCTE Committee on Classroom Practices in Teaching English (Ouida Clapp, Chair). Urbana, IL: National Council of Teachers of English, 1977 (pamphlet).

Templeton, S. "Synthesis of Research on the Learning and Teaching of Spelling." *Educational Leadership* 43(March 1986):73–78.

If students have repeated opportunities to write and speak for their own purposes and to work together to discuss, edit, and refine their written work, they will gradually develop solid foundations and will become more consistent and precise in their use of language.

9 Grammar and Language Usage

The terms *grammar* and *usage* may have different meanings for different people. Some apply the term *grammar* to all aspects of language study, from learning rules and principles to considering how different people speak and write. From this viewpoint, usage is considered a facet of grammar. To other people, grammar generally means the way we *ought to* speak and write, whereas usage means the way we *do* speak and write. Still others make no distinction between the two terms. When teachers discuss grammar and usage, they need to make sure that they have defined the terms.

Grammar is defined here as a systematic, explicit description of word form and structure (morphology) and of the arrangement of words in sentences (syntax). Teaching grammar means both having students identify various language elements and having them analyze how sentences are formed. For example, a grammar exercise might require students to identify the subject and predicate of a sentence or to distinguish between adjectives and adverbs. In contrast, usage is defined as the way people express themselves in speech and writing. Teaching usage means helping students to express their ideas with greater dexterity and refinement. For example, a usage exercise might ask students to recognize that "Them are the ones" is not acceptable in some circles or that the following sentence needs to be revised if it is to convey the intended meaning: Coming home late from work, my dog had destroyed the living room curtains.

Understanding the difference between language acquisition and language learning helps to clarify the distinction made here between grammar and usage. As many researchers have observed, one's native language is *acquired* naturally, through communication with one's parents and others. Speech is shaped when one listens to others and imitates what is heard. The process is intuitive in that one does not consciously study a system of rules or principles. Language *learning,* on the other hand, is a conscious study of language, of either one's own native language or a second language. Acquisition and learning are thus distinct processes (Krashen, 1981).

Krashen posits *monitor theory* to explain the relationship between acquisition and learning in language performance. The basic principle here is that we use what we have *acquired* to initiate an utterance; consciously *learned* knowledge is brought into play only as a "monitor" to reshape or to correct first attempts (see also Krashen and Terrell, 1983). According to monitor theory, the acquisition process is the more important in developing one's ability to speak and write well habitually. The monitor has limited value because, as a checking mechanism, the consciously learned knowledge will not be used in many communication settings. For example, when people are speaking or writing rapidly and are eager to express their ideas, they are usually oblivious to the form their words take. They may easily misuse or misspell words that are not well entrenched in their speaking or writing vocabularies. In contrast, the monitoring of form requires conscious attention and reflection; people must review what they have said or written with a critical ear or eye to reshape and refine.

Usage habits are, to a great extent, the result of the acquisition process, whereas formal knowledge of grammar is the result of learning. The knowledge of grammar may serve the monitor but will not necessarily affect the spontaneous usage that is based on acquired habits. For instance, through studying grammar learners will discover that *them* is an objective case pronoun and that *they* is the corresponding pronoun in the nominative case. The learners would thus come to recognize that in the sentence *Them are the ones,* "them" is being used atypically as the subject. Yet if this is what the learners are used to saying, the formal knowledge alone will not affect their usage (though it may convince them that their usage should be changed). If they wish not to say *Them are the ones,* they must acquire a different habit.

Not all educators differentiate between grammar and usage, but the distinction can be useful because it helps teachers clarify their instructional goals for oral and written expression. The distinction will be maintained in this chapter as we consider issues of grammar and usage.

Grammar

Different schools of thought have produced different ways of analyzing and describing language. Traditional grammar emphasizes categorizing elements into eight parts of speech and analyzing (often diagramming) sentences. Structural grammar stresses form class words (similar to parts of speech) and sentence patterns. Finally, transformational grammar draws a distinction between the surface structure (word order) and the deep structure (underlying meaning) of sentences; it also emphasizes discovering the *phrase structure rules* that determine how sentences are generated. (See Appendix D for a more complete description of these three grammars.)

Different grammars take different perspectives, but all are alike in that they provide a way of analyzing language. Such analysis requires the person to think abstractly. The student must recognize patterns and relationships, must label elements, and must learn basic rules or principles. Nonetheless, the object of scrutiny is a mental process, one which the student has used successfully since infancy without really giving the process a second thought. As Petrosky (1977) points out, the purpose of learning grammar is to "describe . . . primarily unconscious workings and translate them into conscious exercises" (p. 86).

The study of grammar can become an extremely puzzling endeavor, especially for those students who cannot yet deal with the high level of abstract thought required if they are to consider words as members of linguistic categories. Asking students to analyze language is, in a way, like asking them to analyze their drawings in terms of the principles of line and color that they use intuitively. We do not ask children to analyze and label what they do when they draw a path narrower and narrower as it goes off into the distance. We accept the fact that children represent the world as they see it, to the best of their abilities. We leave more sophisticated consideration of drawing principles (and the corresponding vocabulary) for later years.

Requiring children to identify subjects and predicates or to learn phrase-structure rules will put most of them in the awkward position of having to deal with a familiar, intuitive behavior as a set of rules and categories that have little to do with how language is used or might be used. Realizing that we employ adverbs and prepositional phrases in our discourse does not change our speech or writing, just as simply learning the term *perspective* has little effect on our ability to draw a tapering path. In other words, a knowledge of grammar does not necessarily affect usage. Pence points this out in the preface to the first edition of his grammar book:

> a knowledge of grammar does *not* in itself guarantee that even the serious-minded student will thereby become a master of correct English. One can know all about grammar and still make stupid blunders, just as one may know nothing of the technique of the subject and yet never make a mistake. Indeed, a *formal* study of grammar would certainly be an inefficient means by which to learn how to avoid errors. (Pence and Emery, 1963, pp. iv–v)

Research findings support this viewpoint (see, for example, Harris, 1962; Braddock et al., 1963; Elley et al., 1976). Indeed, there seems to be little justification for widespread teaching of formal grammar at any level. The younger the children are (and thus the less able they are to engage in abstract, analytical thinking), the less reason there is to devote extensive instructional time to this discipline.

"Formal" and "extensive" in this context need definition. An example will illustrate. Assume that during the year, a language arts class devotes well over half of its class time to the study of grammar. Working with lists of sentences, the students identify sentence elements (e.g., subjects, predicates, phrases, clauses) and determine how words and phrases function in sentences (e.g., as nouns, verbs, adjectives, adverbs). The teacher explains the principles; the students apply the principles by examining sentences prepared by the teacher or presented in a grammar textbook. The emphasis is on analysis, though students are occasionally asked to produce sentences to illustrate principles (e.g., they are asked to write a sentence with a noun clause as the subject). This approach is "formal" in that grammar is studied systematically as an end in itself. The time is "extensive" in that more than half of the total class time is given to analyzing and describing the language.

Such concentrated effort to learn rules and labels may make students adept at analyzing sentences, but it will have very little effect on students' ability to acquire better language habits or to use the language more skillfully.

This is not to say that there is no value in the study of grammar. Some learning of terminology and principles is desirable during the elementary and middle or junior high school years. It is sometimes helpful for students to have labels for the language elements they use. A common vocabulary makes communication about language easier when, for instance, students and teachers discuss how to revise a piece of writing. However, the more formal and extensive the instruction, the more students will tend to perceive grammar as an isolated subject that has little relevance to their communication ability. Learning grammar is not a prerequisite to speaking and writing well; it should not be taught as such. Only when students have a good grasp of language, having comprehended and used a variety of language structures, should they be asked to learn the labels that a grammar assigns to the elements of those structures.

Grammar instruction will be most appropriate and effective if it is marked by these features:

1. Grammar is taught in the context of a strong expressive language program.

Whenever grammar is presented, it should be subordinate to the more important goal of having students speak and write to express their ideas. For instance, when students work together to revise public writings, they will have many opportunities to improve their expression by rewriting and polishing their sentences. To help them consider alternatives, the teacher may select sentences or passages from their papers and have the group discuss different ways of stating the ideas. At these times, the teacher may easily introduce grammar terms and spend a few minutes explaining them. However, the goal is to help students improve their expressive abilities, not simply to have them learn descriptive terms.

2. Grammar is allocated less time in the curriculum than writing, reading, or any other language art.

At all grade levels, it is more important for students to comprehend and use language than to analyze and describe it. Instructional units may include the content of grammar, but time-consuming grammar units, per se, should be avoided. Thus, students may profitably spend a few days noting how adjectives and adverbs are used when the class is reading and writing descriptive pieces, but students do not need to spend several weeks studying adjectives and adverbs in isolation from coherent texts.

3. Students study what they are ready for and capable of handling in each grade.

Students in each grade will be at different levels of readiness for grammar, just as they are at different reading and spelling levels. For instance, in a single class there may be some students who can readily identify all the parts of speech and others who are just beginning to recognize the difference between nouns and verbs. As such different levels of readiness become apparent, the teacher must tailor instruction accordingly.

To summarize, grammar has been defined here as a system for analyzing and describing the sentences people produce. When teachers ask students to identify and label sentence elements or to learn the rules that govern sentence formation, the emphasis is on teaching grammar so that students can describe the language. This emphasis on description, though useful to some extent, is not as important for children as is guidance to help them express their thoughts effectively in writing or speech. It is the way students use language, not what they know about it, that determines the effectiveness of their communication.

Language Usage

Children come to school with different levels of facility with language. Some have extensive vocabularies and an easy command of sentence structure; they speak fluently and well for their age. They do so because they have had good models. Typically, they come from homes that are filled with lively conversation and good books that are much in use. Other children have limited vocabularies and are less adept at expressing their ideas. They may not use complete sentences and may not even be able to say with clarity what they think. These children tend to come from homes in which conversation and reading aloud are limited; a few characters from television programs may be the most influential language models that some of these children have. The purpose of usage instruction is to help all these students speak and write with greater dexterity and refinement.

Skillful language use is acquired gradually through repeated exposure to good oral and written language. The teacher's language, the language of peers, and the language of books all serve as models for the child in school. If the models are exemplary, they will reinforce the habits that well-spoken children have acquired and will help the less articulate children gradually improve their language versatility and control. By surrounding students with good language models, the teacher can foster the natural, intuitive process through which language habits are acquired. The students will be unaware of being taught directly, but they will imitate what they hear and read and thus come to extend and refine their expressive abilities.

While providing good language models, the teacher can also help students learn new vocabulary, manipulate sentence structure, and master various conventions. Direct instruction can make students aware of new ways of using language. They may then adopt these ways in their speech and writing. Thus, there are two goals for teaching usage: to provide students with language experiences that will encourage the acquisition of good habits, and to give direct instruction that will show students how they might purposely refine their speech and writing.

Providing Experiences with Language

At all levels, immersion in language can be accomplished with a number of enjoyable activities. The key is to have students hear, read, say, and write as much exemplary language as possible. Through listening and reading, students become aware of the way others use language and can put to use what they have heard and read. Activities that make connections between receptive and expressive language are ideal for developing the intuitive sense of language that contributes to skillful usage.

Reading aloud and storytelling provide many opportunities for students to hear and use well-wrought language. In the early grades, children should be exposed to a variety of books. They should be told stories and should be encouraged to participate orally. Hearing and speaking story language can help young children acquire versatility in their use of sentences and vocabulary. For example, when listening to *The Old Woman and the Red Pumpkin* by Betsy Bang (Macmillan, 1975), children will eagerly repeat the old woman's chant: "Pumpkin, pumpkin, roll along. I eat tamarinds, I do. I eat plums and rice, I do, while I sing my song." Or when listening to *Stone Soup* by Ann McGovern (Scholastic, 1968), they will enjoy chiming in on the repeated refrain, "Soup from a stone! Fancy that!" Many other books and folk tales include delightful language of this sort that invites oral participation and that can influence spontaneous usage. One second grader, for example, quite enjoyed the story "Stone Soup" and went about saying "Fancy that!" for several days. It is not unusual for children to imitate story language playfully in this way, making the words and patterns their own.

Dramatizing favorite stories allows children to try out different "voices" and styles of speaking as they take characters' parts. The literature provides the model that can be imitated or altered according to individuals' interpretations. For instance, one group of first graders enjoyed taking turns enacting "The Three Billy Goats Gruff." The first "troll" used the exact language of the teacher's telling to send the first two goats on their way: "Well, then, be off with you!" The next "troll" tried his own version: "All right, I'll let you cross my bridge this time!" This deviation prompted a discussion of other statements the troll might make at this point in the story, and the other "trolls" in the group then tried some of these. The experimentation gave everyone a chance to consider how the troll might best give his grudging permission. The dramatizing provided good language practice and led to a greater understanding and appreciation of the original concise and forceful words.

In the upper grades, storytelling and reading aloud continue to provide excellent models of language and exposure to vocabulary. Discussion can give students a chance to reflect on the language as well as on the content of the story. If students are encouraged to write, the tone and style of the literature may well affect their work. For example, after hearing the Grimm Brothers' tale "The Boy Who Wanted to Learn How to Shudder," one group of sixth graders wrote new scenes that could be incorporated into that suspenseful story. Here are portions of two of the papers. The excerpts reflect the mood that was created and the kind of language used during the telling:

The boy sat by the flickering fire, warming himself from the freezing night air. The fire cast a ring of light, which seemed to make the surrounding darkness even more ominous than it already was. Strange, unsteady shadows were cast by the fire, and the glowing embers were so hot they were almost white. The fire danced and flicked, almost as if it had a will of its own.

The time was nearing midnight when James heard the unmistakable sound of rocky, wet concrete grating and grinding against rocky, wet concrete.

Choral speaking or reading of poetry helps students to hear and use varied vocabulary and sentence structure while they enjoy the rhythm and sounds of poetic language. There are many poems that lend themselves to choral speaking or reading, from nursery rhymes in the early grades to ballads, lyrical poetry, or humorous works in the upper grades. Poems used for these purposes should have strong rhymes, pleasing rhythms, and repetitive language patterns. They should also evoke clear, vivid images. Young children will enjoy chanting familiar nursery rhymes like "Hickory Dickory Dock" or the poetry of pattern books such as *Brown Bear, Brown Bear* by Bill Martin, Jr. (Holt, Rinehart and Winston, 1970). Other poems that many children enjoy include these:

"At the Garden Gate," by David McCord in *Far and Few, Rhymes of Never Was and Always Is* (Little, Brown, 1952).
"The Pickety Fence," by David McCord in *One At A Time* (Little, Brown, 1977).
"Shop Windows," by Rose Fyleman in *Time for Poetry,* edited by M. H. Arbuthnot and S. L. Root, Jr. (Scott, Foresman, 1968).
"Trains," by James S. Tippett in *Crickety Cricket! The Best-Loved Poems of James S. Tippett* (Harper & Row, 1973).
"What the Gray Cat Sings," by Ogden Nash in *Everybody Ought to Know* (Lippincott, 1961).

Each of these books includes many other poems that lend themselves to choral speaking or reading. Other suitable poems may be gleaned from the works of Rosemary and Stephen Vincent Benét, John Ciardi, Eugene Field, Aileen Fisher, Langston Hughes, Henry Wadsworth Longfellow, Eve Merriam, A. A. Milne, Jack Prelutsky, Carl Sandburg, Shel Silverstein, and Robert Louis Stevenson, among others. Almost all poetry collections include several works that may be used for these purposes.

Independent reading provides children with yet other models of language that can affect their own usage. While engrossed in a good story, an exciting true-life adventure, or a book of poetry, children will encounter words and modes of expression that they may not hear in the classroom or at home. Those who read widely take in a much greater variety of language than those who read very little. Though not conscious of learning anything specific, the wide readers will still be positively influenced by the exposure.

At all levels, the language of literature is inspiring to students. It stimulates them to savor words and rhythms and to experiment with new forms of oral and written expression. The effects on their language usage are sometimes obvious and immediate, as when students' speech or writing clearly shows the influence of the language patterns they hear and read. But the effects are also subtle and cumulative. Years of exposure to literature will result in an ever-growing intuitive command of vocabulary and syntax that will contribute to children's general expressive abilities.

Teaching for Refinement

To help children develop versatility and control, teachers must also encourage students to be consciously attentive to the way they use language. As their intuitive sense of language grows, they also need to learn how to develop greater command of syntax, vocabulary, and the generally accepted conventions of oral and written language usage. The terminology of English grammar may be introduced in these kinds of lessons, but the primary goal should always be to help students improve their language usage rather than to master terminology.

Improving Syntactical Versatility   Young children who are just beginning to write typically string ideas together, using "and then" or a similar repetitive phrase as the major device for connecting a series of simple sentences. They are writing their thoughts as they would speak them. As they mature intellectually, internalizing language structures that they hear and read, their speech and writing also mature naturally (Britton, 1982). For instance, a very young child might write the following:

I rode my bike to the park. And then I met my friend. And then we rode our bikes. And then we played baseball. And then I went home and then I watched TV.

An older student might express the same sequence in this way:

I rode my bike to the park, where I met my friend. We rode together and played baseball. When I got home, I watched TV.

To a great extent, then, syntactical versatility is a function of cognitive growth and experience with language. Children will come to write with greater maturity whether or not we give them specific instruction. However, as Mellon

(1969) and O'Hare (1973) point out, sentence-combining activities do show children how to form more sophisticated sentences consciously.

Typically, sentence-combining activities present several simple sentences that may be combined in various ways. Here is an example:

- Mrs. George is an old woman.
- Mrs. George has white hair.
- Mrs. George owns a parrot.
- The parrot's name is Sherlock.
- Sherlock is green and yellow.
- Sherlock talks.

The sentences may be combined in any of these ways:

- Mrs. George, an old woman with white hair, owns a parrot. The parrot, who is green and yellow, is named Sherlock. Sherlock talks.

- Mrs. George, an old, white-haired woman, owns a talking parrot named Sherlock. Sherlock is green and yellow.

- Sherlock, a green and yellow talking parrot, is the pet of Mrs. George, an old woman with white hair.

Here is another example, one that requires attention to sequence rather than attributes:

- We had a game today.
- It was a baseball game.
- Henry hit a home run.
- The crowd cheered.
- We won the game.
- We celebrated.
- We ate cookies.
- We drank soda.

Possible combinations include the following:

- We had a baseball game today. When Henry hit a home run, the crowd cheered. We won the game. We celebrated with cookies and soda.

- In our baseball game today, Henry hit a home run. The crowd cheered. After the game we celebrated. We had cookies and soda.

- When Henry hit a home run in our baseball game today, the crowd cheered. We won the game and celebrated with cookies and soda.

Sentence combining is almost like a game, the object of which is to find many ways to put the ideas together sensibly. In introducing this activity, the teacher needs to show students what to do, giving examples. Students may work individually or in pairs on lists of simple sentences, sharing their results with the rest of the class.

When students first begin to manipulate sentences in this way, their products may be awkward. However, the goal is not for them to create the perfect sentence; their aims are just to see that there are different ways of stating the same ideas. Whatever students write should be praised so that they will be encouraged to do more. As children practice and mature, their efforts will improve. With each exercise, of course, the teacher may contribute one or two suggestions to stretch the group's awareness of the possibilities. During these lessons, the teacher may also explain what certain words or structures are called in terms of grammar.

Most children catch on rather quickly to sentence combining. They enjoy playing with sentences, especially if the exercises are on topics that interest them. The experience is useful, for it shows students that they have alternatives when they write. Over time, the practice will have an effect on their compositions. At some point, in fact—usually in adolescence—many students will begin to write very complex, even ponderous sentences, and they will need help in the other direction—simplifying for clarity and style.

Another activity that can give students greater versatility is imitation writing (see Chapter 7). Students put their own ideas in the form of the model and gain practice in using specific syntactical structures. Their purposeful imitations of interesting sentences, poems, or stories contribute to their sense of how language might be used. When guiding imitation writing, the teacher can easily introduce selected patterns to stretch and challenge children's imagination and ability. Again, grammar terms may be introduced in these lessons. For instance, asume that students have created a number of different sentences in imitation of this one: When the clock struck midnight, Cinderella's coach turned into a pumpkin. After displaying and discussing the students' imitations, the teacher might point out that the first part of each sentence is called an adverbial clause. The learning of grammar is thus tied to the task of writing, and the lesson will probably be meaningful because the students have created their own examples.

Developing Vocabulary   Just as maturity and language experience affect syntax, children's oral and written vocabularies are a result of their cognitive growth and their reading and listening. Hearing and reading stories, interacting with adults and peers, and watching films or television all naturally contribute to children's vocabulary development. As is true for adults, however, children understand many more words than they use in daily speech and writing. We all have a vague understanding of certain words (the ones we keep meaning to look up in the dictionary), but we only *use* those words that we know well.

To help children use more precise vocabulary, the teacher needs to provide many opportunities for them to learn word meanings. After a time, the students will rather naturally use the words orally and in writing.

Cullum (1967) gives an illustration of vocabulary learning in kindergarten that is a good model for any grade level. In his chapter called "Kindergarten Chatter," he describes the visits that he made to one class expressly to introduce new "big" words to the children. One one occasion, Cullum brought a box of small change into the class and had the children examine the contents. He told them that the pennies, dimes, and quarters were called *coins,* a new word for most of the class. He describes what they did next:

> Each child . . . had a chance to shake the coins. Later that morning we practiced a little speech. Someone would go out in the hallway and knock on the door.
> "Come in!" we all yelled.
> Billy entered and said, "Trick or treat. I am collecting for UNICEF. Do you have any coins to contribute to UNICEF?"
> Everyone again had a chance to jangle the coins in the box. (p. 61)

Cullum introduced the word, illustrated it, gave the children repeated meaningful practice using it, and accomplished all these activities in the context of a delightful game. He tells of the results of his work as the year progressed:

> It was exciting to see them go home during the school year as twenty-two eerie apparitions, twenty-two well-trained pachyderms, twenty-two proud, snorting stallions, and twenty-one (one absent) crowing chanticleers. They carried their big words home to astounded parents, grandparents, and older brothers and sisters. They were proud of their new words. Together we had added sixty new words to their speaking vocabularies. At the end of the year I devised a test to see how well they had retained their big words. Without any review, over 90 per cent of the class scored 100! The words were still alive! (p. 65)

Interest and enthusiasm for words can be contagious in the right kind of environment, as Cullum so aptly demonstrates. We can learn much from his example. The teacher who *assigns* words to be learned will not build vocabulary as effectively as the one who *teaches*—demonstrating, explaining, repeating, and encouraging meaningful use. Other worthwhile activities include these:

1. *Word of the Week.*   Clear a space on the bulletin board for a "Word of the Week" display. Choose any word that seems interesting, perhaps one from that week's reading unit. Spend some time each day talking about the word and having students use it in meaningfully repetitive situations, such as skits. Keep a master list posted, adding a word each week and occasionally reviewing previous entries. Encourage students to bring in interesting words that they find when reading independently.

2. *Sentence Elaboration.*   Post a simple sentence on the board, with each word written on a separate card. For instance: The cat jumped. Divide children into small groups and give each group a stack of blank cards. Some groups can brainstorm words to describe the cat, others the way the cat jumped, others where the cat jumped. Give them some examples to get them started. On the cards, have them write the best words they can think of, one word per card. Then each group can add cards to the original sentence. When the class is finished, they might have a sentence like this:

> The furry, gray, green-eyed cat jumped quickly, softly, and stealthily onto the garbage can, the car, and the wall.

Keep the sentence posted, and encourage students to alter it as they encounter new words in reading and listening activities.

3. *Inventing Words.*   Introduce two words that are loosely related. Discuss their meanings. Have students suggest ways to combine the two, inventing new words. For instance, *bleak* and *dreary* might suggest *dreak*. If they come up with a word that exists (*bleary*), they will probably be very interested to learn that one, too.

4. *Word Books.*   Have students record interesting words in special notebooks. The words may be alphabetized but may also be simply listed in the order in which they are encountered through reading or listening. Students may write definitions or may include the sentence in which the word was found. Occasionally, students may share their words by exchanging books and discussing their word collections.

5. *Teacher's Word.*   Choose a word to concentrate on for a day. Announce the word early in the morning and use it as often as possible during the day. If the word is *exasperated,* for instance, have fun claiming to be exasperated at small irritations. Students will soon imitate, using the word in their own contexts, having fun, and getting meaningful practice.

6. *Choosing the Best Word.*   Give children several sentences in which there are words that might be added or changed to convey different nuances of meaning. One such sentence, for example, might be: The lame old man walked slowly down the street. Encourage students to picture the old man and suggest alterations in the sentence to convey what they are thinking of. Students may then discuss how the different words they think of convey slightly different meanings. (The elderly man limped slowly down the street. The man, aged and lame, shuffled down the street.) Exploring word meanings through writing and talking will give students experience in choosing words carefully to express just what they intend to express. Students may wish to consult a thesaurus for this kind of activity.

With regular, enthusiastic attention to vocabulary, children will learn new words and be eager to use them in their speech and writing. They will gradually see the importance of a well-chosen word and, with practice, will be able to help each other with word choice in their writing response groups.

Dealing with Non-Standard English   Some students' language deviates significantly from Standard English. Teachers thus need to decide how to handle what may be considered to be errors. On the one hand, teachers want students to gain respect as educated people. People are judged at least partly by their language usage, and so educators have a hard time not correcting children who say "brang" instead of "brought," or "Me and him are friends," or "I ain't got no idea." On the other hand, teachers must realize that disapproval of language can easily be interpreted as disapproval of the student who uses it. As Moffett (1968) observes,

> The student [who is being corrected] is being asked, in effect, to prefer the dialect of a speech community to which he does not belong and to disavow, in some measure, the way of talking that he learned from his parents and from other people upon whom his sense of personal and social identity depends. A lot more than variation in linguistic forms is entailed in this sort of correction. . . . Actually, to preserve his own sense of integrity, [the student] has a powerful motive not to adopt this alien grammar. (pp. 156–57)

Zealous correction of students turns the teacher into a critic, but adopting a laissez-faire attitude does not help students achieve greater linguistic versatility and power. A sensitive balance must be maintained between cheerfully accepting students' language and gently intervening to help them improve.

Young children, who are still experimenting with language, seldom need direct attention called to their usage. They make many errors that they literally outgrow. For instance, it is common to hear little ones say things such as "Mommy drived me to school today." Having realized intuitively that *ed* is often used to form the past tense, they apply the knowledge to all verbs. With a little more experience as listeners and speakers, they will abandon the anomalous form quite naturally. Almost without exception, children in the early grades do not need instruction to correct their language. They just need more experience in interacting with well-spoken models—parents, teachers, peers—and in listening to a variety of books and other sources of good language so as to acquire good habits.

Older students may have developed more ingrained habits of non-Standard English usage. Gentle intervention may be desirable. More important than correcting errors, however, is the process of making these students aware that they have choices when they use language and that their choices affect both the tone of a message and way it will be received. Students also need to realize that language is most effective when it is used with a keen awareness of the communication context.

One way to illustrate these points is to have students contrast Standard and non-Standard English statements of the same ideas as they might be used in different contexts. For instance, the non-Standard statement *It don't matter to me* is prevalent in many people's daily speech. It would be useful to evaluate this as a bantering negation among friends, as a response to an employer who offers options in the workplace, and as a reply to an elegant hostess who asks one's beverage preference. The use of "it don't" is also prominent in the lyrics of many popular songs and is appropriate to the character, tone, and rhythm of those songs. Students need to realize that in some situations "it don't" may be acceptable, whereas in others the pattern would be considered highly inappropriate. Such comparisons avoid condescension toward the non-Standard English speaker while helping students see that an unthinking use of language may have undesirable consequences.

Works of literature, articles in periodicals, and television programs offer many opportunities for students to consider the various forms that language can take. Students may be encouraged to evaluate literary characters in terms of the language they use. They can discuss how readily speech gives clues to personality, social station, motivation, and purpose. Television dialogue or discourse from the daily paper might also be examined for students to compare how different speakers and writers use language. Such comparisons should be made not simply to illustrate what is right and wrong but to demonstrate that language not only conveys content but also reveals information about the user.

The study of Standard versus non-Standard English might extend to works in which the non-Standard form is used purposely for special effect. For example, consider the following two passages. (A) is the opening of the Declaration of Independence, and (B) is the opening of H. L. Mencken's "The Declaration of Independence in American."

> (A) When in the course of human events, it becomes necessary for one people to dissolve the political bands which have connected them with another, and to assume among the powers of the earth, the separate and equal station to which the Laws of Nature and of Nature's God entitle them, a decent respect to the opinions of mankind requires that they should declare the causes which impel them to the separation.
>
> (B) When things get so balled up that the people of a country got to cut loose from some other country, and go it on their own hook, without asking no permission from nobody, excepting maybe God Almighty, then they ought to let everybody know why they done it, so that everybody can see they are not trying to put nothing over on nobody. (For the full text see *A Mencken Chrestomathy,* Vintage Books Edition, 1982, p. 583.)

Mencken intended to create a down-to-earth tone that would amuse the reader. He purposely deviated from the Standard English he knew and could use with precision and elegance. Students need to realize that there is a difference between knowingly using the double negative (or other non-Standard forms) and doing so out of ignorance. In most situations, the former will be accepted, whereas the latter will be criticized or disparaged.

By examining and discussing different language forms in these ways, students can gradually become aware that language is "right" only to the extent that speakers (writers) make choices that are appropriate to the situation and to their purpose. As this awareness grows, students should be encouraged to tailor their language consciously to suit different situations.

Skits can be an enjoyable medium for this kind of language practice. The teacher introduces a specific non-Standard English construction and a counterpart in Standard English—for example, "I don't want no more" and "I don't want any more." Students can plan and perform skits to show how each statement would probably be received in different contexts: by friends and family at the dinner table, at a social gathering of people one hopes to impress, by an old-time frontiersman at the campfire, at a White House reception, and so on. Students might also think of similar statements that convey the same tone ("I ain't got a hankerin' for no more of that" or "Thank you, but I do not care for any more right now"). Conducted with a spirit of fun, such activities can make the point without demeaning anyone who commonly uses the non-Standard form.

Yet another activity that can help students gain conscious awareness of language usage is a more formal kind of ear training. The teacher reads aloud several sentences, which students judge as Standard or non-Standard. For instance, the students can evaluate these sentences:

1. He don't know what he's talking about.
2. She don't talk right.
3. That doesn't make sense to me.
4. It don't make any difference anyway.
5. Jack doesn't understand the rules.
6. Mother don't take her medicine when she should.
7. It doesn't look as if it will rain today.
8. It don't look as if it will snow either.
9. She doesn't have a chance to win.
10. Terry doesn't know what's good for her.

Students may occasionally be encouraged to write their own contrasting sentences and take turns reading them aloud for classmates to judge. Such practice, which need only take a few minutes from time to time, helps students make distinctions between usage patterns. The children will become more aware of the language they hear and use daily. Listening attentively for differences, as well as purposely writing and stating different patterns, can help students acquire greater versatility with usage.

When concentrating on specific non-Standard English constructions in this way, the teacher should be highly selective, giving attention only to the more glaring anomalies that many students use regularly. As Loban (1966) found in an extensive study of children's language, students from kindergarten through grade twelve actually revealed surprisingly few deviations from Standard English in their speech. Most of their language deficiencies were "matters of sensitivity to clarity and precision of communication" (p. 47). Thus, small doses of ear training, skits, and other enjoyable activities should be targeted to those deviations that seem most serious in a class. The large majority of time should be given over to matters of overall clarity and precision, such as word choice, clear syntax, and effective organization of ideas.

Punctuation and Capitalization   The conventions of punctuation and capitalization are to writing what intonation and pause are to speech. They provide clues to understanding the message, and they give signals to facilitate communication. Children need to see these conventions as an integral part of writing, as ways to make their strings of words "work." The standards of form should not be perceived as a set of rules to be memorized but as aids that help writing make sense.

These skills are best learned gradually as part of an ongoing program that provides frequent opportunities for students to read and write for varied purposes. When children read widely, they will inevitably acquire a sense of how written ideas are conventionally marked. When they write often, on many topics, they will have a need for and an interest in knowing how to punctuate and capitalize correctly. If specific instruction is given as children see a use for it—to make their writing readable—they will understand it and apply it. As they develop writing fluency through repeated practice, their use of these mechanics will improve.

Children may be introduced to punctuation marks and capitalization in the earliest grades. They will have seen these conventions in the first books they encountered and will have accepted the odd squiggles and different kinds of letters as part of written language. As reading instruction begins, children learn to differentiate words from one another and to examine text more closely. They come to see that there is a purpose to these special marks. They soon realize that a capital letter indicates the beginning of a sentence, and that a period signals the end.

The use of dictated stories in the reading program (see Chapter 3) offers particularly good opportunities for introducing these writing mechanics to the young reader; this is because the children watch as the teacher transcribes their words. Recording contributors' names along with their statements, for instance, also illustrates different uses of capital letters and several marks of punctuation:

> Tony said, "We played the hopping game." Terry said, "We hopped and hopped like a bunny." Sam said, "The principal came in to watch."

After a group has finished reading a story, the teacher may ask such questions as Where is Tony's name? What letter does Tony's name begin with? Is the *T* like the *T* in Terry's name? These questions can lead to a discussion of the use of upper-case letters in proper nouns, a concept that young readers will quickly internalize. Further examination of the story can call attention to other details that are easy to understand because the written text was created from the spoken

The standards of form should be taught as aids that help writing make sense. The use of dictated stories in the reading program offers particularly good opportunities for introducing writing mechanics to the young reader, because children watch as the teacher transcribes their words.

language. Children will come to know that upper-case letters are used in their names and at the beginnings of sentences, that a period is used to indicate when someone stops dictating, and that quotation marks set off each contribution. This knowledge is reinforced when children read other-author materials that follow the same conventions.

As children develop reading ability and become more attentive to how written texts look, they will want their own writing to be right—that is, to look and sound like the writing in books. They will begin to demonstrate their knowledge of the conventions by using both capital and lower-case letters and various marks of punctuation. They may apply their knowledge inconsistently at first, using capital letters in the middles of words as well as at the beginnings of sentences, or inserting marks of punctuation in odd places. They may also overemphasize what they know; for instance, beginning writers will often place enormous dots at the ends of their sentences, as if to make it quite clear that they know how to use periods.

Teachers can capitalize on this interest in correctness by giving editorial assistance and instruction as questions arise. Generally, advanced skills (such as those involving the use of commas) should be taught only after beginning skills (using periods to end sentences) have been mastered. However, the best time for teaching any specific element is when children ask, "How do you do this?" Usually, students raise questions only about things they are actually ready to learn, so instruction based on student-generated questions will rather naturally follow a progression from the easy to the difficult. Such instruction will be particularly meaningful because it will solve genuine problems that arise in the group.

One fourth-grade teacher took advantage of just such a situation. Ray, a student, had written a story about a time when he was responsible for watching his three-year-old brother while Mother cooked dinner. Absorbed in a favorite television program, Ray did not notice Tommy sneak a piece of cake into the living room. The toddler, sitting under a table, spread crumbs liberally on the carpet as he enjoyed his unsupervised snack. Now, as a writer, Ray wanted to know how to punctuate his *I yelled, Tommy said,* and *Mother called.*

The teacher helped Ray, explaining where each mark belonged and why he needed to indent his lines with each new speaker. Then, because there were other children in the class who were also trying to write dialogue, the teacher asked Ray if he would be willing to share his edited story. On the following day, using an overhead transparency, Ray proudly explained how the exchanges in his story were punctuated. Many children were interested; more questions arose. The teacher decided it was time for a series of activities that would provide a forum for learning to write dialogue. The group spent several days engaged in these tasks:

1. The teacher dictated a short paragraph that included dialogue. Children recorded the dictation in pencil, punctuating it as they wrote. Then the teacher displayed a transparency of the paragraph, without punctuation. Students consulted their papers and, through discussion, agreed about where the various marks should go. As they made their decisions, the teacher placed the marks on the transparency for all to see. Students who had made some errors on their papers corrected their own work.

2. Children were given paper and pencil and were sent about the school as "reporters." Their assignment was to record the exact words from at least one conversation. On their return, they worked in pairs to rewrite and punctuate their notes. As they worked, a few questions came up, and these were discussed among the whole class. The properly punctuated conversations were placed in a folder for all to read and enjoy. The collection was often used as a reference in later weeks.

3. The teacher provided pictures that showed two or more people involved in the same activity. Again working in pairs, children decided what *was* happening in the picture, what *had* happened, and what *might* happen next. After discussion, each individual wrote a piece to describe the action, including made-up conversation. Before the pictures and writing were displayed together, partners helped each other proofread and edit their writing.

4. The teacher read aloud an event from a story in which conversation was implied. The children rewrote the event as if the story characters were addressing one another directly. The need for accurate punctuation was reinforced when these pieces were read aloud.

5. Children were asked to look in their writing folders for a first draft that contained dialogue. Individuals checked their own work for accuracy of punctuation. They made revisions and reviewed the work with at least one other student.

A common element in several of these activities was the pairing of children to work on a task. Working together promoted active involvement because the children had to think through the problems, share knowledge, defend their ideas, and learn from each other. Whenever children are learning specific skills, even skills that seem to involve a good bit of rote memory (such as punctuation), the teacher should provide many opportunities for children to help each other. Learning will be more thorough and more meaningful when, after the teacher's instruction, students discuss the issues among themselves, explaining concepts to each other in their own words.

Although the five activities given as examples all involve punctuating dialogue, similar tasks may be used to teach any element of punctuation. These kinds of activities should be used repeatedly, over several weeks or months, to give children ample practice and reinforcement to overlearn the concepts. When correct punctuation becomes almost automatic, the writer becomes ever more fluent and confident.

As students master various conventions, the class may work together to compose a set of standards for all to follow. They should decide which features they consider most important and should make a list with the teacher's help. (One item on such a list might be: The first word of a sentence starts with a capital letter.) Along with their standards, students may want to include examples of more complicated conventions, such as those used in dialogue. Such a list of standards and examples may be maintained as a chart and may be used as a reminder when students are preparing final drafts. Because they work together to create the chart, the students will be more likely to understand the standards and adhere to them than they would if they were expected to use a list of someone else's rules.

To summarize, here are five principles for teaching punctuation and capitalization that hold true at all grade levels:

1. Teach these writing conventions within meaningful contexts. A few well-planned activities, directly connected with what students are reading and writing, will be much more effective than an extensive punctuation unit featuring drills and exercises that are unrelated to immediate student needs.
2. Emphasize that punctuation and capitalization are used to make a writer's meaning clear. Avoid presenting the conventions as sets of rules to be memorized.
3. Allow plenty of time for the use of easier conventions to become practically automatic before teaching more advanced ones.
4. Whenever possible, teach specific conventions when students start to use them on their own in their writing.

5. Teach for transfer. Develop assignments and practice activities that students can readily use in their own writing.

Expressive Skills: Some Conclusions

In many schools, spelling, grammar, and usage are taught through use of commercial materials that include carefully sequenced lessons and practice activities. The assumption is that students will learn to speak and write well by working their way through such programs, most of which involve paper-and-pencil, short-answer drills with specific elements. A different viewpoint has been expressed here: Competent use of oral and written language is acquired through varied language experiences as much as it is learned through direct instruction and practice in specific skills.

Students need to hear literature and other modes of discourse so as to acquire a sense of how words may be used and sentences may be formed. They need to read widely to acquire the same intuitive sense of good usage and also to develop familiarity with the conventions of written language (e.g., spelling and punctuation). They need to speak and write purposefully to varied audiences so as to have good reasons for speaking and writing well and to have the chance to imitate and apply what they have acquired through listening and reading. Specific skill work can be useful to help students refine the abilities they acquire, but direct instruction and skill practice should always be integrated with activities that encourage purposeful listening, reading, speaking, and writing.

When commercial materials are used, they are best used as resources, not as complete programs that must be followed exactly as presented. Published series can give teachers ideas about how to introduce certain concepts, but the sequence and even the content will usually need to be modified to suit the observed needs of the students. For instance, the best time to give instruction about quotation marks is when students begin to notice them in print and use them in their own writing, even if the available published series would introduce them at a later date. Similarly, if many students are writing stories about a favorite fictional character, it makes sense to add the character's name to their spelling lists, even if it is not on the high-frequency list for that grade level. Skill instruction in all these areas is best when the teacher has long-range objectives in mind but is flexible enough to plan specific lessons to match observed needs and interests among the students.

As is true for many kinds of learning, students will make progress and will also have setbacks before finally achieving competence with the skills of oral and written expression. For instance, many first graders quickly learn how to begin a sentence with a capital letter and end it with a period. In a few years, however, as they become attentive to more complex conventions, they may lapse into seeming ignorance of capitals and periods. Older students, who are concentrating on more difficult concepts (and using more complex language structures as well), may temporarily forget the first things they learned and seem to regress. This is not an unusual phenomenon for learners of any skill at any age. Teachers must always be prepared to review and reinforce previous learning, from one lesson to the next and from one school year to the next. They can seldom assume that students have mastered a specific form or convention. However, if students have repeated opportunities to write and speak for their own purposes and to work together to discuss, edit, and refine their written work, they will gradually develop solid foundations and will thereby become more consistent and precise in their use of language.

Suggested Activities

1. (a) Teach a lesson on sentence combining to a group of students who have limited language facility. Conclude the lesson by having them use sentence combining to revise a first-draft piece of writing.
   (b) Compare your lesson to one in which students complete exercises in a grammar book that focus on subordination. What kind of learning experience would students have in each situation?

2. Identify a syntactic element and plan an imitation-writing lesson to help students use the element in their own writing. (See page 297 for an illustration.)

3. Examine a language arts text for a primary or intermediate grade. If this text were among the curricular materials provided for your classroom, how would you use it?

4. Plan a lesson to teach vocabulary to a group of primary-grade students. Use children's literature as a springboard.

References

Braddock, R.; Lloyd-Jones, R.; and Shoer, L. *Research in Written Composition.* Urbana, IL: National Council of Teachers of English, 1963.

Britton, J. "Notes on a Working Hypothesis about Writing" in G. Pradl, ed., *Prospect and Retrospect: Selected Essays of James Britton.* Montclair, NJ: Boynton/Cook, 1982.

Cullum, A. *Push Back the Desks.* New York: Citation Press, 1967.

Elley, W. B.; Barham, I. H.; Lamb, H.; and Wyllie, M. "The Role of Grammar in a Secondary School English Curriculum." *Research in the Teaching of English* 10(Spring 1976):5–21.

Harris, R. J. "An Experimental Inquiry into the Functions and Value of Formal Grammar in the Teaching of English, with Special Reference to the Teaching of Correct Written English to Children Aged Twelve to Fourteen." Unpublished doctoral dissertation. University of London, 1962.

Krashen, S. D. *Second Language Acquisition and Second Language Learning.* Oxford, England: Pergamon Press, 1981.

——————, and Terrell, T. D. *The Natural Approach: Language Acquisition in the Classroom.* Hayward, CA: Alemany Press, 1983.

Loban, W. *Problems in Oral English: Kindergarten through Grade Nine* (Research Report No. 5). Urbana, IL: National Council of Teachers of English, 1966.

Mellon, J. *Transformational Sentence-Combining.* Urbana, IL: National Council of Teachers of English, 1969.

Moffett, J. *Teaching the Universe of Discourse.* Boston: Houghton Mifflin, 1968.

O'Hare, F. *Sentence Combining: Improving Student Writing without Formal Grammar Instruction* (Research Report No. 15). Urbana, IL: National Council of Teachers of English, 1973.

Pence, R. W., and Emery, D. W. *A Grammar of Present-Day English.* New York: Macmillan, 1963.

Petrosky, A. R. "Grammar Instruction: What We Know." *English Journal* 66(December 1977):86–88.

Suggested Readings

De Beaugrande, R. "Yes, Teaching Grammar Does Help." *English Journal* 73(February 1984):66–69.

Goodman, Y.; Haussler, M.; and Strickland, D. (eds.) *Oral and Written Language Development Research: Impact on the Schools.* Urbana, IL: National Council of Teachers of English, 1982.

Gordon, K. E. *The Well-Tempered Sentence: A Punctuation Handbook for the Innocent, the Eager, and the Doomed.* New Haven, CT: Ticknor & Fields, 1983.

——————. *The Transitive Vampire: A Handbook of Grammar for the Innocent, the Eager, and the Doomed.* New York: Times Books, 1984.

Halliday, M. A. K. *Learning How To Mean.* London: Edward Arnold, 1975.

Irmscher, W. F. "The Teaching of Writing in Terms of Growth." *English Journal* 66(December 1977):33–36.

A Language for Life. Report of the Committee of Inquiry appointed by the Secretary of State for Education and Science under the Chairmanship of Sir Alan Bullock FBA. London: H.M.S.O., 1975.

Mitchell, R. *Less Than Words Can Say: The Underground Grammarian.* Boston: Little, Brown, 1979.

Newkirk, T. "Grammar Instruction and Writing: What We Don't Know." *English Journal* 67(December 1978):46–48.

Teaching the Basics. NCTE Committee on Classroom Practices in Teaching English (Ouida Clapp, Chair). Urbana, IL: National Council of Teachers of English, 1977 (pamphlet).

V

Language Arts Program Design

In earlier chapters of this book we explored the dynamics of listening, speaking, reading, and writing. The chapters in this section extend those discussions by considering how to use this information in planning the overall program. To design a good program, the teacher must understand the workings of each language-thinking process and also understand the overall patterns that emerge when those processes are purposely used in coordination with one another. In a way, teachers must be like master chefs who have a thorough knowledge of basic ingredients and can mix them in any number of ways to create a variety of tasty dishes. The "chef" in the classroom designs a good program by making expert blends of reading, writing, speaking, and listening. The students are often unaware of the separate "ingredients"; they know only that the learning is enjoyable and challenging.

Program design must begin with decisions about basic goals and evaluation strategies. An instructional goal or objective is simply a statement of what the teacher hopes the students will accomplish. Goals should be set in advance so that classroom activities will be purposefully geared toward the goals. The necessary concomitant to goal-setting is

311

evaluation. That is, the teacher needs to decide how to judge the extent to which students are reaching the goals that have been set. Neither goals nor evaluation strategies should be rigid; there may be good reasons to modify either in the course of working with children. However, the teacher must at all times have a clear sense of purpose and direction so as to be able to make good decisions about specific classroom activities.

This section offers suggestions for designing a program with attention to process, integration, and thinking. Chapter 10 explores the issues of setting goals and deciding how to evaluate students' progress. Chapter 11 describes several different instructional units to illustrate what can be accomplished in the classroom.

Instructional goals should determine the type of evaluation that is used; evaluation should reflect instructional goals.

10 Setting Goals and Evaluating Progress

Instructional goals should determine the type of evaluation that is used; evaluation should reflect instructional goals. These assertions may seem obvious, but in reality the critical relationship between goals and evaluation is often overlooked. A teacher may want students to write with vigor but may not quite know how to assess "vigor." He or she may instead grade papers for elements of mechanical accuracy such as spelling and punctuation. Similarly, a teacher may want students to read critically but will grade performance only on workbook exercises that require literal comprehension. In these instances, the evaluation does not match the intended goal, and the discrepancies can easily influence students' efforts. Students are very attentive to grades and will quickly learn what they must do to get high marks. They will tend to work hardest at the things they know will be graded, even if those things do not reflect the teacher's most important goals.

To have an effective program, teachers need to identify what they want students to do and then design the evaluation to measure *that* and not something else. However, maintaining a clear and consistent perspective is not always easy. Report cards may not include spaces for indicating students' progress on some of the goals the teacher has set. There are standardized tests that measure only a limited array of competencies but that are nevertheless considered important evaluation instruments.

Standardized achievement tests evaluate almost all aspects of the language arts curriculum. Tests, or portions of tests, cover vocabulary development, word recognition, reading comprehension, writing, and even listening skills. Most tests measure these areas through a series of multiple-choice items that increase in difficulty from the beginning to the end of the test. Different levels of tests cover the entire grade range. When the tests are originally developed, they are administered to a set of students who have been chosen to represent the range of characteristics of all students who are eventually expected to take the test. The scores from this first set of test takers (the *norming population*) are used to set the standards or *norms* by which the scores of future students taking the tests will be judged.

Standardized test scores may be useful, in certain situations, to compare the achievement of one group of students against that of another group. For example, in a school where three fourth-grade classes have approximately the same student characteristics, standardized achievement scores may provide one way of comparing the overall effectiveness of instruction. In some states, researchers are attempting to do a similar kind of evaluation by comparing scores at schools where student populations have generally the same characteristics. However, even when classrooms or schools have been carefully equated, there may still be unrecognized differences between groups that cause score comparisons to be misleading or inappropriate.

Most standardized achievement tests are not designed to measure in detail the strengths and weaknesses of individual students. This creates problems for the teacher when specific ongoing instructional decisions or curriculum-development goals need to be addressed. Generally, items on a standardized test will not closely reflect the content of a specific language arts curriculum, or include enough items of one type to provide teachers with a valid look at individual students' abilities. In addition, the type of task represented by such a test does not represent much of "real-world" reading, writing, or general language usage. For these reasons, ongoing classroom decisions will usually be best made through the use of informal, teacher-constructed assessment measures that more accurately will represent the actual curriculum's concerns and problems.

Each teacher will struggle with these kinds of problems, and each will find different solutions, influenced not only by personal conviction but also by the traditions, demands, and expectations that exist within the school and the community.

This chapter gives some perspectives and suggestions that may be adapted to different situations. There is a review of each of the language processes, with suggested goals and evaluation strategies for each, as well as an overall perspective based on certain common denominators.

Evaluation of Reading Abilities

Some elements of reading ability may be measured by specific tests. Specific word-recognition skills, for example, may be assessed rather easily with tests that directly follow a classroom lesson. Most basal readers provide mastery tests for these purposes in each instructional unit and/or at the end of the book. Such tests may be adequate for assessing progress in learning specific skills, but there is more to developing reading ability than learning specific skills. Hence, there is more for the teacher to evaluate.

As was emphasized in earlier chapters, a competent reader skillfully uses the reading-thinking process with both narrative and expository text. It is this aspect of reading that is most important to assess, and effective assessment can really only be done through the teacher's careful observation of students as they read. Good observation entails more than getting a general sense of how the students handle themselves. It requires systematic attention to the reading-thinking process that students ought to be using.

The teacher needs to know exactly what to look for in order to monitor the students each time they meet in a group to read and discuss a selection. The teacher also needs to have certain standards in mind, appropriate to the age and abilities of the students, so as to judge how well the students are doing and where they need further instruction. The behaviors that are comprised in the reading-thinking process suggest standards for judging students' achievement.

Predicting   A critical element of skillful reading is the ability to predict while reading a story or an article. The alert reader is always thinking ahead, anticipating what will happen next in a narrative or what information will be presented in a piece of nonfiction. Predictions should be balanced, some arising from the reader's background of experience and prior knowledge, others coming from the information presented in the text. This element of the reading-thinking process can be routinely assessed when students read under the teacher's guidance.

At one extreme will be the reader who cannot or will not make any predictions. Some children are so used to being given a purpose for reading that they are perplexed when someone asks them what *they* think will happen or what *they* might learn. They simply don't know what to say because they have never been asked to think in that way before. Others may have ideas but are too timid to suggest them, either because they are afraid of being wrong or because they think others will consider their ideas foolish. Even if these students can pronounce the words in a reading selection, they will be poor readers, because they have not learned to activate their thinking before and during reading.

The excellent reader is able to make logical, defensible, and sometimes particularly insightful predictions. In fact, the child who makes good predictions but who stumbles over some of the words in the text is actually a much better reader than the one who pronounces the words with perfect accuracy but who looks bewildered when asked to predict the action. The first child is a thinking reader; the second is a word caller who is not comprehending.

Students do vary in their ability to make predictions. Yet their ability can improve with instruction, especially when they are given many opportunities to participate in Directed Reading-Thinking Activities (DR-TAs) that require speculative thinking. As students gain more experience with DR-TAs, they will learn to become actively involved. Their skill at predicting will improve gradually, as will their willingness to risk raising a "foolish" or potentially wrong idea. They will read with spirited eagerness to anticipate and hypothesize.

Listening and Interacting   Another critical element of reading ability involves listening to and interacting with others when a group is discussing a reading selection. Alert readers have something to say about what they read, and they compare what they think with what others think. They can decide whether they agree or disagree with others; they listen, judge, and respond. Discussion refines and extends students' comprehension as they become aware of new perspectives about the material and integrate these views with their own ideas.

Some students have trouble participating in a discussion about a story or article. They do not listen to their fellow readers and thus often cannot say whether they agree or disagree with anyone in the group. They may be politely quiet and look attentive, but they are not really listening if they cannot respond intelligently when asked "Do you agree with that idea?" Some children are so used to attending to the teacher that they do not realize their classmates' comments are also worth hearing. Others may hear what their peers say but cannot integrate the words with their own ideas. They can repeat responses but cannot compare and contrast them with their own. Still others will say they agree with almost every idea that is raised, even when one contradicts another. Not yet thinking for themselves, they will assume that if the teacher accepts an idea then it must be a good one.

Good readers are alert during discussion. They listen to the teacher *and* to their peers. They can explain why they agree or disagree with others, having considered and judged the various ideas raised. Sometimes they change their minds when a new idea seems especially good; sometimes they hold their ground and convince others that they themselves have the best perspective. They participate as thinking individuals.

With DR-TA experience, students will improve their ability to listen and to interact. They will come to realize that their ability to reason is more important than their skill at determining the right answer. They will be alert and willing to participate, eager to exchange ideas with others in the group.

Judging   As students read a selection, they should be able to tell if the text supports their predictions, contradicts them, or has not yet provided enough evidence for them to decide one way or the other. This ability to judge is a critical element of comprehension. It would seem that anyone would invariably be able to make such judgments, but students are not necessarily able to do this consistently.

Some readers will forget their initial ideas, not realizing that their predictions are supposed to serve as purposes for reading. When they finish reading, they may be able to answer the teacher's questions on the selection, but they will not be able to judge whether or not the material confirmed their thinking. These students have not yet learned to read for their own purposes.

Good readers will remember their predictions and will consistently be able to tell whether the text matched or contradicted what they expected. They will also be able to judge when they do not yet have enough information to make a decision. They will have learned that reading involves setting one's own purposes and deciding for oneself if the purposes have been met.

Teachers should not be satisfied to have students simply answer questions after they read. Teachers' questions are limited measures of comprehension that ignore the importance of students being able to make independent judgments about what the text has said, given their expectations. Students should be improving their ability to read for their own purposes.

Justifying   Closely tied to the ability to judge a text in light of one's predictions is the ability to cite specific textual evidence to support those judgments. Readers may know that the text has confirmed or contradicted a prediction, but they should also be able to return to the text and point out the words that caused them to make the judgment. Sometimes the material will give direct justification; often, the reader must infer from the text.

Poor justifiers often do not realize specifically what they have just read. They may, for instance, claim that their prediction was right (when it was) but be unable to cite the relevant piece of text that *proves* they were right. Similarly, they may use textual information to make a new prediction but be unable to tell just what part of the text they have used. Sometimes this weakness results from a lack of practice in skimming a text to find a specific point; the student knows the point is there but just can't find it. Sometimes, the student simply doesn't connect the text with the judgment; he or she is unable to reconstruct and explain the reasoning that led to the judgment.

Alert readers not only make intelligent judgments but can also cite specific, relevant textual evidence to justify their thinking. They consistently say, "I was right because it says right here . . ." or "I think such and such because it says here and here and here." They are skilled both at locating information and at explaining how they arrived at their judgments. When they make an inference, they can cite the information they used and explain their reasoning. They can also help their peers justify and are often able to show other children where the latter got their ideas.

Practice and guidance are critical. When students are expected to justify, and are given regular opportunities to do so, they will find evidence more quickly and learn to explain their reasoning to others.

Revising   Another important element of the reading-thinking process is the ability to revise a prediction, given new information from the text. The ability to revise one's thinking requires flexibility and attention to new information; it is the heart of comprehension. To revise a prediction, the reader must keep an original prediction in mind, must compare it with textual information, and must realize when a change of direction is needed.

There are students who either will not change their minds or who will do so capriciously. Some will keep to an original prediction no matter how clearly the text contradicts an idea, almost as if changing their minds would be admitting defeat. Others will be easily swayed by peers and will relinquish a prediction that is actually supported by the available facts; they may be so unsure of themselves or so inattentive to what they read that they assume they must be wrong. Still others, who are just getting used to the idea of predicting, do not yet realize that predictions may easily be changed at any point during the reading.

Good reader-thinkers will readily be able to say, "Well, here's something I hadn't expected! I guess I'll have to change my mind." Such students realize that predictions are just hypotheses that must be continually scrutinized in light of the material. Often, they are thinking so well of possible alternatives that they notice clues that others miss and come up with particularly insightful revisions.

Skilled readers, of course, also know when revision is not necessary. They do not always change their minds, and they are not easily swayed by others. They revise only when the text suggests it or when they hear a particularly strong argument in favor of change.

With practice and encouragement, students become more skilled at revising their thinking as they read. They listen to others but learn to rely on their own judgments. They attend to the text and learn to look carefully for clues. Sometimes they change their minds entirely; sometimes they modify an original idea; sometimes they staunchly defend their points of view. Whatever their decisions, they are thinking as they read.

Summary Predicting, listening and interacting, judging, justifying, and revising are critical elements of the reading-thinking process. If students do not refine these abilities, they will not develop as readers, no matter how well they master specific skills, and no matter how well they answer questions at the end of a reading selection. They should be expected to use the reading-thinking process when they read and should be observed regularly to see if they are improving.

Table 10.1 summarizes these critical elements, providing an overview of key behaviors that can be observed when students read and discuss. The information in the table may be converted to a simple checklist so that observations may be noted regularly for individual students. For similar perspectives on the evaluation of reading abilities, see Agnew (1982), Pikulski and Shanahan (1982), Moore (1983), Schön (1983), Jaggar and Smith-Burke (1985), and Gillet and Temple (1986).

Students may also be asked to evaluate their own progress. Self-evaluation may be accomplished informally through group discussion. Students may be asked to reflect on the way they handled themselves as they read and discussed a selection. They should consider such issues as these:

- Did we make reasonable predictions based on what we knew and on what we were reading?
- Did we listen to one another's ideas?
- Did we keep our predictions in mind when we read?
- Were we able to judge whether or not the text confirmed our predictions?
- Did we find evidence in the text to justify our thinking?
- Did we use what we read to decide whether to keep or change our predictions? Did we miss any clues that might have helped us make better decisions?

Self-evaluation can help students become aware of how they use the reading-thinking process and what they might do to improve their abilities. Through monitoring their own behavior, students can learn to take responsibility for the way they read, think, and discuss.

TABLE 10.1 Criteria for Evaluating the Reading-Thinking Process

Process	Student Behavior			
	Poor	Making Progress	Good	Excellent
Predicting	Does not predict; says, "I don't know" or "I can't think of an idea"	Occasionally offers predictions, usually wild guesses	Can make logical predictions based on background of experience and text information	Consistently makes logical predictions based on background of experience and text information
Listening and Interacting	Does not listen to others' ideas; cannot agree or disagree with others	Listens to others; waits for others to predict, then agrees with them	Listens to others' ideas; can agree or disagree with others' predictions and reasons	Listens to others' ideas; can agree or disagree with others and tell why
Judging	Cannot tell if a predicton has been supported or contradicted by text	Sometimes can tell if a prediction is supported or contradicted by the text	Can often tell if text supports or contradicts a prediction	Consistently knows if text supports or contradicts a prediction
Justifying	Cannot cite text evidence that supports or contradicts a prediction	Usually says, "I don't know why I think so, I just do."	Can often cite relevant text information that supports or contradicts predictions	Consistently cites specific, relevant text information in discussion; often notices clues that others miss
Revising	Cannot revise a prediction using new textual information	Does not usually revise predictions; may keep to an original idea despite evidence to the contrary	Revises predictions in accordance with text	Consistently revises predictions in accordance with text; also recognizes when predictions may be sustained

Independent Reading   Another facet of evaluation in reading involves assessing students' independent reading. Reading is taught not only to help students comprehend school texts but also to introduce them to the enjoyable world of books. Teachers should not just want students who are capable of reading but who read because they like to read. Because independent reading is an important goal, teachers should evaluate how well students are acquiring the habit of reading for pleasure.

Assessment of independent reading can be simple and straightforward. The teacher may set up a class chart, with space for each student to keep a cumulative record of books read. The student should either list titles or simply add a mark (in colorful ink or with a sticker) for every book read. Or, students might keep individual reading records, using a standard form that the teacher will provide. Some classes also enjoy maintaining a group record. For instance, some classes create a book "worm" that snakes its way around the walls, each construction paper segment representing a book that a student has read.

Besides noting the quantity of books read, the teacher will also want to assess students' attitudes toward independent reading and the types of books they choose. Several qualitative dimensions may be noted, for instance:

1. *Degree of interest.* How much interest does the student show in reading for pleasure? When time is available, does the student readily pick up a book or turn to another activity? When asked "What are you reading now?" does the student respond with a shrug or the name of a book?
2. *Overall breadth of selections.* Does the student tend to read the same kinds of books or select a wide variety?
3. *Length of books chosen.* Does the student tend to read short selections, long selections, or a combination of both?
4. *Level of difficulty of choices.* Does the student tend to read relatively easy books, relatively difficult books, or a mixture of both?

It is useful to incorporate these dimensions when observing and describing students' independent reading. By doing so, teachers will gain a better picture of the kinds of readers they have in class and can more easily suggest books that will develop or sustain the children's interest in reading. Knowing that a child enjoys mysteries or adventures or biographies or horse stories will allow the teacher to tempt the reader with particularly good books that are in line with a favorite interest. Some teachers like to keep track of the kinds of books students read so as to discuss a child's reading habits with parents. The teachers get and give advice on how the child may be encouraged or challenged through independent reading.

Although qualitative assessment of independent reading is valuable, teachers must be careful about judging students on the kinds of books they choose. Taste in reading is a personal matter that develops differently among individuals.

Again, evaluation should match instructional goals. If the goal is to encourage students to read for pleasure, then the amount of pleasure they take in their independent reading is more important than the degree to which their choices match adult standards of "good" reading habits. It is more important for a child to be an avid reader than it is for the child's pattern of reading to conform to what adults consider good.

Wide differences in tastes are easily observed among mature readers of all ages. Some individuals read fiction almost exclusively, whereas others prefer nonfiction, and still others most enjoy poetry, drama, or some other mode of discourse. At any stage in life, a reader may become fascinated with a single topic or author and may seek works relating only to that one interest. Others will skip, almost randomly, through a wide variety of books. Some readers thoroughly enjoy the classics of literature, whereas others read current authors almost exclusively. Adults have preferences in reading (which change periodically), and they explore new authors or new kinds of reading matter only when they are ready to do so.

Children, too, have preferences that ought to be respected. One child may enjoy reading many types of books and will move from fiction to nonfiction to poetry rather naturally, dipping into a wide variety of authors and topics. Another will prefer reading the same types of books or the same author for long stretches of time. One of these children is not a better independent reader than the other. If both read regularly and take pleasure in the books they choose, both are developing the habit of independent reading, even though their tastes are developing differently.

Teachers can certainly try to influence students' reading interests and tastes (within the bounds that are acceptable to their parents) by giving lively book talks, by reading tempting passages from good books, and by making a wide variety of enticing books readily available in the classroom. But it seems unreasonable to expect children to read books for which they show very little enthusiasm. For instance, requiring that every child read a predetermined variety of books in a given time may have a negative effect on many children's attitudes toward the very books teachers hope to encourage them to read. It is disconcerting to hear, "Now, you must read a biography [fantasy, book of poetry, etc.] before the end of the marking period!" Gentle suggestions, given with sincere enthusiasm, will do more to affect students' reading interests than insistent reminders about requirements can do.

In evaluating students' independent reading, teachers should keep track of books read and note how readily students engage in free reading. Teachers should also observe students' habits, interests, and tastes in reading and should discuss these regularly with parents. But teachers should be cautious about assigning grades based on the kinds of books students choose to read. What is right for one child in a class is not necessarily right for another. Real readers develop; they are not coerced.

Evaluation of Writing Abilities

Just as there is more to reading than specific word-recognition skills, there is more to writing than spelling properly and getting the punctuation marks right. As with reading, the mechanical skills of writing may be assessed with relative ease, using commercial materials available in the classroom or planning a regular testing program, such as the one suggested for spelling in Chapter 8. What is more difficult to manage, and yet is more important, is a program of writing evaluation that goes beyond the mechanics to judge both how well students develop their thoughts in writing and how well they use the critical elements of the writing process.

Traditionally, teachers have evaluated writing products—the students' papers—without attending to the process by which they were created. Too great an emphasis on product can skew the writers' values toward mechanical accuracy and can lead students to write just to please the teacher. Certainly teachers should evaluate the products, but they also need to evaluate the process by asking how well students are learning to behave as writers. Here are a few ways in which both facets of a writing evaluation program might be handled.

Evaluating Process

Teachers must consider what they want students to be doing when writing. Teachers should then design a system of evaluation to measure those behaviors. Here are some key writing behaviors and suggestions as to how they may be assessed through careful observation.

Initiating   One important element of writing is the ability to initiate one's own writing. A student should develop enough confidence and resourcefulness to get started with minimal help or prodding. This is not to say that good writers are always self-sufficient and never need encouragement. They are, however, generally able to proceed on their own, and they usually welcome opportunities to have their say in writing.

Poor initiators resist writing and usually write only when the activity is required. They may lack confidence in their ability or they may believe that they have no ideas worth writing about. Some may be discouraged because they have been severely criticized for poor spelling or other mechanical failings. Others may be capable mechanically but do not yet value their writing as a legitimate form of communication, one that will interest an audience.

Good initiators are usually eager to write, even if they sometimes have trouble thinking of subjects. They are confident that their ideas will be well received; they want to reach their audience. They welcome encouragement and suggestions, but they are not overly dependent on teacher or peers to get started. They are happy to have writing assignments, but they are also self-starters who often choose to write when they have a free choice of activities.

Without a fair amount of initiative, student writers will not devote enough time to their writing to profit from the benefits of practice and instruction. Many students need extra support and encouragement to gain confidence and enthusiasm; a sensitive teacher will give these insecure students special help so that they can overcome their unique "blocks." Regular opportunities for private writing (for instance, those provided by journals and learning logs) help students develop initiative and confidence. The degree to which each child attempts these kinds of tasks should be monitored and assessed.

Developing Fluency   Fluency is an important feature of skillful writing. Students cannot improve their ability to write if they write only a few words and then claim to be finished. To a large extent, students who are self-sufficient initiators will rather naturally develop writing fluency; they will want to write, they *will* write, and they will become fluent as a result. Gradually, they will be able to write longer pieces as they mature. But initiative and fluency do not necessarily go hand in hand. Some students are eager to write, but they quickly run out of ideas or confidence.

Nonfluent writers often claim that they cannot think of anything to say. They write very little and then stop. Because they have trouble generating ideas, they often ask for help, saying, "What should I write next?" They are quite dependent on the teacher or on peers for encouragement. These students may write mechanically accurate sentences, but they write very few of them.

Fluent writers usually generate ideas as they write. They become involved with their work, developing momentum after they get started. They enjoy comments and suggestions as they are working, but they are not dependent on these to sustain their effort. They may reread their work as they write, in order to build on the ideas they have already recorded. They are often attentive to how much they write, and they take special pleasure in producing especially long pieces.

With regular practice, especially involving such private writing as is found in journals, students can improve their writing fluency. Assessing progress can be a straightforward process; the teacher or students may simply check units of work regularly, keeping track of how many words (or sentences, or pages) are written.

Working with Peers   The writing process includes both getting response from fellow writers and giving response in turn. Only when students work with each other do they develop a clear sense of audience and learn to consider writing as a way to communicate. A critical behavior, especially for public writing, involves being a functioning member of a response group.

Some students are inordinately passive in writing response groups. Probably they have not yet grasped what it means to write for an audience or to respond to someone else's writing. They may never have been expected to write for anyone other than a teacher or to read anyone else's work in progress, so they may not see the sense of peer discussion. They may consider response-group activities nonessential, not worth the effort. Many passive students just do not know what to say about someone else's work. They need considerable guidance to learn techniques for responding.

Good responders are generally active in response groups. They value comments from peers and eagerly offer their own viewpoints. They realize that an audience can help a writer achieve writing purposes; they welcome an audience and try to be helpful in return. They may not know enough about writing to ask the most useful questions or to give excellent advice, but they will gradually improve when given opportunities to work in response groups.

Responding ability is not necessarily correlated with writing ability. Some average writers are excellent responders; some good writers are poor responders. Specific directions in the form of writing response guides can provide help for the students who require it. Also, students should be given many opportunities to work together on their writing so that through experience they can improve this aspect of their writing behavior.

Revising and Polishing   Another critical feature of the writing process involves revising and polishing a piece of public writing. This part of the writing process is influenced by the writer's attitude and by his or her specific knowledge of the techniques of revision. Revision can be tedious or difficult, so a writer has to have a reasonably positive outlook and must be confident about continuing to work on the project. The writer also has to have some idea of how to do the following: change words, elaborate, cut, reform sentences, and alter sequence.

Some students lack the confidence, the knowledge, or both. They resist revision, claiming they have done enough by writing a first draft. These students may lack confidence or may find the physical and/or mental act of writing extremely difficult. Others claim they do not know what they might do to improve a piece; usually they are right, for they need guidance and practice before they can gain the knowledge and, to some extent, the intuition about what might be improved.

Skill in revising and polishing develops gradually, with experience and practice. Young writers will not usually be able to improve every word, sentence, and paragraph of a first draft, but they can develop greater sensitivity to their work. The teacher's expectations will be different for each child. Progress for some students may entail finding and correcting several misspelled words in a first draft, whereas other students will be able to make significant improvements in the organization and wording of ideas. The teacher needs to consider each child's capability and to encourage each child to make the appropriate kind of revisions. Students should be engaged in the process of responding to one another's work and making revisions that are in line with those responses.

The extent and quality of revisions will improve gradually over time when students have regular experiences in reworking first drafts.

Summary   Initiating, developing fluency, working in response groups, and revising public writing are all important writing behaviors that should be monitored and assessed regularly. Table 10.2 summarizes the key features of each of these behaviors. The information in this table may be converted to a checklist for use in evaluating individual students on the various process dimensions (see Figure 16). For other suggestions on evaluating the writing process, see Cooper and Odell (1977), Graves (1983), and Jaggar and Smith-Burke (1985).

As students become actively engaged in the writing process, the teacher may also give them opportunities for evaluating their own progress. This self-evaluation may also be accomplished informally, through teacher-student conferences. Issues for the student to consider include the following:

- Am I able to get started with a piece of writing fairly easily? If not, what might help me get started more easily?
- When am I able to write most fluently?
- What do I most enjoy writing about?
- What do I do best in my writing?
- What do I have the most trouble with?
- How have I been able to improve my first drafts by working with my response group?
- What else would I like to improve with the help of my peers?
- What do I contribute to my response group?

Through discussing such issues, students can become more aware of the way they use the writing-thinking process and what they might do to improve their abilities. Also, such self-examination can encourage students to take responsibility for recognizing their own strengths and weaknesses rather than relying on the teacher as the only source for this information.

Evaluating Products

When students submit public writing for the teacher's evaluation, he or she should know what to look for and should use consistent standards when evaluating the papers. Each teacher should think the issues through individually, should try out various approaches, and should make decisions accordingly. Though teachers must work out their own procedures for reading students' papers, they will benefit enormously from working together, as a faculty (or a school district), to set basic standards. A schoolwide (or districtwide) evaluation system will insure consistency not only within a classroom but also within and across grade levels.

Such an evaluation system usually begins with an examination of students' writing samples. This will enable teachers to describe good, average, and poor

TABLE 10.2. Criteria For Evaluating the Writing Process

Process	Student Behavior			
	Poor	Making Progress	Good	Excellent
Initiating	Writes only when told to; generally resists writing	Sometimes wants to write; initiates some writing	Often eager to write; often initiates own writing	Obviously enjoys writing; often initiates own writing; chooses writing over many activities
Developing Fluency	Limited fluency; writes very little; claims to have "nothing to say"	Writes with some ease on certain topics; usually needs encouragement to keep writing	Often writes with ease; sometimes needs encouragement to keep writing	Consistently writes with ease; has much to say; seldom needs encouragement
Working with Peers	Passive in writing response group	Gives limited response to others' work; sometimes wants response to own work	Often makes good comments in response group; interested in response from others	Consistently makes good contributions to group; eager to get response from others
Revising and Polishing	Does not revise work; resists rereading or rewriting	Sometimes willing to revise; can make some changes to improve work	Sees need to revise; improves parts of work	Eager to revise; consistently improves work by rewriting

writing at each grade level. Teachers work together to read the papers, making overall (holistic) judgments about the quality of individual papers. When all papers have been categorized into one of several qualitative levels, teachers describe each level in terms of specific elements that are observable in the papers. These descriptive criteria are tried out on new writing samples and are revised until the teachers are satisfied that the criteria are clear. Once criteria are established, they are used by all teachers to assess the quality of first-draft writing. A detailed description of these steps is given in Appendix E. More information about this kind of evaluation strategy may be found in McCaig (1972, 1976) and White (1984).

Although this process is somewhat time-consuming, it has great value for monitoring overall progress from the beginning of the year to the end. When all teachers use the same standards and procedures, the grade level, the school, and/or the district may also keep track of group achievement from one year to the next. Because the teachers themselves determine standards, they feel quite comfortable using them. They are not likely to feel that unfair criteria have been imposed on them from the outside. Also, because teachers work together to define what good, average, and poor writing is at each grade level, they find that their instructional programs gain new direction and purpose. After going through this evaluation process, teachers usually claim that they find renewed enthusiasm for teaching writing. They develop clear ideas about what they want their students to be able to achieve. Holistic scoring of student writing is a very useful evaluation strategy for assessing final draft work as well (Diederich, 1974; Lloyd-Jones, 1977; Kirby and Liner, 1981). The teacher is able to read papers efficiently and yet can feel confident that each has been judged fairly. Individual students' progress may be monitored by periodic assessment throughout the year.

Besides judging the overall quality of student writing, teachers must also consider how they will react to specific elements in individual papers. Making specific responses requires considerable sensitivity. When students submit papers they have usually worked hard on them, done their best, and are eager for praise. Even those who haven't worked very hard will still want their efforts recognized. If students are to keep writing and improving, teachers must be cautious in giving criticisms.

The following are suggestions for marking papers. They are based on the assumption that the classroom is like a writing workshop in which students are writing regularly for both private and public purposes and are submitting only some of their public work to be marked by the teacher.

- *Use writing folders.* Have students keep first drafts in individual writing folders. After they have written several drafts, have each choose a good one to revise and submit for evaluation. Giving children a choice of what they want the teacher to read involves them in the evaluation process. They will feel more confident about their work if they have some control over what they hand in.

- *Use response groups.* Set up writing-response groups and give students time to meet regularly to revise and polish the papers they will submit. Working together, students will find that editing proceeds more easily. Their final drafts will be better when several peer editors have helped out.
- *Allow pencil.* Encourage students to write in pencil so that when they revise a paper to hand in, they can make changes and corrections more easily. It is discouraging for students to have to copy an entire page in order to correct a few misspelled words or alter a few sentences, but pencil work can be readily erased. Work may be recopied in ink *after* the teacher has seen it and made additional suggestions. Indeed, ink copies are not really necessary unless the work is to be published in some way (such as on the board for a parents' meeting, in the school newspaper, or mailed to a correspondent).
- *Introduce word processors.* If the budget allows, bring word processors into the classroom and let students prepare final drafts on the computers. After a response group has discussed a paper, a student can quickly and easily make changes and corrections before printing out a final copy for the teacher. Of all the uses of computers in education, word processing in the writing program is one of the best. Rewriting and correcting can be done quickly and easily on a word processor; most students will actually come to enjoy editing. Their work improves dramatically when the tedium of copying and recopying by hand is reduced.

If students have been given adequate time and guidance in preparing final drafts, the teacher's task of reading and marking the papers should go rather easily. The students will have taken care of many problems on their own. Here are some more suggestions for the next stage, when the teacher has judged a paper holistically and now wants to attend to specific elements.

- *Limit what you mark.* It is very discouraging for a student to receive a paper from the teacher if the work is covered with corrections. Only the most confident, secure young writers will be able to withstand meticulous attention to their failings. Most students will become discouraged and will want to stop writing altogether. Pay attention to a few of the weaknesses that you consider most important; ignore the rest. If you like, jot a note at the bottom of the paper suggesting that the writing could still use some more editing. Let the students decide whether or not to submit the work again.
- *Tell what you will be looking for.* As students prepare the final drafts, tell them what you will especially be looking for. If you have been emphasizing spelling, tell them to pay particular attention to this. If you have been teaching sentence combining, tell them you will be looking for evidence of that. If you have been teaching certain elements of capitalization or punctuation, tell them you will concentrate on these when you read the papers. As you read, keep the announced goal(s) firmly in mind and respond accordingly.
- *Note errors in the margins.* Develop a code to indicate specific items. For instance, let *sp* mean misspelled word, *cap* mean capitalization, *c* mean comma error. Post the code in a visible place or give each student a copy. When you read a paper, write code symbols in the margin, on the lines in

which the anomalies occur. When students receive their papers, they can consult the code to see what you have noted.

This practice makes the teacher's error-spotting less intrusive than it would be if the problems were noted on top of the students' words. The method also gives students extra proofreading practice. When papers are returned with notes in the margins, students must look across the line(s) to find the problems the teacher noted. If students have written in pencil, they can make corrections easily and then cut off the margin, giving them a neat, corrected paper that may be taken home with pride.

• *Make positive comments.* Balance corrections with praise for good work. Write positive comments about good ideas, word choice, well-formed sentences, choice of details, use of dialogue, or any other commendable features. Students will be encouraged to write if they know the teacher is interested in what they have to say and sincerely appreciates the good things they have done.

Assessing Process and Products

To assess both process and product, teachers may wish to construct a summary form to keep track of students' progress in writing. Students may be assessed on each of several dimensions of writing; their scores may then be averaged and translated into letter grades. The items to be scored may vary, depending on the teacher's goals, but the grades should reflect equal attention to process and product.

One such summary sheet is shown in Figure 16 based on the process items in Table 10.2 and on selected items relating to writing products. This summary sheet is a modified version of a checklist that was developed and used in the Avon Grove School District, West Grove, PA. Scorable items are defined as follows:

1. Initiating Writing
Level of initiative, judged according to the standards given in Table 10.2
2. Developing Fluency
Level of fluency, judged according to the standards given in Table 10.2 with particular attention to the student's quantity of private writing (journals and/or learning logs)
3. Working with Peers
Quality of work in writing response groups, judged according to the standards given in Table 10.2
4. Revising and Polishing
Ability to edit and revise public writing, judged according to the standards given in Table 10.2, with particular attention to the student's willingness to revise and rewrite
5. Public Writing
An average of holistic scores given to papers the students submitted for teacher evaluation

	Initiating Writing	Developing Fluency	Working with Peers	Revising and Polishing	Public Writing (Holistic Score)	Specific Skill Improvement	TOTAL	AVERAGE
Susan	3	3	5	4	3	4	22	3.6
Ben	5	5	3	3	5	5	26	4.3
Joe	1	1	3	2	2	3	12	2
Alice	2	4	2	2	3	1	14	2.3
Bobby	3	5	5	2	3	5	23	3.8
Fran	5	5	5	3	5	5	28	4.6
Edith	3	1	1	3	2	3	13	2.1
Sam	5	5	5	5	5	4	29	4.8

FIGURE 16   A summary sheet for evaluating students' writing

6. Specific Skill Improvement

This is a variable item from one marking period to the next; it may change as the teacher's goals change. Spelling, word choice, sentence variety, elements of usage, or any other specific skill may be listed here. Students are assessed on the level of their achievement in that skill, as reflected in their writing during the marking period.

The recorded student scores are based on a scale of 1 to 5, 1 representing the lowest score, 5 the highest. To use the form, the teacher observes how students perform throughout the marking period on each of the items listed and decides on an overall score for each item. Scores are then averaged and converted to letter grades. Any item may be weighted to influence the total score more heavily. For instance, if the class has concentrated heavily on learning to work in response groups, the working-with-peers score may be doubled, or if the teacher places particular value on private writing to build fluency, then the developing-fluency score may be doubled.

Quantifying student progress in this way is useful not only for obtaining grades but also for obtaining an overview of the class. It furthermore enables the teacher to note specific strengths and weaknesses of individuals. For instance, among the eight students listed in Figure 16, there are two who are doing quite well (Fran and Sam), three who can be considered average to good (Susan, Ben, and Bobby), and three who are having trouble (Joe, Alice, and Edith). Yet individual profiles within each group reveal differences. Although Alice and Edith are both having trouble, Alice is a much more fluent writer than Edith, but Edith does a better job of improving specific skills.

The suggested form may be modified to suit the needs of other teachers and students. Other dimensions of the writing program may easily be added or substituted as scorable items. The important principle behind this method is that effective writing evaluation balances assessment of process and product. Students are rewarded by praise and grades not only for good final drafts but also for successful use of the process by which first drafts are composed, revised, and edited. Private writing is assessed simply and informally; for instance, journals are monitored to see that they are being written regularly and to see if students are gradually improving fluency. Students are given credit for their efforts at private writing—for their journals, learning logs, and other kinds of writing that are not submitted for evaluation. Public writing products are assessed according to specific, consistent standards. Evaluation based on these principles makes for a sound program.

Evaluation of Oral/Aural Abilities

Listening and speaking skills may be evaluated by the same principles that are used to judge reading and writing. Again, that which is assessed should be those behaviors that match the teacher's instructional goals. The teacher must consider what the students should be doing and then design evaluation to assess those behaviors. Here is a review of the critical elements of listening and speaking, with suggestions about how these may be used for assessment.

Attending As both listeners and speakers, students must learn to sustain attention. The listener must be attentive to the speaker; the speaker must be attentive to the listener. Students' abilities may be assessed in various oral and aural situations that are typical of classroom activities at each grade level. For instance, listeners should improve attention skills when they are listening to stories, oral directions, teachers' lectures, students' presentations, and group discussions. Speakers should improve their attention (their alertness and consideration of the audience) when they are contributing to discussions, making presentations, and helping classmates with various learning activities (such as responding to a piece of writing during a group conference).

Attention skills are best assessed through systematic observation of students in different situations. For instance, the storytelling teacher can evaluate listening attention during story time. Students should be able to increase their attention spans gradually through the year, and the teacher can note progress as longer and longer stories are told. Similarly, as students listen to directions, view films, and participate in other listening activities, their attention may be monitored and assessed informally.

When students work in groups or make presentations to the class, the teacher may also note improvement in their attentiveness as speakers. Students should improve their ability to keep track of what they are saying. They should notice if listeners are confused and perhaps need more information; they should speak loudly enough to be heard; and they should express their ideas clearly.

Interacting   Listeners and speakers must learn to interact effectively. Whether working in small, independent groups or as a whole class under the teacher's direction, students should use and improve interaction skills. For instance, when students are having a discussion, the following behaviors should be in evidence:

- Being polite (not interrupting or poking fun)
- Taking turns in making contributions
- Contributing purposefully
- Being able to state what someone else has said
- Elaborating on what someone else has said
- Recognizing agreement and disagreement in the group
- Respecting other points of view
- Responding directly to others (rather than only to the teacher).

These behaviors may be assessed through regular, careful observation by the teacher. When students are participating in a DR-TA, for instance, the teacher will have a good opportunity to evaluate group interaction. Writing response groups may also be monitored for the teacher to see how the students interact in that situation. Whenever students are having a discussion or are working together, the teacher may note how well they interact.

Listening and Responding Critically   With some kinds of material, especially with the teacher's lectures or demonstrations, students should be able to listen and respond critically, using several different kinds of thinking:

- Setting purposes for listening (using prior knowledge and experience to predict what will be learned)
- Recognizing when purposes have been met (recalling and discussing information that supports or contradicts prelistening predictions)
- Reviewing and applying new learning (discussing new material so that students can recognize, summarize, and apply what has been learned)
- Raising new questions based on what was learned

These are critical skills for listening and responding. They are similar to those required by the reading-thinking process. Students improve their listening-thinking abilities with practice and instruction. Basic competence may be assessed through the teacher's observations in a variety of informational listening activities that take place during the language arts period and during content-area instruction. The information in Table 10.1 may be adapted for use in assessing listening-thinking abilities. Essentially the same criteria may be used to rate students' reading or listening skills when they are participating in an instructional group.

Listening and Responding Creatively With other kinds of material, especially with oral literature, students should be able to listen and respond creatively. Rather than learning information, they will be interpreting and savoring language, following a story line, understanding characters, grasping the significance of various story elements, and forming their own views of what the story means.

Their creative listening abilities may be assessed during the telling of the story. The teacher can note facial expressions and spontaneous contributions the students make, both of which demonstrate clearly how well the students are understanding and interpreting. After the story, students may be asked to do any of the following activities, all of which require creative response to a work of literature:

- Discuss the story, bringing out personal interpretations
- Retell the story
- Draw a favorite scene (or a sequence of scenes)
- Enact the story
- Write about the story
- Make up a new scene (or a new ending).

Speaking Effectively Almost all students can improve their speaking abilities. Each student will have specific strengths and weaknesses that may be assessed through the teacher's observation. These are some of the elements of speaking ability that might be considered:

- Confidence in speaking out in front of classmates
- Courtesy in allowing others to speak
- Fluency (ability to speak at some length with reasonable ease)
- Precision (command of vocabulary and syntax)
- Language usage (application of appropriate vocabulary and syntax for the situation)
- Volume (use of appropriate volume for the situation).

Speaking abilities should be assessed in a variety of situations. The child who is confident and fluent in a small group may become timid and hesitant in front of the whole class. A child may speak with precision and confidence about a familiar topic but may grow imprecise and anxious when trying to explain something unfamiliar. It is thus unreasonable to evaluate speaking abilities only when students are giving oral reports to the class on new material they have been learning. The teacher should observe students in one-to-one conferences, in small groups working independently, in teacher-directed groups, and in whole class discussions. For other perspectives on evaluating oral language abilities, see Genishi and Dyson (1984) and Jaggar and Smith-Burke (1985).

Evaluation of the Whole

Reading, writing, speaking, and listening can be evaluated as separate abilities to the extent that each has unique features. However, development in each is related to and influenced by corresponding development in the others. In fact, teachers should only be satisfied if students make connections—using vocabulary in their writing that they learned by reading, improving their speech by hearing good models, and in other ways making smooth transitions that show their growing competence in their comprehension and use of language.

When language is being used most purposefully, distinctions among skills are blurred. When students are working in a writing-response group they are reading, writing, listening, and speaking. We miss the point of evaluating growth if we continually think of the four langauge arts as separate entities.

Teachers miss the point of evaluating growth if they continually think of the four language arts as separate entities, each made up of separate, specific skills. Such fragmentation leads teachers to look only for improvement in discrete elements (for example, in phonics, spelling, and knowledge of grammar). Specific skill assessment has its place, but teachers should also be concerned with the degree to which the students use the language arts in purposeful, integrated ways.

In fact, when language is being used most purposefully, distinctions among skills become blurred. Labels such as *reading activity* or *writing activity* are not accurate descriptors for many tasks. For instance, when students are working in a writing response group, they listen to or read each other's papers, discuss things among themselves, and make suggestions for revision. They are reading, writing, listening, and speaking. All four abilities are equally important to accomplishing the task at hand, and students must move from one to the other smoothly and efficiently.

Certainly the most interesting and valuable activities are marked by natural integration. The following projects show the combination of language processes:

- A reading group discusses a basal reader story, rewrites it as a play, and acts it out.

- Students pair up to collect information for saturation reports (see Chapter 7). Each pair discusses their findings and prepares a joint report, which is read and discussed by classmates.

- Students interpret a folk tale, told by the teacher, in a series of creative dramas.

- Students listen to a favorite story, dictate their own version of it, and use the dictation as material for a reading lesson.

- Students read about zoos, take a trip to the local zoo, interview the staff, and write an account of what they learned.

These are only a few of the kinds of activities that are most challenging and interesting to students because they require meaningful, integrated application of specific abilities. Good teachers intuitively prefer these to drill and practice on isolated skills.

If purposeful integration is an instructional goal, then the evaluation must match that goal. Teachers must pay some attention to assessing the whole. It is not necessary to create new batteries of tests to do this. What teachers do need is a sense of common denominators. Some common denominators are evident among the evaluation criteria listed in the previous sections of this chapter—those that are recognizable as different modes of thinking. For instance, skill in predicting is essential for effective reading and listening, and interaction skills are basic competencies of speaking and listening. Predicting and interacting require the individual to go beyond rote learning to exercise cognitive abilities at higher levels. Using *thinking* as a common denominator, consider the following possible configuration of basic abilities, with some suggestions as to how these would be revealed in specific language arts activities:

Anticipating
- Predicting the outcome of a story in a reading group
- Predicting what will happen in the science experiment the teacher is demonstrating
- Chiming in during storytelling to say the next few words before the teacher does
- Writing a story that will make others laugh

Gathering Evidence
- Reading to find out if a prediction was right
- Listening to find out if a prediction was right
- Interviewing an expert to get answers to questions
- Writing notes to use in a report

Interacting
- Reading an article and getting angry with the author
- Listening to a peer to decide if one agrees with him or her
- Telling a peer why one likes his or her idea
- Writing a letter to a pen pal

Revising
- Changing a prediction after reading the first page of the story
- Changing a prediction after viewing the first five frames of a filmstrip
- Saying an idea again, in different, clearer words
- Adding more specific details to a paragraph

Reasoning
- Drawing one's own conclusions after reading an article
- Making inferences when listening to a speaker
- Explaining why one thinks an experiment didn't work
- Writing an essay to convince others of a point of view·

Reflecting
- Rereading a story to consider how the author created suspense
- Listening to a poem again to savor the language
- Telling about a personal experience that taught one a lesson
- Writing in a journal about why one got upset

Judging
- Reading a story to decide if a younger child would enjoy it
- Listening to two words to decide if they rhyme
- Telling an opinion of the class play
- Writing an opinion of a book one read

This is only one configuration of the kinds of thinking that are basic to a variety of classroom language activities (indeed, to a variety of human endeavors). Others have suggested different arrays (see the Suggested Readings at the end of Chapter 1). Thus, this compilation should not be adopted as the definitive list. But teachers may use the following process by which this list was created:

1. Decide what students should be doing in the language arts classroom. Describe the behaviors that should be evident when they read, write, speak, and listen. For example, should students be able to predict outcomes when they read a story? use more precise words when they write? listen to one another more attentively during discussion?
2. Decide which activities will encourage students to use the behaviors identified in step 1.
3. Analyze the activities. Which ones require students to use the same thinking processes? Categorize the activities accordingly.
4. Consider how the activities in each category will provide opportunities to observe and assess students' thinking.

When different teachers follow these steps, they may compile lists that are different from the one suggested here. Their results will depend on their instructional priorities, their philosophies of teaching, and their perceptions of the fundamentals of cognition. But when they have made their decisions, they will have guides for assessing students that go beyond a fragmented view of the language arts as four separate skill areas. The identified common denominators will allow the teachers to observe progress in thinking as they observe progress in reading, listening, speaking, and writing.

Suggested Activities

1. Use the information in Table 10.1 to develop a checklist for evaluating the reading performance of an individual student. Conduct or observe a DR-TA and use your checklist to evaluate one student's performance.
2. Design a bulletin board display to record the books read by the students in a class.
3. Collect writing samples from at least ten students in a class. Sort the writing into four categories, ranked from poorest (1) to best (4). Identify

the strengths and weaknesses of the writing in each category. For suggested descriptors, see Appendix E.

4. Read aloud a story to a small group of bilingual students. Evaluate their listening skills. Base your evaluation on the students' responses to the story as they engage in one of the activities listed on page 334.

References

Agnew, A. T. "Using Children's Dictated Stories to Assess Code Consciousness." *The Reading Teacher* 35(January 1982):450–54.

Cooper, C. R., and Odell, L. *Evaluating Writing: Describing, Measuring, Judging*. Urbana, IL: National Council of Teachers of English, 1977.

Diederich, P. B. *Measuring Growth in English*. Urbana, IL: National Council of Teachers of English, 1974.

Genishi, C., and Dyson, A. H. *Language Assessment in the Early Years*. Norwood, NJ: Ablex, 1984.

Gillet, J., and Temple, C. *Understanding Reading Problems*. Boston: Little, Brown, 1986.

Graves, D. M. *Writing: Teachers and Children at Work*. Portsmouth, NH: Heinemann, 1983.

Jaggar, A., and Smith-Burke, M. T. (eds.) *Observing the Language Learner*. Newark, DE: International Reading Association, 1985.

Kirby, D., and Liner, T. *Inside Out: Developmental Strategies for Teaching Writing*. Montclair, NJ: Boynton/Cook, 1981.

Lloyd-Jones, R. "Primary Trait Scoring" in C. R. Cooper and L. Odell, eds., *Evaluating Writing: Describing, Measuring, Judging*. Urbana, IL: National Council of Teachers of English, 1977.

McCaig, R. A. "What Research and Evaluation Tells Us About Teaching Written Expression in the Elementary School." Paper presented at Western Michigan University Elementary/Middle School English Conference: March, 1976 (available from the Department of English, Western Michigan University, Kalamazoo, Michigan).

————. *The Writing of Elementary School Children: A Model for Evaluation*. Grosse Point, MI: Grosse Point Public Schools, 1972.

Moore, D. W. "A Case for Naturalistic Assessment of Reading Comprehension." *Language Arts* 60(November–December 1983):957–69.

Pikulski, J. J., and Shanahan, T. *Approaches to the Informal Evaluation of Reading*. Newark, DE: International Reading Association, 1982.

Schön, D. A. *The Reflective Practitioner*. New York: Basic Books, 1983.

White, E. M. "Holisticism." *College Composition and Communication* 35(December 1984):400–09.

The language processes need to be related to one another, and these relationships should be used to improve communication and thinking in all subjects.

11

Integrating the Language Arts

Reading, writing, listening, and speaking are related processes. Acquisition of competence in these areas is a requirement if students are to master other subjects. The issue of integrating the language arts is thus twofold: The language processes need to be related to each other, and these relationships should be used to improve communication and thinking in all subjects. Illustrations throughout this book have emphasized such purposeful integration within the language arts and across the curriculum. This chapter provides a few examples of extended units that elaborate the principles. Some of these examples are curriculum-centered, based on content objectives in various subjects. Others are student-centered in that the students choose the content and direction of their studies.

Curriculum-centered Instruction

These units were designed for large-group (whole class) instruction. The teachers began by selecting key concepts from a major subject area—such as science or social studies—and by choosing key language skills to emphasize. Instruction took place during a language arts reading period and/or during the time allotted to the content area. The brief descriptions here include those of major activities. Activities and materials could be modified to suit the needs and abilities of students at other grade levels.

A Week with the Stars (Grade 4)   A class spent five class periods completing these activities. The lessons developed science concepts while promoting critical and creative thinking and giving practice in reading, writing, speaking, and listening.

The science concepts to be developed were these:

1. What a star is.
2. What light years are.
3. What constellations are.
4. Why groups of stars are named.

Day 1. Students began by predicting answers to these questions:

1. What do you think a star is?
    Predictions: sun, stones that give off light, fiery gases
2. How fast do you think light travels?
    Predictions: 1 mile per minute, 1 mile per 14 minutes, 1 mile per 25 minutes
3. What do you think constellations are?
    Predictions: connected stars, pictures of stars, stars with tails

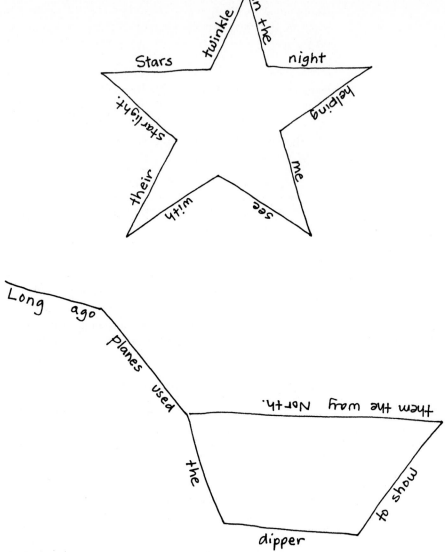

FIGURE 17 Fourth-grade concrete star poems

Students read to find out if their predictions were right. The material was in an article called "Stars" in *The Golden Book Encyclopedia,* Book 14 (Golden Press, 1960). The class discussed their reading in light of their predictions, developing answers to the initial questions by using material from the text to revise their first hypotheses. Writing in their learning logs, students then recorded what they had learned. Here are a few of the entries:

A constellation is a group of stars that some people say looks like a picture. It takes more than four years for star light to reach us. Stars are round balls of fire like the sun. The sun and stars are alike because both are burning suns.

The sun is a star. When we see stars we think we see pictures but we don't. There are millions and millions of stars. The stars are in groups that move around during the night. When light hits the dust particles in the atmosphere it bends the star which makes it twinkle.

Stars are bright. They make a big dipper. They are neat to me. The sun is a star. The stars make streams of light.

Some stars are bigger than the sun. Stars give off light. When the light from a star hits a little dust particle, it makes the end bend to go around it and it twinkles. If the nearest star's power was turned off, it would take over four years for us to know it.

Day 2. Using a battery-operated planetarium in a dark room, the teacher helped the students locate Polaris (North Star), Ursa Major (Big Dipper), Ursa Minor (Little Dipper), Cassiopeia, and Orion. While pointing to each constellation, the teacher told a myth that accounts for the name of each star cluster. Children observed the constellations, discussed what they saw, and talked about the myths, which fascinated them.

Day 3. Using overlay transparencies, the teacher again exhibited the constellations. Students discussed the names of the star clusters, recalling the myths associated with them. Students talked about their own star gazing and then wrote concrete poems in the forms of stars or constellations. They edited and corrected their work and then copied the poems on blue paper to display on the bulletin board. (See Figure 17 for some of these poems.)

Day 4. Using selected paragraphs from the first day's reading material, the teacher developed a modified cloze activity. (The term *cloze* refers to a reading passage from which some words have been deleted.) Working in pairs, students completed the passage, applying context clues and recent learning to fill in the blanks. As a class, students discussed the words they supplied and the context clues they used to complete the passage. See Figure 18 for the cloze passage used in this part of the lesson:

Day 5. Students wrote on the topic of stars, choosing from these topics that the teacher suggested:

1. What you learned about stars
2. A fantasy story about stars
3. A personal experience with stars

STARS

The words "sun" and "star" mean the same. All stars are _____. And our sun, along with all other suns, is a _____. But when people talk about the stars, they usually mean all stars except our _____.

The sun is about 93,000,000 miles from the earth. Even the _____ star is much farther than that. _____ travels 186,000 miles a second. From the _____, light reaches the earth in 8 minutes.

Sirius, the Dog Star, is the brightest _____ in the sky. It takes nearly nine _____ for light from this _____ to reach us. If _____ should explode _____, it would be nearly _____ years before we saw the explosion.

When we _____ that anything is star-shaped we mean that _____ has five points. But _____ are really big round _____ like our sun. People got the idea that stars have _____ because they twinkle. It is the _____ in the air that makes them do so. If we could _____ them from the moon, where there _____ no air, they would _____ with a steady light.

The _____ we see are not spread evenly over the _____. Instead they are in groups, called _____. The people of long ago thought that the different _____ made pictures in the sky. The names they gave the constellations tell us what _____ they saw.

FIGURE 18   Modified cloze activity (Stars unit)

Students read their accounts to each other and then placed their papers in the writing folders used for storing first drafts (a source of material for possible revision later). Here are samples of some of the first drafts:

THE STARS

One night I went outside to look at the stars. I saw the big dipper and the little dipper in the sky. It was hard to find it the first time. Then I found the little bear and then I saw the big bear. Then I looked very hard and I found Cans Minor the little dog. Then I remember that Cassiopeia was in a "w". I looked and looked for a "w" then I found it. It did look like a lady in a chair. All the stars look pretty.

STARS

Stars are big round balls of fire like our sun. They look like they have five points but they just twinkle. Some stars form pictures called constellations. It takes light from the nearest star four years to reach the earth. Light travels 186,000 miles per second. The north star is the brightest star we can see. The north star does not move it stays in one place. The big dipper and the little dipper are also called Ursa Major and Ursa Minor. It is fun to see constellations.

STARS

I lernd that Sirius is the closest star to the earth and the sun is a star. I also lernd that if Sirius wold burn out it wold take us nine years to now it. I lernd that it takes light at least eight minuts for the suns light to reach earth.

Summary. A Week with the Stars included this sequence of language activities:

- Oral speculation to set reading purposes
- Reading for specific information
- Oral review of predictions and text information
- Learning log writing to summarize reading
- Discussion based on observation of planetarium
- Teacher storytelling of star myths
- Oral review of learning
- Discussion of personal experiences with star gazing
- Poetry writing
- Reading/writing cloze activity to review learning
- Discussion of cloze activity
- Writing based on unit activities.

One activity led to another in a natural progression. Learning was reinforced through the students' active involvement in a variety of language and thinking activities. Content was covered, but students also had excellent opportunities to read, write, speak, and listen.

Betsy Ross and the American Flag (Grade 3) This was a three-day unit that jointly emphasized language arts skills and concepts from the social science curriculum. The social science concepts to be developed were these:

1. Why a country would want a flag
2. Betsy Ross's role in American history
3. The features and significance of the first U.S. flag

Day 1. Students first predicted answers to these questions:

1. Why would a country want a flag?
    Predictions: to fly on holidays, to use for armies when they go to war, because every other country has one

2. Who made the first American flag?

     Predictions: Clara Barton, Betsy Ross, Martha Washington, a factory in Washington

3. What did the first flag look like?

     Predictions: blue with a circle of stars, fifteen white and red stripes, stripes with an English flag in the corner, red with a circle of stars

Next, the teacher told the legend of Betsy Ross, including the following information along with additional historical facts. The teacher also used dialogue and other personal details to make the story interesting.

Betsy Griscom, born in 1756, grew up in Philadelphia. She learned needlework and was very good at it, even winning a prize for a sampler she once made. When she grew up, she married John Ross, an upholsterer. They opened a shop, but John died at 36. Betsy kept sewing to make a living for herself. One of her customers was General George Washington.

When the colonies went to war, Washington stressed the need for a flag, citing several reasons; for instance, the men needed the motivation, and the flag they were using looked too much like a British flag. Washington designed a flag with thirteen stripes and thirteen six-pointed stars. Betsy agreed to make it but suggested five-pointed stars. Betsy sewed the flag in secret; the Continental Congress would have to approve it before it could be shown.

The lawmakers eventually agreed and wrote the flag's design into the Congressional Record. No one is sure that Betsy actually made the first flag, but that is the legend.

Students reviewed their predictions and established correct answers to the prelistening questions by discussing what they learned from the teacher's story. Then they wrote for ten minutes, summarizing what they had learned. They read these accounts to each other at the end of the lesson. The reading aloud prompted further discussion. These are a few of the students' papers:

John Ross got killed by an explosion of gun powder. Betsy Ross made the first flag. I wonder if she had any children.

We don't know if Betsy Ross made the first flag. Betsy Ross could not wear bright colors, she had to wear gray dull clothes. When she grew up, George Washington asked her to make a flag, but we don't know if that is true or not.

Betsy Ross was very important to America. Because she made the first flag for us. I'm glad that George Washington picked her to make the very first flag for the United States of America. I also learned that England owned a lot of American colonies. But I just don't understand why they had to have a war. Why couldn't they just talk things out?

Betsy Ross was a Quaker. When she was a little girl, she could sew really good. She couldn't wear bright colors. When she was grown up she married a man. His name was Mr. Ross. He put the cloth on furniture. So she worked with him. One day John Ross was killed by exploding gun powder. Betsy Ross made the first flag. It was red, white, and blue. It had 13 stripes and 13 stars. I'd like to know what else Betsy Ross made and did she have any children.

Although the teacher emphasized the country's need for a flag in her telling, and the group discussed this concept after listening, many students did not write about that issue. Students seemed much more interested in reflecting on the life and personality of Betsy and her husband, John. However, the teacher's presentation and the group discussion introduced the most important flag-related concepts, which were then reinforced over the next few days.

Day 2. The teacher reminded students of the skimming techniques they had been learning in their reading groups. The class then skimmed through Chapter 6 in *Pennsylvania Primer* (Penns Valley, 1960) to find out how Betsy Ross made a five-pointed star. Students discussed their findings.

The teacher demonstrated how to make a five-pointed star, asking children to watch carefully so that they could then write their own directions for creating one. Each student then independently wrote a set of directions. They discussed the process, referring to their notes. Then, as a group, the class composed a set of instructions that the teacher wrote on the board.

Students then made a five-pointed star, following their group-dictated directions. The completed stars were used to make a Continental flag on the bulletin board.

Day 3. Students recalled and discussed the reasons why a country needs a flag. The teacher recorded the information they gave in a cluster outline on the chalkboard. Then, with the diagram erased, each student tried to reconstruct it from memory. Next, as a group, the children reconstructed the cluster, with the teacher writing on the board while the students referred to their own outlines. Finally, the students added forgotten details to their individual outlines. (This sequence gave students meaningful reviews of key facts and concepts. They were actively involved in remembering details and noting relationships, working both individually and as a group to learn the material.)

Students wrote for ten minutes, summarizing what they had learned. They then read their accounts to one another. Here are some of the papers:

If a ship is at sea, you turn the flag upside down if you need help. Other ships will see it and come and help. Ships also can tell if another ship is a friend or foe, like a pirate would be an enemy. A flag says people belong to a certain country.

> A country needs a flag because they need something to plant when they claim a spot. We should have pride in our country. The flag can separate armies and it is a national symbol. We can claim a spot, for instance Penn did, Columbus did, and so did Neil Armstrong. The flag is important. What would we do without a flag?
>
> A country needs a flag to separate armies like the British and the Americans. People needed a flag to follow, to know where their own soldiers were. At sea if the flag is upside down, that means the ship is in trouble. It also tells who the ship belongs to. We need a flag to claim a spot. Men on the moon claimed a spot, so did Christopher Columbus. A flag is a symbol that people can be proud of.

These accounts, like those written on the first day, do not reflect all that students had grasped from the activities. But they do show which concepts and facts seemed most significant to the children. The exercise gave each child a chance to express learning individually.

Summary. Betsy Ross and the American Flag included this sequence of language activities:

- Oral speculation to set listening purposes
- Listening for enjoyment and specific information
- Oral review of predictions and new information
- Writing to summarize
- Reading aloud to share written summaries
- Skimming a text to find specific information
- Discussion of text information
- Listening to and viewing a teacher demonstration
- Writing directions individually
- Discussing directions
- Rewriting directions as a group
- Following group-composed directions to make stars
- Discussing (with the teacher recording main points)
- Reconstructing board notes individually
- Reconstructing board notes as a group
- Rewriting individual notes
- Writing to summarize learning.

Students were actively involved throughout. They were thinking both critically and creatively and were using language for varied purposes to master the material.

Other Integration Strategies   Whatever the content, the language arts may be integrated in a considerable number of ways to make learning meaningful and enjoyable. Here are a few activities that promote an integrated use of language skills. They may be adapted to suit the needs and abilities of students in various grades.

- Students read books of their own choosing and share their reading through book talks, skits, art projects, or writing.

- Students interview family members to find out what life was like a generation ago. They write up their findings, meet in writing groups to revise their work, and prepare a class book of their papers.

- Working in small groups, students design and create board games that are based on the information in a unit of study.

- Students view a film, discuss it, and write letters to pen pals to describe what they saw and what they especially liked.

- A reading group discusses which stories they like best in their basal reader. They explain why these stories appeal to them. Then they write letters to the publisher, to give their opinions.

- Students plan a Picture Book Day for children in a lower grade. They write letters to the other class, choose favorite picture books, practice reading, and travel to the other room for one-to-one book sharing.

- Students keep a class journal to record each day's most interesting or memorable occurrences. Pages may be posted in sequence around the walls or may be kept in a special class diary. The class must discuss what will go in the journal; individuals (or small groups) may take turns as recorders.

- Students work in small groups to write and act out skits or plays based on what they are studying in the content areas.

- Students plan, write, and illustrate their own filmstrips or mural versions of favorite fairy tales.

- Students interview the principal, teachers, and other adults in the school to find out about their hobbies or special interests. They write up their findings for the school newspaper or a special class publication.

These are only a few of the kinds of activities that keep students meaningfully involved in language and thinking. All are fun, certainly, but each also requires attention to skills and content. A typical integrated learning unit might include several of these types of activities. The teacher can meet various curriculum objectives and can help students refine their abilities in the language arts. For more perspectives on strategies for integration see Newman (1986) and Atwell (1987).

Student-centered Learning

When students choose the topics and ask the questions, they not only have a better chance of understanding whatever they study (Asher, 1980), but they are also immediately engaged in the one process that makes them learners in the truest sense. This process is called *inquiry*. As Holt (1964) observed: "The only answer that really sticks in a child's mind is the answer to a question that he asked or might ask of himself" (p. 119).

Study based on self-selection is the most meaningful learning of all; it is what teachers want students to do when they leave the classroom and what they should be doing in school. John Dewey recognized this principle many years ago. Its significance and relevance have been confirmed repeatedly through the years by such educators as Kelley (1951), Stauffer (1969, 1975), Moffett and Wagner (1983), and Torbe and Medway (1981).

A plan for student-centered study, modeled after Stauffer's inquiry reading (or individualized DR-TA), includes these four basic features:

1. Students select a subject for study. Topics may be suggested by the teacher but are not assigned.
2. Students pose questions to guide their research. The teacher may help them formulate questions but does not tell them what they should ask.
3. Students look for information in a variety of print and nonprint sources. Their goal is to find answers to their own questions.
4. Students present their findings to the class. Their work culminates in a creative sharing of what they have learned.

Each of these steps requires the teacher's guidance to help students work effectively. Lessons in specific skills may be needed at different times during the unit to help students accomplish their study efficiently.

To illustrate, here are the details of one group's fifteen-day period of study that was spread over four weeks. Each "day" consisted of a one-hour session with the teacher; students did additional work on their own time. The teacher kept a log of the group's activities. The log is given here, along with some samples of student work.

> There were fifteen fourth graders in the class who were able but reluctant readers. They were ready to learn research skills, but they also needed to become more excited about books. I planned this unit to teach them some basic skills and also to show how pleasurable reading can be. Each day before we started, I read aloud from a different book. There was a sudden demand in the library for some of those titles! I also found that the extra time spent reading to them enhanced their anticipation of our group meetings, and that carried over into an eagerness to get on with the regular lesson. These usually reluctant readers also became more and more interested in the unit activities because they were allowed to choose their own topics for study.

Day 1. Today we explored ways to identify a topic. I decided they needed some practice in this before I could expect them to select a workable topic for extended study. I mentioned ideas at random and asked the students what they might want to learn about those topics. This was a real brainstorming session! Here is one list we came up with:

Indians

famous Indians	early history
how to trap animals	where they lived
homes	food
smoke signals	weaving
trade	ceremonies
learning to hunt	making traps
peacepipes	names of tribes
Squanto	Apache
how they traveled	life span
crops	money
jewelry making	making weapons
making pueblos	making arrowheads

The discussion was lively. I was glad to see how well one student's thinking stimulated another's. They began to see that with some time spent thinking, they can come up with many interesting things to learn about.

Day 2. We took the original lists we made yesterday and did some classifying. I wanted the group to practice relating topics to one another and distinguishing between broad headings and details. First we grouped similar things together and came up with headings. Here is an example:

- how to trap animals
- how to make arrowheads
- how to learn to hunt
- how to make weapons
- how to make traps
- *Heading:* Hunting

Then we chose a rather broad topic and found or thought of subtopics related to it. Here are two examples:

Apache

where they lived
famous Indians
homes
how they traveled
food
money/trade
ceremonies
how they learned to hunt

Famous Indians

Squanto
Pocohontas
Sacejewea
Geronimo
Sitting Bull

Then I had them think of specific questions they could ask about a particular topic. This is one example.

Sitting Bull

Why is he remembered?
Was he good or bad?
Where did he live?
What kind of home did he have?
Which tribe did he belong to?

We did several of these exercises, grouping and regrouping the first ideas we had come up with and adding new thoughts as they occurred to us. They're beginning to understand how to narrow a topic and think of specifics related to a general idea.

Day 3. More practice thinking of topics, but today I also had the group think about what they knew and didn't know about a few subjects. This helped them see that a good part of research is adding to what you already know. The group thought of topics and, together, listed things they knew and things they wanted to find out. Here are two examples:

Hurricanes

What we know:
    They destroy buildings.
    They kill people.
    They make whirlpools.
    Whirlpools take boats down.
    Tidal waves wash out homes.

What we want to learn:
    What makes a whirlpool go around?
    How deep can a whirlpool be?
    How do they name hurricanes?
    Where do hurricanes happen?

Pearls

What we know:
    They're used in jewelry.
    They come from oysters.
    They're white and pinkish.
    They're smooth and round.

What we want to learn:
    How does an oyster make a pearl?
    Where do you find pearls?
    What does a pearl diver do?

After doing several exercises like this, I gave them their assignment for tomorrow: Each of you come to class with a topic *you* want to learn more about. I told them they could choose things we had already talked about but that I hoped they would have many more ideas of their own.

Day 4. After three days of talking about topics, no one seemed to have any trouble coming up with an idea. In class I had each pose one good question about the chosen topic and encouraged them to help one another do this. The three days of preparation showed. They were able to think of many questions—some very broad, some very specific—and select one that would guide their coming studies. Here are the questions they settled on:

CATHY: What are the names of the parts of a horse's body?
FRANK: How are monkeys like people?
SCOTT: What is a warhorse?
ED: How are wild pigs different from tame pigs?
KEN: What are the names of the bones in a man's body?
RUSS: Why did the dinosaurs die out?
JERRY: Why do people like to race stock cars?
JACK: How did the modern wheat combine develop?
EMILY: How does a hot air balloon fly?
BOBBY: How did the Greek myths explain people's lives?
PAM: What were some famous Indian ceremonies?
BILL: Why do we remember Sacejewea?
PETER: Where do sharks live?
RICHARD: How is a bobcat different from a lion?
NICK: What plants grow in the ocean?

I wrote the questions on the board as each made final decisions. Group members sometimes suggested rewording questions, and everyone became very interested in the great variety of things the group would be studying. As they decided on their questions, I had them write down what they already knew and what they would like to find out. Here are a few examples of that work.

Scott: What is a warhorse?

What I Know

Knights rode warhorses.
Warhorses wore armor.

What I Want to Know

What did warhorses carry?
Who used warhorses?

Jack: How did the modern wheat combine develop?

What I Know

> What it looks like
> How it works
> Big ones cost $40,000

What I Want to Know

> How many men does a combine replace?
> Who invented the first harvester?
> What did the first one look like?

Bobby: How did the Greek myths explain people's lives?

What I Know

> Pandora's box explains troubles.
> Zeus was king of the gods.
> Apollo was the sun god.
> Greeks worshipped gods.
> They had lots of gods.

What I Want to Know

> How the gods made the seasons
> How the gods made day and night

Day 5. We hit the library. The students were ready and eager to see what kind of information was available. It was not surprising to see everyone head for the shelves of encyclopedias. Richard quickly found "bobcat" in an encyclopedia and asked if he should copy the article there or take the book back to the room. I told him to look for more materials before worrying about taking notes. Others, too, seemed to have forgotten their questions, bent on copying the first piece of information they found. I decided to spend tomorrow on notetaking, as opposed to copying, and urged everyone just to look for good sources.

Eventually, Richard found two animal books, each with a page about bobcats, plus a *National Geographic* article on wild cats. He acted as if each were a prize. His excitement at finding several relevant sources made his eyes shine! I circulated and helped, and by the end of the hour, each student had at least one or two potential sources. As I watched them search, I saw they needed help with skimming as well as notetaking.

Day 6. A day of practice. I took a set of encyclopedias to the room. Each child chose a volume, opened the book at random, and found something to read about. I talked about key words and skimming, and we did some examples on the board. Then I walked around the group, found out each student's topic, and asked questions so they could practice looking for key word clues. We did this several times, each time with a different reading passage. I showed them how to pace quickly with their fingers, using the analogy of a helicopter: You move along swiftly until you see a landing place (an information clue), then drop down, check it out, and up and away, home if you got your information, on to the next clue if you did not.

We spent about half an hour with this, and then each student tried it with the sources found yesterday in the library. In order to search effectively, however, many of their original questions had to be narrowed still further. The children soon saw the need for this themselves, saying things like, "What's a good clue word if. . . ?" Frank, who wanted to find out how monkeys are like people, soon thought of two more questions: How do monkeys use their hands? What do monkeys eat? He decided on the key words *hands* and *food.* Bobby had a tough time with his question about the Greek gods. Finally he decided he could look for stories that used words like sun, thunder, spring and winter.

Day 7. Each child had some (though not enough) source material in the classroom, so I postponed another trip to the library until we could do some work on notetaking. I made sure each had a clear question in mind before beginning to read. Pam was reading to learn what Indian corn dances were like; Scott was reading about Genghis Khan's warhorses; Nick wanted to know where conditions are right for algae to grow, and so on. I told them all to read until their heads were full.

In fifteen minutes I stopped them, had them close their books, turn to a neighbor, and tell as much as they could from their reading. After three minutes, the neighbors got their turns. Then everyone took paper and pencil (books still closed) and wrote for fifteen minutes. After this, they returned to their books and added information they had forgotten but wanted to include.

We talked about the advantages of reading, thinking, and talking before taking notes. I stressed how important it is to have notes in your own words. I also reminded them to write down the book title and page number of what they had just read, in case they ever wanted to return to that source for more details.

The brief time spent on notetaking strategies had helped them learn to put things in their own words. Here are some of their notes, which they wrote impromptu, following the few minutes of talking with classmates immediately after reading.

Richard: The bobcat is smaller than a lynx. It is about as big as a house cat. The bobcat weighs 20 to 25 pounds. The lynx is almost twice the size of a house cat and weighs about 60 pounds. The bobcat is a meat eater. He will attack deer and sheep. He is enemies with the fox and the great horned owl.

Bill: Sacejewea was an Indian girl. She was a Shoshoni Indian. She was famous for guiding the Lewis and Clark expedition. They traveled for two years. When she saw a mountain she knew, she said that is the land of my people. Sacejewea had a baby named Pomp. She carried him on her back.

Nick: Underwater plants are many different colors, different shapes, different sizes. There are some that grow 400 feet long. Some you can eat, some are poisonous. Some are pink or yellow, seaweed is green or brown. All the plants have names. Algae is one of the names of underwater plants.

Emily: The first balloons were filled with smoke. Now they use hot air. The name for the basket is gondola. The gondola is made of wicker. The tallest balloons are about six stories high. The taller the balloon the more weight it can carry. A lot of people can ride in a balloon.

Day 8. We talked a little more about taking notes, the importance of putting down your own version of the information, and the need to note the source and page number for future reference. Then it was back to the library. Here are some observations that I jotted down while the students worked.

Frank is using key words to find out if all monkeys have fur. He's looking through many books to see if he can find the word *furless.* He says if he can find no mention of furless monkeys, he's going to conclude that all monkeys have fur.

Cathy checked the card catalogue for books on horses. After looking at each one listed (all fiction), she decided that an encyclopedia would be best after all. She's busy with words like *fetlock* and *withers.*

Ed is comparing domestic and wild pigs. He has been looking for litter size and has been unable to find information about a specific number of newborns. He has a one-track mind! No other basis for comparison is important until he gets this one straight. Finally he found the statement (for Hampshires) that they have "as many as twenty in a litter." We talked about this until he saw that this meant a maximum number. He is persistent and keeps looking.

Emily had a ride in a hot air balloon, and she is as interested in telling about this as she is in finding out why they go up. She was excited to find a *National Geographic* article with photos, and she went from one child to another, showing the pictures and telling her own story.

Peter is absorbed. He's supposed to be looking for the habitat of sharks, but he is too taken with all the shark pictures he has found to be much concerned with habitats for now.

Nick is businesslike. How quickly he has grasped the idea of looking for a specific piece of information. Jerry got carried away by all the racing car books, and it was Nick who said, "You're interested right now in stock car racing, aren't you? Well, what do people win if they win a stock car race—ribbons or money?"

Jack was surprised when I suggested that his grandfather might know a lot about early farm machinery. I don't think it had occurred to him that one can find this kind of information outside a library. I found a story about Cyrus McCormick in an old basal reader for him, and he is busy with that.

As a whole, the group is making good progress. I am pleased that they are showing some real enthusiasm about the books they are using to find information.

Day 9. The students continued reading, some in the library and some in the classroom. Emily came today full of first-hand information about hot air balloons. She had gone with her mother to a nursing home where she had talked to a man who had once owned a balloon. She had a whole string of new words like *burner, lift-off,* and *guy wires,* which she proudly used to continue her commentary on the pictures she had found.

Ken was looking for skeletal nomenclature and got detoured. He found a series of acetate overlays in a book about muscles, organs and bones. Immediately he said, "Now if I lift this up, I can slide my hand in here and reach the heart to fix it!"

I can see real progress in this group. Most are using the read-talk-take notes strategy I showed them. They are spending a good bit of time explaining what they read to each other and then writing it in their own words. Also, I see that although they are sticking to their original questions quite well, they are also delving deeper into their topics and finding information they hadn't even thought to look for earlier.

Day 10. Some children are ready to plan for sharing. Emily is reading *21 Balloons* by W. P. DuBois, which I brought in for her; her research is completed. Ken is back on track. I taught him "Dry Bones," and he is now chanting as he memorizes *clavicle, radius,* etc. He decided he wanted to be able to recite all the bones on demand.

I talked about sharing, explaining that when you have the answers to your questions, you are ready to present your findings to the whole group. I also pointed out that there is no need to explain everything you have found and that it is best to select the most interesting or important pieces of information. I gave them several choices of ways to present, stressing that each would have to decide how to share their learning in a way that would interest the rest of the class:

- game using vocabulary learned
- three-minute "radio" spot on tape
- poster to accompany a "lecture"
- demonstrations with props
- anything else with my approval

To help the group see what to think about, I chose Ken and had a conference with him in front of the group. With my encouragement, he decided to dress up in a white coat and make a reflector on a headband for his head—doctor's apparel. He also decided to make a poster of the bones of the body to aid his explanation. Our conference helped the others see what they would need to consider as they planned what and how to share.

Day 11. Some children are still reading; some are planning their presentations. I had conferences with those who were ready. About three days of actual researching was all these students could sustain, understandable since this was really their first experience with individualized, independent work.

Day 12. Jack gave his talk today. He is a farm boy who has first-hand knowledge of modern farm machinery. He showed a very detailed, complex model of a combine that he built himself with his Lego pieces. It had a detachable cutter and roller bars and many other moveable parts. The children were fascinated. He also showed a picture of McCormick's first reaper as a comparison.

Jack's grandfather had supplied answers to his questions on labor-saving. (Two men, one driving a combine and one with a truck for the grain, replace from ten to fifteen laborers and several different operations, such as stacking wheat and hauling sheaves.) In a farm magazine Jack found pictures depicting the evolution from reaper to combine. He also read about Cyrus McCormick and John Appleby. This was his first experience with biography, and he has since started a fictionalized biography of Paul Revere.

Days 13 and 14. The rest of the presentations were done on these two days. The talks were short, a few minutes each, but the students were very well prepared and spoke confidently about what they had learned. Visual aids were selected or prepared with care. Here is a summary of what several showed and did:

Cathy. Poster of a horse with parts labeled to accompany a well-organized talk explaining names and functions.

Frank. Talk on the characteristics of man and monkey, with a large, clear chart organized like a checklist.

Scott. Card game using vocabulary associated with war horses, which he demonstrated with a few volunteers to help. Scott had stumbled onto a book which depicted warhorses through the centuries. He was fascinated with Genghis Khan and the story of his sweep through Asia. He ended up concluding that there were always war horses and that they carried whatever needed to be carried. Actually, his incidental learning turned out to be far more interesting than what he set out to learn. For instance, he was amazed to discover that the invention of the stirrup revolutionized warfare, providing, as it did, leverage for throwing weapons while mounted. His card game, similar to Old Maid, included words like coat of mail and endurance.

Russ. Poster with drawings of dinosaurs in a cold world (cloud over the sun, snow on mountain tops, icicles hanging from palm trees) to illustrate his explanation of why dinosaurs died out.

Jerry. List of all the words he could associate with stock cars, which he explained clearly and enthusiastically to the group.

Pam. Poster of five Indian tribes, a ceremony for each illustrated, which she used to enhance her talk.

Bobby. Oral reading of a Greek myth. Bobby really just wanted an excuse to read more mythology, and this is what he did. He found the answer to his first question in the story of Ceres, Proserpine, and Pluto—the explanation for winter and summer. Bobby has great difficulty reading orally, so I was astonished when he decided to read to the class. Such rehearsal! He spent parts of three days (some at home) reading aloud. He went out in the hall so he could concentrate better when he was in school. He read the myth that answered his second question, "Phaeton and the Chariot of the Sun," and did a very fine job.

Emily. Lovely poster of hot air balloons to accompany a good summary of how they work.

Peter. Card game, similar to Old Maid, with different kinds of sharks, which all the group loved. He agreed to leave the game in the room so everyone could play during breaks.

Richard. Simulated TV interview, beginning with his statement, "I'm a big game hunter, but in my spare time I photograph bobcats."

Nick. Detailed, businesslike talk about ocean plants. His poster was excellent, with cutaway sections showing the surface and bottom of the plants he described.

Each student did a fine job of explaining major points. All used their own words and had very little need to refer to notes. They spoke confidently and with enthusiasm, giving evidence of solid learning.

Day 15. We talked about our work over the past weeks. The thing the students seemed to value above all was the chance to choose their areas of interest to study. They also loved the daily reading aloud and liked the hand-picked books I had brought in for them from time to time. The last activity was a fifteen-minute period of writing about their chosen areas—a chance to reflect, mention other ideas, and so on. Several volunteers read aloud what they had written. It gave us all a good sense of closure.

Looking back at our few weeks of work, I saw how valuable certain of our activities had been. One of the best was having the students write following their reading and talking about their topics. I did not grade their notes, but reading them regularly gave me many insights into what the children were learning and, sometimes, when they were heading in the wrong direction. For instance, when Ed was reading about domestic versus wild pigs, he kept getting his details confused. I knew he needed help when I saw in his notes "Hampshires have a sharp razor back."

I also found that the students loved making up lists of all kinds. They eagerly kept lists of words related to their topics, and this was a good way to reinforce the vocabulary they were learning. For a while I thought that Jerry was just goofing off. Then I saw his comprehensive list of stock car terms (seventy-seven in all) that he had learned and could use with authority.

Although the final presentations were natural outcomes of the children's learning, I also found great value in the informal, day-to-day sharing of information. As they learned new facts, they loved to take turns making up questions to stump classmates. Bobby was continually dropping Greek gods' names that no one else knew and then carefully explaining who they were. He became our mythology expert. We also had our medical authority, several naturalists, and, of course, an enthusiastic source on hot air balloons. It was good to see the students gain confidence in what they knew. Since each had studied a different area, each could be the authority on a different topic.

I also noted many cooperative efforts to make sense of what individuals were reading. The students knew that I couldn't help everyone at once, so they naturally began to help each other. Once Peter was looking for how old sharks get. He read aloud to a few others, "Scientists aren't certain how long sharks live." He commented that he would have to keep looking for the answer, but the group convinced him that if scientists were not sure, he would probably not find the information anywhere. Many other times, too, I found students helping one another figure out words, interpret meanings, and find information. They were learning to rely on themselves as they learned the process of inquiry.

Directing Student-centered Learning

The fifteen-day unit just presented is only one example of organization and direction of student-centered learning. The basic principles behind such units hold that students should think and use language in new and challenging situations. Students are moved temporarily away from structured textbooks to be guided by their own purposes for learning. Such study allows for considerable skill development in each of the language arts.

Students set purposes for reading. Next, they locate information. They do not always find answers to their questions right away and may need to check several sources. They must distinguish between relevant and irrelevant information. They read a variety of materials, often finding books related to their studies that they explore simply for enjoyment. They write for different purposes—to take notes, to compose summaries, and to prepare for their presentations. Writing is directly tied to what they are reading and discussing, so the writing process, in this context, is especially meaningful. As students read and share their knowledge informally with classmates, they explain orally what they are learning and must listen to others' explanations. The final sharing, too, requires prepared speakers and attentive listeners. Most important, students' learning stems from purposes they set themselves, based on questions they raise about areas of genuine interest.

In the unit just described, each student selected a different area to study; the work was completely individualized. The same kind of unit can also be conducted with several groups of students, each group pursuing an area of mutual interest to its members. This arrangement has obvious advantages. Students learn to work together, divide tasks, discuss progress, and help each other out. Monitoring students' work can also be easier for the teacher if there are several groups to follow rather than twenty-five or thirty individuals.

Grouping based on areas of interest will usually be different from grouping based on skill needs or ability levels. Sometimes the most able students in the class will be interested in the same areas as the poorest achievers. The newly formed groups will offer good opportunities for all to learn how to take advantage of each person's strengths. The slow reader may have creative ideas for sharing; the one who has trouble writing may be a whiz at finding information. Students will have to break away from their usual ability-group routines to deal with peers in new ways. Sometimes groups will form based on friendship alone;

In student-centered learning, students think and use language in new and challenging situations, guided by their own purposes for learning.

this, too, can be advantageous to learning. When students work with close friends, they may accomplish more because they get along and enjoy being together.

There are no hard and fast rules for deciding how to reorganize the class for student-centered learning. Sometimes, there will be a few groups working together and a few individuals striking out on their own. The key is to make sure that students choose to study what interests them and feel comfortable working together. Students should not be assigned to groups; groups should form naturally on the basis of students' stated areas of interest. Individuals should be allowed to work on their own if they desire.

The most important thing the teacher can do during one of these units is to keep watch over the students' work. The teacher should know when to help, especially when students need direct instruction in specific skills. As the illustrative log revealed, the fourth graders needed help in skimming and taking notes. This situation became evident to the observant teacher when the class first started searching for information. The teacher thus planned lessons on the spot to introduce necessary skills. These lessons were particularly useful because they were geared to students' needs and were also applied immediately as students continued their work.

Each group will perform differently and will require a different schedule of work. Skill instruction, too, must be tailored to the observed needs in the group. Hence, it is difficult to suggest exactly how such a unit should be conducted. But here are some basic considerations and suggestions about what the teacher can do at different stages of the process:

Setting Purposes   The first step is to have students select topics. The teacher in the example, who knew that the students were inexperienced, accordingly spent a few sessions developing the concept of *topic*. The students practiced thinking about topic selection; brainstorming and classifying gave them the needed practice and stimulated thinking. The time devoted to these initial activities paid off; students had little trouble selecting a topic when it was time to do so.

Another approach is to use a basal reader or content-area textbook as the foundation. Class work in a regular text provides background and can generate interest in certain areas of study. Most basal units and textbook chapters are organized around themes. When students delve into a thematic unit, they will often be eager to investigate certain concepts in greater detail. During regular unit work, spare moments might be spent in discussions about possible directions for future study. An end-of-unit review might also serve to set purposes for continuing investigations.

Another approach is to reserve a special place on the classroom bulletin board for posting articles, pictures, and memorabilia related to students' interests. If everyone is encouraged to bring in interesting material, the board will soon be filled with photographs, maps, flyers, and clippings. This collection can stimulate topic choices when the time for student-centered work arrives. The picture of an erupting Mt. St. Helens will lead to questions about volcanoes; an article about raccoons will stimulate curiosity about these creatures; a postcard of a faraway place will generate questions about the people there. Students are curious about many things. With minimal effort, teachers can uncover those interests and use them to encourage further learning.

After students choose their topics, they must ask pertinent questions. This may be a difficult task for some. Because teachers seldom ask students to raise these kinds of questions, it may be a new experience for many. At first, they may ask questions that are hopelessly broad (How do they live in Japan?), self-evident (Do birds fly?), or impossible to answer (Where do the stars stop?). But if teachers recognize that asking good questions is, itself, a skill to be developed, they can be more patient with those students who have difficulty. Exercises in asking questions are helpful, even if the answers are not sought. Experience is also useful. Most students learn from one unit to the next what a fruitful question is. Most useful are the teacher's and group's reactions to questions; these help students narrow broad questions and identify the real interest behind awkward ones. Sometimes questions should be left as is so that looking for answers will, in itself, stimulate needed revision.

The teacher must also be prepared for students who are interested in areas about which the teacher knows nothing and for which he or she has no standards to judge the quality of their questions, their background of experience, or, ultimately, their findings. When encouraged to explore, students may venture into territory that is quite unfamiliar to the teacher. This can be a very healthy exercise if the teacher maintains the right perspective. The teacher will have to be able to say, honestly, that he or she does not know but will use his or her greater experience to help the students explore and find answers. The teacher will have to be comfortable with uncertainty and must be willing to risk making mistakes; this simply means that the teacher will have to become a learner too. Working with a teacher who is also learning can be a refreshing change for students. It can also be a pleasure to the intellectually curious teacher.

Some students pose only questions for which they clearly know the answers. Even when encouraged, they will claim no other interest except in one narrow topic, about which they already have a good deal of information. Sometimes these students will have extremely limited interests or will have anxieties about confronting anything unfamiliar. Some students respond in this way because, to them, answering questions correctly is the point of being in school, so they pose only questions they can answer with certainty. There are no easy solutions for dealing with these students. It may take several units to encourage the unresponsive students into revealing their interests and admitting to real curiosity. Some will make very little progress, even after several units, and their efforts will be meager at best. However, the goal of teaching students to direct their own learning is an important one, even if its means struggling with those who have difficulty or who are reluctant.

As questions are determined, it is a good idea to have students think about what they already know and what it is, specifically, that they want to find out. Making these distinctions helps students to see that their prior knowledge is relevant and useful. Students are also encouraged to reexamine what they already know. They may not be certain, once they think about it, of what they do know. All this also gives the teacher insight into how much students know about their topics. Some may know a good bit already; they can be guided to more detailed sources of information or be encouraged to delve more deeply into the topic. Others may be investigating an area they have just discovered; they may need guidance in finding relatively simple sources of information so as not to become overwhelmed.

Gathering Information   Once preliminary thinking and purpose setting are completed, students will be ready to search for information. During this time there will be many opportunities to challenge thinking and build important language skills. Most inexperienced students will approach research as Richard in the example did—they will head for the encyclopedia, or another single source, and begin to copy. It is extremely important to show students other tactics. There are several ways to do this:

1. Collect books on the chosen topics and bring them to class. Have students look through several sources before they take any notes. Supervise these first steps carefully to make sure they are searching for information. They should not be writing at this point.

2. As students find information, have them explain it orally before they write it down. This technique counteracts the tendency to copy, as was pointed out in Chapter 7 and in the illustrative log.
3. Help students find films or other audiovisual sources; do not expect them to find all their information in books.
4. Stress the value of people as sources. Help students find experts in the school or community; arrange for phone calls, visits, or an exchange of letters to get information.

When students realize that searching for information is as important as writing down what they find, they will be slower to copy and less satisfied with a single source. A few examples will illustrate the variety of sources that can be used. In each of the following situations, the students were so involved in learning that they were not tempted to rely on the first piece of information they found.

A fifth-grade boy was interested in learning how pinball machines actually worked. With the teacher's help, he located a pinball repair service in the Yellow Pages of the telephone book. A short in-school phone conversation led to an after-school visit to the shop in a nearby city. The child was able to have a very informative talk with the mechanic. The boy also borrowed some printed information; this was useful because the school library had no material on pinball machines.

A second-grade group, all avid baseball fans, was interested in learning more about their favorite game. The teacher knew that a major league player lived in the area and wrote to him of the group's work. He volunteered to come to the class to give a talk. The visit was arranged and was an exciting event because the player came in uniform and brought souvenirs for everyone. He began his talk, giving general information that he thought would be of interest to the whole class. He was surprised and delighted when the study group (all wearing baseball caps) interrupted him politely to say that they had some questions they very much wanted to ask. They proceeded to read from their prepared list, having selected and phrased their questions carefully, and listened eagerly and attentively to his answers. They were thrilled to see a hero but they had not forgotten that he was an excellent source of information.

A third-grade girl, interested in tropical fish, and finding only one book on the topic in the school library, posted a request on the teachers' notice board. One of the teachers had a home aquarium full of tropical fish and an extensive personal library. The teacher lent the girl several books to help her out.

A fifth-grade group, interested in grizzly bears, got together to watch a television program about those animals. They watched with more than usual attention because they had a set of questions for which they were seeking answers. Although the program provided some answers (which the students related enthusiastically in school the next day), it did not give information about all of their questions. The surprised students pursued books with greater interest the following week.

The search for information can be exciting, especially if students are encouraged to go beyond readily available sources. The library may be the first place to check, and sometimes there will be a wealth of information there. But there are many other possibilities that can lead to good information and, sometimes, to memorable experiences.

When students are searching in books, specific skill lessons may become necessary, as the illustrative log showed. Students may need help in using a card catalogue, an index, a table of contents, and other such guides. Practice in previewing, skimming, notetaking, and keeping track of sources may all be necessary. None of these skills can be taught thoroughly during the unit, but some short and relevant exercises can be scheduled as needs arise. Skill lessons should not dominate the unit; the most important goal is to find information. More extensive teaching and practice can be done after the unit is completed and before the next unit begins.

Vocabulary and comprehension skills will be exercised to the fullest extent as students search for answers. Generally, they will gravitate toward books they can read easily, but they may end up using some materials that are difficult. Students may be puzzled or confused from time to time with unfamiliar words and language patterns. There are several ways to smooth the way. It is most valuable for the teacher to encourage students to share, informally, what they are learning *as* they read. In-progress sharing accomplishes these ends:

1. Explaining what they have learned to others reinforces students' learning.
2. When talking to classmates informally, students will use their own words. They will be "translating" the material and thus building comprehension.
3. Students' explanations help the teacher see what learning is occurring. If a student gives an erroneous, vague, or confused explanation, the teacher will know that help is needed to clarify word meanings or textual information.
4. If given a chance to explain a point, show a picture and describe it, or define a new term, students will derive satisfaction in being the authority on that issue.

Written records of learning are also valuable during the research stage. Students might keep logs of their work, in which they write about what they are finding. As the students' personal records of learning, these do not need to be graded or revised. Students might also keep vocabulary lists, recording words that are new, interesting, or particularly important to the area being researched. More organized notes can also be kept of information obtained from the various sources. The type and extent of writing in these units should match the students' ages and abilities. Older, more experienced students can be expected to keep more extensive records than young students who are just learning how to write and do independent work.

Sharing   Informal, day-to-day sharing of information keeps students actively involved in learning. A more formal presentation at the end of a unit has additional advantages and can be a pleasurable activity. The most important reason for end-of-study sharing is that students are given a chance to tell what they have learned to a wide and receptive audience. The final activity becomes not a report that the teacher alone will see and evaluate but rather a presentation to peers of what one has learned. Students understand the special importance of their work, and most learners will relish the chance to speak to the class on a favorite topic. Sitting back to listen helps students appreciate other children's efforts, too. The fun of planning something unique, with props or costumes or special effects, also adds to the enjoyment.

During the school day, a reasonable amount of time must be devoted to planning for final sharing. These tasks need to be done:

1. Students must go over information they have found and must decide which material to present to the rest of the class. They are not obligated to show or tell everything they have learned; rather, they need to review their findings to choose the material that they consider to be the most important and interesting. This process encourages students to evaluate their information in a new light. They learn to organize findings in such a way that their knowledge will be clear to those who do not know as much.
2. Students must decide how to show others the facts effectively. A presentation mode must be selected, and necessary audiovisual aids must be chosen or designed and made.
3. Rehearsals must be scheduled. Students must practice before making a presentation to the class.

Some of this work can be done at home, but the more that is done in school, the more the teacher will be able to monitor progress and make suggestions. Sharing is a vital part of the learning process. It should be given serious attention by the teacher.

These strategies help students make successful presentations:

1. Give students a few ideas for planning how to share their findings. Suggest several ways, but do not overwhelm them with choices. For a start, choose four or five of these activities:

- Do a demonstration
- Build a model and explain how it works
- Summarize facts on a chart or poster
- Paint a mural
- Dramatize information in a skit
- Make a filmstrip to show and narrate
- Plan a "TV" show with "celebrities" giving facts
- Take photographs to illustrate; make a display

- Plan a puppet show to present findings
- Plan a lecture
- Write a book to read aloud and donate to the class
- Make a diorama
- Make a movie
- Design a game that will teach facts or vocabulary
- Bake a cake with a frosting illustration.

2. Be available to help students select information they plan to share. Discuss which concepts, facts, or processes would probably be most interesting to the class. Help them to determine which information is the most important. Let students make choices, but provide help when they are uncertain.

3. Organize a schedule for the presentations, based on what students plan to do. Have them estimate how much time they will need, after the first rehearsal or two. Allow time for setting up; make sure everyone has plenty of time and all goes smoothly.

4. Be alert to various students' needs for help at different stages. Provide encouragement, support, and suggestions as they plan. Help them see how to make their presentations as successful as possible.

As they prepare, students may encounter unexpected problems that can present new opportunities for learning. For instance, a group of fourth graders was once planning a talk on the planets. They had organized their information well; each had a well-defined part to play in the presentation. They had only one problem—their model of the planetary system just was not working. They had decided to form the planets from clay and suspend them on strings inside a cardboard box that they had painted to resemble outer space. They planned to point out the planets as they told about them. Unfortunately, Jupiter and the other large planets kept sliding off their strings and smashing to the floor of the box. The group held several conferences and experimented with alternatives (thicker string, a sturdier box). Finally they hit on the idea of fastening paper clips to the ends of the strings to stop the clay balls from sliding. The plan worked! Their satisfaction at solving a critical problem, on their own, was great. Their problem-solving skills turned the obstacle into an excellent thinking exercise. As students plan presentations, they must figure out how to design visual aids or costumes, make workable models, or write detailed scripts for skits. Each presentation will present unique problems that need to be solved. Students continue to learn even when their research is over.

More Examples and Some Final Thoughts

Individualizing the thinking and learning process can be accomplished at all grade levels with all types of students. The time allotted to such a unit can vary, depending on the ages, abilities, and experience of the students. Those who have few independent skills and limited attention spans should probably start with units that require a few days' work from start to finish. Purposes can be limited; research time can be a day or two; presentations can be simple and easy to plan. More experienced students may be able to spend several weeks at individual work; these students may plan more elaborate presentations because they will have more information to study and share. To illustrate the variety that is possible, here are brief descriptions of several different units that were done in a variety of schools:

A sixth-grade group of seven chose to study the assassination of John F. Kennedy. They were especially curious about the tragedy because it had occurred during the year they were all born. They interviewed parents and teachers, read many books, and gathered a remarkable amount of information in about three weeks' time. To share what they had learned, they enacted the Dallas scene, conducted interviews with "witnesses" and finally discussed several of the still-unsolved mysteries of the incident. Their presentation required about a week of planning and rehearsing and took a half hour to do.

A first-grade boy wondered how cats meow. He spent some time each day for a week, reading several books about cats and asking people who had cats what they knew. He explained his findings simply and clearly, using a diagram of a cat's vocal cords (which he drew himself) to enhance his three-minute talk.

A fourth-grade boy, with limited verbal skills and very little experience with independent work, spent two days researching information about clams. He had posed one good question (How does a clam move?) and found his answer. He drew a simple but careful picture of a clam, with parts labeled, to use with his very brief talk. (This was the first time that the boy had shown such initiative and motivation in school. His work brought him deserved praise from his teacher.)

An eighth-grade group of six students studied the local trash disposal system. They were prompted by curiosity about where the garbage trucks disposed of their loads. The students called local trash collectors and public officials, obtained pamphlets, and found newspaper articles about the process. They also looked into systems in neighboring localities and became genuinely concerned about the problems associated with dumps. With help from parents and teachers, they arranged a visit to the local dump and made a short 8mm film there to demonstrate the different stages of the process. They showed their film and explained in detail what they had learned for their half-hour presentation. They gave the class updates from time to time.

Having recently acquired a puppy, one second grader had questions about pet care and chose to read a series of books about caring for puppies. For her presentation, she showed how to give a dog a bath. She used a live dog, a wash tub, water, soap, and flea powder. The teacher had arranged for the class to move outside to a grassy area for the demonstration. It was a memorable experience for all.

Three eighth graders worked together on a project done jointly for their English and social studies classes. They chose the Civil War as their area of interest and decided to share their knowledge with the class through a series of short plays, which they wrote and performed. The dialogue from one of these, depicting their interpretation of a shift in the North's attitude toward the war, clearly demonstrates the kind of sophisticated thinking that inquiry units promote. The students had collected information, sifted through it for key ideas, and translated what they judged most significant into dramatic form:

Scene I [soon after the start of the Civil War]

Private Smith: I remember one day when Private Jones and I were called into General Grant's office. . . .

General Grant: Private Smith and Private Jones, come in here! [Privates salute] At ease. I've called you in to talk to you about last night's incident regarding the southern property. I'd like to read you some orders I received from Commander Halleck. [General Grant reads] "Brigadier General Grant, I'm distressed to hear of all the looting and burning of southern property. I wish this to be stopped at once. It is not military-like behavior. We are not at war to destroy southern property but to get them to become citizens once more. The penalty for looting is a $50 fine. A second offense will cause a person to be demoted one rank. You will follow these orders." [General Grant talks to privates] Go tell the other soldiers about this because Commander Halleck has been talking about making the penalty stiffer. Is that clear?

Privates: Yes, sir!

Scene II [6 months later]

General Grant: Lt. Smith and Lt. Jones, come in here. [Lieutenants salute] Do you remember when I called you in several months ago?

Lieutenants: [in unison] Yes, sir.

General Grant: I wish you to disregard all previous orders about southern property. Take your troops into the south. Destroy property and live off the land. Is that clear?

Lieutenants: [in unison] Yes, sir!

General Grant: Dismissed.

Independent research like this may sometimes provide teachers with the only hint of a student's true ability. One fourth-grade boy was in a classroom in which several student-centered projects were undertaken during the year, sometimes in conjunction with social studies or science units, sometimes involving any topics the students chose to pursue. Guided by his own questions about topics that truly interested him, this boy was persistent and skillful in finding information and presenting it creatively. One of his presentations involved writing, producing, and starring in a play based on a book of famous FBI cases; another involved building a working barometer that the class used daily for several months to record the atmospheric pressure. Unfortunately, the curriculum did not allow much time for self-selection. Unmotivated by the usual routine, the boy did not fare well most of the time and was not recommended for promotion to fifth grade.

The most critical features of an inquiry unit are the teacher's attitude and behavior. Teachers who value student inquiry will be the most successful at directing independent study. For these teachers, student-centered learning is always a goal; having students select topics of interest is only an extension of the search for meaning and relevance that is at the heart of every class period. Postman and Weingartner (1969) describe several features of this kind of "inquiry teacher," among which these are particularly significant:

> The teacher rarely tells students what he thinks they ought to know. He believes that telling, when used as a basic teaching strategy, deprives students of the excitement of doing their own finding and of the opportunity for increasing their power as learners.
>
> His basic mode of discourse with students is questioning. He emphatically does not view questions as a means of seducing students into parroting the text or syllabus; rather he sees questions as instruments to open engaged minds to unsuspected possibilities.
>
> Generally, he does not accept a single statement as an answer to a question. In fact, he has a persisting aversion to anyone, any syllabus, any text that offers The Right Answer. Not because answers and solutions are unwelcome—indeed, he is trying to help students become more efficient problem-solvers—but because he knows how often The Right Answer serves only to terminate further thought. (p. 34)

This kind of teacher will be capable of meeting the demands of a student-centered unit of study. And such learning *does* demand teacher effort. Supervising independent learning is not as easy as sticking to the curriculum guide. The territory of student inquiry is uncharted and unfamiliar to all teachers; there are surprises at every turn each time. Students may choose a topic for which no information seems to exist within a 250-mile radius of the school. Some will become discouraged, anxious, or even angry when they cannot find answers easily and immediately. Some will declare their work finished after they have read one article, and no amount of patient encouragement will induce them to look seriously for more information. For every student who is eager, curious, and hard working, there may be one who is listless, bored, and hostile. Mediocre, mumbled talks will share the spotlight with delightful student-produced plays. Everyone will need different kinds and amounts of help, and the classroom will not be orderly, quiet, and predictable. The teacher must be tolerant of different rates, intensities, and extents of learning.

Student-centered learning does not instantly turn passive students into industrious seekers of knowledge. There is no guarantee that introducing such a venture will produce spectacular results. But such activity is the most significant we can provide for our students—problems, setbacks, and failures included. Kelley and Rasey (1952) urged teachers to take a new perspective on learning. Their message is just as meaningful decades later:

> We will have to stop foisting subject matter upon learners because we think it is good for them. We will need to begin consultation with learners as to what is to be done, in order to take advantage of the individual paths of energy pointed out by individual purpose. (p. 74)
>
> It is unthinkable, when one stops to reflect on it, that a group can enter into an enterprise when only one in the group knows what is to be done and has made the decision all by himself. Whenever a group of people start to do anything, consultation is required if the project is to be anything but authoritarian. Without consultation he [the student] feels that this is the teacher's show, and he has no responsibility for its success or failure. When the teacher does all the planning, he also assumes all the responsibility. As a result he is liable to get apathy on the part of the learner at best, if not active resistance. (pp. 148–49)

Teachers must not foster active resistance. They must stimulate active involvement in language and thinking so as to have a hand in developing inquiring minds.

Suggested Activities

1. Plan a three-lesson unit of study in science, social studies, or another content area. Integrate several language activities into your plan. Consider how you will meet the special needs of individual students.
2. Teach the lesson you planned for activity 1. Evaluate the students' performance and consider how you might alter your plan if you were to teach the unit again.
3. As a follow-up to a unit in a basal reader, help a group of students brainstorm a list of topics for further study. For several of the topics, help students pose questions that could serve as purposes for research.
4. Guide one academically talented student through a student-centered research project. Include topic selection, a search for information, planning and rehearsal for sharing, and sharing. Keep a log of this experience.

References

Asher, S. R. "Topic Interest and Children's Reading Comprehension" in R. J. Spiro et al., eds., *Theoretical Issues in Reading Comprehension*. Hillsdale, NJ: Erlbaum, 1980.

Atwell, N. *In the Middle: Writing, Reading, and Learning with Adolescents*. Portsmouth, NH: Heinemann, 1987.

Holt, J. *How Children Fail*. New York: Dell, 1964.

Kelley, E. C. *The Workshop Way of Learning*. New York: Harper and Brothers, 1951.

—————, and Rasey, M. I. *Education and the Nature of Man*. New York: Harper and Brothers, 1952.

Moffett, J., and Wagner, B. *A Student-Centered Language Arts Curriculum, Grades K–13: A Handbook for Teachers*. Boston: Houghton Mifflin, 1983.

Newman, J. M. (ed.) *Whole Language: Theory Into Use*. Portsmouth, NH: Heinemann, 1986.

Postman, N., and Weingartner, C. *Teaching as a Subversive Activity*. New York: Dell, 1969.

Stauffer, R. G. *Teaching Reading as a Thinking Process*. New York: Harper & Row, 1969.

—————. *Directing the Reading-Thinking Process*. New York: Harper & Row, 1975.

Torbe, M., and Medway, P. *The Climate for Learning*. Montclair, NJ: Boynton/Cook, 1981.

A Selection of Wordless Picture Books

Alexander, M. *Out! Out! Out!* New York: Dial, 1968.

——. *Bobo's Dream.* New York: Dial, 1970.

Anderson, L. *The Package: A Mystery.* New York: Bobbs-Merrill, 1970.

Anno, M. *Anno's Journey.* New York: William Collins & World, 1978.

——. *Anno's U.S.A.* New York: Philomel, 1983.

——. *Anno's Flea Market.* New York: Philomel Books, 1984.

Ardizzone, E. *The Wrong Side of the Bed.* New York: Doubleday, 1970.

Asch, F. *The Blue Balloon.* New York: McGraw-Hill, 1971.

Barton, B. *Elephant.* New York: Seabury, 1971.

Bollinger-Savelli, A. *The Knitted Cat.* New York: Macmillan, 1971.

Briggs, R. *The Snowman.* New York: Random House, 1978.

Carle, E. *A Very Long Tail.* New York: Thomas Crowell, 1972.

——. *A Very Long Train.* New York: Thomas Crowell, 1972.

Carroll, R. *What Whiskers Did.* New York: Walck, 1965.

——. *Rolling Downhill.* New York: Walck, 1973.

de Paola, T. *Pancakes for Breakfast.* New York: Harcourt Brace Jovanovich, 1978.

——. *Sing, Pierrot, Sing.* Harcourt Brace Jovanovich, 1983.

Fuchs, E. *Journey to the Moon.* New York: Delacorte, 1969.

Fromm, L. *Muffel and Plums.* New York: Macmillan, 1973.

Goodall, J. S. *The Adventures of Paddy Pork.* New York: Harcourt Brace Jovanovich, 1968.

——. *Creepy Castle.* New York: Atheneum, 1975.

——. *An Edwardian Christmas.* New York: Atheneum, 1978.

——. *Above and Below the Stairs.* New York: Atheneum, 1983.

Hamberger, J. *The Lazy Dog.* New York: Four Winds/Scholastic, 1971.

Heller, L. *Lily at the Table.* New York: Macmillan, 1979.

Hoban, T. *Look Again!* New York: Macmillan, 1971.

Hogrogrian, N. *Apples.* New York: Macmillan, 1972.

373

Hutchins, P. *Changes, Changes.* New York: Macmillan, 1971.

Keats, E. J. *Skates.* New York: Franklin Watts, 1973.

Krahn, F. *A Flying Saucer Full of Spaghetti.* New York: E. P. Dutton, 1970.

————. *Sebastian and the Mushroom.* New York: Delacorte, 1976.

————. *The Mystery of the Giant Footprints.* New York: E. P. Dutton, 1977.

————. *Catch That Cat!* New York: E. P. Dutton, 1978.

McCully, E. *Picnic.* New York: Harper & Row, 1984.

Mari, I., and Mari, E. *The Apple and the Moth.* New York: Pantheon, 1970.

————. *Chicken and the Egg.* New York: Pantheon, 1970.

Mayer, M. *A Boy, a Dog, and a Frog.* New York: Dial, 1967.

————. *Frog Where Are You?* New York: Dial, 1969.

————. *Frog Goes to Dinner.* New York: Dial, 1974.

————. *The Great Cat Chase.* New York: Four Winds, 1975.

————. *Ah-Choo.* New York: Dial, 1976.

————. *Oops.* New York: Dial, 1977.

Meyer, R. *Vicki.* New York: Atheneum, 1969.

Olschewski, A. *Winterbird.* Boston: Houghton Mifflin, 1969.

Ringi, K. *The Magic Stick.* New York: Harper & Row, 1968.

————. *The Winner.* New York: Harper & Row, 1969.

Schick, E. *Making Friends.* New York: Macmillan, 1969.

Spier, P. *Peter Spier's Christmas.* Garden City, NY: Doubleday, 1983.

Schweninger, A. *A Dance for Three.* New York: Dial, 1979.

Sugita, Y. *My Friend Little John and Me.* New York: McGraw-Hill, 1973.

Turkle, B. *Deep in the Forest.* New York: E. P. Dutton, 1976.

Ward, L. *The Silver Pony.* Boston: Houghton Mifflin, 1973.

Wezel, P. *The Good Bird.* New York: Harper & Row, 1966.

Wildsmith, B. *Brian Wildsmith's Christmas.* New York: Franklin Watts, 1970.

Winter, P. *The Bear and the Fly.* New York: Crown, 1976.

B Teaching Word-Recognition Skills

As students develop their ability to read, they also need to become adept with the mechanics of reading. They must learn the word-recognition skills that will enable them to decode words independently and to improve their reading fluency. At any grade level, the amount of time spent on teaching word-recognition skills should not exceed the amount of time devoted to having students read connected discourse. Too great an emphasis on decoding can lead youngsters to think that reading is simply a matter of identifying words correctly. They must realize that reading also involves responding to the ideas presented by an author. Comprehension and appreciation of the text should be the priority; specific skill instruction should be introduced as a means to read interesting and enjoyable materials more effectively.

There are two main word-recognition strategies to be learned. Students must acquire a sight vocabulary (words that are recognized immediately at sight), and they must develop a repertoire of skills for figuring out words they do not recognize immediately.

Building a Sight Vocabulary

Building a sight vocabulary is, to a great extent, a feat of memory. Good readers have a great number of words stored in memory; they seldom stumble because they know so many words well at sight. But, though memory plays an important role, sight vocabulary is not acquired with rote memory. That is, learning words is not like memorizing a telephone number or a grocery list or the names of the presidents of the United States.

Acquiring a sight vocabulary is similar to acquiring an oral vocabulary. An infant, learning language orally, hears words over and over in real communication contexts. Parents hold up favorite toys, household objects, or foods while stating the names of these things. Or parents describe the ongoing situation ("Now let's put on your mittens" or "Here comes Grandma"). The child learns to associate words with the objects or concepts they stand for. After hearing the same words repeatedly, the child learns them and uses them; they become meaningful words, stored meaningfully in memory. In learning to read, the child must make associations between printed words and their oral counterparts. Again, repetition in meaningful contexts is important so that the words become stored meaningfully in memory.

These are simplified explanations of complex cognitive processes. Building oral and reading vocabularies depends on the individual's ability to make associations, remember learned words, and apply that learning in a variety of novel situations. However, although we may not know exactly how the mind works to do these things, the processes are rather easily used by the large majority of individuals. Children become attentive to oral language rather soon after birth, learning to speak within a year or two, and most children become attentive to written language not long after. In fact, many children acquire their first sight words before they come to school. They recognize their own names, the titles of favorite books, or other familiar words in their daily environments.

Though we can marvel at the complexity of the processes, we cannot overlook the fact that learning to recognize and attach meaning to words, both oral and written, is a natural and relatively easy process for so many individuals. Children need meaningful contexts for learning and opportunities to reinforce their learning by seeing words in new contexts. Given these conditions, most children will acquire sight vocabularies rather easily.

Meaningful Contexts for Learning

Children come to school with sizeable oral vocabularies. The words they know orally provide the most important foundation when they learn to recognize words in print. For most children, nouns will be particularly meaningful because they can be readily associated with the objects or people named. The child's experiential background provides the context for learning these words. Pictures, objects, and discussion will all prompt children to use that background to attach meaning to nouns in print. Certain nouns will be especially meaningful—a child's own name, for instance, or other words that are associated with favorite objects or activities. *Puppy* may be highly meaningful to one child, *salamander* to another; *chocolate, cowboy,* or *barn* may carry the most meaning for others.

Less meaningful will be function words, such as conjunctions, prepositions, or auxiliary verbs, because these, although seemingly easy words, cannot be associated with concrete things. However, the child's familiarity with the language provides a meaningful context for learning these words. For instance, a word like *has* carries little meaning in and of itself and may be relatively difficult for a child to learn (in comparison with the child's name, for instance), but seeing the word in sentences that follow the child's usual way of speaking will help the child recognize it.

Providing meaningful contexts thus involves matching the words to be learned with what children already know about the language and the world. Basal reading programs systematically introduce words that are part of most children's knowledge of the world and of the language; if taught conscientiously, these programs provide adequate meaningful contexts for children to acquire sight vocabulary. Children's own dictated stories (see Chapter 3) provide other, often richer contexts for learning words. A print-rich environment provides yet other meaningful contexts for learning words. Labeled objects and books with captioned illustrations will stimulate word learning, as will many other print materials, including something as routine as the day of the week written on the board.

Reinforcement

Most children, especially beginning readers, need to see a word several times, in different contexts, before they will learn it well enough to recognize it instantly whenever it appears. This aspect of acquiring a sight vocabulary is much like learning other skills—the learner needs practice.

Basal reading programs provide built-in practice; a word is introduced and then repeated several times in the pages that follow its introduction. Workbook exercises also reinforce sight vocabulary learning. The amount of repetition in these programs is usually adequate for most children to learn a word well, but some children may need more practice. When children learn words from materials other than a basal program, some amount of reinforcing repetition is needed to promote solid learning.

Whether the class is working with a basal program or is following another approach to reading, the best kind of repetition comes when children simply read self-selected materials for their own purposes. Each time children delve into books and magazines they really want to read, they will see many words that they have seen before. Reading independently, they cannot help but give themselves meaningful practice, and they will become more and more sure of the words they encounter. This is general practice, to be sure (the teacher may not know just which words will be encountered when children select their own reading material), but it is important practice, nevertheless. Children reinforce their word learning no matter which words they read.

Other kinds of activities provide focused practice, giving children meaningful repetition of certain words the teacher particularly wants them to learn.

Word games and various exercises may be used for this purpose. A few examples of these include the following:

1. Childen search through old periodicals, cutting out words they recognize and pasting them on a bright piece of construction paper to make a word collage.
2. Children play Concentration with a deck of pairs of previously learned words. The usual rules apply. Each player turns up two cards and says the words. If they match, the pair is kept; if not, the cards are returned to their original places, and it is the next player's turn. The winner is the one with the most pairs after all cards have been removed from the array.
3. Children search through a word card deck, finding words that fit various categories—for example, things to eat, things to wear, things that are alive, things that are smaller (or larger) than a sandwich.
4. Children play Old Maid with word cards, matching pairs according to the rules of that game.
5. Children match words cards with pictures that represent objects, actions, or events.

All these activities require children to associate the printed word with its oral counterpart repeatedly. An additional feature of each activity is that it is designed to appeal to the learner, to be fun. Children might also learn a number of words if the teacher simply prepares word lists or flash cards and drills the students regularly with these. However, drill with words in isolation requires considerable use of rote memory. Consequently, the learning may take longer and may not endure over time. Also, such strategies would not be nearly as enjoyable as activities that are more like games, where practice is part of a pleasurable endeavor.

Figuring Out Unknown Words

While acquiring a sight vocabulary, students should also be developing strategies for identifying unknown words. Even highly skilled readers encounter unfamiliar words in print. Beginning readers, who have limited sight vocabularies, will find unfamiliar words quite regularly. Students need to know what to do in these situations if they are to become independent and effective readers.

There are four main strategies for identifying an unfamiliar word: using context clues, sounding the word out, recognizing familiar structural elements such as roots and affixes, and using the dictionary.

Using Context Clues

Probably the most powerful aid to word identification is to use the context in which the word appears. A context may be as straightforward as a picture with a label or an accompanying text, but usually the context is a *language* context—the other words in the sentence or the paragraph give clues to what the unfamiliar word is.

If you see an unfamiliar word in absolute isolation, you can only guess wildly what it is. For instance, here is a word you know orally that has been disguised with asterisks. What do you suppose it is?

$$*****$$

It could be any one of thousands of words at this point. Let's add a bit of context:

$$an *****$$

The number of possible choices becomes limited at once. Now you know that the word is a noun (marked by an article) and that it also begins with a vowel because the article is *an* rather than *a*. Let's add a bit more context:

$$An ***** is good to eat.$$

Now your choices are limited still further. Of all possible nouns, you are dealing with something that is edible, and good at that. Still more context gives further clues:

An ***** is good to eat. It is a red (or yellow or green), crunchy fruit that is harvested from trees and often is used to make pies that are a favorite American dessert.

With this amount of context, you probably had little trouble deciding that the word is *apple*.

What you did is what children are capable of doing, too. Let us examine the knowledge and experience you used that children also are able to use. First, you used your knowledge of the language that you have acquired through experience: Nouns are signaled by articles; the article *an* precedes words that start with vowels. (You did not recite these rules to yourself; you just used them.) Next, you used your knowledge of the world, also acquired through experience: you know what is edible, what is a red and crunchy fruit, and what is used in a favorite American dish. (You may also have used your considerable knowledge of words you know in print; the number of asterisks corresponded exactly to the number of letters in the word, so you, an experienced reader, had an additional clue that would not be meaningful to beginning readers.

For words that are well-known orally, a full language context is usually sufficient to help the reader identify the word in print. But there are other strategies that are useful when the context does not immediately lead to identification. One of these is to sound out the word—to use phonics.

Using Phonics

Using phonics requires knowing letter-sound associations—the sounds represented by different letters. With this knowledge, a reader can sound out a word. Sounding out a word can be a useful aid to recognizing the word. Consider again a word disguised by asterisks:

*****

Again, this arrangement could be any one of numerous words. But with even one letter revealed, the choice becomes limited:

h****

With a second letter revealed, the field becomes narrower still:

ho***

With each new letter, your certainty becomes greater:

hor**
hors*
horse

Using phonics is similar to using context clues: knowing letter-sound associations helps the reader identify a word by reducing the number of possible choices. As with acquiring a sight vocabulary, learning phonics is easiest when the learning occurs in meaningful contexts and when the students are given adequate practice.

The issue of meaningful contexts for learning phonics is a particularly important one, starting with the most critical context—the overall reading program itself. Some programs are planned with the mistaken assumption that children must learn all the letter-sound associations before they can read. Phonics becomes the priority; phonics exercises are given more time and attention than any other reading activity. Children spend most of their time dealing with individual letters or small letter clusters, only occasionally confronting whole words and seldom reading connected prose. In such an instructional context, children can easily lose sight of the point of their efforts. When asked what they think of *reading,* they may express either negativity or indifference, because, to them, reading is just a puzzle of letter exercises. Learning phonics has become an end in itself for these children, not a means to an end.

A healthier context for learning is one in which phonics plays a subordinate role to reading for pleasure and information. Children need to learn phonics skills while they are learning to read. They should not learn them before, because phonics is not a prerequisite for reading. Phonics is only a useful strategy that *readers* use to figure out unknown words. Students need to realize that reading is a process for making sense of text; phonics is simply a way to sharpen a reader's skill.

There are numerous phonics programs available on the market, from those that are a part of a basal reading system to those that are designed solely to teach sound-letter associations. Many different approaches are available, and each experienced teacher probably has a favorite. But the essence of phonics instruction involves learning to associate sounds with letters or clusters of letters. Students need to be able to do the following:

- discriminate visually among letters
- discriminate auditorily among sounds
- match letters with the sounds they represent
- use what they know about letter-sounds to figure out words

The most sensible way of teaching these skills is through a systematic program that gives children repeated instruction and practice in each skill as it applies to the various letter-sound associations. Examples of teaching strategies for each include these:

1. Visual discrimination.
   a. Show children a letter. Have them find its match in an array of several letters.
   b. Show children a word. Have them find other words that begin (or end) with the same letter.
2. Auditory discrimination.
   a. Pronounce pairs of words. Have children tell if each pair starts (or ends) with the same sound.
   b. Pronounce pairs of words. Have children tell if the words rhyme or not.
3. Matching letters with sounds.
   a. Pronounce a word. Have children find other words in print that start (or end) with the same sound.
   b. Have children categorize words in print according to beginning sounds, ending sounds, and/or vowel sounds.
4. Applying learning to new words.
   Print a word the children know (*ball*). Change a letter to make it a different word they probably have not seen (*mall*). Have them pronounce the new word.

Phonics activities vary in difficulty. The easiest are those that require children simply to choose between alternatives; more challenging are those that require students to produce examples of some kind. A good program will include a balance of easy and difficult activities, involving both auditory and visual skills, chosen to suit the level of challenge that students can handle. Here are various phonics activities categorized according to difficulty. In each instance, the teacher presents either auditory or visual information, and the child's response is either auditory or visual.

1. Choice activities.
   a. Auditory-auditory. Pronounce pairs of words. Have students tell if they start (end) with the same sound.
   b. Auditory-visual. Make a list of words that students know orally. Give each child a pack of word cards that begin (or end) with the same sounds as the words on your list. Children should know the words in their decks as sight words. (Target sounds may be spelled differently; for instance, children may have word decks that include words such as *Cindy* and *sand* to represent the beginning *s* sound.) Pronounce words from your list and have students find words in their packs that start (or end) with the same sounds.
   c. Visual-auditory. Write several words on the board. Have children find and say the words that start (or end) with the same sound.
   d. Visual-visual. Write several words on the board. Have children look through packs of word cards to find words that start (or end) with the same sounds.
2. Production activities.
   a. Auditory-auditory. Pronounce several words, one at a time. Have children think of and say words that start (or end) with the same sounds.
   b. Auditory-visual. Pronounce several words, one at a time. Have children write words that start (or end) with the same sounds, or have them write only the letter-sound they hear at the beginning or end of each word you say.
   c. Visual-auditory. Write several words on the board. Have children think of words that begin with the same sounds.
   d. Visual-visual. Write several words on the board. Have children write words that start (or end) with the same sounds.

All these activities (except for the very first letter-discrimination task) require children to deal with letter-sound associations within the context of whole words. This is a feature of all good phonics instruction. It is not very useful to teach children isolated sounds (e.g., *b* says *buh* or *d* says *duh*) because letter sounds appear in words and work together as a unit. For instance, *bad* is pronounced in the way we say *bad,* not *buh-a-duh*. Emphasizing sounds in isolation can lead children to approach words laboriously, letter by letter, resulting in reading that sounds like this:

Thuh-uh duh-aw-guh ā-tuh thuh-uh buh-ō-nuh.
(The dog ate the bone.)

In fact, too much emphasis on phonics instruction of any sort can lead children to rely too heavily on phonics as a way of figuring out new words. *Sounding it out* is not the most reliable or efficient way of identifying most unknown words, because pronouncing a word does not necessarily result in proper identification of the word. For example, there are a number of words that can be pronounced in at least two ways, depending on the way the word is used. *Read* and *wind* are only two examples. Also, there are many irregular words that do not follow the usual rules of pronunciation (e.g., *once, was, do, own*). And, most important, as children mature, they will encounter more and more words that they will not understand even if they do pronounce them correctly. Sounding out a visually unfamiliar word leads to recognition only if the reader already knows the word orally. (If you do not know what a *basilisk* is, your understanding is not increased much when you pronounce the word.) More is needed to identify these words properly.

One way to maintain a balanced perspective is to make sure students have ample opportunities to use phonics and context clues together. Although some classroom time can be devoted to pure phonics activities (such as those listed above), most of the time children should be figuring out words in the meaningful contexts of sentences and paragraphs and stories, where letter-sound associations and meaning clues, provided by the surrounding words, are used simultaneously and provide a check on one another. One suitable activity is a kind of cloze exercise.

Children are given passages from which parts of some words have been replaced by blanks:

> Peggy decided to take Pepper for a walk in the woods. She put on her c____t and hat because it was cold outside. Then she put the leash on the d____g. Out they went, and soon they were running among the tr____s. They saw squirrels and b____ high in the branches. They saw a r____ running through the bushes and a tiny ch____ m____k, too.

Children read the passage, saying or writing the words that have been altered. They must use the sense of the sentences *and* the letter-sound clues to figure out the words. In this passage, for instance, the context alone would suggest several words that would fit in the second sentence: sweater, scarf, mittens. But with the first and last letter given, the reader inevitably decides that *coat* is the missing word. Conversely, the word b____, seen alone, could be any one of many words, but the context immediately suggests *birds*. Balanced use of both kinds of clues together makes for more efficient and accurate word recognition.

Another way to keep from emphasizing phonics too heavily is to teach children to use other strategies for identifying words. Two useful strategies are structural analysis and dictionary skills.

Structural Analysis

Structural analysis refers to dividing a word into its constituent parts, usually syllables, using meaning clues within the word to identify it. Many words are composed of root words and affixes (prefixes and suffixes) that carry their own meaning. Some knowledge of these meaning-bearing word parts is useful to readers, because knowing what the elements of a word mean can help them figure out what the word as a whole means. For example, knowing that the prefix *trans* means across is useful when the reader encounters *transinternational, trans-Atlantic,* or *transcontinental.* The prefix also gives clues to the meaning of *transcribe, transgress,* and *transilluminate.* Breaking a word into its parts is also a useful aid to pronunciation; dividing a word into syllables brings a long word under control when the reader attempts to say it.

At beginning levels of reading, word parts such as *s, ed,* and *ing* endings will be most useful to learn, as will the recognition that some words are compound words: note the words *something, grandmother, baseball,* and *seahorse.* At later levels, children may be introduced to common prefixes, suffixes, and roots. Basal reading programs usually include systematic attention to word structure at each level, but some teachers supplement these materials with their own practice exercises.

Some important principles to keep in mind when teaching structural analysis are these:

1. Children must be able to hear the number of syllables in words before they can be expected to divide a word into syllables. Repeated auditory practice is usually necessary to develop this syllable sense. The teacher needs to give many examples of one-, two-, and multisyllable words orally, exaggerating the parts as children are first learning to hear them: *grandmother, grand-moth-er, grandmother.* Children need to repeat the words after the teacher says them, listening for the parts as they repeat them. Children may also be asked to clap or tap their desks as they say each part, to reinforce their auditory attention to the syllables.

2. As children learn to hear syllables, they also need to see a word divided into syllables. The teacher can put different known words on the board, intact and divided into syllables, and have the children read the words, listening for and noting the syllable divisions.

3. When specific roots and affixes are taught, several examples of illustrative words should be given so that children can see how the root or affix carries meaning in each.

4. While learning a root or affix, children need practice in using the information to figure out unknown words. For instance, a suitable exercise might look like this:

inter:	a prefix meaning between
interact =	to act on each other (action between)
	Tom and Agnes talked to each other; they interacted.
intervene =	to come between
	If you two keep fighting, I will have to intervene!
interrupt =	to get in the way of
	May I interrupt your conversation? I have something to say.

If *inter* means between, what do you think the underlined words mean in these sentences?

- The Enterprise is an *interplanetary* spaceship.
- The President of the United States went to the *international* meeting.
- It was an *interschool* track meet.

In this exercise, students are given examples of words beginning with the prefix (with a context for each to help make the meaning clear) and are asked to figure out the meaning of other words that also are given in the context of sentences. As much as possible, students should be given familiar words that illustrate the root or affix under study. They should also be presented with unfamiliar words to which they can apply their new knowledge. In an exercise like the one just given, for instance, the words in the first part should be familiar, whereas the words in the second part should be unfamiliar.

Having a sense of syllables and knowing the meanings of common roots and affixes provide useful knowledge, but, as with phonics, these aspects of reading instruction should not dominate the program. Children should not spend undue amounts of time at paper-and-pencil syllable exercises. Their best practice will come when they encounter an unfamiliar word in the context of something they are reading and use structural analysis along with phonics and context to identify the word.

Using Dictionary Skills

Of all the word-recognition skills, those relating to dictionary use have probably the most long-lasting value for students. Though skilled, mature readers may use context, phonics, and structure to figure out unfamiliar words, these individuals also rely heavily on a dictionary to determine both pronunciation and meaning. This is not surprising, because mature readers know almost all of the words they read; when they encounter an unfamiliar word, they usually have neither seen nor heard it before. Mature readers can only approximate its sound and sense until they check the dictionary. (Of course, even then, they may not be absolutely confident in their knowledge of that word.)

Using a dictionary is a useful habit to acquire, and it *is,* more than anything else, a habit. It takes effort to use a dictionary (it is so much easier to skip the word or to vow to look it up later and then never get to it). So, from the earliest days in school, children should be aware of dictionaries and should see adults consulting dictionaries regularly so that using a dictionary becomes, to them, an integral part of reading. Even in kindergarten and first grade, the wise teacher will have several dictionaries in the room and will make a point of checking them regularly, if only to demonstrate how they are used.

Instruction in dictionary use can begin quite early, with picture dictionaries. Commercial picture dictionaries are available, often as part of a basal reading program, but children also enjoy making their own. They can compile dictionaries of the words that they are learning. They can draw or cut out pictures to illustrate words and bind the pages together in some simple way.

As they mature, students need regular practice in dictionary skills. These skills involve the following:

1. Learning that dictionaries adhere to alphabetical order.
2. Learning what is contained in a dictionary entry; this may differ from one dictionary to another
3. Learning how to interpret diacritical markings in terms of the pronunciation key at the bottom of the page.
4. Learning how to use guide words to find the right page quickly.
5. Learning how to skim a page to find the word quickly.
6. Learning how to find a word in the dictionary that the student doesn't know how to spell. (This skill is discussed in relation to Spelling in Chapter 8.)

Each of these skills needs to be taught and practiced repeatedly so that students will feel at ease with the dictionary and can build up reasonable speed at finding words. When they can use a dictionary skillfully, they will be more likely to develop the habit of consulting the dictionary regularly.

Many basal reading programs provide exercises in dictionary use, and many of the upper-grade books include glossaries, which children can also use to develop their dictionary skills. But experienced teachers like to supplement the regular program with specific dictionary exercises. Here is one example of a series of activities involving the use of guide words. These activities would be most suitable for upper-level elementary students.

1. The teacher explains the principle of guide words, having students examine a dictionary or glossary page as an example.
2. The teacher puts two guide words on the board, along with a number of other words, some of which would be on that dictionary page, some of which would not. The group decides whether or not each word would be included on the page. (This activity is done several times over the course of several days, with different sets of guide words, until students seem to have grasped the principle.)
3. Children are given several follow-up exercises that are comparable to the group exercises. For example:

Guide Words: car   clam

Circle the words that would be on this dictionary page.

city	clang	choke
choose	circle	cow
centipede	common	cut
calendar	center	club
class	circus	comet

4. Students play Dictionary Race. The teacher puts a list of words on the board. Students must find them in their dictionaries, writing the page number for each word as they find it. The winner is the one who finishes first (and has found the proper pages). Invariably, the winner will have been the best user of guide words.

Dictionary skills must not be overemphasized in the reading program. For mature readers, it is just as inefficient to check the dictionary for every unknown word while reading as it is to try to sound out every word. Students, who are developing reading skills, need to learn to use a dictionary smoothly, but they also need to learn that sometimes, for words that seem of minor importance, a good reader uses context clues to get the general sense of the word and moves on quickly, purposefully intent to discover the overall meaning of the passage. The dictionary is consulted later, to refine the reader's understanding of the word.

A Balanced Strategy

Context, phonics, structure, and the dictionary are the tools of the skilled decoder, but the efficient reader selects only those tools that are needed to get the job done quickly and smoothly. A good reader uses as few as possible. The decisions are made rapidly, often without conscious attention, because the aim is not just to recognize the words but to use the text to make the words meaningful.

Practice with individual decoding skills is valuable, to learn each one's use well, but the reader must also learn that a proper balance is necessary. Too heavy a reliance on context clues leads to a lack of precision, while too great a dependence on phonics leads to inefficient word-by-word (even letter-by-letter) reading. Too much emphasis on structural clues or the dictionary can lead to a sacrifice of the overall meaning as the reader stops to ponder individual words. Yet too little attention to these aids results in imprecise understanding of word meaning. The efficient reader uses the right tools at the right time. Developing this skill requires experience and wise guidance from the teacher.

Selected Picture Books for Writing Models*

Anglund, J. W. *A Friend is Someone Who Likes You.* New York: Harcourt, Brace & World, 1958.

—————. *Look Out the Window.* New York: Harcourt, Brace & World, 1959.

—————. *Love is a Special Way of Feeling.* New York: Harcourt, Brace & World, 1960.

Baylor, B. *Guess Who My Favorite Person Is.* New York: Charles Scribner & Sons, 1977 (illustrated by R. A. Parker).

Bendick, J. *A Fresh Look at Night.* New York: Franklin Watts, 1963.

Charlip, R. *Fortunately.* New York: Parents Magazine Press, 1964.

Collins, D. *If I Could I Would.* Champaign IL: Garrard, 1979 (illustrated by K. Oechsli).

de Regniers, B. *A Friend?* New York: Atheneum, 1964 (illustrated by B. Montresor).

Hoffman, B. G. *Red Is For Apples.* New York: Random House, 1966 (illustrated by D. Bolognese).

Lexau, J. *That's Good, That's Bad.* New York: Dial, 1963 (illustrated by S. Hoff).

—————. *I Should Have Stayed in Bed.* New York: Harper & Row, 1965.

—————. *The Homework Caper.* New York: Harper & Row, 1966.

O'Neill, M. *Hailstones and Halibut Bones.* New York: Doubleday, 1961 (illustrated by L. Weisgard).

—————. *People I'd Like to Keep.* New York: Doubleday, 1964 (illustrated by P. Galdone).

—————. *Words, Words, Words.* New York: Doubleday, 1966 (illustrated by J. Piussi-Campbell).

Viorst, J. *Alexander and the Terrible, Horrible, No Good, Very Bad Day.* New York: Atheneum, 1973 (illustrated by R. Cruz).

* This list was compiled by Julie Slocum-Nuckolls with help from the members of the 1983 California South Coast Writing Project Fellows and is used with permission.

————. *My Mamma Says There Aren't Any Zombies, Ghosts, Vampires, Creatures, Demons, Monsters, Fiends, Goblins, or Things.* New York: Atheneum, 1974 (illustrated by K. Chorao).

————. *Rosie and Michael.* New York: Atheneum, 1974 (illustrated by L. Tomei).

————. *Alexander Who Used to be Rich Last Sunday.* New York: Atheneum, 1978 (illustrated by R. Cruz).

Williams, B. *Kevin's Grandma.* New York: E. P. Dutton, 1975 (illustrated by K. Chorao).

Zacharias, W. *But Where is the Green Parrot?* New York: Delacorte, 1965.

Zemach, H. *The Judge.* New York: Farrar, Straus & Giroux, 1969 (illustrated by M. Zemach).

Three Approaches to Grammar

Traditional Grammar

Traditional grammarians describe the English language by defining elements of the sentence and by analyzing sentences to explain the relationships among words, phrases, and clauses. A sentence is said to be made up of at least one subject and one predicate, either of which may be a single word or a group of words. Sentences are classified into three types:

Simple

A simple sentence is made up of a main clause, containing a subject and a predicate and any words that qualify (modify) either. These are simple sentences:

- Dogs bark.
- Raising his head high, the dog barked loudly at the man in the truck.

Complex

A complex sentence is made up of one main clause and at least one subordinate clause. The main clause would be grammatically complete on its own. The subordinate clause(s) would not be grammatically complete alone. These are complex sentences:

- As the game began, I found a seat.
- As the game began, I found a seat that provided an excellent view of the field.

Compound

A compound sentence is made up of at least two main clauses that are connected with a coordinating conjunction. Subordinate clauses may be included with either main clause. These are compound sentences:

- He went, but I stayed.
- He went, but I stayed until I had finished eating.

In this approach to grammar, words and groups of words are classified into the following eight parts of speech. Each part of speech may be used in various ways in sentences. Some examples are given here.

Nouns

A noun names. The words that name people (*Betty*), places (*Alaska*), concrete objects (*computer*), or abstract concepts (*liberty*) are all nouns. These are the most common ways in which nouns are used:

1. Subject of a sentence (The *engine* started.)
2. Object of a preposition (The boar crashed through the *jungle.*)
3. Appositive (Mr. Fogg, the *mayor,* led the parade.)
4. Direct address (*Irma,* what is your last name?)
5. Direct object (Larry planted a *tree.*)
6. Indirect object (I gave *Spencer* a dollar.)
7. Objective complement (They elected Hans *president.*)
8. Subjective complement (Football is my favorite *sport.*)

Pronouns

A pronoun is a word used in place of a noun. A pronoun designates a person, a place, a concrete object, or an abstract concept without directly naming it. These are some of the words that are often used as pronouns: *he, they, anyone, that, it.* Pronouns are used in the same ways as nouns as the subjects of sentences, the objects of prepositions, and so on.

Verbs

Verbs describe action or state of being. Verbs may be distinguished from one another in these main ways:

1. Principal verbs and auxiliary verbs.

    The principal verb expresses the main action or state of being; auxiliary verbs, when used, are helpers. In the sentence *You should have arrived sooner,* the main verb is *arrived; should* and *have* are auxiliary verbs.

2. Transitive and intransitive verbs.

    Transitive verbs take direct objects. (The catcher *hit* a home run.) Intransitive verbs do not take direct objects. (The moon *shines* faintly tonight.) Some intransitive verbs are called linking verbs. These verbs link the subject with a word that renames or describes the subject. (I *am* the winner. I *am* thrilled.)

3. Verbs in the active and passive voice.

    A verb is in the active voice if the subject of the sentence performs the action or is in the state of being described by the verb. (Al *carried* Bob.) A verb is in the passive voice if the subject of the sentence receives the action described by the verb. (Bob *was carried* by Al.)

4. Verbals.

    There are three forms derived from verbs that are known as verbals: participle (*Carrying* the laundry, I crossed the street.), gerund (*Swimming* is an Olympic sport.), and infinitive (*To eat* well is his goal in life.). A verbal has the sense of a verb but functions as some other part of speech; for example, a participle functions as an adjective.

Adjectives

Adjectives qualify (modify) nouns or pronouns by describing attributes of the nouns or pronouns. (A *fluffy, white* dog greeted us at the door.)

Adverbs

Adverbs qualify (modify) verbs, adjectives, or other adverbs, giving information about how, when, where, or to what extent. (The sun shone *brightly.* He is *very* tired. We walked *quite* slowly.)

Prepositions

Prepositions function in (prepositional) phrases to join nouns or pronouns to the rest of the sentence in some way. Usually, prepositional phrases (a group of words introduced by a preposition) serve as adjectives or adverbs. (The man *in the trench coat* is looking for evidence. The rain came *through the roof.*)

Conjunctions

Conjunctions connect words, phrases, or clauses, showing their relationship. There are three kinds of conjunctions: coordinating conjunctions (Ralph *and*

Pete took the train, *but* Grant drove. We ran over the hill *and* through the meadow.), subordinating conjunctions (I will go *if* you will. *Although* it was raining, we continued the game.), and correlative conjunctions (*If* he bought a ticket, *then* he is entitled to a seat. It is *either* this one *or* that one.).

Interjections

Interjections are usually exclamations that do not have any grammatical function in sentences. (*Oh,* I see. *Goodness!* This room is cold.)

This traditional approach to English grammar is based on Latin grammar. Latin is a highly inflected language; that is, words change form to signal shifts in meaning and to indicate their grammatical relationships within sentences. Because of the extensive inflections, there is a fixed, correct way to form Latin words and to use them in sentences.

By contrast, English is more flexible. A few inflectional changes do occur in English; for instance, many words have different forms for singular and plural (*cat, cats; child, children*). Also, some words change form as they are used in different grammatical positions (*I* own a dog; the dog barked at *me.*). But English requires many fewer such changes than Latin, and words are used in English sentences with relative freedom. For instance, a word that is a noun in one sentence can easily be an adjective or a verb in another sentence without changing form (I will go to the *store* for milk; I will *store* the milk in the refrigerator.). These kinds of shifts, as well as the ease with which English speakers can combine words, alter existing words, and invent words contribute to the flexibility of English.

Traditional grammarians accommodate to this flexibility of form and function by stressing that an English word, unlike a Latin word, cannot be classified as a part of speech until it is used in a sentence, when its function will then determine how it should be classified. The basic terminology of Latin grammar is retained, however, to analyze word forms and the structure of sentences.

This approach has been criticized on the grounds that the application of Latin rules to English is forced and that emphasis on such rules in English leads to rigid prescription of fixed usage. The dissension over *It is me* versus *It is I* illustrates the basis of the criticism. According to Latin-based traditional grammar, *It is me* is wrong because the objective-case pronoun *me* cannot properly serve as a predicate nominative. However, the critics claim, language grows and changes through the years; *It is me* (or often *It's me*) is gaining acceptance as a proper English statement and there is no reason to disallow it simply because it violates rules that are based on Latin grammar.

Structural Grammar

Structural grammar was invented to avoid the prescriptive rules that follow logically from traditional grammar. The structuralists put aside the Latin-based system to look at the way people actually use English. Studies of extant usage yielded basic sentence patterns, which were offered simply as descriptions, not as prescriptions. Examples of a limited number of these discovered basic sentence patterns follow:

1. Noun Phrase + Intransitive Verb
     Horses gallop.
     The bees swarmed.
2. Noun Phrase + *Be* Verb + Adjective
     The rabbit is hungry.
     The driver was tired.
3. Noun Phrase + Linking Verb + Adjective
     The lion seems angry.
     The waiter became obsequious.
4. Noun Phrase + Transitive Verb + Noun Phrase/Direct Object + (Adverb)
     The robin ate the berries.
     The shortstop caught the ball deftly.
5. Noun Phrase + Transitive Verb + Noun Phrase/Indirect Object + Noun Phrase/Direct Object + (Adverb)
     The personnel director gave me an application.
     The general awarded him a medal proudly.

In structural grammar, words are classified in a way roughly analogous to the method used for traditional parts of speech. However, to avoid applying a prescriptive, Latin-based classification system, the structuralists examine the way words are actually used in sentences, investigating both the forms they assume and their syntactical functions in basic sentence patterns. This approach takes into account the high degree of flexibility within English.

The structuralists posit *form classes* as the basis of word classification. Words are categorized according to the affixes they may assume and the positions they may take in sentences. The major form classes are nouns, verbs, adjectives, determiners, adverbs, and function words (such as prepositions).

A word is categorized into a form class mainly through an examination of the place it assumes in a sentence. For instance, the word *running* may be identified as a verb in one sentence (I was *running* down the street.) and as a noun in another (*Running* is a popular sport.). Words are also categorized according to their form. Certain affixes, which are used to form words, are clues to a word's form class; for instance, the suffix *-tion* suggests that a word is a noun (*celebration, demonstration*).

In many ways, structural grammar is similar to traditional grammar, and much of the terminology is the same (e.g., nouns, verbs, adjectives, adverbs). The major difference between the two is that structural grammar explains word and sentence formation on the basis of current English usage. It does not attempt to be prescriptive, whereas the traditionalists apply historical precedent and thus tend to prescribe usage.

Transformational Grammar

Transformational (or generative) grammar was invented to improve on structural grammar. It was argued that the structuralist scheme—of observing language users and categorizing their sentences by pattern—led to certain problems. For instance, the structuralist approach led to the difficulty of tracking down all the sentences that people might use so as to provide a complete list of basic patterns.

Rather than examining actual usage, transformational grammarians posit a theory to explain how sentences are generated. The theory assumes that a sentence has both a deep and a surface structure. The deep structure is the underlying meaning of the sentence, whereas the surface structure is the form of the observed utterance. Sentences may have the same deep structure but different surface structures (*Mary opened the book; the book was opened by Mary*), or they may have the same surface structure but different deep structures (*Mary is easy to please; Mary is eager to please*).

The deep-structure system carries the core of meanings from which a language user draws. The sentences that are generated adhere to predictable surface structures, described by *phrase structure rules*. Some examples of phrase structure rules are these:

1. Sentence ⟶ Noun Phrase + Verb Phrase
(A sentence includes a noun phrase followed by a verb phrase.)
2. Noun Phrase ⟶ Determiner + Noun
        Proper Noun
        Pronoun
(A noun phrase may include a determiner followed by a noun, a proper noun, or a pronoun.)
3. Verb Phrase ⟶ (Auxiliary) + Verb
(A verb phrase includes a verb and may include an auxiliary.)
4. Verb ⟶ Transitive Verb + Noun Phrase
        Intransitive Verb
        Linking Verb + Complement
(A verb may be a transitive verb followed by a noun phrase; an intransitive verb; or a linking verb followed by a complement.)

Besides adhering to phrase-structure rules, sentences are also subject to the processes of transformation, elaboration, coordination, and subordination. These processes result in the great variety of utterances that may be generated from the kernel sentences of the deep structure system. Some examples follow:

1. Transformation

Kernel sentence:	Jack ate the pie.
Negative transformation:	Jack did not eat the pie.
Passive transformation:	The pie was eaten by Jack.
Question transformation:	Did Jack eat the pie?

2. Elaboration

- At three o'clock in the morning Jack ate the cherry pie.
- Hungrily, Jack ate the entire cherry pie in twenty minutes.

3. Coordination

- Jack ate the pie, and Mary ate the cake.
- Jack ate the pie, but Mary ate the cake.

4. Subordination

- When Jack ate the pie, Mary ate the cake.
- If Jack ate the pie, then Mary ate the cake.
- Although Jack ate the pie, Mary ate the cake.

Like structural grammar, transformational grammar avoids prescribing how words and sentences ought to be formed. The emphasis is on explaining how sentences are generated to convey the user's intended meaning.

Developing a Writing Evaluation Program

This is a suggested procedure for setting up a schoolwide or districtwide writing evaluation program. The basic principle here is that teachers must examine their own students' first-draft work to establish baseline data. Only by knowing specifically what their students can do readily on their own will teachers be able to assess improvement after instruction and practice. Here are the steps to follow.

Developing Standards

Obtain writing samples from all the students involved. To do this, teachers will have to agree on two or three topics that all will use for the assignment and will have to agree to get the samples from their classes during the same time period.

All students should be given the same kinds of directions for writing. Again, teachers should discuss this issue and should agree on a standard procedure. It is important to give the students just enough direction to get them started; the samples should reflect what they can do on their own with minimal teacher intervention. The papers will be first drafts; no rewriting or correction by the teacher or by the students is involved.

Students should be given a number to put on their papers. They should not write their names. (The papers need to be assessed as objectively as possible; omitting names makes this easier.) Things will be less confusing if each teacher has his or her own set of numbers to use. For instance, Mr. Brown's class might use the numbers 1–30; Mrs. Smith's class would use 31–60; and so on. Or each teacher might be assigned a code letter to be used with the same set of numbers; one class's papers would thus be numbered A-1, A-2, and so on; another's would be numbered B-1, B-2, and so on.

Teachers get together to read the papers. They should first select a random sample of twenty-five papers from each grade level. (The rest of the papers should be saved for later steps.) At least two teachers should read each set of papers. It is best if first-grade teachers read first-grade papers, second-grade teachers read second-grade papers, and so on. While reading, a teacher should make an overall judgment on each paper, not stopping to react to errors. The reading should proceed briskly, with the teachers making overall, relatively intuitive judgments. This kind of assessment is based on principles of holistic scoring, which was discussed in Chapter 10.

Each paper should be put in one of several piles, corresponding to the overall judgment. For first-grade papers, four piles is usually enough: 1 = poor, 2 = below average, 3 = average, 4 = good. In higher grades, where there will be more variability among students, seven categories may be used. The poorest papers go in the pile marked 1; average papers go in the pile marked 4; the best go in the pile marked 7. Piles 2 and 3, 5 and 6 are for the in-betweens.

When teachers finish a set of papers, they should mark the score for each paper on a master list. Thus, when both teachers have finished reading the same set, each paper will have two scores. If the teachers disagree on scores, they should get together to discuss those papers (perhaps with a third teacher sitting in) and agree on a single score for each paper.

When each paper has been assigned a single score by at least two readers, teachers should carefully examine the papers piled in each score category in order to decide which attributes constitute that category—that is, what it is about each paper that makes it fit in its category. This step will take a fair amount of time. The papers in each pile, though somewhat similar, will have areas of difference. Working from the specific elements in the papers, teachers must identify the characteristics that constitute a *1* and a *3* and so on. The descriptions for a given number category will, of course, differ at different grade levels, because what is generally considered excellent writing in second grade may be only average or poor in fourth grade.

Trying Out and Revising Criteria

Select a second set of twenty-five papers at random from the original set. Read these papers as before, rating them 1–4 or 1–7, according to the standards that were established. Trying out the criteria in this way will invariably reveal the need to have more specific, clear standards. Revisions can be made accordingly.

Using Criteria for Evaluation

When teachers are satisfied that they have established workable criteria, children's first-draft writing can be judged periodically. (Teachers should realize that such assessment is only valid when the writing situation is like that which was used to obtain the samples on which the criteria were based.) By noting specific strengths and weaknesses, the teacher can plan for ongoing instruction. The teacher can also note students' progress over time.

This system probably is most valuable for establishing baseline data for evaluating students' writing from the beginning of the year to the end, and from one year to the next. As students receive more practice and instruction, writing scores in each grade improve steadily. For instance, here is a typical set of third-grade scores from a school district:

	Levels						
	1	2	3	4	5	6	7
September	9%	10%	16%	42%	17%	3%	2%
May	6%	9%	10%	29%	21%	15%	10%

At the beginning of the year, for eample, 42 percent of the third graders were rated as Level 4 writers; by the end of May, 29 percent of the same students were rated as Level 4 writers. As a group, these students improved their performance in writing during the year. In schools using such a system, teachers find that most students do move up at least one level in writing competence by the end of the year. Noting scores in this way, teachers and students will see tangible evidence of improvement in writing.

Here is one example of the criteria that one group of teachers came up with for second grade (Avon Grove School District, West Grove, Pennsylvania).

LEVEL 1

Garble, absence of any reconstructable thought

[A garble is a word or group of words that cannot be interpreted. A reconstructable thought is a group of words which can be reconstructed, by supplying words and interpreting spelling, into a sentence as intended by the child.]

LEVEL 2

One to three thoughts, possibly mixed with garble; some reconstruction necessary.

LEVEL 3

At least three related thoughts requiring minimal reconstruction

LEVEL 4

Level 3 criteria, plus:
> a sense of relatedness with movement of thought through the writing, or
> a summary idea

LEVEL 5

Level 4 criteria, plus:
> at least one complex sentence, and
> development of one or more good ideas

LEVEL 6

Level 5 criteria, plus:
> elaboration on idea(s), and
> one item from the list of desirable characteristics (below)

LEVEL 7

Level 6 criteria, plus two items from the list of desirable characteristics (below)

DESIRABLE CHARACTERISTICS

> an attempt to communicate with the reader (such as addressing the reader directly)
> imaginative/creative qualities
> exceptional vocabulary
> figurative language
> humor
> expression of feelings
> introduction of character
> a literary device, such as dialogue or a parenthetical expression

It is noteworthy that these second-grade criteria do not include elements of mechanical accuracy such as spelling or punctuation. Examining their student papers carefully after scoring them holistically, the teachers realized that most of the best papers were inconsistent mechanically. The good writers in second grade, on their first drafts, used many invented spellings, for instance. The teachers realized that, though they valued spelling and taught it regularly, their writing program goals went beyond conventional spelling in first drafts.

In fact, these teachers worked on many aspects of writing in second grade that are not reflected in these evaluation criteria. The teachers set basic standards for good (Level 4 +) first-draft writing that make sense to them and that most or all of their students can meet by the end of the year with regular instruction; some children exceed the standards considerably. When the children move on to third grade, expectations are higher, the third grade writing criteria being somewhat more stringent.

These standards are good ones because the teachers in that district worked them out together, based on their own students' actual performance. Transferring the criteria as is to another group of teachers would not improve the writing-evaluation system in that other school. The teachers in any school or district need to go through the process on their own, basing their judgments on what *their* students are doing.

Index